A SHEARWATER BOOK

THE
EMPTY
OCEAN

THE
EMPTY
OCEAN

PLUNDERING THE
WORLD'S MARINE LIFE

Written and Illustrated by

RICHARD
ELLIS

ISLAND PRESS / SHEARWATER BOOKS
Washington • Covelo • London

A Shearwater Book
Published by Island Press

SHEARWATER BOOKS is a trademark of The Center for Resource Economics.

Library of Congress Cataloging-in-Publication Data
Ellis, Richard, 1938–
    The empty ocean / Richard Ellis
        p. cm.
    Includes bibliographical references and index.
    ISBN 1-55963-974-1 (alk. paper)
        1. Marine animals. 2. Endangered species. I. Title.
    QL 121.E5794 2003

                                                            2003002077

British Cataloguing-in-Publication Data available
Book design by Joyce C. Weston
Printed on recycled, acid-free paper
Manufactured in the United States of America

10 9 8 7 6 5 4 3 2 1

CONTENTS

Few modern ecological studies take into account the former natural abundances of large marine vertebrates. There are dozens of places in the Caribbean named after large sea turtles whose adult populations now number in the tens of thousands instead of the tens of millions of a few centuries ago. Whales, manatees, dugongs, sea cows, monk seals, crocodiles, codfish, jewfish, swordfish, sharks, and rays are other large marine vertebrates that are now functionally or entirely extinct in most coastal ecosystems. Place names for oysters, pearls, and conches conjure up other ecological ghosts of marine invertebrates that were once so abundant as to pose hazards to navigation, but are witnessed now only by massive garbage heaps of empty shells.

—Jeremy Jackson et al., "Historical Overfishing and the Recent Collapse of Coastal Ecosystems," 2001

PREFACE

While immersed in other projects and adventures, I kept bumping into stories of overfishing, overhunting, and other depredations that ocean life has been subjected to. As I read the voluminous literature and listened to the cries of despair, I realized I had found the subject for my next book, one that seemed as necessary as a fire alarm in a burning building. Through carelessness, ignorance, greed, or just plain stupidity, we have squandered our precious marine heritage—in some cases beyond salvation. I have written about all sorts of things that live in the sea, from sperm whales to great white sharks, from giant squid to deep-sea viperfish, but never before have I felt such a pressing need to get the information out. Some of the situations are already hopeless: millions of whales, dolphins, seals, sea lions, and sea otters have been killed in the name of fashion or commerce. We will never again see a living great auk or Steller's sea cow; the barndoor skate is history. But this is only the beginning of the end, as it were. Poisoning, overfishing, and extinctions are on the increase around the world. If we are not to repeat the history we did not understand, perhaps this warning will alert the fire department, and maybe—just maybe—we will be able to avoid greater calamities in the future.

I began this book many years ago, when I thought the world needed a book about the Atlantic Ocean. Among the subjects I addressed was the history of the cod fishery, and I did a lot of research on this significant episode in American and Canadian maritime and economic history. *The Atlantic Ocean* never got written (by me, anyway), but pieces of it were eventually incorporated into various other books. For instance, the part about Atlantic sea monsters became the basis of my 1994 study *Monsters of the Sea,* and the chapter on the giant squid in that book led to my writing an entire book about *Architeuthis,* the huge squid that, up to the time *The Search for the Giant Squid* was published (1998), had never been seen alive by a human

being. (It now has—at least in larval form—an event that could conceivably
lead to yet another book.) My history of the Atlantic cod fishery has been
recycled and updated, and it appears in this book as the paradigm of careless
overfishing.

I began *The Atlantic Ocean* long before Mark Kurlansky published *Cod:
A Biography of the Fish That Changed the World*, and I'm glad that worked
out the way it did. His book, published in 1997, was particularly helpful to
me. Other books that I found useful are mentioned here in the text or listed
in the bibliography. Many people contributed to my work in this book,
advertently or not, including Paolo Guglielmi of the World Wildlife Fund;
Carl Safina of the National Audubon Society; Ole Lindquist of Iceland; Carl
Luer of Mote Marine Laboratory in Sarasota, Florida; Alida Bundy of Fish-
eries and Oceans Canada; Heather Hall, Amanda Vincent, and Sara Lourie of
Project Seahorse at McGill University in Canada; Paul Bowser and James
Casey of Cornell University's College of Veterinary Medicine; John
Richardson of the *Portland* (Maine) *Press Herald;* George Balazs of the
Honolulu Laboratory of the Southwest Fisheries Science Center (National
Marine Fisheries Service); Peter Harrison and Shirley Metz of Zegrahm
Expeditions; Daryl Domning of Howard University; James Porter of the
University of Georgia; Andrei Suntsov of the Russian Academy of Sciences
in Moscow; and Andrew Baker, Peter Benchley, Briton Busch, James Carlton,
Phil Clapham, Malcolm Clarke, Osha Gray Davidson, Rodney Fox, Errol
Fuller, Burney LeBoeuf, John McCosker, Ed Melvin, Michael Novacek, Seiji
Ohsumi, Hideo Omura, Roger Payne, Bill Perrin, Karen Pryor, Rhys
Richards, Joan Rose, Dick Russell, Victor Scheffer, Leighton Taylor, Carl
Trocki, Craig Van Note, E. O. Wilson, Bernd and Melany Würsig, and Charles
Yentsch.

From 1980 to 1990 I served as a member of the American delegation to
the International Whaling Commission, the organization chartered in 1949
to oversee the whaling industry, but which, in recent years, has served as the
battlefield for worldwide whale conservation. During that ten-year period, I
came to know many of the players on this international stage and, through
them, expanded my knowledge of the history and politics of whaling. To
most of us—indeed, to most of the world—the passage of the moratorium
on commercial whaling in 1982 signaled the end of whale-killing for profit. I
thus resigned from my position in 1990, believing that the anti-whaling
forces had won the war. But as with most wars, it wasn't over when the
shooting stopped; as of this writing, the Japanese and the Norwegians are

still whaling, under various loopholes in the quota system. Although my remaining on the delegation probably wouldn't have changed anything, I now believe I should have stayed the course, if for no other reason than to watch what was happening from within.

I participated in countless "save the whale" campaigns, including some in which I stood on street corners in Manhattan soliciting signatures on anti-whaling petitions, which we planned to bring to the Japanese and Soviet embassies, and others in which I drew the whales for consciousness-raising bumper stickers, T-shirts, and newspaper ads. I painted portraits of the ten species of great whales, and these were published in a 1975 issue of *Audubon* magazine. I am not a field researcher—I classify myself as a library or Internet researcher—but I have been a student of marine life for four decades, and in my travels I have seen in the wild many of the species discussed in this book. I have also visited fishing villages in Connecticut, Massachusetts, Rhode Island, Maine, California, Hawaii, Newfoundland, and Quebec. For nearly twenty years, I have lectured on cruises sponsored by organizations such as Sven Lindblad's Special Expeditions, the American Museum of Natural History's Discovery Tours, and the Explorers' Club Travel Program. To the people who put me on these ships, I am eternally grateful: Penelope Bodry-Sanders, Liz De Gaetano, Pam Fingleton, Julie Kohn, and Alicia Stevens. Through their good offices I traveled to many of the places mentioned in this book: Spitsbergen, Franz Josef Land, Bering Island, the Kamchatka Peninsula, the Kurile and Aleutian Islands, the North Pole, the Pribilof and Diomede Islands, South Georgia Island, the Falkland Islands, the Antarctic, Baja California, the Great Barrier Reef, Norfolk Island, Lord Howe Island, Indonesia, Iceland, and Alaska. On my own, I visited South Africa, Australia, New Zealand, Hawaii, Bermuda, Newfoundland, Nantucket, the Azores, Patagonia, Japan, Scotland, Ireland, Norway, Iceland, and the Galápagos Islands, all places that appear somewhere in the history of whaling, sealing, fishing, or all three. Almost everywhere, I found helpful and cooperative people, even when they realized I would be writing about the sometimes awful things they had done in the name of commerce.

This book was in the works for some time, and many people I consulted during the process died before the book was published. They were friends as well as colleagues and advisors, and I will miss them: Bill Dawbin, Ricardo Mandojana, Masaharu Nishiwaki, Ken Norris, and Bill Schevill.

Throughout the long, difficult process that miraculously results in a book, I relied heavily on those who make up my support system. As a newly minted research associate at the American Museum of Natural History, I am grateful to just about everyone there but especially the library staff, who abetted me in my endless searches for obscure references. I can't thank the Internet, but I'd like to anyway. My trusty agent, Carl Brandt, watched me sink into the bottomless Atlantic and come up sputtering something about "emptying the ocean," and he found Jonathan Cobb and Todd Baldwin of Island Press, who were willing to publish this book. I believe this book would have been vastly inferior without Jonathan Cobb's incredible attention to detail and his organic understanding of what makes a narrative flow. He once told me that he sees a manuscript as music; I wrote the score, but he conducted the orchestra.

Once again, Stephanie has been there to add new meaning to the words *support, patience,* and *loyalty.*

THE EMPTY OCEAN

INTRODUCTION

～ 1 ～

GRAY WHALES
IN THE ATLANTIC

Once upon a time, gray whales fed in the cold waters off Iceland and Greenland and migrated south—perhaps to the Bay of Biscay or even to the English Channel—to breed. Morphologically, they were the same whales (now known as *Eschrichtius robustus*) as the better-known California gray whales, which confine their migratory meanderings to the Pacific coast of North America, annually swimming south from the Bering Sea to Baja California and back again. No living person has seen an Atlantic gray whale, but we do have suggestive historical and conclusive paleontological evidence to confirm the existence of the creature that whale-hunters used to call "devil-fish."

The earliest mention to date of what may have been the Atlantic gray whale can be found in an Icelandic bestiary from about A.D. 1200 that describes some different kinds of whales, but not accurately enough for modern cetologists to identify them as to species. The *Konnungs skuggsjá* (King's Mirror), a thirteenth-century document written in Norwegian probably as a set of instructions for a king's son, lists twenty-one sea creatures, some of which can be referred to as living whales, dolphins, and pinnipeds, and some of which—mermaids and mermen, for example—are clearly mythological. Although it is not clearly identified, the gray whale is thought to be one of the whales mentioned.

A seventeenth-century Icelandic work by Jon Gudmundsson (quoted in Hermannson 1924) contains a list of various whales that might be found in nearby waters, and one of these is the *Sandlaegja*, which has been translated as "sand-lier." The description—translated from Icelandic—is as follows: "*Sandlaegja*. . . . Good eating. It has whiter baleen plates, which project from the upper jaw instead of teeth, as in all other baleen whales. . . . It is very tenacious of life and can come to land to lie as a seal to rest the whole day. . . . *Sandlaegja*, reaches 30 ells [an ell is about thirty inches], has baleen and is well edible." Although other whale species share some of these attributes, many of these characteristics, such as the "whiter baleen plates" and the sand-lying behavior that gave it its name, would appear to refer to the Atlantic gray whale, which does indeed have short, whitish baleen and a habit of entering very shallow water.

The historical literature I've mentioned so far is inconclusive, but we know from other sources that before the modern era gray whales swam in the Atlantic Ocean. Fossil remains of a species similar to—perhaps identical with—the Pacific gray whale have been found in western Europe (Sweden, England, and the Netherlands) and on the eastern coast of North America from New Jersey to South Carolina. The Atlantic gray whale fed in cold northern waters (perhaps off Iceland and Greenland) and then moved south to breed and calve. (There also used to be a sizable western Pacific population of gray whales, summering off Siberia and wintering in the breeding grounds off Korea and Japan, but during the past century this population was all but eliminated by Japanese and Korean whalers.) Extrapolating from comparable Pacific data, we can assume that during summer the Atlantic gray whales fed in deep, cold northern waters and then, with the coming of autumn, headed south, probably to Spain, France, or England on one side of the Atlantic or America's eastern seaboard on the other. In protected bays, the cows most likely would have delivered their calves and become impregnated prior to the northward journey in the spring.

More suggestive historical accounts also exist. For example, as James Mead and Edward Mitchell point out in their 1984 study of the Atlantic gray whale, there are the orders the directors of the Muscovy Company gave to

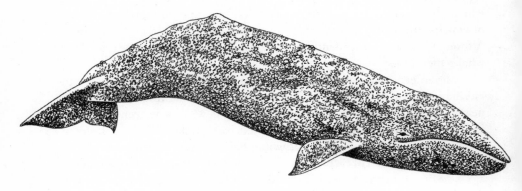

GRAY WHALE   (*Eschrichtius robustus*)

Thomas Edge in 1611. These instructions include descriptions of whales Edge might look for, including one, the *Otta sotta,* described as being "the same colour as the Trumpa [sperm whale] having finnes in his mouth all white but not above a yard long, being thicker than the Trumpa but not so long. He yeeldes the best oyle but not above 30 hogs' heads." And in the *Philosophical Transactions of the Royal Society of London* for 1725, Paul Dudley described the "scrag whale," with characteristics applicable to no other species but the gray whale: "The Scrag whale is near a-kin to the Fin-back, but instead of a Fin on his Back, the Ridge of the After part of his Back is scragged with a half Dozen Knobs or Knuckles; he is nearest the right Whale in Figure and for Quantity of Oil; his bone is white but won't split."

The most thorough account of the Atlantic gray whale in the historical record is Ole Lindquist's "The North Atlantic Gray Whale (*Eschrichtius robustus*): An Historical Outline Based on Icelandic, Danish-Icelandic, English and Swedish Sources Dating from ca 1000 A.D. to 1792," published in 2000. The author reads Icelandic, Danish, and Swedish and therefore found many more sources than those of us who relied upon earlier, mostly English-language, authors. One such source is a 1657 work by Thomas Bartholin, a University of Copenhagen professor, called "Record of the Fishes of Iceland," which contains this description:

> The fifteenth type is the *sandlaegja*. It is twenty or nearly thirty ells long and lies quietly in the sand. It takes the greatest possible pleasure in sand and greedily seeks out the tiny little fish which are abundant there. It is equipped with horny plates, and although it is eaten by humans, it does not have a pleasant taste, nor is it particularly fat. It is difficult to kill and dies slowly as seals do. It is happy to rest on land. If one comes upon it in the sand, one cannot get near it because it throws up the surrounding sand and moves vigorously in an extraordinary way. But once the force of the waves had driven it into the shallows and it has been run through in several places by spears, it lies dead.

An Icelander named Theodor Thorlacius (1637–1697), bishop of Skáholt, wrote of the *Sandlaegja* in 1666: "It takes its name from the sand in which it loves to lie, because it is generally seen on the shore. All these have [baleen] but lack teeth. Its flesh is very beneficial to health and perfectly suitable for eating." In 1706, another Icelander, Thormod Torfaeus, wrote *Groenlandica anttiqua,* in which he described the *Sandlaegja* thus: "They have a large tongue and taste good, something they have in common with all those endowed with gills. Their fat is more easily melted than those of the lean ones." These descriptions, Lindquist remarks, "reflect the Icelanders' knowledge of gray whales as it was around 1650."

Especially in the lagoons of Baja California, Pacific gray whales inhabit fairly shallow waters, and they have been known to strand themselves on beaches or sandbars, but no living whale habitually comes ashore. To do so would mean almost certain death, for whales are ill equipped to move on land, and a whale on the beach in the sun is a whale that cooks in its own blubber insulation. It is therefore curious to read the Icelanders' descriptions of the habits of the *Sandlaegja,* almost every one of which alludes to the whale's habit of lying in the sun like a seal. Lindquist mentions Swedish clergyman Olaus Magnus (1490–1557), who wrote of a whale "clearly distinguishable from the walrus, which comes on to the beach in sunshine where it sleeps soundly like the seal and which people frequently manage to capture by tying it with ropes." Lindquist wrote that "the only cetacean that has a habit like that is the gray whale," but even if the Atlantic version regularly came ashore, as the Icelanders said it did, its Pacific counterpart does not engage in such self-destructive behavior.

In *Sea of Slaughter,* an impassioned condemnation (written in 1984) of humankind's ecological excesses in the North Atlantic Ocean, Farley Mowat gives us a most dramatic version of the disappearance of the gray whale, which he calls *Otta sotta.* Something, or some groups of hunters, eliminated the Atlantic gray whale, but Mowat's hard evidence is thin and hard to track down. In his view, at least, the *Otta sotta* was "the favorite prey of the Basque whalers until they exterminated it, relegated it to historical oblivion." The more cautious Ole Lindquist concludes that

> the North Atlantic gray whale was hunted primarily by coastal
> inhabitants (a) around the North Sea and the English Channel, from
> prehistoric times at least into the high Middle Ages; (b) in Iceland, from
> about 900 A.D. until about 1730; and (c) in New England by European
> settlers from the mid 17th century until about the same time, possibly
> also by Indians there; secondly that it was caught by Basques in the latter
> half of the 16th century and in the early 17th century.

We have no way of knowing whether the Basques and the Icelanders by themselves hunted the Atlantic gray whale to extinction. Its numbers might have been low before the first Basque *chaloup* was launched. We do know that these very whalers wreaked havoc on the right whale populations of the Bay of Biscay and then headed across the North Atlantic, where they did the same thing. Yet for all this killing, the right whale is not extinct. During the past two centuries, it appeared for all the world as if the idea were to kill all the whales, but despite our massive, concentrated efforts, we failed to eliminate a single great whale species. If industrial whaling could not eliminate any species of whale, how could seventeenth-century open-boat whalers armed with hand-thrown harpoons have accomplished what the diesel-powered catcher boats armed with exploding harpoons could not? It would have been an extraordinary accomplishment for the early hunters to kill *all* the Atlantic gray whales, but even if they didn't, they could have so stressed the population that it became vulnerable to other deadly forces, such as disease or climate change. To imperil (or even eliminate) a species, we don't have to administer the final coup de grâce ourselves.

There is no more poignant example of the agonizing inadequacy of humankind's approach to marine mammals than the disappearance of Steller's sea cow. When Commander Vitus Bering's ship *St. Peter* was wrecked on a remote western Aleutian island in 1741, the surviving crew members found there, in addition to bewhiskered sea otters, immense "sea cows," which were subsequently named for Georg Wilhelm Steller, the naturalist on the voyage. Bering died on the island, but Steller survived and reported the existence of fur seals, sea otters, and the sea lions that now bear his name. Returning sealers killed the huge, slow-moving, oil-rich "manatees" with such fervor that there were none left by 1768.

We have entered an era in which the lesson of the sea cows has been ignored, usually in the name of short-term profits. Whalers, fishermen, and sealers have systematically destroyed the fisheries that sustained them and have then been surprised that they could not pass on their legacy to those who followed. Gone are the days when cod fishermen on the Grand Banks, off the southeastern coast of Newfoundland—once the world's richest neighborhood for *Gadus morhua*—could lower a basket on a rope and bring it up filled with wriggling cod. Only recently have biologists come to understand the intricacies of fish breeding, recruitment, and migration, and for many species the revelations have come too late.

So many of the inhabitants of the oceans have been depleted—fishes, sharks, whales, dolphins—but so have many creatures that spend only a part of their lives in the water yet depend on the oceans for their very existence. The semiaquatic seals and sea lions feed and travel in the water but come out to breed and give birth, as does the sea otter. Perched as he is at the pinnacle of the food pyramid, *Homo sapiens* has made a career of eliminating those on the lower tiers. Even the most powerful of the ocean's predators—the sharks, tunas, billfishes, whales, and dolphins—have fallen before the fishers' and hunters' relentless determination to wrest a living from the sea's bounty. Some of these creatures were hunted for food, some for fur, some for oil. Some species of aquatic birds died by the thousands because they were trapped in nets meant for fishes, and some, like the flightless great auk, were hunted for food and clubbed out of existence. Our ability to affect the life and death of sea creatures—the subject of this book—acutely underscores our responsibility to the creatures that share our planet. In that sense—and *only* in that sense—is it our planet.

We are stranded on shore, watching as the bountiful sea life disappears before our uncomprehending eyes. For many species, what we do—or don't do—in the coming years will make the difference between existence and extinction. In some cases, it is too late to do anything; the sea cows, great auks, Labrador ducks, and Caribbean monk seals are gone, probably to be followed into the black hole of extinction by barndoor skates, thorn-back rays, Patagonian toothfish, Chinese river dolphins, Ganges River dolphins, and the little Gulf of California porpoises known as vaquitas. Weep for them—and listen to the words of William Beebe: "The beauty and genius of a work of art may be reconceived, though its first material expression be destroyed; a vanished harmony may yet again inspire the composer; but when the last individual of a race of living things breathes no more, another heaven and another earth must pass before such a one can be again."

EMPTYING THE OCEAN

~ 2 ~

DECLINE OF THE FISHERIES

Abundant signs of the biosphere's limited resilience exist all around. The oceanic fish catch now yields $7.5 billion to the U.S. economy and $82 billion worldwide. But it will not grow further, simply because the amount of ocean is fixed and the organisms it can generate is static. As a result, all of the world's seventeen oceanic fisheries are at or below sustainable yield. During the 1990s the annual global catch leveled off at about 90 million tons. Pressed by ever growing global demand, it can be expected eventually to drop. Already fisheries of the western North Atlantic, the Black Sea, and portions of the Caribbean have collapsed. Aquaculture, or the farming of fish, crustaceans, and mollusks, takes up part of the slack, but at rising environmental cost. This "fin-and-shell revolution" necessitates the conversion of valuable wetland habitats, which are nurseries for marine life. To feed the captive populations, fodder must be diverted from crop production. Thus aquaculture competes with other human activity for productive land while reducing natural habitat. What was once free for the taking must now be manufactured.

—Edward O. Wilson, *The Future of Life*, 2002

The marine ecosystem has traditionally been considered safe from human degradation, mostly because of its size and depth. There was just too much of it for our puny efforts to have much of an effect, and the creatures that lived in it seemed infinite in variety and endless in number. John Seabrook noted in a 1994 *Harper's* magazine article:

Marine-fishery management has always rested on the assumption that the number of fish in the sea is limitless. Other of our natural resources—timber, bison, land, wild horses—used to be managed in the same way, and each time we neared the end of the resource the philosophy changed. Ocean management has not yet changed, although

11

it has begun to adapt. The ocean is still free, as it has been forever. Traditionally, if you wanted to buy a factory trawler, hire a crew of a hundred men, and go out and catch tens of thousands of fish a day, you didn't have to pay the government anything for the use of the resource—no rent, no special taxes. In fact, the government would help set you up in business with tax incentives and low interest loans.

At his inaugural address to the International Fisheries Exhibition in London in June 1883, Thomas Huxley spoke of the state of the fisheries. Not even a salmon river could be exhausted, he said, because the men who fished the river were "reachable by force of law." That is, they could be restrained by law if the fish population was seen to be threatened. He continued:

> Those who have watched the fisheries off the Lofoden Islands on the coast of Norway say that the coming of the cod in January and February is one of the most wonderful sights in the world; that the cod form what is called a 'cod mountain' which may occupy a vertical height of from 20 to 30 fathoms—that is to say, 120 to 130 feet, in the sea, and that these shoals of enormous extent keep coming in in great numbers from the westward and southward for a period of something like two months.

On these and other grounds, it seemed to Huxley that "this class of fisheries—cod, herring, pilchard, mackerel, &c.—might be regarded as inexhaustible."

In 1961, Hawthorne Daniel and Francis Minot published *The Inexhaustible Sea,* a book described on the jacket as "the exciting story of the sea and its endless resources." But Daniel and Minot hadn't been reading the newspapers carefully: while they were writing their book, journalists were reporting that the anchovy population off the coast of Peru was crashing. Anchovies (genus *Engraulis*) and sardines (genera *Sardina* and *Sardinops*) are among the most important of all commercially fished species. The California sardine fishery, celebrated by John Steinbeck in his 1945 novel *Cannery Row,* peaked at 1.5 billion pounds in 1936 but had ceased to exist by 1962. Anchovetas (*Engraulis ringens*) were so abundant off Peru Current in such vast numbers that they once headed the list of largest commercial catches: more than 12.1 million tons were caught in 1967. But this fishery completely collapsed in 1973 (a result of not only overfishing but also the El Niño of that year), and the anchoveta, once considered the most numerous fish in the world, is now greatly reduced in numbers. And the codfish, responsible for the discovery and early industrial success of New England, is essentially gone, its "inexhaustible" fishery closed indefinitely.

At four o'clock every morning of the year, the Tsukiji Fish Market in Tokyo opens with five acres crammed with sea life of every description: fin-fish, sharks, octopuses, squid, sea urchins, shrimp, lobsters, sea cucumbers, seaweed, and some things that appear to defy categorization. By ten o'clock, everything is gone, the market has closed, and workmen are swabbing the wooden floors of the buildings. Every day, it looks as if the fishermen have vacuumed another part of the ocean to fill the market's stalls with an incredible display of sea life.

The fishermen are fishing as if there were no tomorrow. An article titled "Diminishing Returns" in the November 1995 issue of *National Geographic* begins with these words:

> The unthinkable has come to pass. The wealth of oceans, once deemed inexhaustible, has proven finite, and fish, once dubbed "the poor man's protein," have become a resource coveted—and fought over—by nations.

Even this is an understatement. The fishing off Japan, the decimation of the California sardine fishery, and the crash of the Peruvian anchoveta population are just a few moments in a process that has been going on for decades at an accelerating pace. Throughout the world's oceans, food fishes once believed to be immeasurable in number are now recognized as greatly depleted and in some cases almost extinct. A million vessels now fish the world's oceans, twice as many as there were twenty-five years ago. Are there twice as many fish as before? Hardly.

Close to the precipice of extinction, if not already over the edge, is the white abalone (*Haliotis sorenseni*) of Mexican and California waters. It was said to have occurred in densities of as many as 10,000 individuals per hectare less than half a century ago (a hectare equals 2.47 acres). By the early 1970s, "ab divers" were harvesting these small abalones in substantial quantities because their tender meat made them even more desirable than the larger and tougher pink, red, and green abalones. In 1972, seventy-two tons of white abalone were landed, but after that the catch steadily dwindled; by the early 1990s, the species had virtually disappeared. For almost two years, biologists and divers Gary Davis, Peter Haaker, and Daniel Richards searched areas of "suitable habitat" that were known to have supported this species, and in that time they managed to find only three live individuals, approximately one per acre. "The prognosis for white abalone recovery," wrote Davis and his colleagues in 1996, "is poor, even with immediate active intervention. Wild white abalone broodstock needs to be located quickly and protected, and additional broodstock needs to be produced before significant restoration effort can begin. Population recovery without human intervention is highly unlikely, and white abalone extinction appears imminent." By 1999, the picture had not improved, and in an article titled "Extinction Risk in the Sea," Callum Roberts and Julie Hawkins listed *Haliotis sorenseni* among the soon to be missing. The following year, the National Marine Fisheries Service (NMFS) made it a candidate species under the Endangered Species Act of 1973, and in May 2001, the white abalone became the first marine invertebrate to receive federal protection as an endangered species.

In the past, fish populations were depleted by the simple but lethal expedient of catching too many of the target species, thus reducing the numbers available for future capture and breeding. The introduction of new fishing technologies in the latter half of the twentieth century changed the nature of the industry. Now fishermen deploy longlines that may be a hundred miles long and hung with thousands of baited hooks, which may be intended to catch a particular kind of fish—marlins and swordfish, for example—but catch everything else too, including thousands of unwanted species of fish, sea turtles, dolphins, and seabirds. Drift nets and gill nets sometimes float unattended for years, killing fish and other ocean wildlife that no one will ever harvest. Bottom trawlers scrape the seafloor clean of every living thing, from bottom-dwelling fishes to corals.

No phase of the industry exemplifies "progress" better than the tuna fishery. Once upon a time, tuna of various species were commercially caught on hook and line, with men lined up along the rails of the fishing boats dropping unbaited hooks into a frenzy of feeding tuna, which would snap at anything. The hooked tuna were then yanked from the water, high over the shoulders of the fishermen, and dropped onto the deck. "Their great weight and strength," wrote Robert Morgan (1955), "often make landing by one man with a line impossible . . . and therefore, each hook is operated by two and sometimes three men." In some regions today a similar technique is employed, but the hooks, lines, and jigs are mechanized and there are no fishermen, just a battery of rods bobbing and yanking tuna out of the water and onto the deck.

The biggest change in tuna fishing, however, came with the introduction of the purse seine. Here, a motorboat dispatched from a larger fishing boat encircles a school of tuna with a net, and when the school is completely surrounded, the net, which is closed at the bottom like a colander, is "pursed"— the lines around the top are pulled together—and everything in the mesh is trapped and hauled aboard. Purse seining revolutionized the tuna fishery, particularly in the eastern tropical Pacific, producing catches that dwarfed all previous efforts. But the expeditious capture of albacore and yellowfin tuna had an unexpected downside: for reasons not clearly understood, herds of spinner and spotter dolphins associated closely with the schools of tuna, and when the nets were pursed, the dolphins were trapped too. The term used for the unintentional capture of species not targeted by the fishery is *bycatch*, perhaps the most insidious euphemism in the modern fishing lexicon.

Bycatch refers to the unwanted fish hauled in with the nets, species or sizes that are not marketable—young fish, for example, that have not reached breeding age and thus will never mature and propagate. The term also applies to animals other than fish that are caught in the nets, such as seabirds, dolphins, whales, and turtles. Between June and December 1990, U.S. observers from the National Oceanic and Atmospheric Administration (NOAA) traveling aboard Japanese ships in the northern Pacific sampled 4 percent of the fleet's catch. In addition to catching 7.9 million squid (the target species), seventy-four Japanese vessels took in a bycatch that included 82,000 blue sharks, 253,000 tuna, nearly 10,000 salmonids, 30,000 birds, 52 fur seals, 22 sea turtles, 141 porpoises, and 914 dolphins. Many of these animals are airbreathers; entanglement in fishing nets prevents them from surfacing to breathe, and as a consequence they drown. In the Bering Sea, fishers discarded 16 million undersized red king crabs in 1990—more than five times the number of crabs they were able to bring to market.

The most visible of all bycatches, of course, was the hundreds of thousands of dolphins that were trapped and killed in the tuna nets of eastern tropical Pacific fishermen in the 1960s and 1970s, but this was far from the most harmful and wasteful example. "For every 10 pounds of Gulf of Mexico shrimp scraped from the sea floor," wrote Sylvia Earle in 1995, "80 to 90 pounds of 'trash fish'—rays, eels, flounder, butterfish, redfish, batfish, and more, including juveniles of many species—are mangled and discarded, in addition to tons of plants and animals not even considered worth reporting as 'bycatch,' i.e., starfish, sand dollars, urchins, crabs, turtle grass, seaweed, sponges, coral, sea hares, sea squirts, polychaete worms, horse conchs, and whatever else constitutes the seafloor communities that are in the path of the nets." In a 1996 discussion of the Gulf of Mexico shrimp fishery, NMFS fishery management specialist Steve Branstetter reported in a similar vein that "shrimp constituted 16% of the total catch by weight, other invertebrates 16%, and finfish 68%." The most abundant species in the bycatch were longspined porgy, brown shrimp, croakers, lizardfish, pink shrimp, and butterfish. Juvenile red snappers made up only 0.4 to 0.5 percent of the total catch by weight, but this percentage was calculated to number between 10 million and 35 million individuals annually, which indicates the incredible extent of the bycatch problem in this region.

With reported landings of 154,083 tons in 1999, shrimp is among the most valuable commercial food fisheries in the United States. According to a statistical database of the Food and Agriculture Organization of the United Nations (FAO), the world's shrimp fisheries hauled in 4,423,673 tons of shrimp and prawns in 1999. If other shrimpers are as efficient as Americans operating in the Gulf of Mexico, that adds as much as 30 million tons—*60 billion pounds*—of wasted fishes, sharks, rays, turtles, starfishes, sea anenomes, and cephalopods (squid and octopuses) that are bycatch in the shrimp fishery.

Stretching as far as a hundred miles, longlines consist of thousands of baited hooks for tuna, swordfish, and other billfishes. But longlines also kill young tuna, swordfish, and marlins that should be allowed to grow and breed, as well as sharks, birds, and other sea life in large quantities. Swordfish can be caught with harpoons, and tuna can be caught with hook and line, but these older ways require more work and are therefore less cost-effective. And if there was ever an industry based on cost-effectiveness, it is the modern fishery. Often marginal, and even more often unprofitable, modern mechanized fisheries are driven to wring every dollar, yen, or kopeck from the sea before the fish populations crash or before interfering legislators make them follow regulations that might actually protect the stocks of fish.

Longline fishing is an especially powerful threat to almost all of the twenty-four recognized living species and subspecies of albatross. Baited hooks are "set" from the rear of the fishing vessel, and before these hooks sink to their optimum fishing depths, the albatrosses dive for the still-floating bait, become hooked, and are dragged underwater and drowned. Each year, the Japanese fishing industry alone sets 107 million or more hooks and is responsible for at least 44,000 albatross deaths. Additional losses are caused by fishing fleets from Argentina, North and South Korea, Indonesia, Uruguay, New Zealand, Taiwan, Peru, Brazil, Hawaii, Namibia, and Australia. At least 60,000 albatrosses and other seabirds may be hooked and drowned by longline fishing vessels engaged in the pirate fishery for Patagonian toothfish, which sets anywhere between 50 million and 100 million hooks in the Southern Ocean each year.

Between 1980 and 1986, the southern bluefin tuna fishery may have accounted for an annual mortality of 2–3 percent of adult wandering albatrosses and 14–16 percent of immature birds nesting on South Georgia Island (Croxall et al. 1990), in addition to numerous deaths at the Crozet Islands in the South Indian Ocean. It is estimated that as many as 1,500 Tasmanian shy albatrosses, out of a total breeding population of 12,000, are killed each year on longlines. Long-lining contributes to the observed decreases of other albatross populations as well, including the black-footed and Laysan albatrosses of the Northern Hemisphere, especially in the northern Pacific Ocean, the Bering Sea, and the Gulf of Alaska. In recent years, an estimated 4,500 black-footed albatrosses have been killed annually by longline vessels fishing in Hawaiian waters alone. Given the circumpolar distribution of the black-browed albatross and the overlap of its range with fishing efforts, this species may face the greatest threat from fisheries of any albatross. Many of the dead albatrosses (of all species) appear to be inexperienced young birds in their first years of oceanic wandering, which means that the albatrosses lose the young of previous seasons and therefore lose potential breeding adults, leaving a dwindling, aging population. As Carl Safina (2002) pointed out:

> At one time, albatrosses survived extermination only by being at sea. Today, most albatrosses are safe only on land—where they spend just 5 percent of their lives. Hunting and killing on land in decades past was certain to miss at least some islands and some nests and some birds. But nowadays, every albatross, no matter how remote its nest, finds numerous opportunities to die on a longline. If it does and it has a chick on the nest when that happens the chick starves.

There is some cause for hope, however. A new device developed by Ed Melvin and others at the Washington Sea Grant Program could substantially reduce the number of albatrosses caught by long-liners. Each long-liner would be required to fly streamers suspended from strings behind the boat that would flutter in the wind and keep the birds from snatching at the baited hooks. In their 2001 report, Melvin and his colleagues commented, "In 2000, paired streamer lines virtually eliminated both Laysan albatross and northern fulmar attacks on baited hooks, and completely eliminated the albatross and northern fulmar bycatch." Safina, in his book titled *Eye of the Albatross: Visions of Hope and Survival,* continues:

> The birds are now reasonably secure on their islands, where once they were hunted mercilessly. The main threat now comes from longline fishing, but where longline fishing pressure has softened, some albatross populations have begun to trend upward. For example, Wanderer populations on Crozet and Kerguelen Islands in the Indian Ocean, which had plunged by more than half between 1960 and 1990, are now increasing because many longline boats have moved away from these birds' main feeding grounds (after depleting the Southern Bluefin Tuna

they'd targeted). Antipodes Albatrosses increased from about eight hundred pairs in the late 1960s to over five thousand pairs by the mid-1990s—by far the greatest increase for any great albatross population. The short-tailed has been increasing at 7 percent per year. Full recovery of these species could still require well over a century, and others are in trouble, but the point is this: these birds were in very bad shape, yet things have changed for the better.

Gill nets, still in common use, are submerged walls of netting whose meshes form a noose around the heads and bodies of fish that swim into them. They are used for surface, midwater, or bottom fishing and can be anchored or set adrift; in the latter case, they are referred to as drift nets. (Drift gill nets, a third type, are attached to the vessel at one end, with the other end drifting behind.) When Japan developed monofilament fibers that could be used in open-ocean drift-netting in the mid-1970s, it introduced the most destructive method of fishing ever devised. Large-scale high-seas drift nets were first used in the North Pacific by fleets from Japan, Taiwan, and South Korea. Because of the huge bycatch of marine wildlife in these nets, they have been labeled "walls of death"; hundreds of thousands of whales, dolphins, seabirds, sea turtles, sharks, and other nontarget species have been killed by them to date. Free from any connection with the boat, drift nets are set with floats at the top and weights at the bottom so that they drift passively in the water and trap fish that swim into them. Traditionally, these were small nets used in coastal waters to catch densely schooling fish, such as herring, but with the introduction of light synthetic netting, drift net fishing underwent a major change. The nets can now be used on the high seas, where they are very effective at catching wide-ranging species such as tuna and squid. Barely visible in the water, these nets are devastatingly effective at catching all other wildlife in their path. Each boat sets as much as forty miles of net, totaling some *40,000 miles* of drift net, every night—enough to circle the earth one and a half times.

Dolphins and porpoises are probably caught in drift nets because they cannot "see" the monofilament fibers. Even though the dolphins' mechanism of echolocation is incredibly sensitive, the thin strands of fiber that make up the drift net may not reflect sound well enough to provide an echo. And even if the dolphins receive a signal, they may not be echolocating at the moment before entanglement. They may well detect the plastic floats at the tops of the nets, but those would very likely appear to them as no cause for concern, and they certainly give no indication of the danger below. Because most dolphin species are gregarious—none more so than spinners and spotters, which aggregate in huge schools that may number in the thousands—if the "lead-ers" blunder into a monofilament net, the rest of the school may follow. The long snouts of these dolphins are pushed through the mesh; because the ani-mals are unable to recognize the nature of the snare, they try to push forward and are trapped and drowned.

By 1987, the Japanese squid fleet consisted of more than 1,200 drift netters, each deploying thirty miles of net nightly during a season that lasted seven months. Various conservation organizations, particularly Earthtrust and Greenpeace, campaigned vigorously against this horrifically destructive method, but it would take years of outrage before anything was done. In 1989, videocameraman Sam LaBudde signed on a Panamanian fishing boat as a cook and surreptitiously filmed nets being hauled aboard with dead baby dolphins trapped in the mesh. The film that resulted, *Stripmining the Seas,* became an important weapon in the arsenal designed to bring an end to drift netting. In April 1990, the FAO announced that drift netting had been found even more destructive than previously reported. Between 315,000 and 1 mil-lion dolphins of various species, the organization estimated, were being killed annually—in addition to the 20,000 dolphins killed every year in the purse seine fishery for tuna. Although the United States and Japan signed a joint resolution to outlaw drift netting in 1991, Taiwan continued to build drift net-ters, deploying them off the coast of Africa to avoid detection and prosecu-tion. Under intense international pressure, Taiwan finally shut down its drift net fishery in 1994.

The United Nations described large-scale high-seas drift nets as "a highly indiscriminate and wasteful fishing method" and adopted a resolution to ban them. In June 1998, the European Union moved to phase out all drift nets by European nationals and ban the use of drift nets in European waters. Despite this international condemnation, high-seas drift nets continue to kill thou-sands of dolphins and all manner of other marine life. In January 1999, NOAA banned the use of drift nets by U.S. fishermen in the North Atlantic swordfish fishery to reduce marine mammal bycatch. Because U.S. fishermen are not permitted to use drift nets in the South Atlantic swordfish fishery, this latest ruling bans the use of drift nets in the swordfish fishery throughout the Atlantic Ocean. Drift net fishing for Atlantic swordfish typically involved ten to twelve vessels per year for approximately fourteen days a year, but high bycatch rates of marine mammals and sea turtles prevented a reopening of the fishery.

A method of commercial fishing common in British waters, known as pair trawling, consists of two fishing boats towing a single gigantic net to ensnare fish between them. (Trawling differs from gillnetting in that the trawl is pulled behind a fishing vessel or vessels; gill nets are set and left to fish on their own.) With pair trawling, each vessel pulls on one side of the net, and by carefully coordinating the speed of their boats, the distance between the boats, and the length of their tow wires, the fishermen can precisely control the net's position. The target species is the sea bass, *Dicentrarchus labrax*, a fish that spawns in the Western Approaches, the area of the North Atlantic immediately west of the English Channel. Hundreds of thousands of sea bass gather between December and March every year, and the fry from their spawnings make their way back to the coast in search of sheltered waters in which to feed, grow, and mature. They are particularly fond of estuaries and even more fond of water warmed by the water discharged by nuclear power stations. The young bass are especially vulnerable in these inshore areas; many were being taken before growing big enough to journey back to the Western Approaches to spawn. "Nursery areas" were designated by the British government to give these immature bass some protection, and the number of bass returning to the spawning grounds increased. So many tons of valuable fish in the spawning grounds, however, proved to be too great a temptation, and the large pair trawlers moved in to exploit this otherwise unregulated fishery. French and Scottish pair trawlers had already devastated the black bream fishery for which they had been built, and now they were making massive inroads into the dolphin populations. As many as fifty common dolphins, harbor porpoises, and, occasionally, bottlenose dolphins may be caught in a single haul. Most of the bycatch in this fishery is unreported, but it has been estimated that as many as 2,400 dolphins are killed each year in this process (Deere-Jones 2001).

Before the advent of industrial fishing, some regions of the ocean were too distant or too deep for fishers to reach, and the fish that lived there remained untouched. But with the introduction of more and more sophisticated gear, no area is safe from human predations. Carl Safina (1998a) wrote: "Nowadays, every kind of seabed—silt, sand, clay, gravel, cobble, boulder, rock reef, worm reef, mussel bed, seagrass flat, sponge bottom, or coral reef—is vulnerable to trawling. For fishing rough terrain or areas with coral heads, trawlers have since the mid-1980s employed 'rockhopper' nets equipped with heavy wheels that roll over obstructions." Fishery workers can fish a mile down; they can locate schools of fish whose presence—whose very existence—was unsuspected; they can stay at sea for months and process the catch on board huge factory ships; they can deploy lines that stretch for fifty miles or nets that fish cannot see; they can see the bottom a mile down and drag their huge trawls over it, destroying an entire ecosystem; and they can completely change the character of the food chain.

Fisheries biologist Daniel Pauly is the author of the phrase (and the concept of) *fishing down the food chain*, which means first taking out the apex predators—large species such as cod, tuna, and swordfish—because they are the most desirable species, then, when they are gone, going down a trophic level and taking out their prey species (plankton-eaters such as anchovies), and then taking what's left. This downward shift has occurred as populations of predator fish have been decimated by overfishing and fishers have been forced to harvest what is left, species of the predators' prey. (From the Greek *trophe*, meaning "food" or "nourishment," *trophic level* refers to the position of organisms within food webs, and ranges from 1 [plant] to 5 [top predators].) To gauge the extent of this shift, researchers have assigned numbers to each trophic level, although the distinctions aren't as clear as one would like, given that many creatures feed at multiple levels. The predators at the very top of the chain, humans, are assigned level 5.0, and piscivorous apex hunters such as tuna and swordfish are assigned level 4.0; then 3.0 is given to the prey of these predators (squid, anchovies, and the like), 2.0 is reserved for the zooplankton (e.g., the copepods on which they feed), and 1.0 denotes the bottom level, the phytoplankton that support the whole structure. "We firmly believe," wrote Pauly and his colleagues in a 2000 *American Scientist* article, "that the mean trophic level of the catch . . . is truly declining":

> It takes very little to convince oneself that this situation is alarming—for seafood lovers as well as for environmentalists. After all, the average trophic level of the global catch has already slipped from 3.4 to 3.1 in just a few decades, and there are not many more appetizing species to be found below this level. [Recall that 2.0 corresponds to copepods and other tiny zooplankton, creatures that are unlikely ever to be filling one's dinner plate.] So if the trend continues, more and more regions are likely to experience complete collapse of their fisheries.

Because the top predators are usually sought first, Robert Steneck, a University of Maine marine biologist, said (1998): "It stands to reason that prey populations and their effects on marine communities will increase after release from predator control. Accordingly, fishing alters the organization and structure of entire marine communities via 'cascading' trophic chain reactions." Because the top predators are the least numerous, as one moves down a food web, biomass increases, but nowadays fish catches have stagnated as fishers have moved from top predators to species at lower trophic levels. Once

a top predator has been depleted or exterminated by fishing, alternative predators, which are of no commercial value, thrive in the absence of competition
and thus deplete the biomass of prey species at lower trophic levels.

"Fishing down the food chain," of course, is not restricted to human fishers, but the concept is important to an understanding of the ripple effect of
overfishing by humans. In Monterey Bay, California, the sea otters were
hunted to near extinction, which meant that the sea urchins on which they
fed could proliferate unchecked. The urchins in turn gnawed on the holdfasts
that anchored the giant kelp, which was thereby cut loose to float on the surface, thus eliminating the entire habitat of the fishes that called these great
kelp forests home. When great whales and sea lions began to disappear from
Alaskan waters (the whales because they were hunted by humans, the sea
lions perhaps because of the removal of pollock, their primary food source),
as argued by James Estes of the University of California, Santa Cruz, and colleagues (1998), the killer whales descended one trophic level and began prey-
ing on sea otters.

In the northwestern Mediterranean Sea, fishing has depleted sea urchin
predators, causing a great increase in the region's dominant sea urchin,
Paracentrotus lividus, which has grazed the seafloor into "a relatively feature-
less and largely inedible crustose coralline community" (Steneck 1998). Sea
urchins, however, though they might have a low trophic level, filling a niche
that has been left vacant by the removal of higher predators, must be recognized as a legitimate part of the marine community, and in some instances
the removal of sea urchins has had a calamitous effect on an ecosystem.
Around 1983, a still-unidentified pathogen arrived in the western North
Atlantic Ocean and began killing off the superabundant sea urchin known as
Diadema antillarum. The herbivorous *Diadema* kept the reefs clean of "turf
algae" and permitted the corals of the Caribbean, the Gulf of Mexico, the
Bahamas, and Bermuda to proliferate. When the urchins died, the algae
enveloped vast tracts of the underwater landscape, smothering the corals.

The tremendous increase in aquaculture (fish farming) in recent years
has been offered as a possible solution to the problems of worldwide overfishing, but aquaculture has its own problems, and in some cases it may be
contributing to, rather than solving, the overfishing problem. The species
most prominently farmed around the world are carp, salmon, trout, shrimp,
tilapia, milkfish, catfish, crayfish, oysters, hybrid striped bass, giant clams, and
various shellfish. Of these, shrimp and salmon make up only 5 percent of the
farmed fish by weight but almost 20 percent by value. Farming is the predominant production method for salmon, and aquaculture accounts for 25

percent of world shrimp production—a tenfold increase from the mid-1970s (Naylor et al. 1998).

By a substantial margin, China leads the world in aquaculture, and most of the fish farmed in China are carp, used for regional consumption in low-income households. In other parts of the world, farmed tilapia, milkfish, and channel catfish have replaced depleted ocean fish such as cod, hake, haddock, and pollock. Worldwide landings for the "capture fisheries" (those in which wild fish are caught at sea) have leveled off at around 85–95 million metric tons per year, with most stocks being recognized as fully fished or overfished. In 1990, the figure for aquaculture was 10 million tons, but by 2000 it had nearly tripled (Naylor et al. 2000). Global aquaculture now accounts for more than one-quarter of all fish consumed by humans.

Each species of farmed fish (shrimp and shellfish are also known as fish in aquaculture-speak) has its own requirements, and it is impossible to generalize about the benefits or detriments of fish farming as a whole. Carnivorous species, such as salmon and shrimp, are usually fed fish meal, made from ground-up fish. The cost of providing food for farmed salmon is nearly as high as the price the salmon can command; moreover, in this case, farming contributes to overfishing because the small fish—such as Peruvian anchovetas—are harvested almost exclusively for fish meal. (It is not only fishes that eat fish meal, of course; most of the processed fish meal is fed to chickens and pigs.) To feed the carnivores, fishermen are fishing for fish to feed to fish.

Carp, tilapia, and milkfish are herbivores and can be fed plant food or prepared fish food not unlike that which hobbyists sprinkle into their home aquariums. Could the vast amount of fishes and other creatures caught incidentally in a particular fishery and usually discarded—the bycatch—be saved and used for fish meal instead of targeted fishery species, such as anchovies? This, unfortunately, would require fishers to use valuable space aboard their ships for storage of bycatch, which are worth less per fish than the expensive fish they are seeking. In a 2001 article on the effects of aquaculture on world fish supplies, Rosamond Naylor (an economist and recognized authority on aquaculture) and two colleagues pointed out:

> Carps and marine molluscs account for more than three-quarters of
> current global aquaculture output, and tilapia, milkfish and catfish
> contribute another 5% of total production. Fed mainly on herbivorous
> diets, these species provide most of the 19 Mt [megatons] gain in fish
> supplies from aquaculture.... But market forces and government
> policies in many countries favour rapid expansion of high-value,

carnivorous species, such as salmon and shrimp. Moreover, fish meal and fish oil are already being added to carp and tilapia feeds for weight gain, especially in Asia where farming systems are intensifying as a result of increased scarcity and value of land and freshwater resources. Given the huge volume of farmed carp and tilapia in Asia, significant increases in the fish meal and fish oil content of feed could place even more pressure on pelagic [open-ocean] fisheries, resulting in higher feed prices and harm to marine ecosystems.

Shrimp farming is one of the phenomenal success stories in aquacultural history. More than 880,000 tons of shrimp are produced annually from 2.96 million acres of ponds around the world. Annual revenues are estimated to exceed U.S.$6 billion, and the industry is said to be particularly beneficial to developing countries, providing jobs, alleviating poverty, and in some cases even putting food on otherwise barren tables. (Many fishers, however, lost their livelihood.) However, because shrimp farming can be a boom-and-bust phenomenon, environmental and socioeconomic disasters frequently accompany this branch of aquaculture. Shrimp farms often displace home owners, which serves to increase poverty and homelessness; and when rice paddies or mangrove swamps are appropriated for shrimp farms, the net loss to the community cannot be overstated. Ponds located inland often seep saline waters into the surrounding area, which affects the growing of rice and other crops. Aquaculture may provide a long-term solution to the problems of overfishing, but as currently conceived, it often raises more problems than it solves. Here are Naylor and colleagues again:

> Growth in aquaculture production is a mixed blessing, however, for the sustainability of ocean fisheries. For some types of aquaculture activity, including shrimp and salmon farming, potential damage to ocean and coastal resources through habitat destruction, waste disposal, exotic species and pathogen invasions, and large fish meal and fish oil requirements may further deplete wild fisheries stocks. For other aquaculture species, such as carp and molluscs, which are herbivorous or filter feeders, the net contribution to global fish supplies and food security is great. The diversity of production systems leads to an underlying paradox: aquaculture is a possible solution, but also a contributing factor, to the collapse of fisheries stocks worldwide.

In late 2001, Rosamond Naylor was flying over Sonora looking for shrimp farms, expecting to find "clusters of scattered ponds separated by huge tracts of sere land." Instead, it looked as if the Gulf of California had risen and swept across more than forty-two square miles of the Sonoran Desert: everywhere were "patches of blue, pools of shrimp, one after another, all down the coast," in the words of Marguerite Holloway (2002). Aquaculture, the "blue revolution" of Holloway's article, is by now "a $52 billion-a-year global enterprise involving more than 220 species of fish and shellfish that is growing faster than any other food industry."

We all know that most of the earth is covered with water, but typically we see only the top of it. Beneath its shimmering surface there is a world of life, more intricately woven than that of any rain forest. The occupants range in size from the great whales, the largest animals ever to live on the planet, to microscopic dinoflagellates and submicroscopic viruses. Humans have taken advantage of the ocean's bounty for virtually all of recorded history, probably starting when a prehistoric beachcomber found a dead fish washed ashore, still relatively fresh. From that innocuous beginning or something akin to it, humans became whalers, sealers, aquaculturists, netters, trollers, purse seiners, long-liners, bottom trawlers, rod-and-reelers, dynamiters, poisoners, and myriad others dedicated to removing living things from the ocean. Sometimes the animals were killed for oil, sometimes for baleen, and sometimes for their fur coats, but for the most part they were used for food, and this seemed more than enough justification for the continuing slaughter of the oceans' wildlife. People had to eat, didn't they? Besides, the ocean was so big and so deep and so filled with edible items that there seemed no end to its productivity. If one population of whales (or seals, or fishes, or sharks) was depleted, the fishers simply moved to another area and attacked another population, or changed the object of the fishery. A number of fish species, previously regarded as so plentiful as to be unaffected by human enterprise, have instead shown themselves to be vulnerable to fishing to such a degree that they are now considered endangered. The idea that Mother Ocean would continue to provide for her dependents forever has shown itself to be another gross misjudgment on the part of those dependents.

THE LOWLY MENHADEN

Almost all species of commercially caught fishes are in trouble. Take the lowly menhaden (*Brevoortia tyrannus*), for example. Also known as mossbunker and pogy, this foot-long, one-pound member of the herring family is found in the continental waters of the United States from Maine to Florida. These fish are too bony and oily to be served at the dinner table, but the menhaden fishery is the largest on the Atlantic and Gulf coasts, exceeding the tonnage of

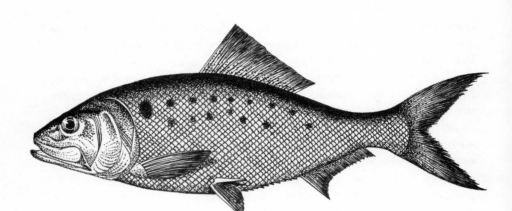

MENHADEN   *(Brevoortia tyrannus)*

all other species combined (Franklin 2001). Menhaden are silvery in color with a distinct black shoulder spot behind their gill opening and a variable number of smaller spots on their sides. They have a deeply forked tail fin, and, like shad and herring, they have a keel of sharp spines on the belly. Menhaden are consumers of phytoplankton and plant detritus and, in turn, are fed upon by almost every species of predatory fish, including striped bass, mackerel, cod, bonito, bluefish, swordfish, and tuna, as well as mammals and birds. Until the human industrialization of fishing, however, their numbers were more than adequate to feed their myriad predators.

In the past, menhaden could be found in immense schools, sometimes numbering in the millions "with their heads close to the surface, packed side by side, and often tier above tier, almost as closely as sardines in a box" (Goode and Clark 1887). The modern menhaden industry emerged in New England early in the nineteenth century, after it was recognized that the species could provide a valuable alternative to whale oil in the production of lubricants, fuel for lamps, soap, and paint. Factories for rendering menhaden were first built on the shores of Massachusetts, Maine, New York, and Connecticut. By the beginning of the twentieth century, menhaden also served as a component of fertilizer and animal feed and was used in the manufacture of substances such as fingernail polish and perfume.

Menhaden taken in Atlantic coastal waters from Maine to Florida and in the Gulf of Mexico provide the major source of fish meal in the United States. The fish are ground, cooked, and processed to yield press cake, fish solubles, and oil. The chicken industry is currently the largest user of menhaden meal, followed by turkey, swine, domestic pet food, cattle, sheep and goats, and, more recently, aquaculture. In Europe, the oil is refined and used extensively in cooking oils and margarine. In 1989, the U.S. Food and Drug Administration (FDA) concluded that fully and partially hydrogenated menhaden oil is a safe ingredient for human consumption. In 1990, the FDA proposed an amendment based on an industry petition to permit the use of marine oils. It was approved in 1997 and could provide a significant new market for menhaden oil, which is rich in omega-3 fatty acids. More recently, it has also been used as a cooking oil and an ingredient in processed foods such as cookies and cakes.

Chesapeake Bay once produced more seafood per acre than any other body of water on earth, and the largest proportion of this seafood was menhaden. The menhaden fishery had spread south from New England after the Civil War, when the purse seine was introduced, allowing the fishery to expand. Coal-fired steamers gradually replaced sailing ships as carrier vessels in the late 1800s; diesel and gasoline engines gradually replaced the steam engines following World War I. The use of purse seines to harvest menhaden continues today, but since the development in the 1950s of the hydraulic power block for pulling up the net, there has been no need for large crews. Other midcentury refinements included lighter, faster, and more maneuverable aluminum rather than wooden purse boats with motors instead of oars; more durable nylon seines instead of natural fiber nets; and large fish pumps, which eliminated the difficult work of transferring the catch from the net into the hold. In addition, spotter planes took over the work of sighting schools of menhaden, radioing locations to captains on board ship. With these changes, harvesting efficiency increased dramatically, with a subsequent drop in catches.

The average tonnage caught from 1996 to 1999 was only 40 percent of the annual take between 1955 and 1961. In the year 2000, the catch was 183,700 tons, the second lowest since 1940, when the National Marine Fisheries Service began keeping records. Maryland has outlawed purse seining in Chesapeake Bay, but Virginia has not. The largest U.S. fisher of menhaden and producer of fish oil and products from it, Houston-based Omega Protein Corporation, founded by former U.S. president George H. W. Bush, accounts for more than 60 percent of the menhaden catch from the Virginia waters of the bay. Omega Protein, which maintains that "the menhaden resource is healthy and self-renewing," is the maker of the so-called long-chain omega-3s that some doctors recommended for self-applied control of cardiovascular disease, cancer, and arthritis.

Despite the company's public optimism, in 2000 Omega Protein laid up thirteen of its fifty-three ships and grounded twelve of its forty-five spotter planes (Franklin 2001). The menhaden fishery has clearly suffered a decline, primarily as a result of international market conditions affecting the price of menhaden products, and, not surprisingly, a shortage of fish. The number of processing plants on the Atlantic coast declined from eight in 1981 to only two at the close of the twentieth century. Still, the menhaden support the largest single-species fishery on the Atlantic coast, the most concentrated fishery in Chesapeake Bay, and, after Alaskan pollock, the second largest fishery in America.

If the mossbunker population is indeed dwindling over the long term, it spells big trouble for Chesapeake Bay. Like oysters in the lower layers, menhaden are filter feeders, removing plankton from the waters of the bay. The Chesapeake Bay oysters have been driven to near extinction; if the menhaden go, there will be nothing to clean the estuaries. Native and alien jellyfish are proliferating, perhaps because the menhaden no longer keep their numbers down by feeding on the larval, planktonic stages.

THE GREAT AND WONDERFUL TUNA

Tokyo, January 5, 2001 (AP). An enormous bluefin tuna—a fish prized as sushi—sold for a record $173,600 Friday in the first auction of the year at Tokyo's main fish market. At $391 a pound, the 444-pound fish was the most expensive auctioned off at the Tsukiji Central Fish Market in years. In 1996, a 250-pound bluefin fetched $44,100. Called *honmaguro* in Japanese, bluefin tuna is popularly served raw as sashimi or sushi in restaurants where a plate of slices can command a bill of more than $100. Both fish were caught in the Pacific Ocean off Aomori Prefecture in northern Japan, an area known for the quality of its tuna. "It's kind of like a brand name," market official Takashi Yoshida said.

Every day in the Tsukiji Fish Market, which handles about 90 percent of the seafood that ends up on Tokyo's tables, the most valuable fish in the world appears as an arrangement of headless, tailless, ice-rimed blocks. These rock-hard carcasses have been trucked in from Japanese ports or flown from the distant waters of New Zealand, Australia, or New England. Here, they are auctioned off to brokers, who will auction them to restaurant owners, who will in turn sell the red, fatty meat as sashimi at upward of $75 per portion. There are a lot of two-ounce portions in a 600-pound bluefin tuna.

The bluefin tuna is probably the most endothermic of all living fishes.

Along with the broadbill swordfish and certain sharks, such as the mako shark, great white shark, and porbeagle, the tunas have developed a circulatory mechanism that enables them to elevate their internal body temperature to as much as twenty-five degrees higher than the water in which they are swimming. The rete mirabile, a sheet of tissue that places the veins and arteries close to each other, functions as a countercurrent heat exchanger. In a 1973 article in *Scientific American,* Frank Carey explained: the "venous blood warmed by metabolism gives up its heat to cold, newly oxygenated arterial blood fresh from the fish's gills. The effect is to increase the temperature and thus the power of the muscle." Heated muscle makes for more efficiency— think of an athlete warming up—and only the sailfish and some of the marlins can equal the estimated fifty-mile-per-hour swimming speed the bluefin tuna may attain. The swordfish, a deepwater hunter, heats up its brain and huge eyes, but tunas and mackerel sharks heat up their brains, their eyes, and their whole bodies. (The differences in these mechanisms have led biologists to suggest that the heat-conservation strategy evolved independently in the sharks, tunas, and swordfish.)

Along with warm-bloodedness, the bluefin has other characteristics that contribute to its speed and efficiency. Whereas the eyes of most fishes protrude, those of the bluefin are flush with its head, further decreasing the drag on what is probably the most hydrodynamically advanced body design of any fish. The bluefin's body is a slick, scaleless teardrop, with slots into which it can fold down its dorsal and pectoral fins. Along its narrow tailstock is a series of finlets; their function is not clearly understood, but they probably help reduce turbulence as the fish rockets through the water. The "drive train" of the tuna consists of a crescent-shaped tail moved from side to side

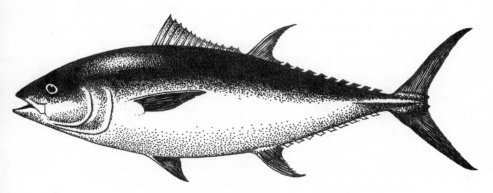

BLUEFIN TUNA *(Thunnus thynnus)*

by powerful muscles. (Most fishes move the after part of their bodies, but the tuna propels itself by moving only its lunate tail.) In his 1991 discussion of the mechanics of swimming, Chris McGowan commented: "The additional drag that accompanies lateral movements of the body is greatest at the tail end, where the displacement is highest, and this explains why endurance swimmers have a narrow caudal peduncle. It also explains why having a stiff tail is more efficient than having a flexible one. The most efficient swimming strategy is therefore to have a stiff body and tail and to allow only the tail to move, as in the tuna."

The largest of the tunas—and one of the largest of all the bony fishes— the bluefin (*Thunnus thynnus*) can reach a length of twelve feet and a weight of three-quarters of a ton. (The International Game Fish Association's record for a bluefin caught on rod and reel is 1,496 pounds.) The word *magnificent* is often applied to the bluefin, and it is exquisitely applicable. They are bluewater (open-ocean) schooling fishes that not only swim incredibly fast but also make some of the longest migrations of any fish. Specimens tagged in the Bahamas have been recaptured in Newfoundland, Norway, and even Uruguay. The northern Pacific bluefin (*Thunnus tonggol*) ranges across the entire northern Pacific, migrating from California to Japan and back (the $173,000 fish was one of these) and sometimes detouring as far south as New Guinea. The southern bluefin, *Thunnus maccoyii*, a very similar species, lives only in the Southern Hemisphere and makes similar migrations. Bluefins feed on mackerel, herring, mullet, whiting, eels, and squid.

Long before the Japanese elevated it to the heights of gastronomic desirability, the bluefin was considered one of the world's premier game fishes. The great weight and sheer power of giant tuna made fishermen eager to do battle with them, even though there were few success stories. Zane Grey, the author of popular western novels in the 1920s and 1930s, was a passionate biggame fisherman, spending most of his not inconsiderable royalties (his books sold 13 million copies) on fishing trips, fishing boats, and fishing gear. In addition to books such as *Riders of the Purple Sage,* he wrote about his fishing experiences. In *Tales of Swordfish and Tuna* (1927), he described his battles with giant bluefin tuna, first in California and then in Nova Scotia waters. After many tries, he hooked one and fought it for four hours:

> To me he seemed enormous, supremely beautiful and unattainable. He
> flashed purple, bronze, silver-gold. When he went under he left a surging
> abyss in the water, a gurgling whirlpool. This sight again revived me. I
> was a new man, at least for a little while. I turned that tuna round. I
> pulled the launch toward him. I held him so that he towed us stern first.

In short I performed, for the time being, miraculous and hitherto unknown feats of rod endurance. I would have cheerfully walked overboard into the sea for that fish.

Brought to the dock, the tuna measured eight feet, eight inches in length and six feet, four inches in girth and weighed 758 pounds. In the prose for which he was famous, Grey described the vanquished fish:

> I was struck dumb by the bulk and beauty of that tuna. My eyes were glued to his noble proportions and his transforming colors. He was dying and the hues of a tuna change most and are most beautiful at that time. He was shield-shaped, very full and round, and high and long. His back glowed a deep dark purple; his side gleamed like mother-of-pearl in a lustrous light; his belly shone a silver white. The little yellow rudders on his tail moved from side to side, pathetic and reproachful reminders to me of the life and sprit that was passing. If it were possible for a man to fall in love with a fish, that was what happened to me. I hung over him, spellbound and incredulous.

Bluefin tuna are still prized as big-game fishes, but it is the Japanese sashimi market that sets the astronomical prices on these fish. When a big, top-quality tuna is caught in New England, Australia, or New Zealand waters, it can sell on the dock for more than an average two-bedroom house, and by the time it is served in a restaurant, its value may have increased tenfold.

Because of the prices they can fetch, bluefins have been overfished, and their North Atlantic breeding populations are estimated to have declined by about 90 percent since 1980. As with all fish populations, exact counts are impossible, so there are vast gaps between the high estimates made—to no one's surprise—by the fishermen and the low estimates made by those who would protect the tuna from overfishing. From dock to cabinet ministry, there have been endless discussions about solving the problem at every level, but few protective measures have been taken because to do so would require unprecedented domestic and international cooperation. There is an organization that is supposed to oversee the tuna industry, the Madrid-based International Convention for the Conservation of Atlantic Tunas, known as ICCAT (pronounced "eye-cat," and ridiculed as the "International Conspiracy to Catch All Tuna"). In response to dwindling catches, ICCAT's twenty-two member countries divided the North Atlantic Ocean into eastern and western sectors, each with its own quota. In 1991, when Sweden submitted a proposal to ICCAT that the bluefin be listed as endangered, it was immediately voted down by the United States and Japan, countries with a strong economic interest in catching tuna. Conservationists, fishermen, and bureaucrats continued to draft position papers and proposals while the tuna populations plummeted and the prices rose. As John Seabrook wrote in 1994, "one reason that the price is so high is that there are so few of them left in this part of the ocean, and one reason that there are so few of them is because the price is so high." If someone is willing to pay $173,000 for a fish, a lot of fishermen will be looking to be the lucky one to cash in.

When Gramps took little Billy to the Old Fishin' Hole, he had a pretty good idea that there would be sunfish or crappies there and it would be a simple matter of dropping in a hook baited with a worm. But commercial pelagic fishing bears no resemblance to a fishin' hole. In order to catch fish—or, for that matter, to protect a species—people have to understand where the fish go and when. Nowadays, every available technological and biological advancement is employed in the never-ending quest to understand the behavior of fish. To locate them, fishers use radar, sonar, loran, and spotter planes; to catch them, they deploy drift nets, gill nets, purse seines, and gigantic trawls; and to process and transport the catch, there are powerful, far-ranging factory ships.

In 1996, Molly Lutcavage of the New England Aquarium, along with Paul Howey of Microwave Telemetry, Inc. in Columbia, Maryland, began to develop microprocessor tags that could be attached to Atlantic bluefins in an attempt to better understand their migration and biology. In previous tagging systems, the tag included only information about where and when it was inserted, so when a fish was caught, the most researchers could learn was how long the fish took to get from there to here. The new tags, however, logged the fish's temperature hourly, averaged the temperatures, and stored the figure. After sixty days, the tiny computer shut down, an electric current was generated to corrode the wires fastening it to the fish, and the tag floated to the surface, transmitting its data via satellite to waiting scientists. Barbara Block of Stanford University launched thirty-seven of Howey's pop-up tags but then employed an "archival" tag, which was lodged in the tuna's abdomen and measured not only water temperature but also light, depth, and internal body temperature until the fish was caught and the tag recovered. Among the more surprising findings revealed by the microprocessor tags was that tuna, long believed to travel and hunt near the surface, made regular dives to a depth of 3,300 feet while feeding on squid and could maintain a body temperature of 80°F or higher in the ink-black, icy cold waters more than half a mile down. (Most other fishes, commonly known as cold-blooded, would have a body temperature of 39°F in 39°F water.)

By 2000, a total of 377 fishes had been tagged along the eastern coast of North America with both types of microprocessor tags, pop-up and archival. In a report published in *Science* magazine the following year, Block and her colleagues showed that the migratory behavior of the bluefin was far more complex than anyone had imagined. Rather than segregating into eastern and western Atlantic populations, the tuna "mixed," which further complicated the already thorny issue of who has the right to catch which tuna. Moreover, this mixing did not occur just near the midline: some tuna were found to have traversed the entire ocean—some 1,670 nautical miles—in less than ninety days' time. Before the tagging data were analyzed, it was thought that perhaps 2–4 percent of the tuna crossed ICCAT's line (the forty-fifth meridian) separating the "American" tuna from the "European." ICCAT had established quotas on the assumption that there were two distinct populations that did not mix, but it now appears that although there are two distinct spawning areas—the Gulf of Mexico and the Mediterranean Sea—the fish migrate across the Atlantic Ocean at will until they attain sexual maturity, at eight to ten years of age, at which time they migrate to their particular spawning grounds. Both eastern and western populations feed at western foraging spots, but they separate for breeding. Moreover, it was not 2–4 percent of the bluefins that crossed the ocean; it was closer to 30 percent.

The tuna of the eastern zone, which are caught by Europeans, are managed under a strict annual quota set by the European Union, whereas those of the western Atlantic, targeted by American fishermen, have been managed under strict catch quotas since 1995. (As we shall see, neither of these quotas includes "farmed" tuna.) Nevertheless, in both areas, the stocks of bluefin tuna have fallen dramatically: there has been an 80 percent decline in the eastern (European) stock since 1980 and a 50 percent drop in the western Atlantic population.

Management is a fine and noble goal, but there has to be something left to manage. During the 1960s, bluefin catches peaked at about 38,500 tons, but less than a decade later, overfishing sent the catch plummeting to less than half of that figure, and a 1964 peak of 22,000 tons in the western Atlantic fell to 6,710 tons in 1978. The collapse of the New England tuna fishery has been comprehensively documented, most eloquently by Carl Safina in *Song for the Blue Ocean,* but where the big fish were before they arrived off Georges Bank is still a mystery. The same is true for the massive schools of tuna that every year entered the bottleneck of the Strait of Gibraltar and swam into the functional equivalent of a gigantic fish trap: the Mediterranean.

For thousands of years, men have fished for tuna in the Mediterranean. In her brilliant little book *Mattanza* (an Italian word that means "the killing"), Theresa Maggio chronicles the long, noble history of *tonnara* (tuna fishing), from the time of the Carthaginians and Phoenicians five centuries before Christ right up to present-day Sicily. "The bluefin were to ancient Mediterranean peoples what the buffalo were to the American Plains Indian," Maggio wrote, "a yearly miracle, a reliable source of protein from a giant animal they revered, one that passed in such numbers that the cooperation of an entire tribe was needed to kill them, and preserve their meat. Around the Mediterranean the migrating bluefin was a staple food for entire civilizations." Oppian, the second-century Greek poet and naturalist, wrote a poem on fishing called *Halieutica*, in which he described a second-century *tonnara*:

> Dropped in the water are nets arranged like a city. There are rooms and gates and deep tunnels and atria and courtyards. The tuna arrive in great haste, drawn together like a phalanx of men who march in rank: there are the young, the old, the adults. And they swim, innumerable, inside the nets and the movement is stopped only when there is no more room for new arrivals; then the net is pulled up and a rich haul of excellent tuna is made.

The *mattanza* of the village of Favignana, located on one of the Egadi Islands off the western tip of Sicily, is the most famous of recent *tonnare* (tuna fisheries) and one of only two remaining. A complex arrangement of gigantic nets is deployed along the tuna's expected route, and the fishermen wait for the great fish to swim into them. The nets are hung from ropes, "arranged like a city" as they were in Oppian's day, and stretched to the bottom by massive anchors. "The trap is oblong," wrote Maggio, "except for a widening at the shoulders that makes it look like a widening coffin. It is divided into seven rooms by net walls with gates in them. . . . It is fifty meters squared." The last "room" the tuna will ever see is the *camera della morte*—the "chamber of death"—the only room with a net bottom, which the *tonnaroti* raise by hand from seventy-five-foot-long open boats.

In *The Silent World*, published in 1953, Jacques Cousteau described his experience in a tuna net in Tunisia, where the death chamber is called a *corpo*:

> Marcel Ichac filmed the spectacle from a boat above the *corpo*, while Dumas and I dived into the net to record it below. Sunk in the crystalline water we could not see both sidewalls of the *corpo*, and imagined that the fish could not, either. We had unconsciously taken on the psyche of the doomed animals. In the frosty green space we saw the herd only occasionally. The noble fish, weighing up to four hundred pounds

apiece, swam around and around counter-clockwise, according to their habit. In contrast to their might, the net wall looked like a spider web that would rend before their charge, but they did not challenge it. Above the surface, the Arabs were shrinking the walls of the *corpo,* and the rising floor came into view. . . . The death chamber was reduced to a third of its size. The atmosphere grew excited, frantic. The herd swam restlessly faster, but still in formation. Their eyes passed us with almost human expressions of fright.

My final dive came just before the boatmen tied off the *corpo* to begin the killing. Never have I beheld a sight like the death cell in the last moments. In a space comparable to a large living room tunas and bonitos drove madly in all directions. It took all my will power to stay down and hold the camera into the maddened shuttle of fish. With the seeming momentum of locomotives, the tuna drove at me, head-on, obliquely and crosswise. It was out of the question for me to dodge them. Frightened out of sense of time, I heard the reel run out and surfaced amidst the thrashing bodies. There was not a mark on my body. Even while running amok the giant fish had avoided me by inches, merely massaging me with backwash when they sped past.

The nets were raised and the struggling fish gaffed as they came to the surface. Cousteau: "The fishermen struck at the surfaced swarm with large gaffs. The sea turned red. It took five or six men whacking gaffs into a single tuna to draw it out, flapping and bending like a gross mechanical toy. The boats rocked with convulsive bleeding mounds of tuna and bonitos." In the Favignana *tonnara* in 1957, at the height of the fishery, 7,480 tuna were killed.

I have never seen a *mattanza,* but I have seen films of one, and the sight of these sleek, graceful creatures being gaffed is heartbreaking. One moment they are on what Cousteau called their "honeymoon," and the next they are thrashing in a panicked mêlée as heavy steel hooks are smashed into their bodies and they are hauled ignominiously from the only element they have ever known into the one where they will die. Bluefins are among the most powerful and beautiful of the oceans' top predators, and seeing them gaffed is like watching a thoroughbred racehorse being hacked to death with an ax. Tuna of all kinds are among the world's most popular food fishes, and people are no more interested in knowing how they die than they are in visiting a terrestrial slaughterhouse. It might change our attitude toward tuna sandwiches or $75 pieces of sushi if we realized that tuna are wild animals, which happen to live in the ocean and therefore cannot be viewed like herds of zebras or wildebeest or packs of wolves. They are the oceans' nobility, described by Carl

Safina (1997) as "half a ton of laminated muscle rocketing through the sea as fast as you drive your automobile[; they are] among the largest and most magnificent of animals."

Tuna fishing was once one of Sicily's most important and profitable industries. Until the first decades of the twentieth century, coconut fiber nets more than a mile in length were deployed by the hundreds, but diminishing numbers of tuna, and market laws that make this fishing technique more capital-intensive, have left only about ten *tonnare* in the Mediterranean region; in Sicily, only Bonagia and Favignana remain. What was once a source of pride and the primary source of income for entire communities is now a tourist attraction, providing a few makeshift jobs for the unemployed in a social context poor in prospects and kept alive by the obstinate will of the remaining *tonnaroti*. The canneries in Sicily are closed; almost all the tuna caught in Favignana is shipped to Japan, where, like everyone else, buyers await the annual *mattanza*. There is a rumor in Favignana that the gaffing will be eliminated and the fishermen will simply wait for the tuna to die in the nets because the gaffs make too many holes in the flesh. "Once," wrote Theresa Maggio (2001), "the tuna snares thrived in Algeria, Corsica, Tunisia, Malta, Dalmatia, and Turkey. In Portugal they were called *armaçoes;* in Spain, *almandrabas;* in France, *madragues.* The cause of abandon: insufficient fish to make a profit. Once there were tonnaras all over Sicily. . . . Gone, all gone."

A loophole big enough to drive a factory ship through has been discovered in the regulations governing Mediterranean bluefin tuna fishing, and it could signal total extinction of the Mediterranean's bluefin population within a few years. Although there are strict quotas on the number of fish that can be caught in nets or by harpoons (*spadare*), no regulation whatsoever applies to "post-harvesting," the practice of catching wild tuna and keeping them in pens before they are slaughtered. Post-harvesting "farms" in the waters off Spain, Italy, Malta, and Croatia account for some 11,000 tons of tuna caught in 2001, compared with a total of 24,000 tons caught throughout the Mediterranean region by direct fishing. More than 90 percent of the post-harvested tuna goes to Japan, where the appetite for tuna belly-meat is insatiable. "If nothing is done," says Paolo Guglielmi of the Mediterranean Programme Office of the World Wildlife Fund (WWF), "wild bluefin tuna will completely disappear from the Mediterranean, perhaps with no possibility of rebuilding stocks" (Tudela 2002a).

Post-harvesting has completely reshaped fishing in the Mediterranean, and the fish are much the worse for it. Not only are the tuna threatened, but the fish caught to feed them while they are in the pens are also being fished to destruction. Almost all the countries that fish for tuna in the Mediterranean are switching over to tuna farming. In each country, purse seine catches have declined while the total catch has increased. The entire catch of the Croatian tuna fleet (which increased from nineteen boats in 1999 to thirty in 2000) consists of undersized fish destined for the pens. According to the WWF report cited earlier, "in the Mediterranean, tuna farming started just a few years ago, but estimated production in 2001 gives an indication of the huge development of this activity in the region. In fact, production in the Mediterranean is likely to make up more than half of the world total and is almost exclusively destined for the Japanese market." Given the eagerness with which Mediterranean nations sell their fish to Japan, it is not a little surprising to learn that Japan maintains a thirty-five-vessel longline fleet in the western Mediterranean, targeting large tuna before spawning. Perhaps they believe they can avoid the cost of the middleman. In a further attempt to avoid European prices, Japan has introduced its own tuna farms, with pens in eighteen Mediterranean locations.

Sergi Tudela (2002b), project coordinator of the World Wildlife Fund's Mediterranean Program, wrote:

> In sum, all the usual ingredients are there in the case of tuna fattening
> farms: privatization of a common good (in this case, with the added risk
> of its probable destruction in the short- to medium-term);
> concentration of the benefits into a few hands; public aid provided to
> pillage a natural resource; dispossession of the traditional resource users;
> social and economic deconstruction of the traditional fishing sector;
> complete lack of a regulatory framework; connivance of the
> administration; ineffectiveness of international supra-Statal
> organizations; and growing demand for the product from a powerful
> market.

This sort of thing seems to have originated a world away from the Mediterranean, in Port Lincoln, South Australia, where the southern bluefin (*Thunnus maccoyii*) is caught and raised—again primarily for the Japanese market. Kiwi White, a pilot for the South Australian Tuna Association, captured the basics in this 1996 account:

> The whole tuna industry now concentrates on catching fresh fish in the
> wild using purse seiners transferring the live fish to huge floating cages
> and then towing these cages with up to 100 tonnes of live fish hundreds
> of miles back to our home port. There are many problems with bad
> weather smashing the cages and huge tides that slow the towing boats

down to less than a knot and it is not uncommon for boats to be actually going backwards. The fish are fed twice a day on pilchards (sardines) and each cage requires 3 or 4 divers to clean out the dead fish, repair any holes, etc. . . . The tuna boat operators now have a supply of fat healthy tuna in the bay so when the fish are needed in Japan a team is sent out to harvest kill and prepare these fish ready to be airfreighted. These fish command huge prices (up to $50 a kilo) and they have been the savior of the fishing industry in Port Lincoln, many people are now employed and the owners are building huge mansions, driving the latest Mercedes and in general spending large amounts around our town.

Good for the fishermen, not so good for the fish. In April 1996, South Australia's tuna industry was crippled by a fierce storm, which caused the deaths of thousands of captive fish that would have been worth more than $55 million. The fish, kept in floating pens and unable to escape the storm, were suffocated as their gills became clogged in swirling clouds of silt, excreta, and sediment. Between 65,000 and 75,000 tuna died, representing about half the population of Port Lincoln's nine farms in Boston Bay. The mass deaths were a serious setback but evidently not a lasting one for the booming Port Lincoln tuna-farming industry, which has grown at a phenomenal rate since the first experimental farm was established, in 1991. The $100 million fish-fattening industry now constitutes a whopping 60 percent of the Australian tuna industry's 5,200-ton annual quota—and it will probably rise even higher.

Whether raised in pens or caught in the open sea, tuna represent Port Lincoln's most important product, celebrated annually in the Tunarama Festival during the Australia Day (January 26) weekend by a fair, a parade, a rodeo, fireworks, a race meeting (for horses), and the World Champion Tuna Toss, the "undisputable highlight of the Tunarama Festival with competitors travelling from far and wide in an effort to gain the coveted title." As noted at the World Wide Web site for the Port Lincoln Visitor Information Centre, the world record for throwing a seventeen-pound tuna 122 feet was set in 1998 by a former Olympic hammer thrower.

Even though post-harvesting is classified as aquaculture, the fish are all wild-caught, just as if they had been harpooned or purse seined. True aquaculture requires that the fish be raised from eggs, not simply moved from one place to another to be fattened, but even though the Australian system (also practiced in the Mediterranean) does not qualify under this strict definition, it demonstrates all the ills that besiege legitimate aquaculture, such as that practiced with Atlantic salmon, as we shall see. Like salmon, tuna are carnivorous, and when raised in captivity they must be fed large quantities of small fishes, which themselves may be threatened by overcollecting. This kind of "farming" thus does not relieve commercial fishing pressure—it increases it. Waste from the pens is another problem, as is their location, close enough to shore and urban centers to disrupt and often pollute the littoral (nearshore) zone. Moreover, because tuna farming falls between the definition of a fishery and true aquaculture, it is completely unregulated on a world scale.

And now tuna farming has come to Mexico. In an article published in the *New York Times* in April 2002, R. W. Apple discussed the "new kind of mariculture" that was taking place off the Pacific coast of Baja California. Mexican fishermen net young bluefins and tow them to special enclosures in Puerto Escondido, near Ensenada, where the fish are kept in circular pens and fed live sardines three times a day for six to eight months. When they reach a weight of about 190 pounds, they are killed and frozen, mostly to feed Japan's appetite for fatty tuna. "Despite the lasting slump in the Japanese economy," wrote Apple, "the meat sells for as much as $45 a pound."

For all their vaunted migratory capabilities, no tuna ever swam from New England to Japan, but, as Safina (1997) wrote, "probably more bluefins from the east coast of North America cross the Pacific because the next step in the transaction is a one-way air-freight ticket to Tokyo." The same is true of the Mediterranean bluefins. The future of the bluefin tuna, then, is written in Japanese. There is a better than fifty-fifty chance that people enjoying *maguro* in Japan are eating fish that were fattened in pens in the Mediterranean. Compared with almost nothing five years earlier, the twelve Mediterranean tuna farms produced 11,000 tons of tuna in 2001, more than half the world's total. It is more than a little painful to realize that *Thunnus thynnus,* the most beautiful fish in the world, is literally being eaten out of existence.

Tuna, and swordfish as well, among the most magnificent fish in the ocean, have the misfortune to be at or near the top of the list of most desirable food fishes. At the dock and in restaurants, prices for these fishes rise as their numbers diminish. This sounds like nothing more than a traditional supply-and-demand equation, but the difference between fishing and manufacturing is that once the fish are gone, you cannot make any more.

THE MIGHTY SWORDFISH

During the latter part of the nineteenth century, the broadbill swordfish (*Xiphias gladius*) was considered one of the world's premier game fishes and had a reputation for unmatched pugnacity. G. Brown Goode, assistant secretary of the Smithsonian Institution and a prodigious author and editor of

American fisheries literature, wrote the following (Goode 1887b) about "the perils and romance of swordfishing":

> The pursuit of the swordfish is much more exciting than ordinary fishing, for it resembles the hunting of large animals upon the land, and partakes more of the nature of the chase. There is no slow and careful baiting and patient waiting, and no disappointment caused by the accidental capture of worthless "bait-stealers." The game is seen and followed, and outwitted by wary tactics, and killed by strength of arm and skill. The swordfish is a powerful antagonist sometimes and sends his pursuers' vessel into harbor leaking, and almost sinking, from injuries inflicted by a wounded swordfish. I have known a vessel to be stuck by a wounded swordfish as many as twenty times in one season. There is even the spice of personal danger to give savor to the chase, for the men are occasionally injured by the wounded fish.

In 1940, E. W. Gudger published a lengthy discussion in the *Memoirs of the Royal Asiatic Society of Bengal* of "the alleged pugnacity of the swordfish and the spearfishes as shown by their attacks on vessels." Beginning with an account by the ancient Greek geographer Strabo of an attack on a fishing boat by a swordfish in the Strait of Messina (located between Sicily and the toe of Italy), Gudger covered Pliny, Aelian, and Oppian, the Greek poet in whose *Halieutica* we learn that those who pursued *Xiphias* did so in "swordfish-shaped boats." He wrote, however, that in later years, some swordfish encounters were collisions with "ships in passage," but "the attacks were mainly on fishing vessels by harpooned fish." Most of these so-called attacks occurred in the western North Atlantic Ocean, "where harpoon fishing for swordfish has been for long, and is today, most extensively carried on." Gudger described no fewer than seven cases of swordfish charging dories. One of these accounts, from 1937, goes as follows:

> We were cruising around off Montauk, about July 12, hunting for swordfish when our lookout at the masthead sighted a fish right ahead. The owner of the yacht ran forward to the swordfish stand and harpooned the fish. But unfortunately the harpoon struck forward of the dorsal fin and near the head. It usually happens that when a swordfish is harpooned in or near the head it seems to go crazy and starts looking for something to attack. This fish came to the surface after the first plunge downward and started cutting circles around the boat. We went onto it again and a second harpoon was driven into it. Still the fish would not go down and I put out in a dory to play it. I hauled on the line from the keg

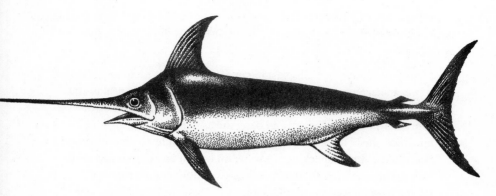

BROADBILL SWORDFISH *(Xiphias gladius)*

till I got within about twenty feet of the fish. Then it suddenly turned and like a flash drove its sword through the dory. Fortunately the sword did not strike me, but that was just my good luck. After striking the dory, the fish thrashed about so hard that it almost threw me out of the dory and did break off its sword at a point just below where it went through the bottom of the dory.

There are occasional modern instances of swordfish attacking boats, such as that in 1967 of a swordfish impaling itself on the submersible *Alvin,* which led to its being brought to the surface and eaten by the crew. But Gudger's description of the swordfish as "a pugnacious and vindictive fish" can only bring to mind the (largely undeserved) reputation of the sperm whale as a menace to the helpless whalers in their fragile boats, who were surprised that the whale would retaliate when it found itself with a spear stuck into its vitals.

If possible, Zane Grey admired the swordfish as much as the tuna. Of the broadbill he wrote in *Tales of Swordfish and Tuna:*

Old *Xiphias gladius* is the noblest warrior of all the sea fishes. He is familiar to all sailors. He roams the Seven Seas. He was written about by Aristotle 2,300 years ago. In the annals of sea disasters there are records of his sinking ships. . . . Tales of his attacks on harpooners' boats in the Atlantic are common. In these waters, where he is hunted for the market, he has often killed his pursuers. In the Pacific, off the Channel Islands, he has not killed any angler or boatman yet, but it is a safe wager he will do so some day. Therefore, despite the wonderful nature of the sport, it is not remarkable that so few anglers have risked it.

Of course, the intrepid Grey was not to be deterred by a fish that fights back; he welcomed the challenge. In 1919, off Catalina Island, he hooked a swordfish:

> First he made a long run, splashing over the swells. We had to put on full power to keep up with him, and at that he took off a good deal of line. When he slowed up he began to fight the leader. He would stick his five-foot sword out of the water and bang the leader. Then he lifted his enormous head high and wagged it from side to side, so that his sword described a circle, smacking the water on his left and then on his right. Wonderful and frightful that sweep of sword! It would have cut a man in two or have pierced the planking of a boat. Evidently his efforts and failure to free himself roused him to a fury. His huge tail thumped out of great white boils; when he turned sideways he made a wave like that behind a ferryboat; when he darted here and there he was as swift as a flash and he left a raised bulge, a white wake at the surface. Suddenly he electrified us by leaping. . . . This one came out in a tremendous white splash, and when he went down with a loud crash, we all saw where the foam was red with blood.

After eleven and a half hours, the line went slack, and Grey lost his giant swordfish. He expressed his admiration for these most worthy of opponents by continuing to fish for them, and later he proudly brought in a 418-pounder. (For some reason, Grey referred to every big fish as "he.") Other big-game fishermen have sought the mighty broadbill, and many have written about their exploits. In 1940, an expedition from the American Museum of Natural History (AMNH) in New York set out to capture some of these "fighting giants of the Humboldt," as they were termed in the title of the *National Geographic* article written the following year by David Douglas Duncan. Because of the upwelling of nutrients there, the Humboldt Current, off the western coast of northern South America, is inhabited by immense schools of anchovetas, which attract swordfish and marlin, the largest of the pelagic predators, and the smaller Pacific bonito, *Sarda chiliensis*. Fishing off Chile, the AMNH expedition caught several broadbills, ranging from 570 to 630 pounds (Mather 1976), and set the stage for fishing in the area now recognized as the best place in the world for big swordfish. The current world's record catch, landed by Lou Marron in 1953 off the coast of Iquique, Chile, weighed 1,182 pounds.

Although swordfish are still considered premier game fish and are eagerly sought as trophies, the large ones are no longer being caught in the North

Atlantic. In the past, swordfishermen hunted their prey by sight, waiting for the telltale sickle-shaped dorsal fin and upper lobe of the tail to break the surface as the big fish "finned out." Then they would harpoon the fish from a specially designed "pulpit" that extended from the fishing boat's prow. The harpoon fishery for Atlantic swordfish was limited to the New England coast in the early 1800s. When David Starr Jordan wrote *American Food and Game Fishes* in 1923, he said this about the swordfish: "The species is rather abundant for so large a fish. Off the New England Coast, 3,000 to 6,000 of these fish are taken every year. Twenty-five or more are sometimes seen in a single day. One fishermen killed 108 in one year." "Them days," as the fishermen say, "is gone forever." Now the broadbill swordfish has been so overfished that it is considered an endangered species and, despite its popularity, there is a full-scale campaign called Give Swordfish a Break, dedicated to getting restaurant owners to take it off the menu.

Found worldwide in temperate and tropical waters, the broadbill swordfish gets its common name from its smooth, flattened bill, which is much longer and wider than that of any other billfish. The bill is used for defense and (maybe) to slash and debilitate its prey, which consists of squid, mackerel, bluefish, and many other mid- and deepwater species. Even today, we don't know how a swordfish uses its bill. The bill is horizontally flattened and sharp on the edges, so it has been assumed that the swordfish enters a school of fishes and slashes wildly, cutting or otherwise incapacitating its prey, which it then eats at its leisure. But since nobody has ever witnessed this activity, the actual use of the sword is conjectural.

In a 1968 study of the "food and feeding habits of the swordfish," W. B. Scott and S. N. Tibbo wrote: "The swordfish differs from the spearfishes (marlins and sailfishes) in that the sword is long and it is dorso-ventrally compressed (hence the name broadbill) whereas the spearfishes have a shorter spear and it is slightly compressed laterally. Thus, the swordfish appears to be more highly specialized for lateral slashing. Such a specialization would seem to be pointless unless directed to a vertically oriented prey, or unless the swordfish slashes while vertically oriented, as when ascending or descending." In contrast to almost every other suggestion about swordfish feeding techniques, Charles Mather (1976) stated, "Essentially a bottom feeder, a broadbill is believed to use his bill as a tool to obtain crustaceans from their cracks or attachments and to enjoy crabs and crayfish," an utterly preposterous suggestion. In *Living Fishes of the World* (1961), ichthyologist Earl Herald wrote, "the sword may be used to impale fishes during feeding," which seems highly unlikely because the fish to be impaled would offer no resistance to the impaler, and even if such a process could be made to work, the swordfish would be unable to get at the dead fishes stuck on the end of its nose.

Since the 1960s, pelagic longlines have been the primary gear used to capture swordfish. The area of U.S. commercial swordfishing has expanded to include the entire U.S. Atlantic coastline, the Grand Banks, the Gulf of Mexico, the Caribbean Sea, and the mid–Atlantic Ocean, making it possible to catch swordfish throughout the year. Today's deepwater swordfishers, like those unfortunate members of the *Andrea Gail*'s crew who did not return from their voyage in the "perfect storm" of 1991, set out miles of baited longlines. The expansion of the fishery into areas of warmer water means that younger, smaller swordfish are more often caught, which reduces the population by removing individuals before they reach breeding age. There is no way to prevent these smaller fish from taking the baited hooks; the only restrictions on the fishermen simply prevent them from selling the juveniles commercially. Whether they are sold or discarded, the younger fish die.

Here is a description of the longline fishery for swordfish by Carl Safina (1998b), founder and director of the National Audubon Society's Living Oceans Program:

> Today, the submarine canyons and banks these animals prowl is so spaghettied with baited lines that more than 80 percent of the female swordfish caught are immature, killed before they can breed. (Female swordfish take at least five years to reach sexual maturity, at which point they are almost six feet long.) With longlines taking 98 percent of the swordfish catch, large adult fish are rare in the North Atlantic. Between the early 1960s and today, the average size of North Atlantic swordfish dropped two-thirds, from almost 270 pounds to 90 pounds. In nursery grounds off Florida, off South Carolina, in the Gulf of Mexico, and elsewhere, longlines catch mostly juveniles. U.S. swordfishers in the Atlantic discard about 40 percent of the swordfish they kill; the fish are too small to sell. In 1996 they dumped 40,000.

In 1969, the U.S. Food and Drug Administration (FDA) discovered that swordfish flesh had a high mercury content, and the agency banned the sale of any swordfish with an excess of five-tenths part per million.* According to

---

*The swordfish scare was initiated by the 1956 discovery that families of fishermen near Minamata on the Japanese island of Kyushu were afflicted by a mysterious neurological disease with symptoms that included loss of coordination, tremors, slurred speech, and numbness in the extremities. The symptoms worsened and led to general paralysis, convulsions, brain damage, and death. A chemical factory belonging to Chisso *(continued)*

Charles Gibson's 1981 history of the North Atlantic swordfish fishery, "in effect, the mercury ban killed the fishery all the way from the Mississippi deltas to the Grand Banks." Massachusetts health authorities examined a piece of preindustrial swordfish and found that it contained the same amount of mercury as fish caught in the 1970s. They also found that the amount of mercury believed to be dangerous to humans was not evident in newly caught swordfish. They therefore ignored the FDA's warnings and allowed swordfish to be landed again. Other states quickly followed, and by 1973 the fishery was fully operational and the fish, which had been briefly spared, were being caught in unprecedented numbers on longlines. But the fish brought in were getting smaller and smaller.

Since the early 1980s, the commercial catch of swordfish has increased eightfold, but the average weight of fish caught has dropped from 115 pounds to 60. As mentioned earlier, many restaurants are refusing to put swordfish on the menu to discourage fishermen from bringing in the smaller fish. (At Manhattan's Fulton Fish Market, swordfish weighing 50 to 100 pounds are called "dogs," those 25 to 50 pounds "pups," and those weighing less than 25 pounds "rats.") Swordfish quotas have now been tied in with quotas for tuna and marlins, and despite the warnings that the North Atlantic stocks are continuing to decline, the U.S. Congress still allows more swordfish to be caught than would enable a declining population to recover. In "Song for the Swordfish," an article published in *Audubon* magazine, Carl Safina (1998b) wrote: "These days, most fishers know swordfish chiefly by their absence, by old-timers' stories and black-and-white photos on the walls of long-established harborside bars. . . . U.S. longliners claim that Atlantic swordfish can't recover unless all the countries catching them agree to coordinated measures. But in the 1970s, when concern over mercury levels in swordfish forced U.S. and Canadian longliners to stop fishing, the broadbills recovered within a decade. They were depleted to current lows after longlining resumed."

In 1990, swordfish and marlins were added to the species overseen by ICCAT. The Spanish longline fleet lands more swordfish than any other party to that convention. In 1997, Spain had a 45 percent share of the Atlantic swordfish fishery, but of the total of 36,378 tons landed in or imported into

Company, Ltd. that manufactured acetic acid and vinyl chloride and dumped its wastes into Minamata Bay was identified as the source of the mercury that had contaminated the fish and shellfish. Even with the source of this crippling and often fatal disease identified, the Japanese government did not order the plant closed until the 1970s. By 1997, more than 17,000 people had applied for compensation from the government. Since 1956, a total of 2,262 people have died of Minamata disease in Japan.

Spain in 1997, almost two-thirds was exported, primarily to Italy, where *pesce spada* is a particularly popular menu item. Although the Spanish catch of swordfish declined slightly in recent years, the Spanish fish-processing industry compensated for the decrease in domestic landings by importing catch from other countries. Spain is also a major player in the eastern Atlantic and Mediterranean bluefin tuna fisheries. Of all bluefin tuna landed in or imported into Spain in 1997, only one-third was consumed in that country, the remainder constituting a valuable export and one acknowledged to be a primary factor in recent increases in bluefin tuna catches in the Atlantic and Mediterranean.

The so-called regulatory agencies—ICCAT, the European Commission, and the General Fisheries Commission for the Mediterranean—have done little to stem the rising tide of swordfish overexploitation. In Spain, the power of the peso (now the euro) obliterates environmental concerns. Protests from conservation organizations, such as the World Wildlife Fund (WWF), Greenpeace, and the Asociacíon de Naturalistas del Sureste (ANSE) of Spain, have made people aware of the problems but otherwise have accomplished little. In April 2002, representatives of WWF, Greenpeace, and ANSE sailed to the fattening facility at Cape Tiñoso to protest, in that case, not swordfish but Mediterranean bluefin tuna farms. The Spanish navy in Murcia stopped the environmentalists' sailboat and prevented them from approaching.

In the United States, where the problem was first identified, a concentrated campaign to protect the swordfish seems to have worked. In 1998, the organizers of the Give Swordfish a Break campaign, SeaWeb and the Natural Resources Defense Council (NRDC), along with other conservation organizations, successfully advocated recovery measures to restore North Atlantic swordfish. The campaign was launched in January 1998 when twenty-seven leading East Coast restaurateurs announced the removal of swordfish from their menus. Leading cruise lines followed suit. By November 1999, ICCAT was forced to acknowledge the campaign, and for the first time it adopted quotas. The campaign officially ended in August 2000 when the U.S. government closed swordfish nursery areas to fishers in U.S. waters, thus meeting the second goal of the campaign. In October 2002, ICCAT announced that over the previous three years North Atlantic swordfish had recovered to 94 percent of levels considered healthy. On the recovery, an editorial in the *New York Times* of October 13, 2002, commented:

> This is the best news for fish since the striped bass recovery of the late 1980s, and the lesson for future recoveries is much the same: if you leave the fish alone, or at least give them some space, they will repay the effort.

The recovery of the swordfish is one of the few bright lights in the otherwise dismal story of overfishing the fishes at the top of the trophic pyramid. By and large, the hunters have become the hunted. No group of fishes, cartilaginous or bony, is more readily identified as apex predators than the sharks, and no group of fishes is in greater danger.

SHARK-EATING MEN

There are some 350 species of shark in the world's oceans, and most of them do not fit the public's preconceptions of large, toothy predators cruising menacingly offshore ready to gobble somebody up. Most living shark species are less than two feet long and are harmful only to the small fishes and cephalopods that make up their usual diets. (There are even sharks, known as heterodontids, whose teeth aren't sharp at all but are pavement-like, enabling them to crush the shells of bivalves.) Many of these mini-sharks are deepwater inhabitants whose populations would be only minimally affected by fishermen even if they were deemed edible. But some of the larger species *are* edible or otherwise desirable to humans and are found in nearshore waters, which puts them at risk. Indeed, an important 1999 analysis of the world's shark populations by José Castro, Christa Woodley, and Rebecca Brudek of the National Marine Fisheries Service laboratory in Miami concludes that "nearly all species for which we have catches and landings data for more than ten years are in severe declines."

Sharks (and other elasmobranchs—"strap-gills"—including skates and rays) are particularly vulnerable to overfishing. They are what biologists call K-selected, which means they have large young, slow growth rates, late sexual maturity, and long lives, all of which result in low rates of population increase. Moreover, shark fisheries have expanded worldwide, as pointed out in a 1998 report by Merry Camhi and colleagues for the International Union for Conservation of Nature and Natural Resources (IUCN):

> Shark fisheries have expanded in size and number around the world
> since the mid-1980s, primarily in response to the rapidly increasing
> demand for shark fins, meat and cartilage. Despite the boom-and-bust
> nature of virtually all shark fisheries over the past century, most shark
> fisheries today still lack monitoring or management. . . . As a result,
> many shark populations are now depleted and some are considerably
> threatened.

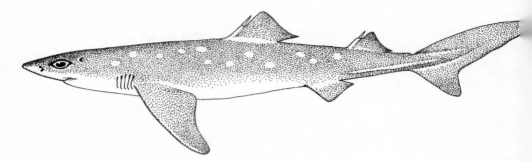

SPINY DOGFISH *(Squalus acanthias)*

Among the most numerous of all sharks, the spiny (piked) dogfish (*Squalus acanthias*) aggregates in large schools throughout its cold- and temperate-water range around the world. It is fished heavily and used widely, in the words of Leonard Compagno (1984a), "fresh, fresh frozen, smoked, boiled, marinated, dried, salted, and in the form of fish cakes for human consumption; it is also utilized in liver oil, pet food, fishmeal, fertilizer and leather." It's no accident, then, that its numbers are in free fall. Castro and his colleagues classify the piked dogfish as a Category 4 species ("substantial historical declines in catches and/or locally extinct"). The spiny dogfish has the longest gestation period of any vertebrate—twenty-two months—so removal of adult females (which are larger than males and therefore more desirable to fishermen) is extremely hazardous to the population.

Spiny dogfish were long considered trash fish—those inadvertently trapped in nets set for other species and sometimes destroying the nets in their unwillingness to be caught. In the early 1990s, however, New England fishermen searching for alternatives to depleted stocks of cod, haddock, and flounder began fishing for the more plentiful, and unregulated, dogfish. Fishermen teamed up with politicians to promote dogfish consumption, in the process giving the species the more appetizing name of "cape shark." With the help of steady European demand—particularly in Great Britain, where the species constitutes a large proportion of the fish in fish-and-chips—the dogfish experiment quickly grew into a fully developed fishery, and that soon became a disaster. In 1998, scientists declared the northwestern Atlantic spiny dogfish population overfished, reporting dramatic declines in the number and size of mature females. After years of stalling, in March 2000 the New England Fishery Management Council submitted its final plan to the NMFS to restrict fishing for this species. But by then, Massachusetts fishermen had so overfished the little sharks that the secretary of the U.S. Department of Commerce, William Daley, imposed quotas of 4 million pounds effective May 1, 2000. Four million pounds may appear to be the opposite of a reduced quota, but the Atlantic States Marine Fisheries Commission (ASMFC) is under pressure to increase the quota for adult females after the emergency ruling expires in 2003. In October 2002, despite alarming scientific reports of an absence of dogfish pups, the commission voted overwhelmingly to double current dogfish quotas.

So far, Castro and his colleagues (1999) have not placed any shark species in Category 5 ("rare throughout the ranges where they were formerly abundant"), but several species other than dogfish qualify for Category 4. These are the thresher shark (*Alopias vulpinus*); the shortfin mako (*Isurus oxyrhinchus*); the porbeagle (*Lamna nasus*); the tope (*Galeorhinus galeus*); the leopard shark (*Triakis semifasciata*); the dusky shark (*Carcharhinus obscurus*); the sandbar shark (*Carcharhinus plumbeus*); and the night shark (*Carcharhinus signatus*). Individuals of all these species are relatively large, and all have been the object of a directed fishery. In every case, the sharks are caught for food, but sometimes leather and liver oil are by-products of their use.

A particularly insidious threat to shark populations is finning, the practice of catching sharks, cutting off their dorsal and pectoral fins, and then throwing them back in the water to die. The fins are used to make shark's fin soup, an expensive delicacy in China, Singapore, Hong Kong, and other Asian countries. In some restaurants, shark's fin soup may sell for $100 a bowl. Many shark fisheries around the world—in Mexico, for example—are in business largely to supply fins to this market. In some parts of the world, finning is so widespread that local shark populations have become endangered. In Honolulu, 2,289 sharks were landed in 1991. By 1998, the number had leapt to 60,857—a 2,500 percent increase—and of that total, 99 percent was for fins. Introduction of the Shark Finning Prohibition Act on March 13, 2002, banned U.S. fishing vessels—anywhere in the world—and foreign vessels fishing in U.S. waters from possessing fins unless the rest of the shark's carcass is also on board (Raloff 2002). In August of that year, U.S. Coast Guard officers boarded the Honolulu-based *King Diamond II* off Acapulco and found 64,000 pounds (32 tons) of fins and no other shark parts. The *King Diamond* had not actually caught the sharks; the Korean fin broker on board had evidently bought them from Asian vessels plying the eastern South Pacific around Fiji and the Solomon Islands and was planning to sell them in Guatemala. The fishing vessel was escorted to San Diego and the cargo confiscated. In the Pacific, where most finning takes place, there are no restrictions on finning or on bringing in severed fins, with or without the car-casses. (Fins can sell for a wholesale price of $200 per pound, whereas shark meat might bring 50 cents per pound, demonstrating the unfortunate eco-nomics of finning.)

Star of four Hollywood movies, the great white (*Carcharodon carcharias*) is the most famous shark of all. Although its anthropophagous inclinations were greatly exaggerated in *Jaws*, the great white actually does attack people every once in a while. Peter Benchley's 1974 novel (and the subsequent movies) assigned the shark such a reputation for malevolence that people decided the oceans would be safer if no great whites were around to threaten them. The vendetta against *C. carcharias* that commenced soon after publica-tion of the novel is still going on. Brave fishermen set out to capture "the man-eater" to prove their manhood and to display mementos of their tri-umph above their fireplaces or around their necks. (A good white shark tooth, which could be more than two inches in length, sells today for about $150; a set of jaws might fetch more than $3,000.) A vengeful, dedicated hunt, conducted on a largely inshore species, has not benefited the scattered popu-lations of *C. carcharias*. Castro and colleagues (1999) placed the great white in Category 3 ("species that are exploited by directed fisheries or bycatch and have a limited reproductive potential") and observed that "populations may be small and highly localized and very vulnerable to overexploitation." Although we still know too little about the migratory habits of the great white, it is now protected in those waters where it is most likely to show up. White sharks were first protected in South Africa in 1992; since then, Namibia, the Maldives, Malta, Florida, and California have fully protected the species, with fishermen no longer allowed to catch them.

Because of their cosmopolitan distribution, it might be possible to reduce or even eliminate a local shark population without raising the specter of global extinction. "Local extinction," wrote Castro and colleagues (1999), "refers to the disappearance of a species or population in a given geographic area, while the species is still extant in the rest of its range. Extinction refers to the disappearance of the species on a global scale. . . . There are few recorded cases of local extinction of sharks or elasmobranchs in general. . . . Nevertheless, it is possible that given enough time and sufficient fishing pres-sure, some sharks could become globally extinct." Jack Musick and Beverly McMillan (2002) asked, "What are the chances that some species of sharks, or many, will go extinct?" Their answer:

> Some scientists argue that it is impossible to drive widely distributed
> coastal shark species, like sand tigers and the handsome duskies that

used to be regular visitors to the Virginia coast, to extinction. [We] believe they are wrong—that there is a point of no return at which remnants of populations become so few that there are not enough breeders to continue. We may be on the brink of finding out just where that point is.

Perhaps the greatest misconception about sharks is that they are particularly dangerous to people. The truth is closer to the opposite. Twenty-five years after the publication of *Jaws,* Peter Benchley wrote an article for *Audubon* magazine titled "Swimming with Sharks," in which he noted: "Somewhere between 40 million and 70 million sharks were killed in 1994. The International Shark Attack File estimates that for every human being killed by a shark, 10 million sharks are killed by human beings." Contrary to conventional wisdom, conflicts between man and shark almost always end in favor of the man, especially if the man is in his own element and not the shark's. Under those circumstances, the conflict is known as "fishing."

That there *is* a Shark Attack File speaks volumes about the nature of the eternal conflict between humans and sharks. Now housed at the University of Florida, the file was originally produced by the Shark Research Panel, founded in 1963 by the Office of Naval Research and the American Institute of Biological Sciences. Its mandate was to record as accurately as possible shark attacks around the world, with the idea that some attacks could be prevented if we had an idea of why they occurred in the first place. Coincidentally, the same year *Jaws* was published, H. David Baldridge (1974b) analyzed the accumulated data and published "Shark Attack: A Program of Data Reduction and Analysis," which showed that shark attacks occurred much less frequently than people thought they did, but people were frightened in anticipation of them out of all proportion to their frequency or the actual danger involved in swimming where sharks were known to be present.*

As the author of *Jaws,* however, does Benchley accept any responsibility for the shark mania that swept the country after the book (and four related Hollywood movies) appeared? No, nor should he. He was writing fiction, not a scientific treatise. In his 1998 *Audubon* article, he stated: "Now it is widely accepted that sharks in general, and great whites in particular, do not target

---

*In the same year, Baldridge also published a popular version of this report. Titled *Shark Attack,* it bore this line on the cover (which of course featured a photograph of a great white shark): "True tales of shark attacks on man—facts more terrifying than the fiction of JAWS." Obviously, the public hungered for more accounts of gory shark attacks, but without the graphs and tables.

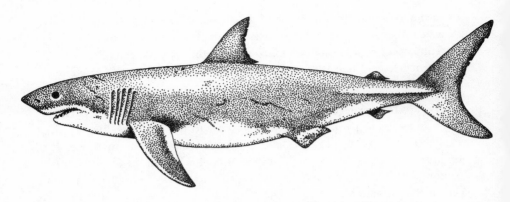

GREAT WHITE SHARK *(Carcharodon carcharias)*

human beings. When a great white attacks a person, it is almost always an accident, a case of mistaken identity." In the summer of 2002, with attendant publicity and appearances on every network television talk show, Benchley published *Shark Trouble,* in which he commented:

> Shark attacks on human beings generate a tremendous amount of media coverage, partly because they occur so rarely, but mostly, I think, because people are, and always have been, simultaneously intrigued and terrified by sharks. Sharks come from a wing of the dark castle where our nightmares live—deep water beyond our sight and understanding—and so they stimulate our fears and fantasies and imaginations.

The success of *Jaws,* both book and movie, is attributable to Benchley's imagination and skill as a writer of thrillers, but another element raises it above most other horror stories: unlike the giant gorilla in *King Kong* or the assorted Godzilla monsters, the villain of *Jaws* really exists. There really *are* large great white sharks out there, and though it doesn't happen very often, they have attacked enough people to make all of us pause—if only for a moment—before going for a swim. As I commented in *Great White Shark* (Ellis and McCosker 1991), "anything that can provoke that same brief, dark thought in all of us is a powerful force indeed."

For many years, "shark tournaments" were held in various locations on the Pacific and Atlantic coasts of the United States in which the object was to catch as many sharks of as many species as possible; winners were chosen on the basis of accumulated poundage caught, largest single shark of a particular species, and so forth. In the early days of these tournaments (the 1960s and

1970s), the carcasses were weighed and measured and then discarded at sea or in garbage dumps. (Some fishermen might have saved the jaws, and Asian restaurateurs might occasionally have collected the fins, but for the most part, the entire shark was wasted.) Scientists subsequently realized that these sharks represented a potential treasure trove of data on growth rates, reproductive biology, distribution, and dozens of other useful subjects, so they began attending the "shark derbies," cameras and calipers in hand, and recording information that would otherwise have been lost.

In a 1973 article co-authored with his wife, Claire, Perry Gilbert, a shark expert and, later, director of Mote Marine Laboratory in Sarasota, Florida, sang the virtues of sharks:

> The shark, with a modicum of fine traits, might be considered one of the
> most successful animals that has ever lived. To other animals it is far
> from delicious. Its tough hide makes it almost inedible, and while it has
> the grace that sheer power bestows, it is not really beautiful. . . . It has,
> however, one enviable attribute and this has contributed greatly to its
> success. . . . Cancer is virtually absent from its primal myomeres.

Some researchers decided that shark cartilage contains a protein that inhibits the angiogenesis (development of new blood vessels) needed to provide nourishment for tumor and cancer growth. Tumors need a large supply of blood to survive, and cartilage contains substances that prevent the formation of blood vessels. Since 1979, at Mote Marine Laboratory, Carl Luer has been exposing nurse sharks and clearnose skates to powerful carcinogens, including aflatoxin B and methylazoxymethanol, and has been unable to get tumors to grow at all. Working with A. B. Bodine, Luer has seen that the carcinogens reach the DNA of the elasmobranch cells, but the cells seem to repair themselves before any sort of mutation can result. In an article in the *Journal of the National Cancer Institute* in 1993, James Mathews wrote, "Most researchers agree that continued study of the shark's intriguing anatomy may yield answers to treating cancer in humans." Certainly an animal that is so successful in resisting cancer is worth more to medical and pharmaceutical researchers than to those who would hack off its fins to make soup out of them.

Despite the total absence of evidence, someone, somewhere was going to cash in on the possibility that shark cartilage could prevent cancer in humans. First came a New Jersey company called Cartilage Consultants, Inc., which obtained a patent for pills made of powdered shark cartilage. The *Journal of the National Cancer Institute* announced that "there is no proof that it is effective when taken this way," and Luer, in an article written for Mote Marine Laboratory, asserted, "The statements made by cartilage pill promoters that it is cartilage that gives sharks their immunity to cancer, then, are inaccurate and irresponsible." We are still a long way from finding—or even suggesting—a shark-related cure for cancer. Indeed, although irresponsible medical research might serve no useful purpose for humans, it might further endanger the sharks. In February 1993, the television program *60 Minutes* aired a story on shark cartilage as a treatment for cancer in humans, bringing forth an outraged response from the people who were doing the research. In the March 1993 newsletter of the American Elasmobranch Society, Carl Luer wrote, "We cannot support the marketing of shark cartilage for this application, especially since the promoters of the product intend to rely on the natural resource as an endless supply of material." If it were true that shark cartilage could somehow prevent cancer in humans, perhaps the taking of sharks might be justified, but since no such evidence exists, they should not be caught and ground up for their components. In a letter to the same newsletter, Kumar Mahadevan, director of Mote Marine Laboratory, stated, "No evidence—not even a logical connection—exists at this stage to assume that shark cartilage tested on blood vessel growth in the laboratory should produce significant tumor regression when given to cancer patients." Assuming that we could consume shark cartilage to protect ourselves from cancer was like believing that we could eat sawdust made from redwood trees to make ourselves taller.

Regardless of opposition from the scientific community, those who wanted to believe that sharks held the key to a cancer cure continued to do so. In 1992, I. William Lane published a book called *Sharks Don't Get Cancer* in which he argued that shark cartilage is the reason. Perhaps not coincidentally, through BeneFin, a company run by his son Andrew, he packaged and sold powdered shark cartilage made from the skulls and backbones of sharks. Thousands of sharks were being killed annually to provide the cartilage that Lane's company ground up. Lane and his family probably made a lot of money from BeneFin, but did he actually believe it worked? In a well-written summary of the entire shark cartilage story published in the *Amicus Journal*, Michael Rivlin (2000) reported:

> Everything Lane had written led me to think he truly believed that shark cartilage could work miracles. But when I interviewed him, his final comments left me shocked. I had asked him how the cartilage market is holding up, and whether he still has faith in the product. "Cartilage is a faddist industry," he replied. "The fad was real and it lasted a long time.

Now, there are a number of other products that have some effect against cancer, and they're easier to take than shark cartilage." And then he started pitching Lane Labs' newest product, "an incredible immune stimulator" made from rice bran and shiitake mushrooms.

In 2000, a new chapter opened in the shark cartilage story. A study published then concluded that sharks not only get cancer but even get cartilage cancer. Gary Ostrander and John Harshberger found at least forty cases of cancer in sharks and other cartilaginous fishes after surveying scientific papers and tumor samples from the National Cancer Institute's Registry of Tumors in Lower Animals. In an article published in *Science* magazine on April 14, 2000, Ostrander is quoted as saying that he hopes the study will help explode the "huge myth" that sharks are immune to cancer—a misapprehension shared even by "people in my own field." It's hard to believe that susceptibility to cancer can save your life, but that's what happened to the sharks. Chalk up one for the elasmobranchs.

Cancer notwithstanding, elasmobranchs (sharks, skates, and rays) are far from immune to overfishing. The thornback ray (*Raja clavata*) is now considered close to extinction, according to monitors of the North Sea populations. With the decline of cod and haddock, fishers have trawled for bottom dwellers and have virtually eliminated them—as well as destroying the seafloor. Replacing the ubiquitous fish-and-chips, skate-and-chips became for a time a popular menu item, as did skate with black butter; with overfishing, however, these dishes have become as rare as dodo pudding.

Probably the most surprising and unexpected near extinction in recent years has been that of the barndoor skate (*Raja laevis*), which nobody was fishing for at all. For generations, cod fishermen hauled in these unwanted elasmobranchs, which, at a total of sixteen square feet, approach the dimensions of their namesake. Like many elasmobranchs, *R. laevis* is K-selected; that is, it is slow to mature, reproduces slowly, and has offspring that are small in number but large in size. Indeed, newborn barndoor skates are already ten inches across, sizable enough to get caught in trawls from their day of birth and therefore never having a hope of reproducing. "Forty-five years ago," Jill Casey and Ransom Meyers noted in a 1998 *Science* article, "research surveys on the St. Pierre Bank (off southern Newfoundland) recorded barndoor skates in 10% of their tows; in the last 20 years, none has been caught and this pattern of decline is similar throughout the range of the species." What happened? When the distant-water fleets were scooping up codfish, redfish, and everything else that swam in eastern Canadian and New England waters in the 1970s, a large part of the bycatch was barndoor

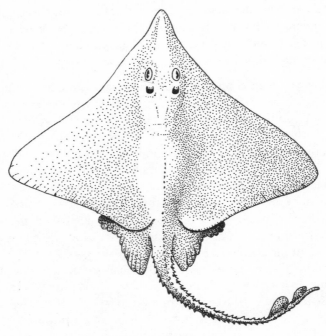

BARNDOOR SKATE
(Raja laevis)

skates. Fisheries biologists, lately studying the decline of more valuable food fishes, didn't notice the disappearance of barndoor skates until it was too late. "If current population trends continue," wrote Casey and Meyers, "the barndoor skate could become the first well-documented example of extinction in a marine fish species."

Carcharias taurus, the grey nurse shark (spelled that way because it is an Australian species), is a popular resident in public aquariums; as it swims slowly around the tank with its baleful, pale eyes and snaggletoothed grin, it is everything visitors expect a shark to look like. Unfortunately, this very "sharkiness" has proved its undoing. Although the grey nurse is not really a threat to divers or swimmers unless provoked, many shark attacks have been incorrectly attributed to this species, perhaps because of its fierce appearance (Last and Stevens 1994). The grey nurse shark's reputation led to indiscriminate killing of the species by spear and line fishers. For years, Australian divers demonstrated their bravery by spearing grey nurse sharks, largely because they *looked* as if they were dangerous. The toothy jaws mounted on a mantelpiece or over a garage door served to show that the diver or fisherman could conquer a "man-eater." This wanton and misdirected slaughter has produced an utterly unexpected outcome.

The grey nurse shark became the first protected shark in the world when the government of New South Wales declared it a protected species in 1984. The species is currently listed as nationally vulnerable under Australia's Commonwealth Environment Protection and Biodiversity Act 1999. It is also protected under fisheries legislation in New South Wales, Tasmania, Queensland, and Western Australia. Globally, the species was listed as Vulnerable in the *IUCN Red List of Threatened Species* in March 2000.

In a way, sharks are bellwethers for the conservation of marine life. They are largely unpopular animals with an almost completely unfounded reputation that includes a nasty disposition, a mouthful of razor-sharp teeth, and an inclination to use them on people. Most of the known shark species are small and harmless; only the great white, mako, tiger, bull, hammerhead, whaler, and oceanic whitetip have ever been implicated in deliberate attacks on people. The number of people attacks on sharks, however, has reduced some shark populations to tatters. With her colleagues from Dalhousie University, Julia Baum analyzed logbook data from shark fisheries and U.S. longline fleets targeting swordfish and tunas in which sharks were bycatch. In *Science* on January 17, 2003, Baum and her colleagues reported that from 1986 to 2000, populations of shark species in the northwestern Atlantic declined by an average of 61 percent. Blues fell by 60 percent, tigers by 65 percent, oceanic whitetips by 70 percent, great whites by 79 percent, threshers by 80 percent, and hammerheads by an astonishing 89 percent.

Before we can protect a species, in the sea or out, we need to realize that it has as much right to be there as we do. To see any animal as inferior insults that species and all life on the earth. A more appropriate view was suggested by Henry Beston in 1928:

> We need another and a wiser and perhaps a more mystical concept of animals. . . . We patronize them for their incompleteness, for their tragic fate of having taken form so far below ourselves. And therein we err, we greatly err. For the animal shall not be measured by man. In a world older and more complex than ours they move finished and complete, gifted with extensions of the senses we have lost or never attained, living by voices we shall never hear. They are not brethren, they are not underlings; they are other nations, caught with ourselves in the net of life and time, fellow prisoners of the splendour and travail of the earth.

THE CODFISH

The codfish (*Gadus morhua*) has historically been one of the world's most important food fishes, and its exploitation has played a significant role in the economic development of the countries that border the North Atlantic Ocean, the home and breeding ground of this species. Among those countries that can attribute a portion of their history to the fortuitous occurrence of shoals of cod are Iceland, Norway, Britain, France, Spain, Portugal, Canada, and, of course, the United States.

The Basques of the tenth century were among the first European fishermen to work North American waters. From their own waters in the Bay of Biscay, the intrepid Basques (also the first people to hunt whales systematically) wandered north, locating and relocating the right whales of the British Isles, Iceland, and Greenland, and eventually fetching up in Labrador, where they pioneered two important industries: whaling and cod fishing. There, at a place called Red Bay, evidence of the first Basque whaling settlement has been found, with ship relics dating from approximately 1540.

A century earlier, a Portuguese named Diogo de Tieve, who discovered the Azorean islands of Flores and Corvo in 1452 while searching for the non-existent "Island of the Seven Cities," found himself off the coast of Newfoundland, and when he returned to Portugal, he reported great schools of cod. This news was welcomed by the Portuguese, who had been catching, drying, and salting the cod caught in their own waters for well more than a century by that time. (Cod are found on both sides of the North Atlantic, but they are far more plentiful in the western quadrant.) No sooner had de Tieve returned from the Grand Banks—for that is surely where he was—than the name *Terra Nova do Bacalhau* began to appear on maps and charts; the New Land of the Codfish was becoming an integral part of the cartography of the known world.

The Black Death ended in England around 1350, and although the documentation is sparse, it is believed that the British resumed sending fishing boats to Iceland as early as 1397. According to historian G. J. Marcus (1981), "during the spring of 1408 or 1409 . . . English fishermen had begun to work the Iceland fishery; and had thereby opened a new and significant chapter in the history of English maritime enterprise." They came in "doggers," craft believed to have been designed for fishing, ranging from forty to eighty tuns burthen. In England and France, a ship's size was reckoned as a function of capacity. A tun was a double hogshead (252 gallons) used for shipping wine, and a ship's burthen was the number of tuns the ship could carry.

Other innovations that affected ship design in the early fifteenth century were the addition of a second mast, which altered the way ships could be sailed, and the introduction of sailing by latitude, which meant the end of "rock-dodging," sailing only with the next landfall in sight or nearly so. Once the British mariners crossed the Atlantic to Iceland, they overwhelmed the Icelandic fishermen and practically turned the cod fishery into an English enterprise. Two centuries later, English settlers (as opposed to adventurers such as John Cabot) made their first landfall in America, at the narrow spit that in 1602 Bartholomew Gosnold christened Cape Cod because the eponymous fish were so plentiful there.

The eating of fish had positive religious connotations for medieval Christians, a factor that had kept demand for the fish high. The initial letters of the words *Iesous Christos Theou Hyios Soter* ("Jesus Christ, Son of God, Savior") are those of *ichthys,* the Greek word for fish. Moreover, fish became a staple of the European diet because eventually it could be eaten regardless of the intricate and variable schedule of fast days, on which people were forbidden to eat meat. (In Christianity's early years, fast days were literally that— the faithful were not to eat anything at all—but later, the days of abstinence were modified so that only certain foods were eschewed.) The most strictly observed of the fast days was Friday, in honor of the Crucifixion, but on occasion they included Wednesday, the day Judas accepted money for his promise to betray Jesus, and also Saturday, the day consecrated to Mary in celebration of her virginity.

Even more important for fish consumption than the weekly fast days, however, were the enduring fasts of Lent and Advent, which ushered in, respectively, the festive seasons of Easter and Christmas. Lent, which lasted for six weeks, was the major fast of the year, and although its observance included cutting down on meals and the amount of food consumed, the major modification in the dietary habits of the populace was the change from meat to fish. Bridget Henisch observed in *Fast and Feast,* a study of food in medieval society:

> Fish, providentially, had escaped God's curse on earth by living in the water. Water itself was an element of special sanctity, washing away the sins of the world in Noah's Flood, and the sins of the individual in baptism. Its creatures might be said to share something of its virtues. Once the choice had been justified, the rest was easy. Fish was plentiful, fish was cheap, and in the season of Lent, fish was king.

Herring was not eaten only during Lent, of course; it was a staple of the European diet throughout the year. After the discovery of the codfish stocks

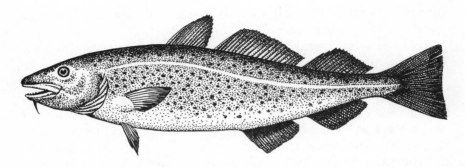

CODFISH (*Gadus morhua*)

of the Grand Banks—and the still-unexplained disappearance of the Atlantic herring in the early fifteenth century—*Gadus morhua* displaced *Clupea harengus* as the predominant fish on European tables. No amount of fancy preparation could make the herring or the cod—or, for that matter, the hake, sole, plaice, whiting, or turbot—tasty or desirable to the medieval palate. They were primarily regarded as Lenten fare and, as such, foods to be *suffered* rather than enjoyed. But suffered or not, cod was in high demand as Lent approached.

Because cod will take almost any bait offered to them, the first Grand Banks fishermen simply baited their hooks with a piece of clam, a capelin, or a squid and hauled in a codfish. The first fishermen—the Basques, for example—fished either from the decks of their vessels or from smaller rowing boats known as *chaloupes,* but the object of their fishery was always the same: the *baccalao** first encountered in such profusion by John Cabot in 1497. (Cabot is said to have fished by lowering weighted baskets into dense schools of cod and simply hauling them up.) By the first decade of the sixteenth century, João Fagundes had traveled the coast of eastern Newfoundland, and the king of Portugal had applied a 10 percent tax on imported cod. (Samuel Eliot Morison—exclamation point and all—referred to this in 1971 as "the first European attempt to protect home industries from American competition!") Fish was also a major element in the diet of sixteenth-century Europeans; it

---

*Although *baccalao* is the Portuguese word for codfish, it is believed to have originated in the Basque language. As Francis Parkman pointed out in *Pioneers of France in the New World,* "if in the original Basque, *baccalaos* is the word for codfish, and if Cabot found it in use among the inhabitants of Newfoundland, it is hard to escape the conclusion that the Basques had been there before him."

was one of the few sources of cheap protein available to them. As historian J. H. Parry noted in 1974, "the import of great quantities of cod was in itself a significant economic event, in a continent where many people lived near starvation level for part of every year." In France, the fish were known as *morue;* in Spain and Portugal, *baccalao;* and in England, stockfish or poor-john.

The cod fishermen were soon to become the most serious rivals of the herring picklers; dried cod is much easier to handle than pickled herring, since the cod can be tossed around like cordwood, whereas the herring has to be stored in a barrel of brine. Once they had learned the basic facts about the natural history of their prey, the fishermen realized that no matter how important it was to be the first ones on the Banks, there was no point in getting there before May, when the capelin swarmed inshore and the cod followed them.*

The codfish is a shallow-water inhabitant; it is plentiful in areas such as the North American continental shelf, where the depth is rarely greater than two or three hundred feet. In the *Encyclopedia Londonensis* for 1810, the habitat and utilization of the cod were described thus:

> They are taken in vast quantities at Newfoundland, Cape Breton, Nova Scotia, and the coasts of Norway and Iceland; also off the Dogger-bank, but their principal resort for centuries past, has been on the banks of Newfoundland, and other sand banks off Cape Breton. That extensive flat seems to be the broad top of a subaqueous mountain, everywhere surrounded by a deeper sea. Hither the cod annually repair, in numbers beyond the powers of calculation, to feed upon the worms that swarm along the sandy bottom. Here they are taken in such quantities, that they supply all Europe with a considerable supply of provision.

As the fish were hauled in, they were gutted immediately, the tongues cut out (and used as counters to record how many fish had been caught by each man), and whatever was in the gut used to rebait the hook. The fish were thrown into the pound amidships, where the header and the dresser performed their functions. When the dresser had filleted the fish, he threw the pieces into the hold through a hole in the deck; there, the salter laid the fish in a bed of salt, where it would remain for twenty-four to forty-eight hours.

---

*The capelin (*Mallotus villosus*) is an incredibly prolific small fish of the smelt family, reaching a maximum length of six inches. In the spring, capelin aggregate in breeding schools that number in the millions and spawn at the surf line, where they are thrown up on the sand to die. On the coasts of Newfoundland, the capelin wash ashore in such quantities that the little fish are used as agricultural fertilizer.

(The salt, obviously one of the most important elements in this fishery, came at first from Brittany or Lower Normandy, but when local taxes made that too dear, the fishermen went to Spain and Portugal to obtain the substance. By the seventeenth century, they were getting their supplies from the salt pans of La Rochelle and its offshore islands, Île de Ré and Île d' Oléron.) The cod roe was kept as a special treat for the crew, the air bladders were made into glue, and the oil from the liver was used for lighting.*

Even more important than the salt cod fishery was the dried cod industry of the sixteenth and seventieth centuries. This fishery, known as the "sedentary" fishery because the mother ship remained anchored, colonized the beaches between Bonavista Bay and Cape Norman on Newfoundland, along the coast of Labrador, and even along the Gaspé Peninsula. The fishery lasted from June to mid-August, but the ships did not head home until the drying was completed, usually around the end of September. The boats were left on the beach, and the dried fish were laid on branches in the holds and transported back to Europe.

Even though John Cabot discovered the Grand Banks and claimed them for England, the British cod fishery began somewhat later than the French and the Portuguese. When John Rut visited Newfoundland in 1527 in the *Mary of Guilford,* he reported "eleven saile of Normans, and one Brittaine, and two Portugall Barkes and all a-fishing." In 1542, Henry VIII criticized his subjects for buying codfish from "Pycardes, Flemynghes, Norman and Frenchmen," and an act of Parliament suggested "the craft and feate of fishing" gave "great welthe to the Realme." Although the French—and, to a lesser extent, the Portuguese—dominated the fishery in the first half of the sixteenth century, the Spanish took the lead in the second half.

When Sir Humphrey Gilbert passed the Grand Banks en route to Newfoundland in 1583, he encountered Portuguese and French fishermen, "sometimes a hundred or more sails of ships; who commonly begin the fishing in April, and have ended by July." Edward Haye, whose account of Gilbert's expedition appears in Hakluyt's *Voyages,* wrote that "cod, which alone draweth many nations thither . . . is become the most famous fishing of

---

*Although the medicinal qualities of cod liver oil were not fully realized until the twentieth century—it is especially rich in vitamins A and D—its virtues were known for hundreds of years to the Lapps, the Norwegians, and the Icelanders. In eighteenth-century continental Europe, it was prescribed by physicians for the prevention and treatment of gout, rheumatism, and even tuberculosis. In later years—much to the discomfort and distaste of innumerable children—it became known as an all-purpose tonic and vitamin supplement.

the world." When Gilbert arrived at Newfoundland, he found an English "admiral" in charge of the camps, and although the fishermen ignored his pomp and circumstance—he had, after all, a patent from the Queen to claim the land for England—Newfoundland became the first English possession in the New World. Gilbert was lost at sea in the *Squirrel* shortly after leaving Newfoundland, but his enthusiastic writings are believed to have inspired another man from the West Country, his half-brother Walter Raleigh, to follow him.

In 1603, the merchants of Bristol sent Martin Pring to check out the stories Gosnold had brought back. "Heere wee found," wrote Pring, "an excellent fishing for Cods, which are better than those of New-found-land and withall saw good and Rockie ground to drie them upon." Pring, a Devonshire seaman, commanded the *Speedwell;* the *Discoverer* was under William Brown. After being detained by the death of Queen Elizabeth on March 23, they sailed from Milford Haven on April 10, 1603, and arrived at Cape Cod Bay in June. Pring landed on Martha's Vineyard, headed south past the mouth of the Acushnet River at what would later become New Bedford, and entered Long Island Sound, opening trade with the Indians there. He sent the *Discoverer* home with a cargo of furs and sassafras and remained behind with the crew and passengers of the *Speedwell* for the rest of the summer, planting wheat, barley, oats, and peas. He arrived back in Bristol in early October, with useful information about "North Virginia," which would not be named New England until John Smith arrived there in 1607.

The colonists tried to set up fishing communities at Weymouth and Cape Ann, Massachusetts, but these failed. The first successful venture was at Salem in 1628, followed quickly at Dorchester, Marblehead, and Scituate. Along with the lumber industry, fishing became the colony's first business, but only after the development of a "winter fishery" around 1630. Farmers who tilled the soil in spring and summer turned to the sea in winter and were thus able not only to feed themselves and their families but also to provide a commodity that could be traded. It was a happy quirk of nature that the cod approached the shores of New England in winter to spawn, since they were much farther offshore in summer, on Georges Bank, the Grand Banks, and Jeffries Bank. The Europeans who held no colonial interests in North America had no such opportunities for a winter fishery, since they would have had to sail across the hostile North Atlantic in late fall, the worst possible time of year.

The Reverend Francis Higginson, the first minister of Salem, died in 1630, but in *New England's Plantation* he left behind a delightful account of the treasures of Massachusetts Bay:

The abundance of sea-fish are almost beyond believing, and sure I
should scarce have believed it, except as I had seen it with my own eyes.
I saw great store of whales and grampusses, and such abundance of
mackerels that it would astonish one to behold, likewise codfish in
abundance on the coast, and in their season are plentifully taken. . . .
Also there is an abundance of herring, turbot, sturgeon, cusks, haddocks,
mullets, eels, crabs, muscles and oysters.

With such variety and abundance, the colonial fishery prospered, especially when it was discovered that the poorer grades of fish could be exported
along with the tobacco that was grown in Virginia. Toward the end of the century, the "triangular trade" was in full swing: New England ships carried fish
and lumber to the West Indies; fish to England, Spain, Portugal, and the
Mediterranean; rum to Africa; and slaves from Guinea and Angola. Cordage,
iron, hemp, fishing tackle, and other products necessary for industry were
exchanged for cod and brought back to the burgeoning colony. In March
1643, a Boston-built ship returned from a voyage to Fayal (in the Azores),
where it had sold fish and pipestaves (the slats used in the manufacture of
barrels, or "pipes"), bought wine and sugar, and sailed for St. Christopher,
where it exchanged the wine for cotton, tobacco, and iron. The premium
dried cod from Massachusetts was sent to France, and the inferior grades
went to Spain and the West Indies. In 1700, with a population of some 14,000
people, Boston had a fleet of about 300 trading and fishing vessels engaged in
commerce with Nova Scotia, Virginia, the West Indies, and Madeira. That
year, the city exported some 50,000 quintals (a quintal equals 100 kilograms,
or what was eventually known as a hundredweight) of winter-cured fish, and
more than three-quarters of it went to the Spanish port of Bilbao, on the Bay
of Biscay.

   By the second half of the seventeenth century, France also had posses-
sions in the West Indies (St. Christopher, Martinique, Guadeloupe, the Tortugas, St. Martin, St. Lucia, St. Croix, Grenada, and St. Bartholomew, in order of
acquisition) and settlements in North America. French shipping was heavily
engaged in the sugar, tobacco, and slave trades—it was estimated that the
sugar plantations of Martinique required more than a thousand new slaves
every year—and these people needed food. The French developed locations
in Newfoundland and the Strait of Belle Isle where they could fish on their
own and not depend on trade from the British or the Americans. One of
these was Placentia, which was particularly desirable because it was free of ice
in the spring. By 1668, the French were loading more than a hundred ships
per year, in contrast with ten or twelve the year before.

Unfortunately, Placentia was on British territory, and the British were not happy about the French settlement there. They tried to oust the French interlopers, but the French dug in and even established stations along the Gulf of St. Lawrence and on Anticosti Island. The French cod fishery peaked between 1678 and 1689, but in 1699 Parliament prohibited settlement on Newfoundland except as necessary to maintain the cod fishery, and for the next 150 years the island was run as a private fiefdom ruled by commercial fishing interests.

As the French retreated from Cape Breton and the Gulf of St. Lawrence, the British moved in. They filled the void and filled their holds in Quebec (the Gulf of St. Lawrence), Newfoundland, and Nova Scotia. With the decline of the French and the New England concentration on Newfoundland, the fishery expanded to the shores of Labrador, and production increased dramatically. In 1763, the Massachusetts fishery brought in an estimated return of £164,000. Marblehead and Gloucester led the way with 150 and 146 vessels, respectively.

Since the New England fishermen were producing so much fish for West Indian consumption, they had to be able to import a commensurate amount of molasses. If the imported molasses was heavily taxed, it meant that fishing had to be reduced, a serious threat to American industry. On May 24, 1764, a Boston town meeting denounced taxation without representation, and by the following year, policies of nonimportation of British goods had begun throughout the colonies. The increasing hostilities between Britain and its colonies in North America were as important to the history of the fishery as to the history of the country. The Boston Massacre occurred in March 1770; the Boston Tea Party, in December 1773. By 1774, as the conflict was heating up, Britain passed the New England Restraining Act, which restricted New England trade to British ports, and then an embargo was placed on trade with Nova Scotia, Newfoundland, and the West Indies. New England fishermen and privateers roamed the coasts of Newfoundland and Nova Scotia capturing British and Newfoundland fishing boats, along with their crews and cargoes, as another device to harass the British.

The war was concluded with the Treaty of Versailles in 1783. The treaty explicitly awarded Americans the right to fish the Newfoundland Banks and take fish on the British portion of the Newfoundland coast, but they were not allowed to dry them there. They were, however, given liberty to dry and cure fish on the unsettled harbors, bays, and creeks of Nova Scotia, the Magdalen Islands, and Labrador, so long as those locations remained unsettled. By the turn of the century, it was becoming apparent that the ships sent over from Europe—especially from Britain—were economically unable to compete with the Newfoundlanders themselves, especially since the Newfoundland "bankers" did not have to make a transatlantic crossing. The Newfoundland residents or settlers, known as "planters," could prepare fish more cheaply than the merchants, since they had no wages to pay. Once again, the specter of war appeared on the horizon, and only twenty-nine years after the Treaty of Versailles was signed, the British and the Americans were at it again, in the war known in Britain as the Anglo-American War and in the United States as the War of 1812.

The rise of a fishery in Newfoundland ousted most of the British ships, and by 1823 the British fishing fleet, which had numbered more than three hundred in 1792, was reduced to some fifteen ships. Newfoundland received a charter (and a resident governor and council) in 1824. The charter was known, significantly, as the Newfoundland Fisheries Act, demonstrating the overwhelming importance of the fishery in the settlement of this island. During the nineteenth century, the cod fishery continued to grow and to dominate the commerce of Newfoundland and New England.

The early 1890s were good years for fishing in Massachusetts, particularly for Gloucester. At the World's Columbian Exposition of 1893 in Chicago, Gloucester mounted an elaborate exhibit featuring a scale model of its thriving waterfront. At the same time, Rudyard Kipling was holed up in Brattleboro, Vermont, writing *Captains Courageous,* the story of the brave Gloucestermen who went down to the sea in schooners. In 1895, fishermen caught 60,000 tons of cod in the waters off New England, including the 211-pound "patriarch" cod, the largest codfish ever recorded.*

By the turn of the century, the stocks of codfish were largely unscathed, and it appeared that the fishery could go on forever. In 1883, Thomas Huxley could say, "I still believe the cod fishery . . . and probably all the great fisheries are inexhaustible; that is to say that nothing we do seriously affects the number of fish." Huxley, one of the late nineteenth century's most eminent scientists and famous for his staunch defense of Charles Darwin's theories, could not have been more wrong. He could not have predicted the effects on the fish stocks of the otter trawl, a British invention introduced around 1880 and adopted by New England fishermen in 1905.† Nine years later, in 1914, the

---

*Nowadays, a cod weighing more than 50 pounds is considered large, and 100 pounds is truly exceptional. Curiously, the cod, which puts up very little resistance when hooked, is considered a game fish by the International Game Fish Association, and the modern record is a 98-pounder caught off New Hampshire in 1969.

†The otter trawl, now the standard bottom trawl, consists of a large, bag-shaped net that is towed through the water with its mouth held open by various ropes, *(continued)*

Commissioner of Fish and Fisheries had appointed a congressional committee to investigate the damage the otter trawl did to fish stocks. Fortunately for
the cod, World War I intervened and the declining stocks had some chance to
recover, but by 1919 the fishers were back in business. In retrospect, their business seems to have been to eliminate the codfish from the North Atlantic. In
1954, they received another enormous boost from technology when the
British factory ship *Fairtry* entered the lists.

At 245 feet in length and with a displacement of 2,800 tons, the *Fairtry*,
built by Salvesen of Leith, was far larger than the largest trawler of the day and
could catch and process cod in unprecedented numbers. The trawl net was
hauled up through a stern slipway, not unlike that of the whaling factory
ships Salvesen also built. On the factory deck of the *Fairtry* there was a heading machine, as well as devices for automatically skinning and filleting the
fish, and belowdecks were two sets of quick-freezers and fully refrigerated
holds. There was also a cod liver oil plant. So as not to be left behind, other
countries commissioned similar factory ships, and soon the Grand Banks
were serving up their cod to the Soviet Union, Germany, Spain, and Poland,
whose fishers were impervious to local restrictions. The catch of cod for 1968
was 810,000 tons, nearly three times the amount caught in any year before the
Fairtry introduced her annihilative technology.

The story of the giant factory ships draining the North Atlantic of its heritage of fish stocks is well told in William Warner's 1977 *Distant Water* and can
only be summarized here. Displacing the fleets of Norway, Iceland, and
Denmark, in whose home waters they were fishing, the distant-water fleets of
Germany, the USSR, Poland, Spain, and Japan took various species of cod and
herring in staggering numbers. The *Fairtry's* displacement of 2,800 tons,
which was once the largest, was soon superseded by Soviet ships that displaced 8,000 tons. (Warner quotes one incredulous observer as exclaiming,
"They're fishing with ocean liners!") The nets used by these factory ships
were enormous; some were large enough to swallow a dozen jumbo jets in a
single gulp. In an hour, these leviathan ships could catch a hundred tons of
fish, as much as a sixteenth-century codfish boat caught in a season.
Increasingly sophisticated technology enabled fleets to process the fish at sea,
not only gutting them but also filleting, freezing, and even packing them.

---

weights, and floats in conjunction with angled "otter boards" (also known as "doors"),
which draw apart as the net is pulled over the seabed. Its depth and distance from the bottom can be controlled by floats. The narrow, tapered end of the net, into which the
trapped fish gather, is known as the "cod end."

It was during this period that the "cod wars" between Britain and Iceland broke out. A "war" between fishing nations was a precursor of things to come; more and more boats would be vying for ever-decreasing numbers of fish. From 1919 to 1951, Iceland's fishery limit was fixed at 3 miles; any nation's boats could fish without protest to within 3 miles of its shores. To protect what it considered its own stocks of cod, Iceland increased the limit to 4 miles in 1952 and to 12 miles in 1958. In 1972, when most other countries maintained a 12-mile limit, Iceland unilaterally increased the limit around its shores to 50 miles. When British and West German trawlers ignored the restrictions, Iceland's coast guard vessels employed trawl-wire cutters to render the fishing gear useless; the British fishing boats tried to ram the coast guard cutters, and Britain sent Royal Navy frigates to Icelandic waters to protect its boats, but luckily no shots were fired. When the British and Icelandic prime ministers met in London to resolve this dispute, the British promised not to send their larger ships into Icelandic waters and not to fish in certain areas. But when Iceland later adopted a 200-mile exclusive economic zone (EEZ), British fishing boats again intentionally violated Icelandic space, and the cod war began anew. British frigates accompanied fishing boats into Icelandic waters, and the Icelanders deployed coast guard ships, planes, and helicopters. Unable to resolve their differences by diplomatic means, Iceland broke off relations with Britain, but in June 1976 the conflict was peacefully resolved, and again Britain agreed to reduce its presence in Icelandic waters.

To avoid such conflicts, the Canadian and U.S. governments contrived to extend their own fishing limits 200 miles offshore, thereby excluding foreign vessels from the productive waters of the Grand Banks. Instead of creating a sustainable fishery for their own fishers, however, the Canadians and Americans engaged in all sorts of "scientific" tomfoolery dedicated to finding out how many cod there had been before the decimation began. They had no way of accurately estimating the actual population, so they began catching the fish themselves in a misguided effort to count them or see how old they were when they died. This, of course, had no appreciable effect on the cod population because by that time—the mid-1970s—the population was so diminished that its recovery was almost impossible. Basing their assessments on the limited knowledge of cod biology at the time, the scientists decided that because the female cod lays millions of eggs every year, it would only be a short while before the population rebounded. For a couple of years, it appeared that the fisheries biologists were right; the catch did increase from its low point of 139,000 tons in 1975. In their wisdom, the Canadian bureaucrats increased the subsidies to fishermen and thereby increased the number of boats fishing for cod. By overestimating the available stock and encouraging more trawlers (the Canadians and Americans never did acquire the factory ship mentality; theirs was more an old-fashioned catch-as-catch-can approach that emphasized the rugged individualism of the fishermen), the government was all but guaranteeing the demise of the codfish—and thereby, of course, that of the cod fishermen.

In time, the fishermen learned new techniques and found new fishing grounds, which made it look as if they were fishing on an increasing stock. Their catches were going up, weren't they? In fact, the cod population was declining at an alarming rate, sliding toward the brink of what had always been held to be an impossibility—extinction. Even with these catastrophic predictions in hand, the Canadian government was more protective of its human population, and not wanting to throw thousands of Newfoundland fishers out of work, it cut the quotas by a skimpy 10 percent. Even with this reduction, however, the fishers continued to *increase* their productivity, with the sadly predictable result that the cod population declined even more precipitously. By 1992, it was obvious that the fishery had run out of fish, and the Canadian government closed it down, not temporarily, but permanently. Of Newfoundland's total (human) population of 570,000, there were 30,000 out of work in 1997.*

And what of New England? Georges Bank and the Gulf of Maine were never as rich in cod as the Grand Banks of Newfoundland, but the United States followed closely behind the Canadians and systematically eliminated the resource that had sustained fishing communities such as Gloucester for two centuries. Foreign trawlers were banned from waters within 200 miles of shore, and the American fishing fleet doubled between 1977 and 1983. In 1982, the American catch reached a high of 53,000 tons, but it began to decline immediately. The Magnuson-Fishery Conservation and Management Act, passed in 1976 to oversee the management of American fisheries, left planning and quotas to "regional councils," which meant that every fishing community could set its own limits—a classic example of the fox guarding the henhouse. The stocks of cod (and also haddock and yellowtail flounder) dropped so precipitously that by 1993, the National Marine Fisheries Service had closed Georges Bank to fishing indefinitely. As of 1995, the U.S. government had paid

---

*Newfoundland seems to be perennially snakebit in its approach to natural resources. First, its pilot whale fishery was deemed ecologically unsound (fishermen drove the pilot whales into shallow water and slaughtered them by the hundreds); its practice of clubbing baby harp seals to death came under intense fire from conservation groups; then, in 1992, Newfoundland's cod fishery, deemed its last safe industry, was closed down entirely.

more than $60 million in subsidies to New England fishermen, and the Canadian government had supported its Newfoundland counterparts to the tune of $600 million.

On the other side of the Atlantic, similar problems were brewing. As of 1997, even though European cod fishermen had reduced their catch by one-third, the young fish had not reappeared. Off the coasts of Britain and Iceland in the 1980s, cod catches averaged 300,000 tons per year, but the total fell to around 100,000 tons. Robin Cook of Scotland's Aberdeen Marine Laboratory said, as quoted in a 1999 Fred Pearce article in *New Scientist,* "Even in the Barents Sea north of Scandinavia, cod are in dreadful shape." The International Council for the Exploration of the Sea (ICES) called for cuts of 40 percent in the North Sea catch to forestall the collapse of the fish—and the fishery. Because cod are a cold-water species, it has been suggested that the general warming of the North Atlantic is somehow responsible, but some fisheries scientists disagree, holding that overfishing is the obvious and primary cause of population reduction.

The primary cause of the decline in North Atlantic cod populations is certainly overfishing, but other factors may have contributed. Recent experiments in his laboratory at the University of New Hampshire have convinced Michael Lesser that reduction of the atmospheric ozone layer has resulted in an increase in ultraviolet (UV) radiation that is deadly to cod larvae. In a 2001 article in the *Journal of Experimental Biology,* Lesser, Julianne Farrell, and Charles Walker pointed out that harmful ultraviolet-B (UV-B) radiation can penetrate to depths of twenty-three meters (seventy-five feet). Although cod usually spawn in deep water, the larvae float up toward the surface, where they are exposed to the UV radiation that can kill or harm them. Even larvae that survived the UV-B irradiation showed damage to their DNA and were smaller than larvae that were experimentally shielded. Under normal circumstances, around 99 percent of the millions of cod eggs and larvae are eaten by predators, but if UV radiation also is killing many of them, the death rate could be even higher.

Some fishermen and government representatives have attempted to blame the crash in cod populations on harp seals, claiming that if the seal herds carry on unchecked, there will be no fish left for anyone. There is no evidence, however, to support such a declaration. In a 2001 report, Alida Bundy of Fisheries and Oceans Canada in Dartmouth, Nova Scotia, wrote: "While groundfish stocks collapsed, seal populations and invertebrates such as shrimp and snow crab increased in abundance. The model predicted these increases, while a simulated increase in harp seals further repressed the recovery rate of cod. It was concluded that these results are consistent with the hypothesis that the collapse of cod was caused by excess fishing and that cod recovery is retarded by harp seals." It must be noted that Bundy's analysis was based exclusively on computer modeling and not on field observations, so the seals' involvement in the decline of cod populations is purely hypothetical.

A more recent report from Bundy puts an even worse spin on the cod situation. When the stocks crashed around 1992, fishing for cod was banned to allow them to recover, but, says the report (Bundy, Lilly, and Shelton 2000), the population dynamics have been so drastically altered that cod may never reappear in their former numbers. Not only cod but virtually all high-quality table fish, such as tuna, haddock, and flounder, have fallen to about 16 percent of what their numbers were in 1990. In a 2002 article in *New Scientist*, Kurt Kleiner quoted fisheries biologist Daniel Pauly: "Jellyfish is already being exported. In the Gulf of Maine people were catching cod a few decades ago. Now they're catching sea cucumber." Reg Watson, Pauly's colleague at the University of British Columbia and another of the report's authors, said, "If things don't change, we'll all be eating jellyfish sandwiches."

"Every nation has its comfort food," observed Debora MacKenzie (2001a). "In Britain, it is a large chunk of white fish, battered and fried, with thick fried potatoes and a sauce made of green peas, all wrapped in paper. . . . Unfortunately, the latest evidence suggests Britain's favourite fish is, after umpteen warnings, really on the road to oblivion." The spawning stocks of North Sea cod have plummeted, from a high of 277,000 tons in 1971 to 59,000 tons in 2001, well below the level at which commercial fishing can be sustained. But commercial fishing not only has not been reduced, it has increased: the depleted stocks mean that more and more fishermen, trying to scratch out a living, are putting to sea in an attempt to catch fewer and fewer fish. Getting fishermen to lay up their boats has proven to be a political nightmare, and the British cod-fishing industry is efficiently putting itself out of business.

At a meeting of the European Union in November 2002, fisheries scientists recommended a ban on almost all commercial fishing in the North Sea because of the imminent collapse of the codfish stocks. In the *New York Times* of November 7, Craig Smith commented, "The cod crisis is one of many facing the international community as countries compete for thinning stocks in the world's once fish-thick seas." For many countries, fishing represents jobs, and few politicians are willing to protect fishes before their constituents. It is estimated that if the North Sea cod fishery is shut down, as many as 20,000 jobs would be lost in the United Kingdom alone. Studies by ICES indicate that unless drastic steps are taken, the fisheries of Europe will follow those of the United States and Canada, collapsing because there are no more fish to catch. "According to scientific surveys and catch statistics," wrote David Malakoff and Richard Stone (2002), "the North Sea's cod spawning schools have dropped to 15% of what they were in the early 1970s." Politicians and fishers argue that a reduction in fishing will enable the stocks to bounce back, but when this kind of short-term solution was applied as a stopgap in New England, it was too late and the fishery collapsed anyway.

"Fishing down food webs (that is, fishing at lower trophic levels) leads at first to increasing catches, then to a phase transition associated with stagnating or declining catches," say Daniel Pauly and his colleagues (1998). "The results indicate that present exploitation patterns are unsustainable." All over the world, people are failing to hear the message. Out of desperation, greed, ignorance, and mismanagement, people are finding the bottom line of fish stocks that once seemed bottomless. Yet it is still shocking that it should have happened to cod—stolid, prolific, resilient, numberless cod, the beef of the sea. Even though we hardly knew them, we took the cod for granted, rather like the buffalo when the prairies were black with them. There is no great mystery about what happened to the codfish of the North Atlantic. The fishermen caught them, and the rest of us ate them.

THE PATAGONIAN TOOTHFISH

On February 11, 1888, the research vessel *Albatross,* working off the southern coast of Chile, hauled in a beam trawl that had been cast into water more than 6,000 feet deep. Among the creatures dumped on deck was a five-foot-long, large-mouthed fish, the likes of which no one had ever seen. Charles H. Townsend and Theodore Gill, ichthyologists aboard the *Albatross,* had it photographed as it lay on the deck; then they had it placed in a rough wooden box and salted, to preserve it for later study. Unfortunately, an overzealous bosun's mate pitched the box overboard, and all that remained of the fish was the photograph. Townsend and Gill named it "*Macrias* with reference to its length as well as its bulk, and the specific name *amissus* is appropriate for it as an estray from its relatives as well as to indicate the loss of the type." *Macrias amissus* was by far the largest of all known deep-sea fishes, and in 1901 Gill and Townsend wrote a brief description of their lost specimen.

Thirty-six years later, Townsend wrote about it again, this time without Gill (who died in 1914), in an article published in the bulletin of the New York Zoological Society. (Townsend was director of the Society's aquarium, then located at the Battery in lower Manhattan.) He had come across the photo-graph in searching through old records of the voyage of the *Albatross,* so this article, titled (as was its predecessor) "The Largest Deep-Sea Fish," included the subhead "A Long-Missing Photograph of the Monster Comes to Light after Nearly Half a Century." And there is *Macrias amissus,* on the deck of the *Albatross.* Townsend said:

> *Macrias amissus* never found its way into the published lists of fishes known to science. Perhaps the ichthyologists will relent when they see the photograph Dr. Gill and I regarded as that of a new fish from the depths and worthy of being described as something new to science, whether we had or had not, the type.

A couple of ichthyologists did relent, but not exactly as Townsend imag-ined they might. When Hugh DeWitt (1962) of Stanford University looked at the photograph, he "was immediately reminded of the illustration of *Dissostichus eleginoides* published by F. A. Smitt in 1898." Because of differ-ences in Gill and Townsend's description (in *Science*) and Smitt's (in a Swedish journal), DeWitt decided that *Macrias amissus* was not exactly like *D. eleginoides,* and he therefore named it *Dissostichus amissus.*

DeWitt's article appeared in the ichthyological journal *Copeia* in 1962, but not many nonichthyologists read it. Somehow, the "*Albatross* fish" became one of the more popular subjects for those who would postulate large, unknown fishes lurking at abyssal depths. For example, Edward Ricciuti's 1973 *Killers of the Seas* has a section titled "Survivors from Past Ages," and there, of all things, is the photograph of the fish from the *Albatross.* The cap-tion reads:

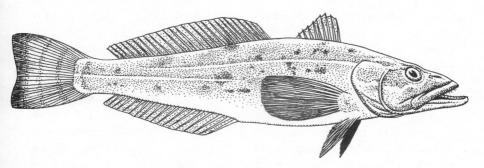

PATAGONIAN TOOTHFISH
(Dissostichus eleginoides)

STRANGE FISH. This fish, about 5 feet long, was dredged from a depth of 6,000 feet by the research vessel *Albatross* in 1888. Shortly after this photo was taken on deck, a crewman tossed the fish overboard, to the dismay of scientists who had never seen anything like it before.

Soviet cetologists, however, had certainly seen something like the *Albatross*'s fish; in fact, *Dissostichus* is a fairly common food item in the diet of Southern Ocean sperm whales. A. A. Berzin's 1972 monograph on sperm whales contains a photograph of a fish with this caption: "Specimen of *Dissotichus* [sic] *mawsoni*, from the stomach of a sperm whale." The stomachs of three sperm whales taken by Soviet whalers in 1963 contained approximately twenty fish per whale measuring seventeen to fifty-three inches long and weighing as much as 100 pounds. It is believed that sperm whales hunt at great depths, but how they are able to catch presumably fast-swimming fishes in the dark is unknown. We may not know how sperm whales catch these fish, but we know how people do, and they do it so efficiently that the fish is on the fast track to extinction.

Now known as the Patagonian toothfish, *Dissostichus eleginoides* was first caught on longlines by fishermen who were randomly fishing the subantarctic waters north of latitude 55° S around Patagonia, southern Chile, and islands such as the Crozets, Heard, Kerguelen, and South Georgia. Today, *Dissostichus* is more familiar to consumers around the world as the Chilean sea bass, black hake, or black cod. In Japan, its highly prized white flesh is known as *mero*. Although hardly any information is available about the growth rate of the fish or the size of the stocks, fishing boats flying the flags of Argentina, Chile, Norway, Denmark, and Spain are hauling in these fishes at a rate so egregious that the Commission for the Conservation of Antarctic Marine Living Resources (CCAMLR, usually pronounced "camel-R") has reported that instead of the allotment, 10,000 tons, fishers are taking more than ten times that. Antarctic and subantarctic waters are mostly outside any country's exclusive economic zone (EEZ) and therefore the limits involve islands owned by various nations, but the far greater problem is that in the Southern Ocean, there is hardly any way to monitor illegal fishing.

Mounting evidence of illegal, unreported, and unregulated (known colloquially as IUU) fishing in the Southern Ocean has forced CCAMLR to propose actions to halt the plunder of these seas. It is estimated that since 1997, IUU fishing for *Dissostichus* species in the Southern Ocean has been on the order of 99,000 tons, more than twice the level of toothfish catches taken in CCAMLR-regulated fisheries. This rate of extraction is unsustainable and has led to a significant and alarming depletion of toothfish stocks in some areas.

The legal fishery for toothfish, mostly in the South Atlantic Ocean and the southern Indian Ocean, is dwarfed by the take of the IUU pirates. Of the 64,900 tons of Patagonian toothfish caught in 1999–2000, the illegal and unreported portion could amount to as much as 36,300 tons. In October 2002, the Australian government announced that it was sending armed patrol boats to the Southern Ocean to protect legitimate Australian fishers and arrest toothfish poachers.

In his discussion of the extinction of the giant birds known as moas by the Maori people of New Zealand, Jared Diamond wrote: "Then, there were no more moas; soon there will be no more Chilean sea bass, Atlantic swordfish, and tuna. I wonder what the Maori who killed the last moa said. Perhaps the Polynesian equivalent of 'Your ecological models are untested, so conservation measures would be premature'? No, he probably just said 'Jobs, not birds,' as he delivered the fatal blow."

"Chilean sea bass" was first served in a Los Angeles restaurant in 1982, and since then, its soft, snow-white flesh and mild flavor have made it one of the most popular menu items in America's finer restaurants. (One Atlanta restaurateur said that he used to go through 1,200 pounds a week.) Because the unfortunate depletion of the world's marine resources is finally achieving a certain notoriety, the reduction in overfishing of endangered species has become a popular crusade in certain circles. One of the best ways to publicize illegal or overexploitive fisheries is to make the buyers of the fish—in this case, the restaurants that serve it—aware of the problems. As was done with the dwindling North Atlantic swordfish populations, a campaign has been started to have chefs remove Chilean sea bass from their menus. Take a Pass on Chilean Sea Bass, a campaign organized by the National Environmental Trust, an advocacy organization in Washington, D.C., claims to have signed on more than 800 restaurants in major cities across the United States. It seems to have worked for the swordfish; let's hope it is not too late for the toothfish.

THE ORANGE ROUGHY

The orange roughy (*Hoplostethus atlanticus*) is a foot-long, big-headed, laterally compressed (like a vertical pancake) deepwater fish that inhabits cold waters over steep continental slopes, ocean ridges, and seamounts. The name is derived from the bright orange or red color of its body and fins, although there are silver tinges on the flanks. Orange roughys have been recorded swimming as deep as 6,000 feet in the North Atlantic Ocean. They are also found in the Indian Ocean and deep below the surface on the continental

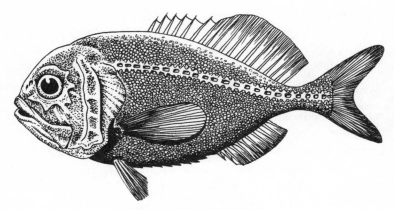

ORANGE ROUGHY
(Hoplostethus atlanticus)

shelf slope between Port Stephens in New South Wales and Cape Naturaliste in Western Australia. They are fished commercially in South Africa, South Australia, and New Zealand. The New Zealand fishery was begun only in 1979; at depths that range from 2,500 to 5,000 feet, it is the deepest commercial fishery in the world.

Orange roughys are among the most long-lived of all vertebrates. They do not mature until they are more than 30 years old, and there are records of individuals that reached 150, which means there are probably orange roughys alive now that hatched before the American Civil War. With advances in deep-sea trawling, fish that could not be caught before were hauled up in great quantities, and orange roughys were extensively exported to the United States. When the fishery began, fishers in Australia and New Zealand were ignorant of the population density and breeding habits of the object of their pursuit, and by the time they learned about the species, intense fishing pressure had seriously reduced the populations. Because orange roughys school tightly, a five-minute tow can fill a trawl net with an astounding ten to fifty tons of fish. This schooling pattern and the slow rate of growth and development make the orange roughy particularly susceptible to overfishing, and catches have fallen to a fraction of what they were earlier. Orange roughy was once a popular menu item in North American restaurants, but as it became scarce, and therefore uneconomical, it was replaced by another exotic Southern Hemisphere fish, the so-called Chilean sea bass. Because of its extremely slow rate of reproduction, the orange roughy will take a long time to recover from the blitzkrieg fishing efforts that nearly drove it to extinction.

SEA HORSES

What tiny fish has a prehensile tail but no tail fin, swims upright, and feeds through a tube? If you answered "Sea horse," you were correct, so here are some more questions: What tiny, slow-swimming fish is found in coastal waters, swims so slowly that it must depend on camouflage for escape, and is affected by pollution, dredging, seaside building, and fishing? The sea horse again. Last questions: What tiny fish is caught by the millions annually, primarily for use in Chinese medicine, but also for the home aquarium trade, and dried as souvenirs? Right. *Hippocampus*. And finally, as revealed in a 1994 *National Geographic* article, what did Amanda Vincent discover was the most valuable fisheries export of the Philippines? You guessed it.

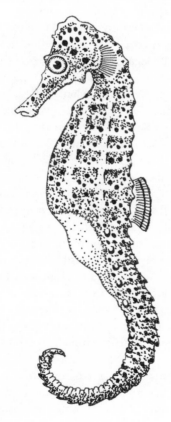

LINED SEA HORSE
(*Hippocampus erectus*)

There are some thirty-five species of sea horse, ranging in size from the tiny pygmy (*Hippocampus zosterae*), which at maturity is less than half an inch long, to the eleven-inch *H. ingens*. Although a single pygmy sea horse wouldn't make much of a meal for a kitten, thousands of them would do, even for people. (In her *National Geographic* article, Vincent reported that she had found wok-fried sea horses on a menu in Hobart, Tasmania.) Sea horses harvested from the waters of Indonesia and the Philippines are used locally in folk medicine, but by far the largest numbers of sea horses are shipped to China (and, to a lesser extent, Korea and Japan), where for five centuries practitioners of traditional Chinese medicine have been using them to cure impotence and asthma and to lower blood levels of cholesterol, prevent arteriosclerosis, and even enhance virility. Dried sea horses are used to make key chains, jewelry, paperweights, Christmas tree ornaments, and other souvenirs. Because they occur in Indonesian and Philippine waters, sea horses are used in folk medicine in these island nations as well.

When Heather Hall began her research on sea horses, she found it "incredible that an animal that is so popular has been so little studied" (Milius 2000). With the support of Guylian, a chocolate company in Belgium that manufactures candies shaped like sea horses, Hall, Amanda Vincent, and Sara Lourie began Project Seahorse, dedicated to the identification and conservation of these little-studied—but utterly familiar—fishes. Even though some of them look like chessmen and others like soda straws or vegetation, all sea horses are proper fishes; they are cold-blooded vertebrates that breathe with gills and swim with fins, just like sardines, salmon, and swordfish. They differ from most other fishes, however, in their upright posture and prehensile tail, and they differ from all other fishes—and most other animals on the earth—in the male's role as incubator of the eggs.

The female produces eggs and deposits them in the male's pouch, where he then fertilizes them. Because the male broods the developing eggs, his condition can correctly be called a pregnancy. After a period that varies among species from ten days to six weeks, the male goes into labor and ejects tiny, fully formed sea horses from his brood pouch. The newborn sea horses receive no further protection from either parent and are potential prey for almost anything that swims in their vicinity.

And their vicinity includes a lot of territory. Sea horses are found in warm, shallow coastal waters of every continent, with most species in the Indo-Pacific region. Many species live among sea grasses, but others can be found in mangrove forests or in areas where sponges and corals abound. Seahorses' tubelike mouths enable them to suck in tiny prey animals, such as mysid shrimp, copepods, and other minute planktonic creatures. Seahorses swallow their prey whole, for they have no teeth and no stomachs. All thirty-five or so species belong to the genus *Hippocampus*.*

Shrimp trawlers using small-meshed nets often collect sea horses as bycatch, and these little creatures ultimately find their way into apothecaries or souvenir shops. Project Seahorse estimates that "total global consumption of seahorses was at least 20 million seahorses in 1995 (more than 56 metric tons) . . . [but] this now appears to be an underestimate; new and very incomplete data from Hong Kong show imports of nearly 13.5 tons from that region alone." At a Web page maintained by Project Seahorse titled "Seahorse Biology and Conservation," Vincent and Hall summarize what is known (and not known) about the sea horse population:

> Extracting seahorses at current rates appears to be having a serious effect on their populations. The impact of removing millions of seahorses can only be assessed indirectly because global seahorse numbers are unknown, taxonomic identities are unclear, geographic ranges are undefined, and fisheries undocumented. Nonetheless, most participants in established seahorse fisheries reported that catches were dwindling markedly. Indeed, fishers' reports and preliminary research indicate that seahorse numbers in sample populations from five countries indicate that seahorse numbers could each have declined by 50% over the past five years. Numbers in the best-understood Philippines populations are reported to have declined 70% between 1985 and 1995.

Neither size nor edibility of a fish is a criterion for its desirability to humans. We catch some species just so we can look at them. The inexpensive technology that makes artificial saltwater systems easily available means that home aquariums are no longer restricted to goldfish, guppies, swordfish, zebra fish, and tetras. Now exotic surgeonfish, triggerfish, butterflyfish, clown fish, and even moray eels and small sharks can be kept in the home, and many of these exotic creatures have to be caught in distant localities such as South

---

*Hippocampus was a mythical sea monster with the foreparts of a horse and the hindparts of a fish or dolphin. The name comes from the Greek *hippos,* which means "horse," and *kampos,* "monster." The sea horse is far from a scary monster, but with its horse-like head, prehensile tail, bony armor, and kangaroo-like pouch, it is a most unusual fish indeed. In the brain, the hippocampus is a horseshoe-shaped part of the limbic system, located in the temporal lobe, that is a center for short-term memory. The hippocampus helps humans construct a three-dimensional "mental map" of our surroundings and is crucial for our ability to move around in the world.

Pacific coral reefs. They are caught in huge numbers, and many of them die long before they reach the distributors. Sea horses, found throughout the world's temperate and tropical waters, are easy to catch and do well in home aquariums. Will the last sea horses be the ones the next generation watches through glass in the sanctuary of their homes?

THE ATLANTIC SALMON

Travelers have left records of the teeming British rivers. For example, the Spanish ambassador Don Pedro de Ayala, who penetrated into the wilds of Scotland in 1498 as far as the Beauly and Spey, was astonished at the immense quantities of fish taken out of the waters. The Elizabethan "water poet" John Taylor noted the hauls from the prolific Tweed. Richard Franck, who made an angling tour of Scotland in the Cromwellian era, reported that at Stirling "the Forth relieves the country with her great plenty of salmon, where the burgomasters as in many other parts of Scotland, are compelled to reinforce an ancient statute that commands all masters and others not to force or compel any servant, or an apprentice, to feed upon salmon more than thrice a week."

—Anthony Netboy, *The Salmon: Their Fight for Survival,* 1974

Found in the eastern North Atlantic Ocean from Greenland to the Bay of Biscay, and in the western North Atlantic from Hudson Bay to New England, the Atlantic salmon (*Salmo salar*) remains one of the world's most popular game fishes. A spindle-shaped, silvery fish, it is blue-gray on the back and freckled with little spots or cross-shaped markings. The world's record—caught in Norway in 1928—weighed seventy-nine pounds, but most are considerably smaller, around ten to twenty pounds. With the exception of some landlocked populations, Atlantic salmon are anadromous: born in fresh water, they migrate to the sea and then return to fresh water to spawn. Unlike Pacific salmon (genus *Oncorhynchus*), which die when they reach their freshwater spawning grounds, Atlantic salmon may repeat the cycle as many as three or four times.

At every stage of their growth, salmon acquire new names. The eggs remain in gravel substrates and hatch during winter, and the newly hatched fish, now known as alevins, emerge in the spring. The next stage is fry, and at the age of two or three months, they are called parrs. After several years in fresh water, they head for the sea as smolts, and they return to their streams of origin as grilse. Only the full-grown fish are called salmon, and these prizes

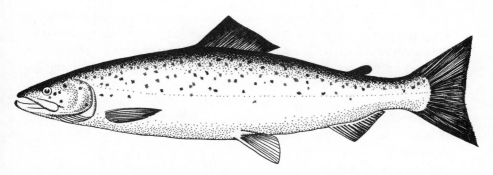

ATLANTIC SALMON
(*Salmo salar*)

are eagerly sought by fly fishermen in freshwater streams and rivers from Scotland to Maine. Because they are regarded as one of the world's premier food fishes, Atlantic salmon are also caught in great numbers by commercial fishermen—particularly gillnetters—leading not only to conflicts with sport-fishermen but also to a catastrophic reduction in the salmon's numbers.

Wild salmon hatch in a multitude of rivers in countries with access to the North Atlantic. The far-flung salmon countries include Canada, the United States, Iceland, Norway, and Russia in the north; the United Kingdom, Ireland, and the Baltic countries in the middle of the range; and France and northern Spain on the southern margin. The young salmon leave their freshwater home and migrate thousands of miles to feed in the rich marine environment of the North Atlantic off Greenland and the Faroe Islands. After a year or more in these feeding grounds, the fish undertake their most impressive return migration to their rivers of origin, where they spawn and complete the cycle.

From time immemorial, the cycle of spawning, ocean feeding, and return migration went on as if the salmon were a permanent feature of the natural world—until the 1950s and 1960s, when developments occurred that began to threaten the fish radically. Their sea feeding grounds, long a mystery, were located, and international exploitation of the fish began at an alarming rate. New types of gear, such as the nylon monofilament net, were introduced, with disastrous results as unregulated ocean fishing fleets began to devastate the stocks of fish at sea. By the mid-1970s, as much as 2,700 tons of salmon were being taken annually from the ocean feeding grounds, and following this massive loss of stock, salmon numbers began to fall precipitously.

The Atlantic salmon's dependence on both fresh- and saltwater habitats has made it especially vulnerable to environmental pressures and overfishing. Over the past half century, the number of adult fish available to return to North American rivers is estimated to have dropped from approximately 200,000 to 80,000. The aquaculture industry's proposed use of foreign imports of farmed fish to supplement depleted ocean stocks poses a further major threat to wild salmon. When farmed fish escape from their sea cages, they invade the closest rivers, bringing with them the potential to transmit disease and parasites and to undermine the genetic diversity of wild salmon populations.

The historical North American range of Atlantic salmon extended from the rivers of Ungava Bay, Canada, to Long Island Sound. As a consequence of agricultural pollution, dam building, and industrial development, most populations native to New England have been extirpated. The remaining native populations of Atlantic salmon in the United States are now found only in eastern Maine.

If dams and pollution are hazards for the Atlantic salmon on its run to the spawning beds, the older and far more insidious problem has been high-seas fishing, which, until recently, was not subject to management regulation. In 1966, when reduced stocks caused concern on both sides of the Atlantic, Canada, the United States, and Spain banned high-seas salmon fishing, although other countries did not join the ban until ten years later. Since 1972, Canada has banned all commercial fishing of Atlantic salmon and, at great expense, has compensated fishermen for their losses. Sportfishing for salmon in the interior of Atlantic Canada and Quebec is now under strict government control.

In the 1970s, 1.5 million salmon made the migration from the sea each year, but since then the number of wild Atlantic salmon returning to spawn has steadily and significantly declined. By 1999, the number had been reduced to 350,000, a decline of more than 75 percent in less than thirty years. The Inner Bay of Fundy group of rivers consists of thirty-three rivers extending clockwise around the Bay of Fundy from the Mosher River in New Brunswick to the Annapolis River in Nova Scotia. Returns of salmon to these rivers are critically low (from a mid-1980s level of 40,000 to a few hundred in 2000), and special measures, including live gene banking, are ongoing to prevent complete extirpation. Largely as a result of legal pressure applied by Trout Unlimited and the Atlantic Salmon Federation, the unique strains of Atlantic salmon found in eight rivers (the Machias, East Machias, Dennys, Narraguagus, Pleasant, Sheepscot, Ducktrap, and Cove Brook, a tributary of the Penobscot) were formally listed as endangered species in November 2000. Yet because these salmon migrate to the feeding grounds off Greenland shared by wild Atlantic salmon from other North American and European rivers, they are still in danger of being harvested.

A number of regulatory schemes have been put in place in both fresh and salt water, but overall, the wild Atlantic salmon population is in free fall. According to the latest report of the Northeast Fisheries Science Center (Kocik and Brown 2001), "the last two decades have seen a period of drastic decline in stock status for all Atlantic salmon populations of the North Atlantic." Angler catches in Maine have averaged approximately 486 salmon in recent years. Declines in runs have led to a no-retention policy statewide; thus, actual landings have been zero. Targeted fishing of Atlantic salmon in Maine was suspended in 2000 and will not be reopened until populations reach conservation targets. The Merrimack River brood stock fishery, which began in 1993, has resulted in an annual catch of approximately 1,000 salmon. The fisheries around Newfoundland and in southern Labrador have been closed under moratorium by the Canadian government since 1992 and 1997, respectively. The only remaining commercial fishery in Canada is a small fishery run by native peoples in Ungava Bay. In May 2001, the Committee on the Status of Endangered Wildlife in Canada (COSEWIC) listed the Bay of Fundy salmon as an endangered species—a species facing imminent extirpation or extinction.

Across the Atlantic, the North Atlantic Salmon Conservation Organization (NASCO) was established in 1983 to "promote the conservation, restoration, enhancement and rational management of salmon stocks in the North Atlantic Ocean through international co-operation." In 1993, a multi-year quota system for the Greenland fishery was agreed on within NASCO to provide a framework for quota setting based on a forecast model of salmon abundance, but the agreement had to be modified to allow for a local use fishery when stock abundance was found to be below recommended conservation levels.

If overfishing was not enough of a threat to the Atlantic salmon, they are now being attacked by disease. In 1998, Paul Bowser and James Casey, researchers at Cornell University's College of Veterinary Medicine, isolated what they believed to be the cause of salmon swim bladder sarcoma virus (SSSV), which, though apparently harmless to humans, was killing wild and farm-raised salmon in New England waters. The infected fish were found in a hatchery operated by the U.S. Fish and Wildlife Service in North Attleboro, Massachusetts, and in the Pleasant River in Maine. Earlier, cancer-like symptoms had been reported in farmed salmon from Scotland as well, but it was not until the development of advanced gene-sequencing techniques that the virus could be positively identified.

In 1984, a new virus was reported on fish farms in Norway and dubbed infectious salmon anemia virus, or ISAV. Then it was reported to have spread through the Bay of Fundy in New Brunswick, where it caused millions of dollars in damage to Canadian aquaculture operations. In an effort to stop further spread, in 1998 the Canadian government paid New Brunswick fish farmers more than $6 million to kill one-third of the province's total production. In early 2000, Eric Anderson, a professor of biochemistry and molecular biology at the University of Maine, warned that the virus might soon infect the aquaculture industry of New England, and that is exactly what happened. In July 2001, a single salmon infected with ISAV was caught in a trap in the Penobscot River in Maine and quickly quarantined, but it was too late. By September, the virus had spread throughout New England, and Maine fish farmers were forced to kill more than 900,000 salmon in an attempt to stop the spread of the deadly virus. Transmitted initially by the sea louse, a small marine crustacean that attacks a salmon's protective mucus, scales, and skin, infectious salmon anemia is highly contagious and incurable, causing massive internal bleeding and death.

In January 2002, 1.5 million farm-raised salmon (out of a state total of 30 million) were slaughtered in Maine to fight the spread of a virus infecting stocks in Cobscook Bay and threatening to spread. According to an article by John Richardson in the *Portland* (Maine) *Press Herald*, the shutdown was to be only temporary, but the fish kill could become a grim metaphor for Maine's aquaculture industry, which is fighting for its young life:

> Salmon aquaculture in Maine is under attack from all directions, with one crisis feeding off another. Infectious salmon anemia spread last year from Canada to Cobscook Bay, where more than half of Maine's salmon are raised. . . . Farmers in Lubec and Eastport killed one million fish by December 2001 to try to slow the spread of the virus. The U.S. Agriculture Department gave the industry $16.6 million over the next two years, to kill the remaining 1.5 million fish and clean out the bay. Most of the fish were too small to be processed into marketable fillets and are being turned into animal feed or fertilizer.

Until recently, the mechanism for the spread of ISAV over large geographic areas was not known, but a recent article in *Emerging Infectious Diseases* indicates that it can be transported in the ships that move fish between sites (Murray, Smith, and Stagg 2002). The authors cite the role of ships in the introduction and spread of the Black Death in fourteenth-century Europe as well as the huge numbers of bacteria, including the agent of cholera (*Vibrio cholerae*), that have been detected in the ballast water of ships.* In Scotland and Norway, "well-boats," which contain massive tanks filled with live fish in water, have been identified more specifically as carriers of ISAV. The salmon die when the virus is introduced with the water; but it is not only fish that are at risk. The authors conclude, "Diseases potentially spread by shipping include waterborne diseases of humans such as cholera and potential viral zoonoses [naturally occurring viruses]."

To date, ISAV has not been reported in wild populations, but the Atlantic salmon, already classified as an endangered species, would be vulnerable to infection by occasional escapees from floating cages. Canada has 15 million farm-raised salmon, compared with 150,000 wild ones. The disease is still a problem for Norway's Atlantic salmon industry and continues to reduce production. Scotland, Canada, and the Faroe Islands have all been affected. Because the Atlantic salmon is such a popular subject for aquaculture worldwide, fish farms have been established far from the fish's nominal home ocean. For example, salmon farming is now well established in Tasmania, earning approximately $100 million (Australian dollars) in 2001. An outbreak of ISAV in Tasmanian fish farms would cause massive economic losses for the island state.

While natural populations are declining, the Atlantic salmon-farming industry continues to increase exponentially. Private aquaculture companies have explored several rearing options for Atlantic salmon, ranging from land-based freshwater rearing facilities to sea ranching and sea-cage rearing. In eastern Maine and the Maritime Provinces of Canada, companies typically rear fish to the smolt stage in private freshwater facilities, transfer them into anchored net pens or sea cages, feed them to accelerate growth, and then harvest the fish when they reach market size. In the northwestern Atlantic, 62 percent of salmon-farming production is based in Canada, with 99.4 percent of that in the Maritimes and 0.6 percent in Newfoundland. The balance occurs in eastern Maine. Production at these facilities and in sea-cage areas has grown enormously: by 1998, there were at least 35 freshwater smolt-rearing facilities and 124 marine production facilities in eastern North America. Since the first experimental harvest of Atlantic salmon in 1979 of 6

---

*Ballast is the additional weight a ship carries to give it stability. In older vessels, ballast sometimes consisted of iron bars, stone, or gravel stowed below, but more recently, ships flood certain designated holds with seawater because it can easily be taken on and discharged.

tons, the mariculture industry in eastern North America has grown to produce more than 32,000 tons annually since 1997. In Maine, production has
exceeded 10,000 tons each year since 1995.

Large-scale salmon farming is practiced in Norway, Scotland, Finland,
British Columbia, Iceland, Alaska, Italy, New Zealand, Australia, Japan, the
Philippines, India, France, Bangladesh, Thailand, and Indonesia, and wherever it exists, there is controversy. Fish inevitably escape from open-water
pens, especially during storm conditions. In some incidents, tens of thousands of farmed fish have escaped into surrounding waters. When fish escape
from farms and survive in large numbers or establish their own breeding
populations, they will compete with wild salmon. Efforts to secure facilities
against these accidents may reduce the size and number of releases, but is
unlikely to stop them altogether. If the escaped salmon are the same species
as the wild salmon (e.g., Atlantic salmon grown in the Atlantic), there is the
possibility of interbreeding between farmed and wild fish. Such interbreeding can significantly alter the genetics of the salmon population. Genetically
engineered salmon in sea-cage farms—a distinct possibility in the near
future—adds another layer of concern with respect to interactions with wild
populations. If interbreeding were to occur as a result of escapes, such genes
could be incorporated into the wild gene pool and possibly diminish the
vigor of the wild population. According to Rosamond Naylor, Susan
Williams, and Donald Strong (2001), "up to 40% of Atlantic salmon caught in
the North Atlantic and more than 90% caught in the Baltic Sea are of farmed
origin. More than a half-million Atlantic salmon escaped on the West Coast
of North America between 1987 and 1997; they have been found in 77 British
Columbian rivers and are spawning in some locations. In the New
Brunswick–Maine region, farmed escapees vastly outnumber wild salmon in
some spawning rivers."

Now there are even Atlantic salmon in the Pacific. *Salmo salar* has been
farmed in Washington State since 1982 and in British Columbia since 1985,
according to research conducted by Skip McKinnell and colleagues (1997). By
1995, more than 10,000 Atlantic salmon had been caught in the North Pacific
out of a total of 140,000 that had escaped from aquaculture facilities in British
Columbia. The majority were caught in the Johnstone Strait area, where most
of the salmon farms are located. On July 2, 1996, high tidal flows destroyed
seven of every ten sea cages near Cypress Island, Washington, releasing more
than 100,000 Atlantic salmon into the sea. Over the remainder of the summer, many of the escapees were caught in the Strait of Juan de Fuca, at the
southern tip of Vancouver Island. A single specimen was caught in a bottom

trawl in the Bering Sea in September 1997 (Brodeur and Busby 1998). "Without improvement in cage design, maintenance and farming procedures to improve containment," wrote McKinnell and colleagues, "the abundance of Atlantic salmon escapees is likely to expand if the industry is allowed to expand." Atlantic salmon roaming free in the North Pacific is but another element in the ecological chaos promulgated by the ignorance and carelessness of the fish farmers.

In the spring of 2002, an estimated 100,000 farmed salmon escaped from pens in the Orkney Islands off the northern coast of Scotland, raising fears that the escaped fish would overwhelm the gene pools of wild fish. In an article published in *Nature* on April 11, 2002, Natasha McDowell commented: "The offspring of farmed fish, some data suggest, are unable to complete the heroic salmon runs by which the natural species navigate between spawning grounds inland and breeding grounds in the ocean. Critics say that, together with the rampant transmission of lice and disease from fish farms to natural stocks, the result is threatening the very survival of natural salmon runs in countries such as Scotland, Canada, and Norway." Studies show that the mixing of farmed and wild salmon populations halves the differences between the two stocks every ten generations, meaning that it is only a matter of time before the wild salmon disappears entirely. Farmed salmon now pose more of a threat to wild ones than any fishermen ever could.

A special report on transgenic salmon was published in *New Scientist* in September 2002. Philip Cohen wrote: "A fierce debate still rages about the effects of releasing various genetically modified organisms. But most scientists and campaigners agree on one thing: GM [genetically modified] fish could create havoc if they escaped and interbred with their wild cousins, or outcompeted native species." Aqua Bounty Farms Inc., a company based in Waltham, Massachusetts, has already engineered fast-growing fish by inserting growth hormone genes into the fertilized eggs of salmon, trout, and arctic char, an intervention that causes the hormone to be continuously "switched on." The salmon reach market size in eighteen months rather than the normal thirty-six, and, according to Aqua Bounty's Web site, "the commercial advantage of this subtle genetic modification is that the fish grow at rates comparable to that of the other competitive types of livestock such as chicken or pigs." William Muir and Richard Howard (1999) identified another possibly disastrous result of producing transgenic organisms. "The transgene," they wrote, "though rare, can spread in a natural population. . . . A transgene introduced into a natural population by a small number of transgenic fish will spread as a result of enhanced mating advantage, but the reduced viability of offspring will cause eventual local extinction of both populations."

In early September 2002, Cohen reported, "Britain's Agriculture and Environment Biotechnology Commission (AEBC) called for a complete ban on GM fish-farming in pens open to natural waterways until there are 'watertight' technologies for preventing fish from escaping and breeding." Aqua Bounty's answer was to further modify the fish to make them all sterile females so they could not reproduce at all, regardless of whether they escaped from the pens.* "Then there's the possibility of human error or just plain stupidity," wrote Cohen. "In Washington state and Oregon, for example, some breeding stations for grass carp were built in flood-prone regions, allowing fertile grass carp to escape during floods." One answer to the problem seems to be raising the fish in closed systems, with a gauntlet of barriers to keep them from escaping. But this would be so much more expensive than floating pens that the ecologically responsible companies would be unable to compete with companies in Chile, Tasmania, and Argentina, and thus their profits—the beating heart of fish farming—would be substantially reduced.

Like many other people, Anne Kapuscinski is concerned about genetically engineered fish. As founding director of the University of Minnesota's Institute for Social, Economic and Ecological Sustainability (ISEES), she has produced the first set of environmental safety guidelines for research on this delicate subject. She wants to see that proper guidelines are followed, mostly to prevent genetically engineered salmon from escaping and interbreeding with wild salmon, which might result in corruption of the wild stock, leading to population declines or even extinction. Introduction of genetically engineered fish into the wild population could also produce a non-native exotic population, the long-term results of which would be unpredictable and maybe even catastrophic to the remaining wild salmon. Quoted in Erik Stokstad's 2002 article in *Science,* Kapuscinski said the only way to keep trans-

---

*Although not mentioned in Cohen's report, this is precisely the method employed by the scientists in Michael Crichton's 1990 novel *Jurassic Park* to ensure that the genetically cloned dinosaurs would not reproduce. As Rob DeSalle and David Lindley noted in *The Science of Jurassic Park and The Lost World* (1997), "The explanation, as Alan Grant [the dinosaur paleontologist in the novel] finally figures out, is that dinosaurs with bits of frog DNA in their genomes can change sex; females can become males because of some environmental influence." The pseudoscience of *Jurassic Park* should not be used to denounce the genetic modifications suggested by Aqua Bounty, but there certainly is an eerie coincidence. In the novel, the dinosaurs overcame the restrictions implanted in their genes and ran wild.

genic fish from interacting with wild populations is to have multiple barriers, such as sterility plus confinement on land.

In a remarkable display of unity and ecological sensitivity, 200 chefs, grocers, and seafood distributors across the United States have announced that they will not purchase genetically altered fish. According to an article published in the *New York Times* on September 18, 2002, "the campaign says it is concerned that if genetically altered salmon are approved by the Food and Drug Administration, they could escape from the pens in which they are raised and interbreed with wild salmon, endangering some species." The author, Marian Burros, points out that one-third of all fish consumed in the United States is farmed, but farmed fish are not necessarily genetically modified fish. The article continues: "Aqua Bounty is also growing transgenic arctic char and trout. Around the world, there are at least 20 fish species that have been genetically engineered. China is raising transgenic carp, and Cuba is raising transgenic tilapia. It is not clear whether any of this fish is being sold." (Stokstad noted in his 2002 *Science* article that the Cuban group—the Center for Genetic Engineering and Biotechnology in Havana—was "a few years away from commercializing the fish.")

Farmed salmon are fed meal and oils from wild-caught fish. Each pound of salmon produced requires at least three pounds of wild-caught fish, challenging the presumption that fish farming necessarily reduces commercial fishing pressure. In fact, there is a net loss of protein in the marine ecosystem as a whole when wild catch is converted into meal for aquaculture consumption. Pens full of salmon produce large amounts of waste—both excrement and unconsumed feed. This may result in unfavorable water quality conditions (such as high nutrient levels and low levels of oxygen) detrimental to both the farmed fish and the natural ecosystem. It is also suspected that nutrients released from salmon farms stimulate microalgal blooms, but proof is lacking because little research has been done. The densely packed conditions in pens promote disease, a common problem in most salmon farms. Furthermore, transmittal of disease from farmed salmon to wild populations has been documented, and the potential effects are serious. Although antibiotics are used to treat some diseases, the potential effects of antibiotic-resistant bacteria on human health are of concern. There has been an emphasis on developing vaccines to prevent specific diseases in order to reduce the need for antibiotics.

In some areas, landowners have opposed the siting of salmon aquaculture facilities near residential shorelines because they are unsightly and odoriferous and they interfere with the natural setting of the seascape. The density of salmon in farms is variable, but the farmer is motivated to pack them in at high densities to increase profits. This exacerbates the problems of pollution and disease and places stress on the fish, which leads to an inferior product. The siting of salmon farms is often problematic, particularly if it does not adequately take into account the proximity to wild salmon migration routes, water flow and circulation patterns, the fate of waste materials, the number of facilities already in an area, and aesthetic concerns.

A salmon is a salmon is a salmon, right? Not exactly. Atlantic salmon live (mostly) in the Atlantic, but there are six species of endemic Pacific salmon: chinook (*Oncorhynchus tshawytscha*); coho (*O. kisutch*); sockeye (*O. nerka*); pink (*O. gorbuscha*); chum (*O. keta*); and cherry (*O. masou*). All occur on both sides of the Pacific Ocean except for the cherry salmon, which is found only off the coast of Japan. All are popular game fishes, and all are commercially fished in great quantities. Like their Atlantic counterparts, Pacific salmon are anadromous, breeding in fresh water, maturing at sea, and then returning to their hatching place to spawn. Pacific salmon species spawn only once and then deteriorate and die. In the process of ascending their natal streams, they undergo drastic physical modifications during which their jaws extend into hooks, their backs become humped, and their flesh and internal organs turn to mush. Even as they become weaker and weaker, they fight their way upstream, often leaping up waterfalls and traversing rapids to get where they are going. When females arrive at their nesting sites, they dig holes in the gravel with their tails and lay their eggs, which are then fertilized by the males. After a period of time ranging from a few days to several years (depending on the species), the young make their way to the sea. In California, Oregon, Washington, and Idaho, the long history of overfishing, the damming of the rivers up which the salmon must swim, and the destruction of breeding streams by timber interests have driven many populations of Pacific salmon to the edge of extinction, and all other Pacific salmon populations except those that breed in Alaska are considered endangered.

While populations of North Atlantic wild salmon have plummeted, more than 100 local populations in the eastern Pacific have disappeared. Salmon are extinct in 40 percent of the rivers where they once spawned along the Pacific coast of North America. The potential for interactions with farmed fish and transmission of disease from farmed to wild salmon is especially threatening in the context of these declines. Governments typically encourage aquaculture because it is viewed as economic development, but this often leads to the intensive, large-scale farming methods most often associated with environmental damage. Because the costs of this damage are not borne by the

industry, nor are the value of ecosystem services factored into the cost of production, there is no pressure on the industry to operate in environmentally
sound ways.

Although farmed salmon accounts for some 40 percent of Scotland's food
exports and is worth £650 million to its economy, the tide of public opinion
in that country is turning against sea-cage salmon farming as people become
aware of its environmental, economic, and social downsides. In May 1998, a
salmon farm at Loch Nevis on the western coast of Scotland reported its suspicions of an outbreak of infectious salmon anemia. The suspicions were
confirmed, and by early 2002 the disease had spread to an additional fifteen
farms, not only on the Scottish mainland but also on Skye and Shetland. A
2001 report by Friends of the Earth Scotland (FoE Scotland) paints a picture
of a vast food industry driven by multinational corporations, heavily dependent on chemicals—many of them deadly—and heavily dependent on public
relations and government protection for its continued expansion. FoE
Scotland maintains that the "alarming rise in the incidence of algal blooms
and shellfish poisoning events have cast doubts on the compatibility of the
two activities" (salmon farming and shellfish farming) and claims that
salmon farming is compromising the high quality of water on Scotland's
western coast. The report says it is not surprising that questions are now
being asked, pointing to a 1999 calculation that for each ton of salmon produced, approximately 100 kilograms of nitrogenous compounds, including
ammonia, were released into the sea.

The coincidence between the areas of the three main shellfish poisonings
and the high density of salmon farms is remarkable. The report goes on to say
that Scottish salmon farming is dominated by multinational companies
driven by short-term economic priorities rather than long-term interest in
the future of Scotland's environment. The estimated waste discharged from
340 Scottish fish farms in 2000, says the report, was equivalent to almost twice
the annual sewage discharged by Scotland's entire human population.
Wherever salmon are farmed, the neighbors are beginning to worry about the
economic, environmental, and physical costs. Aquaculture may indeed provide plentiful salmon for salmon-hungry nations,* but the means by which
this is accomplished are more than a little questionable.

---

*Salmon is one of the foods that supplies the "good" type of cholesterol, high-density
lipoprotein (HDL). The "bad" cholesterol (low-density lipoprotein, or LDL) is believed to
be responsible for clogging blood vessels, and HDL is reputed to "exile" the LDL to the
liver, where it is destroyed. In August 2002, in an article in *New Scientist* titled "The Happy
Fat," Meredith Small identified some ways in which the omega-3 fatty acids *(continued)*

As currently practiced, aquaculture has not provided a viable answer to the world's decreasing stocks of food fish. With invasive fishing practices adversely affecting diminishing populations, it seems only a matter of time before fisheries around the world will crash. Some of these vanishing species—particularly the cod and the salmon—were once paradigms of plentitude. From the mighty tuna to the humble sea horse, from the noble swordfish to the ignoble menhaden, from the menacing grey nurse shark to the harmless orange roughy, species whose numbers we once took for granted are disappearing at an alarming rate. "Give a man a fish," the saying goes, "and you help him for a day. Teach him to fish, and you help him for his whole life." Teach him not to fish so wastefully, and you might help the world.

---

found in fishes such as salmon and menhaden (as well as in flaxseeds, walnuts, and olive oil) are being investigated as an antidote to depression (Hibbein 1998) and even as a possible inhibitor of prostate cancer (Terry et al. 2001). In a 2002 *Newsweek* article about salmon, Jerry Adler wrote, "Even people that don't like salmon know by now that it contains omega-3 fatty acids, which are believed to protect against cancer and cardiovascular disease."

~ 3 ~

THE PLIGHT OF
THE SEA TURTLES

Nearly all sea turtle biologists, sooner or later, become turtle
conservationists, at least by sympathy, and frequently as a major part of
their professional activities. The reasons for this metamorphosis are clear
enough; those who work in the field with sea turtles are inevitably
distressed as the animals they study are slaughtered, often while actually
on the nesting beach. The eggs too are all too frequently raided, either by
man himself or by predators that in many cases have been introduced to
the system by man or allowed to form unnaturally high population
densities as a result of man's tinkering with ecological balances.

—Peter Pritchard, "The Conservation of Sea Turtles," 1980

Modern sea turtles are presumed to have descended from land-based reptiles
that returned to the sea, but hardly any transitional forms have been identified. There are fossil land turtles with columnar legs and feet with claws, and
fossil sea turtles with flippers instead, but nothing that looks like a semi-
aquatic turtle. One view is that sea turtles never left the water at all and developed directly from amphibians or early reptiles in the ocean, but this seems
less likely than the idea that they had terrestrial origins. Robert Carroll, a specialist in the evolution of reptiles, wrote in 1988 that "no trace of earlier or
more primitive turtles has been described, although turtle shells are easily
fossilized and even small pieces are easily recognized. Apparently the earlier
stages in the evolution of the shell occurred very rapidly or took place in an
environment or part of the world where preservation and subsequent discovery were unlikely." Turtles are not dinosaurs; they are not descended from
the first dinosaurs, and they have a shell, which no dinosaur ever had. Turtles
represent a separate group of vertebrates, and one of the oldest of all contin-
uous vertebrate lineages, dating to the Middle Triassic period, about 230 million years ago. Of the living vertebrates, only sharks and bony fishes have a

lineage older than theirs. "Turtles are one of the great success stories of marine reptiles," commented Canadian vertebrate paleontologist Elizabeth Nicholls in 1997; "they are the only living reptiles fully adapted to the marine environment, returning to shore only to lay their eggs." In a 1997 discussion, Peter Pritchard of the Florida Audubon Society nicely captured the basic characteristics of sea turtle survival over evolutionary time:

> The successful penetration of aquatic niches by both early and modern turtles was probably made possible by a remarkable example of preadaptation. Other living aquatic reptiles, including sea snakes . . . marine iguanas, crocodilians, etc., as well as the extinct ichthyosaurs, swim (or swam) by means of body and tail undulations not dissimilar to those of typical fishes. Turtles, on the other hand, lost the capacity for this form of propulsion when they developed the shortened, rigid body form and corselet that has characterized the group since the Triassic. This body form offered armored resistance to attack by predators, but the tradeoff was reduced speed and agility, obliging those terrestrial chelonian species surviving in a world with increasingly sophisticated predators to adopt specialized life styles.

All sea turtles have flippers fore and aft, lightweight shells, and heads that cannot be drawn into their shells. Males usually have longer tails than females and a pair of down-curved claws on both front and rear flippers to help them get a grip on the female during mating. Several males often pursue one female, but only one will succeed in mating with her. The female comes ashore to dig a nest in the sand and lay her eggs, which are round and soft-shelled. Depending on the species, female turtles lay 60 to 120 eggs at a time, and some species do this several times during each nesting session. In *Fire in the Turtle House,* Osha Gray Davidson tells us that both male and female green turtles go ashore to bask, such as these that he describes so vividly: "Five immature turtles lie motionless in the midday heat. . . . The same fine chalky silt that gives the pond its extraordinary color is responsible for the Obake turtles' ghostly appearance. The silt settles on their carapaces and then bakes to a powder as they bask in the brilliant sunlight for up to eleven hours at a time." A stranded sea turtle, however, is usually a dead sea turtle. Except for egg-laying females and hatchlings for a brief time, sea turtles typically are wholly aquatic and are very poorly designed for terrestrial locomotion. Newly hatched turtles scurry toward the sea, and those that survive the predators awaiting them on the beach will spend their entire lives at sea.

The supportive shell of a turtle is composed of hard, bony plates covered by individual horny segments known as scutes, which are made of keratin, the material of fingernails, hooves, and hair. It is the pigment melanin in the scutes that forms intricate designs in some species. The arrangement of the scutes on the upper shell (carapace) and the lower (plastron) differs from species to species and can be used as a key to distinguish one species from another. Differentiation of scutes also applies to land tortoises, terrapins, other reptiles such as snakes and crocodiles, and even a few armored mammals such as armadillos and pangolins. "The turtle lives 'twixt plated decks," wrote Ogden Nash, "Which practically conceal its sex. / I think it clever of the turtle / In such a fix to be so fertile."

Although there is little precise information on longevity, some sea turtles are known—from recovered tags—to live for more than fifty years. They do not have teeth but instead are equipped with a horny beak. Their eardrums are covered with skin, but they hear quite well, particularly at lower frequencies. Their sense of smell is excellent, and they can see well both above and under the water, although they are nearsighted. They spend most of their lives submerged, rising only to take a breath every four or five minutes, but they can sleep underwater for several hours. All sea turtles except the Australian flatback undertake extensive migrations between their feeding grounds and their nesting beaches; the precise navigation required to find a particular beach across thousands of miles of open ocean is an unrevealed miracle. We do not know why turtles nest on some beaches and not on others.

Whatever took out the nonavian dinosaurs 65 million years ago spared several other reptilian groups, including the crocodilians and the sea turtles, which may have been saved by their ability to dive and thus avoid the intense heat, acid rain, volcanoes, or tsunamis. Although ancestral turtles are known from the Middle Triassic, the Chelonioidea, a group that includes both of the two living families of sea turtle (Dermocheylids and Cheloniids), first appears in the fossil record from the early Cretaceous period, 140 million years ago, and is characterized by elongation of the forelimb into a "wing" for underwater flight. (All sea turtles "fly" underwater.)

A hundred forty million years of evolutionary success, however, has done little to prepare the turtles for sharing the planet with a relatively recent arrival; in the twinkling of a geologic eye, *Homo sapiens* has colonized and modified almost every available environment on the earth, and although we haven't quite learned to live in the ocean, that doesn't mean we don't have an enormous effect on the creatures that do. We have destroyed their nesting beaches, stolen their eggs, and slaughtered them by the tens of thousands for meat, fat, soup, shells, leather, and souvenirs; and now we snare them in shrimp nets, run over them in powerboats, pollute and overheat their ocean, and stand helplessly by as they succumb to deadly viral diseases. No living thing can withstand such a frenzied onslaught, and these lovely, hapless, ancient creatures, who watched the dinosaurs, the ichthyosaurs, and the plesiosaurs disappear, may themselves soon vanish, leaving a heartbreaking host of turtle-sized vacancies in the world's oceans.

"There are dozens of places in the Caribbean named after large sea turtles whose adult population now numbers in the tens of thousands rather than the tens of millions," wrote marine ecologist Jeremy Jackson and his colleagues in 2001. Their further loss will not go unnoticed or undocumented. Probably the single most important popular book on sea turtles ever written is Archie Carr's *So Excellent a Fishe* (1967a).* Carr continued researching and publishing thereafter, but this was the passionate rallying cry to save the turtle. In 1979, the World Conference on Sea Turtle Conservation was convened in Washington, D.C., resulting in the 1982 publication of *Biology and Conservation of Sea Turtles,* later revised and reissued (Bjorndal 1995). The National Marine Fisheries Service (NMFS) convenes annual symposia on sea turtles, and the proceedings, published as technical memoranda of the NMFS (and available on the Internet), are among the most comprehensive studies ever done of living animals. Another source of information is the *Marine Turtle Newsletter,* initiated in 1976; it disseminates news of turtles and turtle conservation and is also available on-line (http://www.seaturtle.org/mtn/) for those without easy access to scientific libraries. Countless other Internet sites are dedicated to marine turtles, an indication of the concern that scientists and laypeople have for these imperiled reptiles.

Marine animals have been killed either on land or at sea, but rarely both. Some species of pinnipeds, such as fur seals and elephant seals, were clubbed and shot on land because they came ashore to breed, often in large groups, but sometimes they were shot at sea. Whales, on the other hand, never come ashore, so means of killing them at sea were perfected until they could be shot from a distance and then dragged ashore or onto specially designed ships to be turned into such "products" as meat, oil, and bone. "It remains to be seen

*The title comes from a 1620 resolution of the Bermuda Assembly titled "An Act Agaynst the Killinge of Ouer Young Tortoyses," which shows that even then, sea turtles were being slaughtered with careless abandon: "And at all tymes as they can meete with them, snatch & catch up indiffrentlye all kinds of Tortoyses both yonge and old little and greate and soe carry awaye and devour them to the much decay of the breed of so excellent a fishe the daylye skarringe of them from our shores and the danger of an utter distroyinge and the losse of them."

whether these conceptual generalizations about marine species are applicable to marine turtles," Peter Pritchard commented in 1997, "in that the unavoidable terrestrial ovipositional excursions constitute a special vulnerability to which fully marine species are not subject." The need to come ashore to lay their eggs (resulting in the "unavoidable terrestrial ovipositional excursions") imperils the adult females when they come ashore, the eggs when they are laid, and the hatchlings when they emerge. Most species are so widespread that no single attack can threaten the entire species, so a threatened population in one region may be relatively secure in another, but then the turtles confound the statistics and their own preservation by migrating from relatively safe havens to places where they are in imminent danger. Eight living species of sea turtle are found in the temperate and tropical waters of the world, and they are all declining in number—some to dangerously low levels—largely because of human influences.

LEATHERBACK

The largest living sea turtle is the leatherback, *Dermochelys coriacea,* the sole survivor of a primitive order believed to resemble the earliest sea turtles. Where all other sea turtles have a shell or carapace, the leatherback has smooth, leathery skin that covers prominent bony ridges: seven on the back and five on the underside. Leatherbacks are the only marine turtles whose backbone is not attached to the inside of the shell.

Leatherbacks are turtles whose biology is couched in superlatives: the largest can weigh more than a ton and measure eight and a half feet in length; after the saltwater crocodile, which can weigh a ton and a half, the leatherback is the heaviest reptile in the world. Leatherbacks are the deepest-diving sea turtles, capable of reaching depths of 3,000 feet; of the air-breathing vertebrates, only the elephant seal and sperm whale can dive deeper, and these giant turtles can regulate their body temperature, an accomplishment unique among reptiles. The leatherback's mouth and throat are equipped with backward-pointing spines that enable it to eat its favorite food, the otherwise slippery jellyfish. (Unfortunately, the turtles sometimes mistake floating plastic bags for their usual prey and choke to death on them.) Females gather on the beaches of Indonesia, New Guinea, Central America, the Guianas, and the Pacific coast of Mexico to lay their eggs, and marked turtles of both sexes have been found as far as 3,000 miles from their nesting beaches. Of the two types, the Atlantic leatherback, which ranges from the Gulf of Mexico and the Caribbean Sea to the British Isles in

LEATHERBACK TURTLE
(*Dermochelys coriacea*)

the north, and in the south to Argentina and South Africa, is somewhat smaller than its Pacific counterpart.

On tropical mainland beaches, leatherback females come ashore in groups that can range from 25 to 6,000. They prefer a deepwater approach with a steep, sandy slope, an arrangement that shortens the distance they must travel to get above the storm tide line. The females drag themselves forward with simultaneous movements of their huge front flippers, leaving a track in the sand that can be six feet wide. After laying a clutch of eighty to ninety eggs, they crawl back into the sea, but they return to lay another clutch after only nine or ten days and may repeat the process as many as ten times. With its long hind flippers, a leatherback can dig a deeper nest than most other turtles, and the hatchlings may have to dig through two feet of sand before attempting to reach the sea. As with most turtles, digging out is a group effort, and most of them emerge simultaneously, marginally increasing their chances of getting to the sea without being apprehended by a waiting bird. The tiny hatchlings have scales on the carapace and flippers, but these are soon replaced by the leathery skin, with its distinctive pattern of spots and stripes.

Unless commercial fishing practices are changed, the leatherback turtle will be extinct in the Pacific Ocean by the year 2010, according to a June 2000 report. James Spotila and his colleagues at Drexel University have been studying Pacific leatherbacks in Costa Rica since 1988, and they have observed that far fewer adult females are returning to the beaches to lay their eggs, and consequently there has been a precipitous decline in the number of hatch-lings. In 1988, Spotila and colleagues counted only 1,367 nesting females at Playa Grande; they anticipate that by the year 2004 there will be fewer than 50, which will effectively mean that *Dermochelys coriacea* is extinct in the Pacific. The culprits? Gillnetters from Japan, Korea, and Taiwan, whose nets trap everything that blunders into them, including fishes (many of which are thrown back dead), whales, dolphins, sea lions, seals, seabirds, and the luck-less turtles. (Fewer gillnetters operate in the Atlantic Ocean, so the problem is not as pressing there.)

GREEN TURTLE

The remarkable Archie Carr, born in Mobile, Alabama, in 1909, died at his home near the town of Micanopy, Florida, in 1987. He founded the Caribbean Conservation Corporation (CCC) and served as its scientific director until his death. During a life devoted to research, teaching, and writing, he was responsible for much of what is known today about the biology and life cycle of sea turtles, and he is credited by many for bringing the first international attention to their plight. He wrote ten books and more than 120 scientific papers and magazine articles during a career that lasted more than half a cen-tury. His chapter "The Black Beach" in *The Windward Road,* first published in 1956, won an O. Henry Award, and his *Turtles of the United States, Canada, and Baja California,* published in 1952 by Cornell University Press and still in print, won the Daniel Giraud Elliot Medal of the National Academy of Sciences. In *So Excellent a Fishe,* Carr referred to the green turtle's unwitting role in British colonial history:

> The green turtle was an important factor in the colonization of the Americas. It was herbivorous, abundant, and edible—even when prepared by cooks not aware that it can be made a gourmet's dish. It lived all about the tropical littoral, and grazed in schools on turtle grass pastures that are now mostly vacant. It nested in numbers in places where no turtles ever come ashore today, or come only one on a mile in a year. The British Navy counted on green turtle to extend its cruising in the New World. The Spanish fleets took on turtle for the voyage back home to Cadiz. A green turtle was as big as a heifer, easy to catch, and easy to keep alive on its back in a space no greater than itself. It was an ideal food resource, and it went into the cooking pots of the salt-water peasantry and tureens of flagships alike. It fed a host of people and to some of them became a dish of almost ceremonial stature. In England

the green turtle came to be known as the London Alderman's Turtle, because an Alderman's Banquet was considered grossly incomplete if it failed to begin with clear green turtle soup.

The green turtle (*Chelonia mydas*) inhabits warm, shallow tropical and subtropical waters along reefs, bays, and estuaries throughout much of the world. Second to the leatherback, it is the largest of the marine turtles; adults can weigh 450 pounds, and the carapace has been measured at well more than four feet. (In the past, there may have been green turtles that weighed 900 pounds, but most today are not even half that size.) Green turtles are not actually green—the adult's shell ranges from a rusty reddish brown to light brown with darker mottling—but their fat is, and this has given them their common name.* The most valuable economically of all reptiles, green turtles are killed for their skins, meat, shells, and calipee, the cartilage that is cut from between the bones of the bottom shell (plastron), the vital ingredient in turtle soup. The latter is more valuable than any other part of the green turtle, and poachers often kill a turtle just for the five or so pounds of calipee it will yield, leaving the rest of the carcass on the beach.

Mating occurs in the water off the nesting beaches, and though little is known about the reproductive biology of males, evidence is accumulating that the males migrate to the same nesting beach every year. Females emerge at night to dig a nest in the sand with their hind flippers and then deposit between 110 and 115 Ping-Pong-ball-sized eggs, a process that takes about two hours. Each female will deposit as many as seven clutches at twelve- to fourteen-day intervals, but the average is two or three clutches. Females typically don't produce clutches in successive years; more commonly, two, three, or four years intervene between breeding seasons. The eggs incubate for forty-eight to seventy days. The hatching success of undisturbed nests is usually high, but on some beaches predators destroy a high percentage of nests, and the hatchlings, which weigh less than an ounce and have a carapace only two inches long, are particularly vulnerable to every kind of predator as they emerge from the nest and scurry toward the sea—where more predators await them. Given the number and variety of potential predators of green

---

*The black turtle (*Chelonia agassizi*) is similar in almost all respects to the green, including the greenish fat under the shell, except that it is grayish or black overall, whereas the green turtle is brownish. The black turtle inhabits the coastal waters of the eastern tropical Pacific from southern California to Peru and is not commonly seen in the open ocean; the green turtle lives in temperate and tropical waters around the world *except* for those Pacific coastal waters. Some scientists regard *C. agassizi* as a separate species, and it is so identified in this book, whereas others believe it is just a color morph of the green turtle.

GREEN TURTLE
(Chelonia mydas)

turtles, it is surprising that any survive at all. In the 1990 *FAO Species Catalogue,* René Márquez listed some of those threats:

> The eggs are eaten principally by skunks, raccoons, opossums, coatis, coyotes, badgers, dogs, jaguars, pigs, monkeys, varanid lizards, ghost crabs, dipterous maggots, ants, and beetles; also fungal and bacterial infections are common. The hatchlings, just before erupting from the nest, can be attacked by ants, mites, and fly-maggots, and the nest may be opened by mammals. When the hatchlings emerge from the nest, they race to the sea, and, on the way, they are attacked by mammals, birds, and ghost crabs. In the water, predation continues, by birds at the surface and by fishes in the water column. Sharks and other fishes feed on juvenile sea turtles, but this predation diminishes with growth. Except for man, the worst enemy of adult sea turtles are sharks.

Large numbers of nests may also be destroyed by sea inundation and erosion. One interesting discovery in recent years is that incubation temperatures determine the sex of hatchling turtles; eggs incubated below a critical temperature—which might vary among populations—produce primarily males, and eggs incubated above this temperature produce primarily females.

Green turtles are known to migrate long distances—as far as 1,400 miles —in the open ocean between feeding grounds and nesting beaches, but how they actually accomplish these incredible feats of pinpoint navigation is a mystery. For a long time, no one knew what cues they employed in their pelagic movements, in their movements among foraging grounds, or in their migrations between foraging grounds and nesting beaches. Recently published work, however, suggests that the earth's magnetic field plays a role in these feats. We know that hatchlings and adult females on the nesting beaches orient toward the ocean using light cues. Because green turtles feed in marine pastures in quiet, low-energy areas (with little or no wave action) but nest on high-energy beaches, their feeding and nesting habitats are of necessity located some distance apart. Green turtles that nest on Ascension Island, for example, forage along the coast of Brazil, some 600 miles away.

A recent problem for turtles—as if the long-standing ones were not enough—has been the erection of high-rise buildings along the nesting beaches. In the darkness, after laying their eggs, the females ordinarily head for the ocean, where the horizon is just being illuminated by the rising sun. If hotels and condominiums are brightly lit at night, the disoriented turtles respond by heading toward them and may become stranded and die. The same is true for emerging hatchlings, which may move toward house lights and streetlights and away from the relative sanctuary of the ocean. Hatchlings that fail to find their way to the sea succumb to attacks by predators (which can spot the hatchlings easier in the light), exhaustion, dehydration by the morning sun, or strikes by automobile traffic. Awareness of the problem of beachfront lighting has resulted in some modifications—such as turning lights off at night—but hotels are not designed to function well in darkness, and the problem persists.

During the nesting season of May–October 1997, more than 1,400 hatchlings were found disoriented on the beaches of Volusia County, Florida, which includes Daytona Beach. It is unknown how many more wandered undetected. Private citizens sued Volusia County to prevent vehicles from driving and parking on the beaches where the turtles breed and nest; the suit also held the county responsible for cities' lighting ordinances that harmed the turtles. On August 3, 1998, the United States Court of Appeals for the Eleventh Circuit held that, to be in compliance with the Endangered Species Act of 1973, Volusia County must take additional measures to protect endangered sea turtles nesting on its beaches. In April 1999, the United States Supreme Court declined to hear an appeal of the county council of Volusia County, leaving intact the ruling from the court of appeals. Chalk one up for the turtles. By 2002, Volusia County had become a model for sea turtle protection. The county spent $5,775 to produce a beachfront lighting exhibit at its Marine Science Center to demonstrate turtle-friendly lighting.

Major green turtle nesting colonies in the Atlantic are located on Ascension Island, Aves Island, Mexico's Gulf coast, and Surinam. In the United States, Atlantic green turtles can be found around the Virgin Islands, Puerto Rico, and the continental shores from Texas to Massachusetts. It has been generally accepted, but not proven, that green turtles return to nest on the beach where they were born. Green turtles exhibit strong site fidelity in successive nesting seasons, and Hawaiian green turtles also exhibit site fidelity for their foraging grounds. Important feeding areas for green turtles in Florida include Indian River Lagoon, the Florida Keys, Florida Bay, Homosassa, Crystal River, and Cedar Keys.

The most important nesting site of the green turtle in the Western Hemisphere, however, is Tortuguero ("region of turtles") Beach, on the northeastern Caribbean coast of Costa Rica, approximately fifty miles north of the principal port of Limón. Tortuguero, the location of Archie Carr's green turtle research camp in 1956, was designated a national park in 1975. The park now encompasses more than 46,900 acres and, with the help of the Caribbean Conservation Corporation, protects twenty-two miles of nesting beach from the mouth of the Tortuguero River south to Parisimina. Some 15,000 ecotourists visit the park every year, demonstrating that there are some places where sea turtles are worth more alive than dead.

The Cayman Islands rookery, "possibly the largest green turtle rookery that ever existed" (King 1982), was observed by Christopher Columbus on his fourth voyage in 1503; thereafter, Spanish, French, and English ships periodically stopped there to collect the turtles for meat and eggs. "By 1688," wrote Florida herpetologist F. Wayne King, "a total of 40 sloops from Jamaica were engaged full-time, year round in bringing turtles from the Caymans to Jamaica. . . . This fleet of turtlers returned upwards of 13,000 turtles a year to Jamaica." By the late 1700s, the Cayman green turtles were in danger of becoming extinct, so the turtlers sailed for Cuba and the Miskito Cays of Nicaragua to collect their prey. Although a few green turtles persisted through the nineteenth century, by 1900 the green turtles of the Caymans were a footnote to naval victualing. Bermuda never had such an enormous population, but they too were relentlessly caught and driven to extinction. In "Historical Review of the Decline of the Green Turtle and the Hawksbill," (1982), King reported:

> Most green turtle populations in the Atlantic Ocean, Mediterranean Sea,
> Indian Ocean, and Pacific Ocean are depleted or endangered as a result
> of direct exploitation or incidental drowning in trawl nets. The only
> populations not now declining, and which seem not to be threatened
> with extinction, are those that nest on Europa, Tromelin, and Glorious
> Island in the Mozambique Channel; and on Raine Island, Australia.

Of the eight known species of sea turtle, only Kemp's ridley (*Lepidochelys kempii*) and the black turtle (*Chelonia agassizi*) are not native to Indonesian waters. On the thousands of islands that make up the vast Indonesian archipelago, 143 beaches have been identified as egg-laying sites for the various species. One of these is the island of Bali, where green turtle meat is so highly esteemed that the island cannot supply enough for the culinary demands of the Balinese and brings the turtles in from other islands, such as Sulawesi, Kalimantan, Irian Jaya, Timor, Java, and Flores. Bali is supposed to have an annual import quota of 5,000 green turtles, but it is estimated that at least five times that number come in through the port of Tanjung Benoa, where they are kept in holding pens prior to being slaughtered. Every part of the turtle is used. The shell is a popular tourist item, and smaller pieces of the carapace are made into souvenir items such as matchboxes, spoons, forks, combs, and necklaces. Turtle meat is prepared as satay or *lawar,* a Balinese specialty that consists of turtle meat, coconut, and turtle blood. Deep-fried, the skin is a favorite snack in Tanjung Benoa, and of course the eggs are consumed in Bali just as they are all over the world. An Indonesian conservation group known as KSBK is fighting to have the quotas enforced, but the group believes that thousands of sea turtles—mostly greens—are being killed every year in Bali.

In recent years, more and more green turtles have been found to be infected with the tumor disease known as fibropapillomatosis. It was first described in captured adult green turtles in 1938 by George Smith and Christopher Coates, and it was found again in the late 1970s in mariculture-reared green turtles at Cayman Turtle Farm in the British West Indies. More than half the wild populations in Florida and Hawaii, separated by an entire continent and 1,500 miles of ocean, were estimated to be affected by the disease. In the *Marine Turtle Newsletter* for 1986, George Balazs described the disease as seen in Hawaiian turtles:

> When papilloma tumors develop in predominant fibrous tissue, they are called fibropapillomas. Green sea turtles develop fibropapillomas that appear as lobe-shaped tumors. These tumors can infect all soft portions of a turtle's body. Tumors grow primarily on the skin, but they can also appear between scales and scutes, in the mouth, on the eyes, and on internal organs. . . . Within a year, these white spots usually developed into full blown tumors. The disease frequently affects the eyes first, but we have seen tumored turtles with clean, healthy eyes, so this is by no means a rule. Most of the marine habitats where fibropapillomatosis appears are near areas of heavy human use. Similar tumors are now appearing in loggerhead, olive ridley and hawksbill turtles.

Affected turtles may be extremely emaciated, weak, listless, and anemic. Fibrous tumors may be seen in multiple visceral sites, including lungs, liver, kidneys, and the gastrointestinal tract, resulting in flotation problems, bowel obstruction, renal failure, and pressure necrosis of affected tissues, according to veterinarian Lawrence Herbst (1994). These slow-growing tumors of unknown origin, called green turtle fibropapilloma (GTFP or just FP), have reached near-epidemic proportions. Collective evidence suggests that they result from infection with a tumor-causing virus. Retroviruses, herpesviruses, and papillomaviruses have all been implicated, but definitive proof is lacking.

Although the specific identity is unknown, a herpes-like virus has been identified both in wild green turtles (Jacobson et al. 1991) and in tumor-induced captive green turtles (Herbst and Jacobson 1995). Surgical treatment of individual turtles may be attempted, but it is impractical as a means of control. Because genetic variation in wild green turtles is extremely low, local populations may be at a greater risk of extinction from particular pathogens because of their genetic uniformity. Microbiologist Sandra Quackenbush and some of her colleagues have suggested on several occasions that the disease may threaten this species and others with extinction.* In 2001, they wrote, "FP has appeared worldwide with sporadic but generally increasing frequency in green (*Chelonia mydas*), loggerhead (*Caretta caretta*) and olive ridley (*Lepidochelys olivacea*) turtles and may pose a significant threat to the long-term survival of marine turtles."

KEMP'S RIDLEY

Kemp's ridley (*Lepidochelys kempii*) was named in 1880 for Richard Kemp, a Key West fisherman who supplied specimens to Harvard University laboratories.† At numbers estimated around fifteen hundred, it is now considered the rarest of all sea turtles. It is also the smallest. Full-grown adults weigh less

---

*A researcher with the Florida Marine Research Institute in St. Petersburg, Jan Landsberg, has identified the role of biotoxins—particularly those produced by harmful algal blooms (HABs), the best known of which are red tides—in the death of marine animals. After identifying the dietary factor in a massive fish kill in 1995, she suggested that fibropapillomatosis may be a result of biotoxins that cause immunosuppression, leading to opportunistic infection by the dinoflagellate *Prorocentrum lima* (Landsberg et al. 1999). Not all researchers agree, particularly Lawrence Herbst, who believes that fibropapillomatosis is caused by a herpesvirus and transmitted from infected turtles to uninfected ones.

†Like everyone else, Archie Carr was puzzled by the name *ridley*. He wrote: "What kind of a name is it anyway, and where did it come from? I've traced it all along the coast from Fernandina to Key West and out to Pensacola and people only look vague *(continued)*

than 100 pounds; the carapace is about two feet in length and nearly as wide at it is long. This species nests mostly during the daylight hours (as does the Australian flatback), and mass nesting usually takes place on a windy day. Hatchlings, as they mature, turn from an overall grayish black color to a light olive gray above with a creamy white or yellowish plastron below.

In the past, when these turtles arrived on a beach to lay their eggs (as with other sea turtle species, only the females come ashore), the event, known as an *arribada*—Spanish for "arrival"—was awaited by coyotes, skunks, and coatimundis that would dig up the eggs. But it was awaited much more eagerly by rapacious human *hueveros,* who would do the same on a scale that belies description. A film made in 1947 by amateur cameraman Andrés Herrera showed an estimated 40,000 Kemp's ridleys coming ashore at a place called Rancho Nuevo on the Gulf of Mexico, about 100 miles south of the Texas border. The film was unknown until 1963, when herpetologist Harry Hildebrand discovered it and brought it to the attention of Archie Carr, who watched it in a classroom at Corpus Christi. Carr was astonished:

> The film was short. It was shaky in places, faded with time and rainy with scratches. But it was the cinema of the year all the same, the picture of the decade. . . . For me, personally, as a searcher after ridleys for twenty years, as a chronicler of the odyssey of ridleys, the film outdid anything from *Birth of a Nation* to *Zorba the Greek.* It made Andrés Herrera in my mind suddenly a cinematographer far greater than Fellini, Alfred Hitchcock, or Walt Disney could ever aspire to be. . . . To any zoologist, however, as especially a turtle zoologist and most specifically to me, the film was simply shattering. It still is hard for me to understand the apathy of a world in which such a movie can be so little celebrated.

Rancho Nuevo is still the only place in the world where Kemp's ridleys come ashore to nest, but depleted by the human egg-hunters and despite full protection by the Mexican government since the 1960s, only a small number of females now crawl ashore there. The *Marine Turtle Newsletter* for April 1995 reported that an estimated 580 nests were counted on the beach at Rancho Nuevo, and this was considered good news, since the estimated number of

---

or grieved when I ask about the name. To most people, it's like asking why they call a mackerel a mackerel or a dog a dog. Once in while I run into somebody who knows the ridley as 'mulatto' or 'bastard,' or 'mule-turtle,' but most places the name is ridley and nobody knows why. Maybe one of a couple of dozen fishermen pronounce it 'ridler'; and it may be that this form represents an earlier stage in the etymology of the term, but it seems impossible to confirm this."

nests ten years earlier had been fewer than 200. In *So Excellent a Fishe,* Archie Carr wrote:

> Three years ago I realized that I had heard no definite report of an arribada since some time in the latter part of the 1950s. Now I have just finished canvassing every possible source of information, and it adds up to the dismal certainty that no arribada has been seen for at least seven years. Two or three skipped years might be attributed to chance, because ninety miles is a long beach and there are not really many people there. Now, however, there is no escaping the snowballed evidence that the great arrivals have failed. . . . The fabulous conclaves of former years have gone the way of a thousand other sea turtle colonies before them.

The coyotes and egg-hunters that brought about the original decline are no longer the primary threat to Kemp's ridleys. Now the main problem is "incidental catch" by shrimp trawlers in the Gulf, where the turtles are snagged in nets and drown because they are unable to surface for air. (Even though they can sleep underwater for hours, when they are stressed sea turtles will drown if they cannot get a breath within ten or fifteen minutes.) Between 1,000 and 10,000 turtles of all species, but mostly Kemp's ridleys and loggerheads, are killed in this way each year. Since 1989, all U.S. shrimpers have been required by law to use turtle excluder devices (TEDs), which provide an escape hatch for turtles trapped in nets. However, these are not always in place and sometimes don't work, so thousands of turtles are still being killed "incidentally" every year. Additionally, the United States Congress passed Public Law 101-162, which requires the U.S. Department of State to amend existing treaties and initiate new ones to ensure that TEDs are used on the shrimping fleets of all nations that import shrimp into the United States. Unfortunately, the State Department has not enforced the law in a timely manner, exempting many countries from the shrimp import ban and extending the deadline for compliance well beyond that stated clearly in the law. The United States and 115 other countries, however, have banned the import or export of sea turtle products. It was catastrophic when the eggs were being consumed by the millions and the turtles never got a chance to hatch, but with the killing of so many adults today, Kemp's ridley, with a population of no more than 1,500 adults, is the most endangered of all marine turtles.

Another threat, even more insidious, if that is possible, looms on the ever-decreasing horizon of Kemp's ridley: the two primary feeding grounds for adult turtles are both near major areas of oil exploration and production in the Gulf of Mexico. In June 1979, a well at the Ixtoc site blew and caught fire, burning 400,000 gallons of natural gas per day and producing an oil slick 100 miles long and 50 miles wide. The fire burned for ten months before famed oil-well firefighter Red Adair dropped a gigantic cement plug into the flaming well from the two adjoining wells to seal off the burning gusher. A gigantic oil slick floated ominously off the beach at Rancho Nuevo, and because the hatchlings would have to swim through the oil in July and August, conservationists airlifted 10,000 baby turtles to an oil-free region of the Gulf. The turtles might not be so lucky next time.

OLIVE RIDLEY

The Australian flatback and the olive ridley are the only sea turtles that are not officially endangered, but the status of the olive ridley might not last very much longer. *Lepidochelys olivacea* is the smallest of the sea turtles and one of the most widely distributed. It can be found in tropical regions of the Pacific, Atlantic, and Indian Oceans, but not around Hawaii or the Caribbean Sea. The only known important nesting by olive ridleys in the western Atlantic occurs in Surinam, with small numbers in Guyana. Nesting occurs along the coasts of West Africa and central Africa from Senegal south to Angola; in the Indian Ocean in northern Mozambique, with minor nesting in Tanzania; and, rarely, in South Africa. Minor or moderate nesting occurs on Masirah Island (Oman), the Laccadive Islands, and the Andaman Islands; at several sites around the Indian subcontinent, notably in Orissa State in the northeast; and in Sri Lanka. Little nesting is known in Southeast Asia, with the exception of Trengganu in Malaysia and sporadic records from Burma, Malaysia, Borneo, and Papua New Guinea.

The two ridleys, Kemp's and olive, belong to the same genus (*Lepidochelys*) and are remarkably similar in appearance and habit. The olive ridley, *L. olivacea*, can be differentiated from Kemp's by the presence of six to eight pairs of lateral scutes flanking the central scutes, whereas *L. kempii* has only five pairs (Márquez 1990). In addition, Kemp's is somewhat larger and differs slightly in carapace color, and the two species' nesting grounds do not overlap. (To further confuse matters, Kemp's ridley is sometimes referred to as the Atlantic ridley and the olive ridley as the Pacific ridley.) An obvious behavioral difference is that *L. kempii* nests during the day and *L. olivacea* at night. The etymology of the *olive* part of its common name is somewhat easier to resolve; its carapace is a sort of olive green, whereas that of Kemp's ridley is grayish. Both ridleys are small, as sea turtles go; they rarely measure more than thirty inches along the carapace and never weigh more than 100 pounds. They eat a varied diet of crabs, shrimp, jellyfish, and other small invertebrates, but also fish eggs. Olive ridleys have been captured in prawn trawls at depths below 300 feet, so they are certainly capable of foraging in deep water.

Some authorities consider the olive ridley the most abundant marine turtle in the world. It may also be the most exploited. As with all other turtle species, the major threats to it are the commercial harvesting of adults, incidental catch in shrimp trawls, and rampant harvesting of the eggs from nesting beaches. These factors are of differing significance in different areas, although some populations—the Mexican, for example—are affected by all three. The olive ridley used to be the most economically important sea turtle in Mexico, but legal and illegal fisheries have greatly reduced the large aggregations once found during breeding season.

When population density is high enough, olive ridleys—like their cousins the Kemp's—emerge from the sea in large, synchronized *arribadas* and lay 105 to 115 eggs each. Nesting emergence is mainly at night, but as with Kemp's ridleys, the females sometimes lay their eggs by day. Egg and hatchling predators include a wide variety of birds and mammals, such as hawks, vultures, caracaras, opossums, raccoons, and coyotes. Large *arribadas* now occur only at Orissa State in eastern India (at the head of the Bay of Bengal) and at two beaches in Costa Rica on the eastern Pacific.

Because they are so widely spread, it has been more than a little difficult to get a handle on the status of the olive ridley populations. Tens of thousands die in the nets of Central American shrimp trawlers, and on the Orissa coast of India trawlers have killed more than 50,000 olive ridleys since 1996. In 1997 and 1998, there was no mass nesting at all on Orissa's beaches, and in 1999 another 10,000 turtles died. Although olive ridleys, greens, leatherbacks, loggerheads, and hawksbills are found in Indian coastal waters, the olive ridley is the only species that nests on the eastern coast of India, at Gahirmatha. A quarter of a million olive ridleys once nested there, making it the largest rookery of this species in the world. "At the moment," wrote zoologist Priyambada Mohanty-Hejmadi in 2000, "the threats to sea turtles in India include fishing by trawlers and gill netters in coastal waters, lighting in ports, jetties, industries and coastal development activities, damage by predators and disturbances by local people. Increase in fishing related mortality and no arribadas in two successive years (1997, 1998) are matters of great concern at present." In Mexico, the harvesting of eggs has virtually eliminated the olive ridley. Worldwide, though there are still some undisturbed populations, the general trend is toward reduced numbers.

HAWKSBILL

The hawksbill turtle (*Eretmochelys imbricata*) is a small to medium-sized sea turtle, averaging about thirty-three inches in carapace length and weighing about 150 pounds. The record weight for a Caribbean hawksbill is 279 pounds. Hatchlings are about an inch and a half long, and therefore they are tasty little morsels for any predator, from lizards and rats to birds, from crabs to feral cats and dogs. Hawksbills nest on the beaches of the tropical oceans of the world, frequently sharing their nesting grounds with green turtles. They often nest on small pocket beaches. Because of their small body size and their agility, they can cross fringing reefs that limit access by other species.

Courtship and mating take place in late spring, and nesting occurs between July and October. The behavior of the hawksbill follows the general sequence of that of other species of sea turtle: emerging from the sea, usually at night; selecting a nesting site; clearing the site and constructing a pit; constructing an egg chamber; laying eggs; and filling in the egg chamber, covering over the nest site, and returning to sea. The entire process takes one to three hours. Hawksbills nest, on average, four and a half times per season at intervals of about fourteen days. They have strong site fidelity and are capable of returning to the same place year after year. In Florida and the Caribbean, clutch size is about 140 eggs, which take about sixty days to hatch. Sex determination is very likely temperature-dependent, as in other sea turtles and many other reptiles, but data on this phenomenon are limited.

The carapace of the hawksbill is heart-shaped in the youngest turtles and becomes more elongated as the turtle matures. The hawksbill's name derives from its sharply hooked beak, which it uses to pick at sponges, its primary food item. Hawksbill turtles (and some fishes) are among the few vertebrates that feed on sponges, which are usually considered inedible because of the tiny glasslike spicules that make up most of the sponge's mass. How hawksbills process these glasslike slivers is not known, and rather like the jellyfish diet of the leatherback, there doesn't seem to be much nourishment in a sponge, but hawksbills survived quite nicely until people decided that their shells would make pretty combs.

The unusually thick epidermal scutes that overlay the bones are the "tortoiseshell" so prized by commerce, richly marbled with an irregular pattern of brown and black on a deeply translucent yellow-brown background. (The scutes of the underside, or plastron, are usually clear yellow with little or no dark pigmentation.) In ancient times, hawksbill shells were imported into Rome from Egypt, and in seventeenth-century France, tortoiseshell work was raised to the level of artistry for decorated items such as jewel cases, trays, and

HAWKSBILL TURTLE   (*Eretmochelys imbricata*)

snuffboxes. Hawksbill scutes are imbricate—overlapping like shingles on a
roof—and can be separated from the bony skeleton by heat. The shields are
then flattened by a combination of heat and pressure and the irregularities
rasped away; the material can even be shaped on a lathe. The introduction of
plastic facsimiles in the 1930s and 1940s meant that living hawksbills might
not have to be killed so that eyeglass frames, pocket combs, and hand-mirror
backs could be made, but lately the real thing has become more desirable for
luxury versions of these items, and the turtles are once again at risk.
Hawksbills are also killed for meat, eggs, and leather, and juveniles are sometimes stuffed and lacquered as tourist souvenirs, but it is the desirability of its
shell that most endangers the life of *E. imbricata*.

"Kilogram for kilogram, tortoiseshell is more valuable than elephant
ivory," wrote Wayne King in 1982. The magnitude of the hawksbill trade is
considerable and began to increase in the 1970s, according to David Mack,
Nicole Duplaix, and Susan Wells (1982). In 1967, Indonesia exported less than
22,000 pounds, or 11 tons, of raw tortoiseshell, but nine years later it was
exporting 483,087 pounds, or 241 tons, to Hong Kong, Taiwan, Japan, and
Singapore. Japan is the major consumer of *bekko* (the Japanese word for tortoiseshell), and it is used for everything from cabinets and doorposts to hand
mirrors, shoehorns, eyeglass frames, combs, and cribbage sets. Although
Japan signed the Convention on International Trade in Endangered Species
of Wild Fauna and Flora (CITES), it exempted itself from the ban on hawksbills. Others contributing to the hunger of these Asian nations for tortoise-

shell are Thailand, India, and the Philippines—all countries where hawksbills breed and where the impoverished coastal fishermen will sell anything they can catch to survive. There is significant trade within the Caribbean region as well.* Hawksbill turtles are also hunted for their hides, which are cured for leather. There are recent reports of turtle-leather cowboy boots freely available in Tijuana and of rooms full of confiscated boots on the U.S. border. Even though trade in marine turtles is illegal under CITES, they are stuffed, varnished, mounted, and sold openly as tourist curios in Vietnam, Cambodia, Mexico, and parts of the Caribbean.

Less of a long-distance migrant than other marine turtles, the hawksbill is found in all tropical seas where the water is warm and shallow and where there are reefs, shoals, or estuaries. Hawksbills tend not to congregate in large numbers to nest but instead disperse along many miles of beaches, an inclination that may have saved them from the wholesale destruction visited upon Kemp's ridleys and green turtles. An exhaustive review of the worldwide conservation status (Groombridge and Luxmoore 1989) concluded that the hawksbill is suspected or known to be declining in thirty-eight of the sixty-five countries where information is available. Severe declines have been noted in the western Atlantic and the Caribbean region. Despite protective legislation, international trade in hawksbill shells—both legal and illegal—continues unchecked in many countries and poses a significant threat to the survival of the species in the wild.

The hawksbill is now listed as an endangered species under the Endangered Species Act of 1973, and it is listed as Critically Endangered in the *IUCN Red List of Threatened Species,* maintained by the International Union for Conservation of Nature and Natural Resources. But, as turtle specialist Karen Bjorndal noted in 1999, hawksbill "populations were already greatly reduced or extirpated before they were recorded and/or quantified" by these conservation bodies. Archie Carr and Anne Meylan (1980b) pointed out that because tortoiseshell is a luxury item, as the substance becomes scarcer, the price rises. This encourages fishermen to seek out the few remaining hawksbills, driving

---

*Green turtle farmers on the Cayman Islands—where wild green turtles are extinct—have managed to produce a green turtle whose shell is as ornate as the hawksbill's. The idea was to sell "farmed" green turtle shells in place of those of the endangered hawksbills, thus relieving the pressure on hawksbills. To the untrained or casual eye, the difference between the two is not readily apparent. Ironically, however, this makes it easier for hawksbill shells to find their way to market in the guise of "farmed" green turtle shells. Because the hawksbills don't have to be raised in captivity and are simply caught at sea or on the beach, they are being hunted harder than ever.

the population even lower. In 1991, Japan banned importation of hawksbill shells (Donnelly 1991), a move that was expected to reduce the kill. However, the turtles are still being hunted for food and eggs, and many fishermen view the shells, which can be stored for long periods of time with no danger of deterioration, as simply too valuable *not* to collect. "The scutes are too valuable a commodity," wrote Bjorndal, "for fishermen to stop catching hawksbills because of what may be perceived as just a pause in international trade."

LOGGERHEAD

A loggerhead is a ball of iron on the end of a long handle used in the melting of tar or pitch, or, by extension, an unusually large head. (It was also a wooden bitt or post in a whaleboat, around which the harpoon line was wrapped as it ran out after striking a whale.) The loggerhead turtle (*Caretta caretta*) has an oversized head, hence its unusual name. It reaches a length of 38 inches and can weigh 200 to 400 pounds. It feeds on crabs, mollusks, and shrimp, cracking their shells with its powerful jaws. The loggerhead can also be distinguished from the other sea turtles by the presence of two claws on each of its foreflippers.

Loggerheads can be found in temperate and subtropical waters throughout most of the world. Adults, which usually stay close to mainland shores, prefer to feed in coastal bays and estuaries as well as in the shallow water along the continental shelves of the Atlantic, Pacific, and Indian Oceans. Loggerheads inhabit an enormous range from north to south; in the Western Hemisphere, they are found as far north as Newfoundland and as far south as Argentina. It is interesting to note that some loggerheads live in turbid, detritus-laden, muddy-bottomed bays and bayous of the northern Gulf of Mexico, whereas others choose to live in the clear waters of the Bahamas and Antilles—habitats we more closely associate with tropical marine turtles. Nothing is known about why these creatures would select such vastly different habitats or whether they move from one to the other. The loggerhead is the most common sea turtle in Florida, and indeed, one-third of the world's total population of loggerheads nests there. (Other states with nesting loggerheads are South Carolina, North Carolina, and Georgia.) Extensive ground and aerial surveys performed as recently as 1990 put loggerhead nest estimates at 50,000–70,000 per year in the southeastern United States.

Little is known about the courtship and mating habits of the loggerhead (or those of any other sea turtle, for that matter). In the southeastern United States, adult females begin to nest as early as late April and continue into early

LOGGERHEAD TURTLE
(Caretta caretta)

September, with peak activity during June and July. Loggerheads nest at night, and along the southeastern U.S. coast, females lay an average clutch of 110 eggs. Natural incubation periods range from 53–55 days in Florida to 63–68 days in Georgia. The time eggs take to hatch is inversely related to temperature, and sex determination in hatchlings is also temperature-dependent.

Until recently, no one had any idea where loggerheads spent their first year after hatching. Archie Carr referred to it as the "lost year," but recent studies of tagged turtles (Dellinger 1998) show that the "year" is more like eight years. The young loggerheads drift in ocean currents to areas of seaweed, such as the Sargasso Sea, where they are hard to see in the *Sargassum* weed because of their cryptic coloring. "The early juvenile stages of all species of sea turtles except *Natator depressens*" [the Australian flatback], wrote Karen Bjorndal, Alan Bolten, and Helen Rust Martins in 2000, "apparently occupy the pelagic habitat in the open ocean. . . . Large numbers of small loggerheads occupy the surface waters of the eastern Atlantic, and Brongersma (1972) suggested that these pelagic loggerheads are derived from western Atlantic nesting beaches." After some time in the seaweed, they are passively transported across the ocean by the North Atlantic gyre and pass the Azores and the Canary Islands, subsequently returning across the Atlantic to the Caribbean and the Gulf of Mexico (Musick and Limpus 1997). Even though they accomplish much of their migration by hitching a ride on ocean currents, loggerheads have a fairly specific migratory route around the gyre. Then, as older juveniles, they return to take up residence in shallow coastal areas, typically in North American waters. Ingenious

research by Kenneth Lohmann and colleagues (2001) shows that loggerheads, from the time of hatching, may rely on regional magnetic fields to
navigate the gyre.

The loggerhead was listed by the IUCN in 1978 as Threatened, and it is
now listed as Vulnerable. Recent population studies have concluded that the
number of females nesting in the southeastern United States is in decline.
Because such a significant percentage of the world's loggerhead population
lives in Gulf of Mexico and southwestern Atlantic waters, shrimp fishing, gillnetting, and activities associated with offshore oil and gas exploitation are
particularly dangerous to this species. In the United States, the federal government has listed the loggerhead as endangered worldwide.

With the exception of flatbacks, which have no pelagic stage and spend
their entire lives in and around Australian waters, sea turtles essentially disappear from the time they are hatched until they reach about a foot in length.
Archie Carr (1982) described the problem thus:

> After entering the sea, young turtles of all kinds stay out of human view
> for several to many months. Until lately, this gap in the record of the life
> cycle began just after breakers were passed. What hatchlings did then was
> almost wholly unknown. Did they merely relax or paddle around at
> random, beginning their journey into the limbo of the lost year as totally
> passive plankton?

For loggerheads—and only loggerheads—there seems to be an answer. In
the mid-1980s, Helen Rust Martins, a Norwegian-born biologist at the
University of the Azores, tagged some sea turtles with tags Archie Carr had
provided. When she ran out of tags, she wrote to Carr, requesting more tags
and relating the measurements of the turtles she had already tagged. The "lost
year" turtles had at last been found. Just before his death, in 1987, Carr
hypothesized that the loggerheads that hatched on the beaches of Florida
actually rode the currents in a great transatlantic loop, moving east to the
Azores and Madeira and then back to Florida and the Caribbean. Using tags
and DNA analysis, Karen Bjorndal and Alan Bolten, both of the Archie Carr
Center for Sea Turtle Research at the University of Florida, found that tagged
hatchlings migrated more than 3,700 miles to the eastern Atlantic and the
Mediterranean. The lost loggerheads have been found, but this means that
when turtles protected in Florida by the Endangered Species Act leave
American waters, they can be killed by European fishing fleets. It has been
estimated that Spanish swordfish long-liners alone hook at least 20,000 loggerheads yearly, of which an estimated 20 to 50 percent die. Many of the

turtles hooked are juveniles, and genetic data indicate that some of them hatched in Florida (Wuethrich 1996).

In June 2001, the National Marine Fisheries Service (NMFS) determined that longline fishing practices threatened the existence of Atlantic loggerhead and leatherback sea turtles. The agency concluded that approximately ten vessels were responsible for 75 percent of the loggerheads and 40 percent of the leatherbacks taken as bycatch in the entire U.S. Atlantic longline fleet. To protect these threatened and endangered species, the NMFS closed the area where the bycatch concentration was greatest. The closed area encompasses 2.6 million square nautical miles and covers the Grand Banks off the coast of New England. In response, a fishing industry trade association challenged the decision of the NMFS to close the area to pelagic longline fishing. Then Oceana, a nonprofit international advocacy organization dedicated to protecting the world's oceans, intervened in the case in support of the government's action. On October 3, 2002, Judge Nancy Gertner of the United States District Court for the District of Massachusetts upheld the government's conclusion that pelagic longline fishing would jeopardize the continued existence of leatherback and loggerhead sea turtles, and she affirmed the government's actions taken under the Endangered Species Act to protect these threatened and endangered species. This ruling effectively bans pelagic longline fishing gear from a large area in the North Atlantic Ocean.

New research shows that young loggerheads from eastern Florida, circling the North Atlantic before returning to the eastern coast of North America, rely on "regional magnetic fields" as open-ocean navigational markers. Lohmann and colleagues (2001) exposed hatchling loggerheads that had never been in the ocean to magnetic fields replicating those in three different locations: northern Florida, the northeastern gyre (off Spain), and the southern gyre, roughly midway between northeastern South America and West Africa. Their results showed that "young sea turtles emerge from their nests ready to respond to specific fields with directed movement; these responses are appropriate for keeping young turtles in the gyre system and facilitating movement along the migratory route, which essentially surrounds the Sargasso Sea." At least part of the mystery of loggerhead migrations has been solved.

In the early days of the twenty-first century, loggerheads began dying of unexplained causes in the waters of the Florida Keys. First spotted offshore by boaters, the turtles appeared to be dead or too weak to move. Of the twelve brought to the Turtle Hospital in Marathon, six died and three were in critical condition. Scientists have guessed that they are affected by a previously unknown strain of herpesvirus, but they are not sure. Of course, we see only the sick or dying loggerheads that are picked up or come ashore; no one has any idea how many more incapacitated turtles are still out there.

FLATBACK

Australian waters are home to six species of sea turtle: green, loggerhead, hawksbill, and olive (Pacific) ridley; the leatherback migrates along the eastern coast but does not nest on Australian beaches (Limpus 1995b). An additional species is found in the waters and on the beaches of northern Australia and nowhere else in the world.

The flatback turtle (*Natator depressus*) gets its common name from the smoothness of its shell, which shows little definition of the scales on the carapace. This species used to be known as *Chelonia depressus* (the same genus as the green turtle), but in the 1960s, enough differences were recognized to warrant placing it in its own genus. (*Natator* means "swimmer" in Latin.) Its shell measures about thirty-six inches in length and is noticeably upturned around the edges. Females, which are larger than males and can weigh as much as 175 pounds, can be easily recognized by their shorter tails. Unlike most other sea turtles, flatbacks do not migrate; they spend their lives in and around Queensland, the Gulf of Carpentaria, and the Torres Strait in shallow, soft-bottomed areas away from reefs. Their feeding grounds also extend to the Indonesian archipelago and the Papua New Guinea coast, where these carnivorous turtles feed on squid, sea cucumbers, hydroids, soft corals, mollusks, and jellyfish. Like most sea turtles found in Australian waters, the flatback is hunted for food by Aborigines. On the breeding islands, foxes, dingoes, rats, and monitor lizards dig up and eat the eggs, and rufous night herons can eat entire clutches as they emerge from the sand. Flatbacks lay fifty to sixty eggs per clutch, only half as many as most other species. Despite this, the flatback is the only sea turtle in the world not considered endangered or likely to become so in the near future.

Is there hope for sea turtles? People are the major cause of their problems, and only people can solve them. The concluding chapter in *The Biology of Sea Turtles* (1997), written by Molly Lutcavage and colleagues and titled "Human Impacts on Sea Turtle Survival," ends by eloquently summing up the current predicament of the world's sea turtles:

> There is ample evidence that human activity is seriously eroding once
> abundant sea turtle populations. Much of the impact is unintentional,
> a consequence of the increased exploitation of marine and coastal
> waters—the more intense fishing effort results in an increase in the

incidental catch of sea turtles and a higher risk of entanglement in discarded gear. Debris and pollution in coastal areas take their toll year after year. The inexorable spread of beach development eats away at natural sea turtle nesting habitats and deters nesting females. Even well-intentioned ecotourism programs, which seek to educate visitors to turtle nesting beaches and offer alternative employment for subsistence turtle hunters, have the potential for harm. Poorly regulated foot traffic, noise, and lights create disturbances that may deter nesting females and threaten hatchlings. There are also deliberate threats to sea turtle survival, a consequence of both local economic pressures and international commercial interests which drive continued (even if illegal) fishing for juveniles and adults and a massive taking of eggs. In order to be biologically effective, conservation programs must be firmly based on knowledge of how and to what extent humans are jeopardizing turtle survival. In order to be accepted both politically and practically, conservation programs must also recognize the economic forces behind the disturbing influences. These will be different in different countries and even in different regions, so that implementable solutions are/will be complex. Nevertheless, action is urgently needed to halt the decline and turn the situation around. Otherwise, the extinction of local populations and even some species is inevitable.

~ 4 ~

MISSING MARINE BIRDS

When *Homo sapiens* found the oceans filled with things he could eat, he did not discriminate. He hunted almost every kind of animal that lived in or near the ocean, including fishes, sharks, whales, dolphins, seals, sea cows, sea lions, sea otters, sea turtles, squid, octopuses, and almost anything else that swam under its own power. *Hunting* seems an inappropriate term for the harvesting of marine invertebrates such as clams, oysters, and mussels, which cannot escape, but humans, of course, collected and ate those too. One group of vertebrates, however, was able to escape man's predations because its members could leave the watery realm and take to the air, where hunters could not easily get at them. Some early hunters shot birds with bow and arrow, trapped them on their nests, or hurled things at them to bring them down, but by and large, birds as a group were not threatened. That, of course, was before the invention of the gun. Now hundreds of land-based bird species are extinct, including the dodo, the passenger pigeon, the Carolina parakeet, the ivory-billed woodpecker, and many less familiar types. Albatrosses, sublime masters of the air, are caught on the baited hooks towed behind longline fishing boats, and tens of thousands have been drowned that way. Other aquatic or semi-aquatic birds, such as the pink-headed duck of India and the Laysan teal, are considered threatened, but two waterbirds—one that could fly and one that, unfortunately, could not—are gone forever.

THE LABRADOR DUCK

The Labrador duck (*Camptorhynchus labradorius*) is the only species of marine waterfowl to have become extinct in North America. The drake's head and neck were white, with a black stripe on the crown and a narrow black collar. The back, tail, and underparts were black, and the wings were white. Because of its striking markings, it was sometimes known as the "skunk duck" or "pie duck." John James Audubon's painting of this species shows a black-and-white male and a brownish female, of which he wrote, "The female

119

LABRADOR DUCK
(Camptorhynchus labradorius)

has not, I believe, been hitherto figured." The Labrador duck had a peculiar bill with numerous lamellae (filter plates), and it may have become extinct because it was somehow deprived of its food source—whatever that was. Audubon wrote: "At times it comes ashore and searches in the manner of the spoon-bill duck. Its usual fare consists of small shellfish, fry, and various kinds of seaweeds, along with which it swallows much sand and gravel." The Labrador duck inhabited eastern Canada and the northeastern United States and may not have lived in Labrador at all. Although it was hunted, its flesh tasted strongly of fish, so it was never a popular food item. It seems never to have been plentiful, and it was recorded as rare in 1844. Although the final cause of its demise is not known, it seems likely that hunting of the remaining population was partially responsible. The last one was shot on Long Island on December 12, 1878.

THE GREAT AUK

It is rare to find the entire history of an extinct species in a single work, but Errol Fuller, a young Englishman who evidently has read everything ever written about the great auk, self-published a 448-page coffee-table-sized volume that incorporates practically everything known about *Alca impennis*. He titled this monumental book *The Great Auk* and (assuming he also wrote the flap copy) described it—accurately—as "an astonishingly comprehensive record of a species that is gone forever." The book includes chapters on appearance, lifestyle, and how extinction came about; a complete illustrated catalog of known stuffed specimens; and, in keeping with his description, a catalog of every known great auk egg—also with illustrations.

Crossing the Atlantic Ocean from Iceland in the tenth century, the Vikings were probably the first Europeans to see this great, upright bird. It looked like today's living razorbill (*Alca torda*), but whereas the razorbill stands about sixteen inches tall and can fly, the great auk was more than thirty inches tall and had such tiny wings that it couldn't fly a stroke. It was this helplessness on land that made the garefowl, as it was first known, so vulnerable to hunting; practically everybody who landed on the North Atlantic islands that the great auk called home whacked a few on the head for provisions. The first records of people killing great auks are from 1497, when French ships arrived at the prodigious cod-fishing grounds of Newfoundland. (At this time that the birds were called *pingouins*, the name that would

GREAT AUK
(Alca impennis)

later be applied to the upstanding, flightless black-and-white birds of the Southern Hemisphere.) In 1535, French explorer Jacques Cartier visited an "Island of Birds" (probably Funk Island) off Newfoundland, where his crewmen crammed auks into barrels and collected as many eggs as they could carry. The hapless birds nested on various islands in the western North Atlantic around Newfoundland, including the Magdalens in the Gulf of St. Lawrence, and as far south as the Gulf of Maine and Massachusetts Bay. In the eastern Atlantic, they nested on various islands off Europe, especially St. Kilda (forty miles west of Scotland), and several tiny islands off Iceland. Wherever they were found, they were harvested.

One nesting-ground center was Funk Island, so called because of its overpowering stench ("funk"). The name was probably inspired by the tons of dung that covered every square foot of the half-mile-long island, but some believe the smell to have come from roasting and rotting auks. The first sailors to encounter this speck of land may have found 10,000 breeding pairs there, Fuller suggests:

> Such a convenient larder of fresh meat was bound to be plundered,
> especially by ships that had just made the long voyage across the Atlantic.
> For something like 300 years the larder held up, despite the fearful
> onslaught of the birds. Eaten or used for bait, boiled down for their fat
> or stripped of their feathers, the Great Auks of Funk Island were
> exploited in every way human ingenuity could devise. To facilitate
> removal of their feathers individuals were scalded in vats of boiling water
> and the fires to heat the cauldrons were fueled by fat from already
> butchered birds.

By 1810, Funk Island was the only rookery where any great auks still nested, and sailors returned every spring until they had killed every one.

In Icelandic, the great auk is known as *geirfugl* (hence the term *garefowl*), and several Icelandic islands are known as *Geirfuglasker*. Several of these islands disappeared beneath the sea in 1830 during one of Iceland's frequent volcanic cataclysms, but off Cape Reykjanes at Iceland's southwestern tip, three remain, known collectively as Fuglasker: Geirfugladrangur, Eldeyjardrnagur, and Eldey. Great auks may have remained on some of the more remote outposts, but legend has it that the last living garefowl was killed on Eldey on June 3, 1844, when three fishermen found a breeding pair with a single egg: Jon Brandsson and Sigurdur Islefsson strangled the birds, and Ketil Ketilsson smashed the egg with his boot.

KILLING THE
MARINE MAMMALS

~ 5 ~

STELLER'S LEGACY

In 1648, Semyon Dezhnev, a Siberian Cossack, set sail with seven boats, following the northern Siberian coast eastward from the Kolyma River. Four of the boats were lost before they rounded the Chukotsky Peninsula and one was wrecked there, but the two remaining boats made it as far south as the Anadyr River, which meant that they passed through what would later be known as the Bering Strait. When Dezhnev returned to Moscow in 1662, he filed reports of his journey for payment of accrued salary, so sixty years before Vitus Bering set out, there was evidence that the two continents were indeed separated. Either Peter the Great never saw or heard of Dezhnev's reports or he chose to send Bering anyway, to provide better proof than the reports of an illiterate Cossack.

In 1725, following instructions that Peter the Great signed on his deathbed, Bering headed north from the Kamchatka Peninsula and found an island that he named St. Lawrence, for the saint's day on which he found it. In the little *St. Gabriel,* Bering and his second in command, Alexei Chirikov, actually passed through the fifty-six-mile-wide Bering Strait, which separates Asia from America, but the weather was bad and the fog too heavy for them to confirm the separation of the continents—how could they tell they were not in an enormous bay? Fearing for the safety of the ship, Bering returned to Kamchatka. The government authorized a second expedition in 1740, and this time, with Bering commanding the *St. Peter* and Chirikov the *St. Paul,* they headed eastward, looking for the fabled (but nonexistent) Gamaland, and then continued toward America. The two ships were separated south of the Aleutian island of Amchitka in June 1741 and never reestablished contact. Chirikov made it to Alaska, sighting the Alexander Archipelago on July 15 and then traveling westward before returning to Kamchatka.

Bering's ship, carrying his naturalist, Georg Wilhelm Steller, fared less well. Running low on food and water and with the men falling to scurvy, the *St. Peter* also reached the Alaskan mainland (at Mount St. Elias) and then headed back toward Kamchatka. Bering was now too sick to command the

125

ship; under Sven Waxell, the crew of the eighty-foot-long *St. Peter* passed Kodiak Island without seeing it in the fog, finally reaching the Shumagin Islands and the western terminus of the Alaska Peninsula. As they cleared the islands, with no idea of where they were, a terrible storm arose and blew them westward. Finally, on November 4, 1741, with most of the crew soaked, freezing, and near death, they sighted land, which they believed to be Avacha Bay, their departure point on Kamchatka. It was not; it was the westernmost island in the Aleutian chain, an island home to seals, sea otters, and little blue foxes. Vitus Bering would die there and posthumously give the island his name. The crew anchored the battered ship in a bay, only to have the offshore winds drive the vessel onto shore two days later, burying her keel in the sand.

The arrival of white men on the Aleutians signaled big trouble for the region's marine life. When Bering and Steller were shipwrecked on the barren Commander Islands in 1741, they and the other survivors had to subsist on what they could catch. They began with sea otters and fur seals and initiated what soon became the total elimination of the hapless sea cow. They also found a large, flightless bird ripe for the plucking. It was the spectacled cormorant (*Phalacrocorax perspicillatus*), an ungainly creature that, most unfortunately for its future, had wings too small for flight. Like the sea cow, it was ridiculously easy to kill and tasted good, a combination that almost guaran-

SPECTACLED (FLIGHTLESS) CORMORANT
(*Phalacrocorax perspicillatus*)

teed its demise. In his 1936 biography of Steller, Leonhard Stejneger described the bird:

> The flightless spectacled cormorant is another of Steller's sensational discoveries—sensational not only because its wings were too small to carry its gigantic body, but chiefly because—like the sea cow—it is known only from Bering Island and was exterminated by ruthless hunting. Steller, the only naturalist to see the bird alive, and his comrades were able to vary their fresh meat diet of sea-otter and seal with roasts of this stupid bird, which was as large as a goose, weighing 12 to 14 pounds, "so that one single bird was sufficient for three starving men." Ordinarily cormorants are not considered particularly savory eating, but Steller avers that when properly prepared according to the method employed by the Kamtchadals, namely by burying it encased— feathers and all—in a big lump of clay and baking it in a heated pit, it was a palatable and juicy morsel.

Russian sealers killed off the sea cows within twenty-eight years of their discovery of the cormorants, but it took them more than a century to kill off the birds. There is no question that the sea cows and the cormorants are gone, but Steller observed another creature on this voyage that has not been seen again—not because it is necessarily extinct but because it may never have existed at all. Here is Steller's description of an animal seen in the Bering Sea on the evening of August 10, 1741, included by Stejneger in his biography:

> The length of the beast was about two arshins [5 feet], its head like that of a dog, the ears pointed and erect. On the lower and upper lips on the sides long hairs like a beard, eyes large: the shape [of the body] roundish [cylindrical] and oblong, thicker towards the head, but much slenderer towards the tail. Hair on the whole body thick, on the back gray, but on the belly of a chestnut white, but in the water the said beast appeared entirely like a chestnut cow. The tail [flipper] was divided in two parts, of which the upper was longer. In the meantime the author [Steller] was very much astonished that he could notice on it neither feet nor flippers as in other marine animals. . . . This marine animal, considering its resemblance to a marine ape, might in very truth be called by that name because of its characteristics as displayed by its astonishing manner, tricks and agility. It swam about their ship for more than two hours looking with an air of wonderment now at one person, now at another. At times it came so near to them that it would have been possible to touch it with a pole; at times it went far away, especially when it saw

them stirring about. It raised one-third of its body out of the water, and stood upright like a man and did not change its position for several minutes. Having looked at them attentively for about half an hour it darted like an arrow under their ship and came out of the water on the other side, but soon dived again under the ship and reappeared where it was first seen; and this it repeated about thirty times.

The animal took a long piece of seaweed in its mouth and played with it. After watching the creature for two hours, Steller shot at it, "intending to get possession of it to make an accurate description," but he missed. When the animal reappeared, he took another shot at it but missed again. "However," he wrote, "it was seen at various times in different parts of the sea."

Because no living animal conforms to Steller's description, it has been more than a little difficult to determine what it was. In *Searching for Hidden Animals: An Inquiry into Zoological Mysteries,* Roy Mackal agrees in all particulars with the account reproduced by Stejneger but then disagrees as to how the description is to be interpreted. Mackal, a biologist and cryptozoologist, believes that "the simplest explanation is that the 'sea monkey' actually existed, and that Steller saw it for the first and last time before it became extinct, like the northern sea cow which he was the only naturalist ever to observe. . . . Rational observers are forced to conclude that Steller must have observed a real animal, one that is unidentified to this day." Harold McCracken (1957) believes that Steller merely misidentified a known sea mammal: "Even the eminent naturalist Steller," he wrote, "when he saw his first live sea-otter from the deck of the *St. Peter,* mistakenly called it a 'sea-ape' because of the peculiar antics it performed in the water." Stejneger, on the other hand, thinks that Steller saw a bachelor fur seal, mistook the hind flippers for a two-part tail, and missed the forelegs because "when moving at high speed through the water the fur-seal keeps the fore flippers pressed very close to the body so that they are practically invisible." Stejneger points out (in italics) that up to that moment, Steller *had never seen a fur seal,* but this point is meaningless because Steller had to have written up his observations after the sighting, so it doesn't matter if he hadn't seen one before August 10.

We will probably never know what it was Steller saw that evening, but a clue has surfaced that would seem to tilt the interpretation toward an unknown animal. In 1971, Charles Greer and Victor Scheffer published the text and accompanying illustration of what they believed to be one of the earliest pictures of a fur seal, as it appeared in the 1715 *Comprehensive Pictorial Encyclopedia of Japan and China* by an Osaka physician named Ryoan Terajima. The illustration shows a vaguely seal-like animal, with its whiskers sticking up and with what would appear to be either a three-part tail or small hind legs and a long tail. Terajima's description reads as follows:

> The color of its fur resembles that of a fox, and the shape of its tail is similar to a fish's. Its legs resemble a dog's, but it has no forelegs. . . . Large ones are two to three *shaku* (twenty-eight to forty-two inches) in length. The whole body is that of a fish, and it has a tail, but it is half fish and half beast. Its head resembles a cat's, and its muzzle is sharp. It has eyes and a nose, but no external ears, only small holes. . . . The tail is forked like that of a goldfish and is black in color, but some have a five-forked tail. . . . It has no forelegs, but near the tail there are fins on both flanks, which are black in color, like small legs. These are fins, however, and not legs.

Despite the anomalies, such as no forelegs, no external ears, and a tail like that of a goldfish, Greer and Scheffer read this as a perfectly good description of a northern fur seal, which, they say, was "known to Asiatic peoples . . . long before Europeans came to the North Pacific." The reddish color and forked tail, not to mention the missing forelegs, certainly conform more closely to Steller's mysterious sea monkey than to any known pinniped or sea otter, but the earless nature of this creature differentiates it from Steller's animal. Perhaps there were marine apes with ear flaps, à la Steller, and others with just ear holes, as described by Terajima.

Appending *Steller's* as a prefix to the common name of an animal is tantamount to passing down a death sentence. Whatever it was, Steller's enigmatic sea monkey is gone; his sea cow and cormorant are extinct; his sea lion is in decline (for reasons unknown); only his jay, eider, and sea eagle remain unthreatened. (The sea otter was not discovered or named by Steller; it was known from Kamchatka long before Steller's adventures on the Commander Islands.) There is, however, another bird discovered by Steller that had the name of the great naturalist added to its own, and it too has barely managed to survive.

Of all birds, albatrosses are far and away the least terrestrial—they have been known to spend months or even years riding the winds above the ocean, slowing only to pluck food items from the sea. During Bering's ill-starred 1741 voyage, a large flying bird was sighted, and although Steller thought it was some kind of large gull, it was actually a North Pacific albatross. (The albatrosses of the Southern Hemisphere had been known since navigators rounded the Cape of Good Hope on their way to India, and in 1697 William Dampier identified *algatrosses* as "very large long-winged fowl.") During

SHORT-TAILED ALBATROSS
(Diomedea albatrus)

Steller's time, these birds—now known as Steller's (or the short-tailed) albatross, *Diomedea albatrus*—probably ranged along the northern Chinese
coast, Taiwan, the Kamchatka Peninsula, the ice edge of the Bering Sea, and
the Pacific coast of North America, perhaps going as far south as Baja
California. They were said to follow whaling vessels in order to feed on scraps,
but it was probably their North Pacific habitat that served to identify them,
not their blue-tipped pink bill. (The only other North Pacific albatrosses are
the black-footed and the Laysan, which are dark-backed, whereas the back of
the short-tailed is white.) The name *short-tailed* is misleading, according to
W. Lance Tickell (2000): "Laysan and black-footed albatrosses also have short
tails, and the Galápagos albatross has the shortest tail of all albatrosses."

    The short-tailed albatross is the largest of the North Pacific albatrosses
and also the rarest. Indeed, it is one of the rarest birds in the world, with a

total numbering somewhere around two hundred. Before its decline, *D. alba-trus* was known or suspected to breed in the southern Izu Islands, the Ryukyus, the Pescadores, and the Daitos, but its main area of concentration was Torishima Island in the southern Izus, some 360 miles south of Tokyo. Today, Torishima is the bird's *only* breeding ground.

In 1887, a Japanese firm called the South Seas Trading Company put ashore fifty laborers whose sole function was to kill these *aho-dori*, or "fool birds." The white body feathers were used to stuff pillows and quilts; the wing and tail feathers made dandy quill pens; and some of the larger feathers, known as "eagle feathers," appeared on women's hats in Europe and North America. The fat was useful as food, and the meat was dried and used as fertilizer. Albatrosses are awkward and clumsy on land, and because they show no fear of predators while sitting on the nest, they were clubbed to death as they sat. Japanese ornithologist Yoshimaro Yamashina estimated that 5 million of these birds had been killed between 1887 and 1902, when a volcanic eruption killed all 129 humans on the island at the time. After five years, the island was resettled, and the new homesteaders picked up where their predecessors left off, killing 3,000 birds between December 1932 and January 1933. By April 1933, fewer than 100 birds were left on Torishima. The volcano erupted again in 1939 and then again in 1941, burying the breeding grounds of the short-tailed albatross under thirty feet of ash and lava.

During World War II, the Japanese built an aircraft observation post on Torishima, and the observers reported that a couple of *aho-dori* were breeding there again. In 1946, when Oliver Austin was head of wildlife at the Headquarters of Allied Powers occupying Japan, he tried to visit Torishima, but "available transportation never coincided with freedom from other duties during the breeding season," and he never landed there. Three years later, he sailed around the Bonin Islands whaling grounds on a Japanese whale catcher and "saw no albatrosses whatever." This led him to conclude that Steller's albatross was extinct.

When W. Lance Tickell visited the island in 1973 aboard the British warship HMS *Brighton,* however, he discovered fifty-seven breeding pairs, and he estimated that there had been ten breeding pairs twenty years earlier. A rare bird nesting on a live volcano seems a recipe for disaster. But, as Tickell points out, "Steller's albatross is an oceanic bird and its habitat is not Torishima so much as a wide expanse of ocean not influenced by one small island volcano. No albatrosses are on the island from June to September and throughout the rest of the year, [and] a substantial proportion of the population is always at sea, even at the height of breeding. . . . As long as the island was not blown apart completely, an eruption would merely change the topography; much of Torishima is presently bare ash." Tickell noted the presence of at least one feral cat on the island and commented, "However hopeful we might be for this exceptional bird, there is obviously no room for complacency." Because part of the North Pacific range of the short-tailed albatross includes part of the Hawaiian Islands chain, in November 1998 the U.S. Fish and Wildlife Service proposed listing the species as endangered within the United States.*

Various birds and marine mammals of the North Pacific rim had lived around the Commander Islands, the Aleutian Islands, and Alaska for millennia, undisturbed except perhaps by the occasional native hunter. Avaricious Europeans, eager to reap the rich harvest, followed close on the heels of the Bering expedition, killing and skinning as they came, and had a profound effect on the wildlife of the region. Some creatures, such as the enigmatic sea monkey, may not have been seen then and certainly have not been seen since, but Steller's legacy consists more of the discovery of unexpectedly lucrative creatures. Some were hunted and harvested to such a degree that the species itself was threatened, and one unfortunate creature was exploited right out of existence.

THE LAST OF THE SEA COWS

Humankind's most successful attempt to eliminate a large marine mammal species took place in the icy reaches of the Bering Sea two and a half centuries ago. In 1741, when Commander Vitus Bering's ship St. Peter was wrecked on a remote, rocky island, the surviving crew members found, in addition to bewhiskered sea otters, immense "sea cows," which were subsequently named for Bering's naturalist, Georg Wilhelm Steller. Bering died there of scurvy. (The island on which he died was named Bering Island; with Copper Island, the group is known as the Commander Islands—in Russian, Komandorskiye Ostrova.) On Steller's return to Kamchatka on the Russian mainland, the existence of the sea otters, the sea cows, and the islands themselves was made

---

*I was about as far from the United States as one can get when I saw a Steller's albatross. In the summer of 2001, on an American Museum of Natural History cruise aboard the *Clipper Odyssey,* I sailed from Hokkaido in northern Japan through the Kurile Islands to Kamchatka. One of the other lecturers on board was Peter Harrison, probably the world's foremost authority on seabirds. No sooner had Peter finished his lecture—describing his visit to the isolated island of Torishima to view the only nesting colony of short-tailed albatrosses—than one of these magnificent birds was spotted flying right alongside the ship. For me, this sighting was one of the highlights of a career devoted to looking for sea creatures.

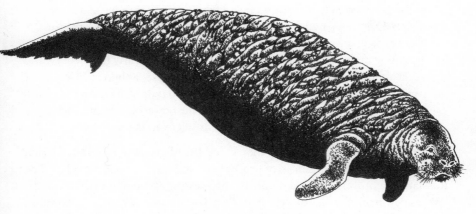

STELLER'S SEA COW
(Hydrodamalis gigas)

known, and Russian sealers began to visit the Commander Islands for the furbearing mammals and for meat and oil for their voyages.

We have no way of knowing how many sea cows existed when Bering landed on these chilly islands, but Leonhard Stejneger, Steller's biographer (and himself a biologist), has estimated that there were about 1,500. They are now extinct, but enough contemporaneous illustrations and descriptions exist to give us ample information about what they looked like and how they lived. As far as we know, *Hydrodamalis* was the only cold-water sirenian (the group that includes the manatees and dugongs, which inhabit warmer waters) and, at a length of thirty feet and a weight of ten tons, the largest. The animal the Russians called *morskaya korova* was an overstuffed sausage of a beast with a small head, pig-like eyes, and skin that was likened to the bark of a tree. It had a forked horizontal tail like that of the dugong (manatees have a rounded, paddle-like tail), and its forelegs were unique in the mammalian kingdom: they had no "finger" bones, and the animal, which probably could not dive below the surface, pulled itself along the shallows on its stumps as it browsed on kelp. Instead of teeth, the mouth of the sea cow was equipped with horny plates, which it rubbed together to grind plant matter into a pulp.

The skin of the sea cow was very thick and could be used for the soles of shoes and for belts. These massive beasts were not killed for their skin, though, but rather for their subcutaneous fat, which could be as much as nine inches thick. In his 1745 description, Steller described the fat:

It is glandulous, stiff, and white, but when exposed to the sun it becomes yellow like May butter. . . . Its odor and flavor are so agreeable that it can not easily be compared with the fat of any other sea beast. . . . Moreover, it can be kept a very long time, even in the hottest weather, without becoming rancid or strong. In flavor it approximates nearly the oil of sweet almonds and can be used for the same purposes as butter. In a lamp it burns clear, without smoke or smell. And indeed, its use in medicine is not to be despised, for it moves the bowels gently, producing no loss of appetite or nausea, even when drunk from the cup.

Once the sealers got started, they killed the huge, slow-moving, oil-rich "manatees" with such insensitive profligacy that by 1768, none were left. The Russian adventurers had taken only twenty-seven years to eliminate the hapless sea cow from the face of the earth. They had no way of knowing, however, that this was the last of them; they probably assumed there were similar undiscovered islands with more sea cows. There were not.

Nowadays, most people attribute the extirpation of *Hydrodamalis* to the Russian sealers who killed every one they found. But mammalogist Paul Anderson (1995) believes that this simple explanation may hide a more complex and interesting truth. His suggestion, evidently first raised by Delphine Haley in 1980, is that their demise involved a chain of events that began with overfishing of sea otters by aboriginal populations from inshore areas inhabited by the sea cows. Sea otters feed on sea urchins, among other things, so the otters' decline led to an exponential increase in sea urchins, which then consumed the algae throughout the sea cows' range. Thus, says Anderson, by the time Bering arrived, the sea cows were restricted to islands such as Copper Island and what would later be known as Bering Island, where algae were still plentiful and there had never been a human population. Isolated on these islands, the sea cows were easy to eliminate. "Sea cow evolution," concluded Anderson, "may have been dependent upon otter predation on urchins, and sea cow extinction may have been hastened by otter declines. The moral may be that extinction is rarely 'simple.'" Regardless of extenuating circumstances, however, the extirpation of the sea cow was brought about by men with spears and knives.

The sea cow is gone, but its cousins are still with us. The Florida manatee (*Trichechus manatus latirostris*) is considered a valid subspecies of the West Indian manatee. The Florida subspecies is found in that state's waters year-round, and during the warmer months its range may extend north to Virginia or west to Louisiana. In Florida, the harvesting of manatees for food has ended, but the threat to their existence has not. Because manatees like to inhabit coastal waterways, they are in constant danger from powerboats: the

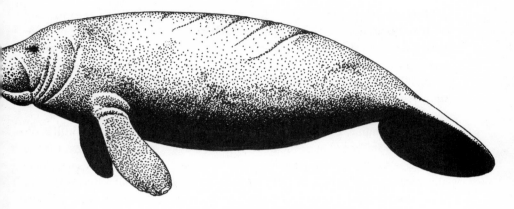

MANATEE   *(Trichechus manatus)*

boats run them over and the spinning propeller slices the animal's back, often fatally.

Florida manatees share their habitat with some of the most avaricious land-grabbers in the history of the United States, and worse, these people want to use the very waterways the manatees call home. John Reynolds and Daniel Odell (1991) tell us: "In Florida, 90% of the human population occupies areas within 10 miles of the coast. That population is growing by at least 800–1,000 new residents each day." When the time came to marshal the environmental forces for preservation of the whales, one thing was clear: living as they did in the open ocean, the whales threatened nobody's way of life. In that sense—and that sense only—it was a relatively easy battle: nobody wanted to live in the middle of the North Pacific Ocean or on the Antarctic ice pack. But a lot of people want to live in coastal southern Florida. The existence of the manatee is therefore in direct conflict with the existence of the developer, and given the history of both species, it is not difficult to guess which will prevail.

In Florida waters, boaters are required to slow down or idle in areas seasonally frequented by manatees, but the collisions continue. Edmund Gerstein of Florida Atlantic University wondered why the manatees wouldn't (or couldn't) learn to avoid the boats: some individuals were being hit two or three times. In 1999, he and his colleagues trained two "teenage" manatees, Stormy and Dundee, to listen to broadcast sounds and then respond by pushing a paddle when they heard (or didn't hear) sounds at certain auditory thresholds. ("It took approximately one year to prepare both subjects for the tests," wrote Gerstein, "and thousands of monkey chow biscuits, along with a great deal of imagination and luck, to keep them interested throughout the subsequent years of training.") Manatees don't hear very well in a world filled with ambient noise, which often masks the sound of an approaching boat, so the researchers designed a device that emitted a sound that the manatees would hear and learn to associate with the boats, enabling them to avoid collisions. Now, if only the boaters will learn to use the warning devices, there may be some hope for this species of manatee.

Halfway around the world from Florida we find the dugong (*Dugong dugon*), the manatee's only living relative. Whereas the manatee's mouth is on the front of its face, that of the dugong is on the bottom of its muzzle, for the dugong is strictly a bottom feeder. It has the same fusiform shape as the manatee (although dugongs are slimmer than their cousins), but whereas the tail fin of the manatee is rounded, that of the dugong is bifurcated, like the flukes of a whale. Unlike manatees, dugongs have incisors, which develop into short tusks in the males. The remainder of their teeth are molars used for grinding plant matter.

The single species of dugong is found in the territorial waters of forty-three countries along the Indian Ocean and western Pacific Ocean. It ranges from Mozambique and Madagascar on the East African coast up through the Arabian Sea, Persian Gulf, and western coast of India through Southeast Asia and Indonesia, all along the coast of northern Australia, and around New Guinea, Melanesia, and the Philippines. With this broad a distribution through some of the most densely populated areas of the world, the problems of the dugong are as wide and diverse as its range.

In most of its habitat, the dugong is considered endangered. A large proportion of the world's remaining dugongs can be found along the mostly uninhabited coasts of northern Australia. There may be 17,000 in the Gulf of Carpentaria and as many as 70,000 throughout Australian waters. Their meat, which is said to taste like veal or pork, is prized by Aborigines, who are permitted to hunt dugongs in their territorial waters, but hunting is otherwise prohibited to Australians. Nevertheless, many of these slow-moving creatures are injured by boats, and many are drowned in shark nets.

An adult dugong will yield five to eight gallons of a high-quality oil, and this oil, used for medicinal purposes, formed the basis of a cottage industry in Queensland from the middle of the nineteenth century until 1960, when the species was protected in Australia. Elsewhere in the region, the dugong's skin is used for leather, the oil for cooking and ointments, and the bones and tusks for carving and ornaments. In Sri Lanka, India, Kenya, and Papua New Guinea, a major cause of dugong mortality is fishnets: because dugongs are slow-moving, they are also vulnerable to boating injuries. Dugongs have poor eyesight and frequently blunder into the nets by accident. The dugong is listed as vulnerable to extinction, and trade in dugong products is monitored by CITES, the Convention on International Trade in Endangered Species of Wild Fauna and Flora. However, it is difficult to keep watch on the small aboriginal villages where dugongs are still speared and netted for food.

"The dugong," noted Fred Pearce in a 1999 article in *New Scientist,* "is the most spectacular casualty of the world wide destruction of coastal ecosystems." In *Dugong: Status Reports and Action Plans for Countries and Territories,* a 2002 study conducted for the United Nations Environment Programme, lead researcher Helene Marsh of James Cook University in Queensland reported that "rising pollution from the land, coastal developments, boat traffic and fishermen's nets are among the threats which are contributing to a decline in the dugong's fortunes . . . hunting for meat, amulets and trophies may be adding to these pressures." The sea-grass beds on which dugongs depend are being cleared for shrimp farms and salt beds or smothered by silt runoff from industrial forestry or farming. And when food is in short supply, dugongs delay reproduction. Marsh and her colleagues also observed that "dugongs appear to have disappeared or already become extinct in some places such as the waters off Mauritius, the Seychelles, western Sri Lanka, the Maldives, Japan's Sakishima Sakoto Islands, Hong Kong's Pearl River estuary, several islands in the Philippines, including Zambalu and Cebu, and parts of Cambodia and Vietnam." For the dugongs of East Africa, the future appears bleak. Few, if any, individuals remain off the coasts of Somalia, Kenya,

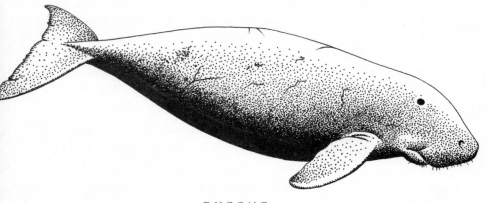

DUGONG
(Dugong dugon)

Tanzania, Mozambique, the Comoros, Madagascar, the Seychelles, or Mauritius.

The ungainly sea cow may already have been on its way to termination, but we will never know, because *Homo sapiens,* the grim reaper for the species, accelerated the process. In an impassioned plea published in the January 1986 issue of the scholarly journal *Marine Mammal Science,* Clayton Ray and Daryl Domning, perhaps the leading authorities on fossil sirenians, proposed that the living manatees and dugongs be given worldwide protection because they are seriously endangered wherever they live. The researchers pointed out that arguably our one lasting interaction with a marine mammal—the direct extermination of Steller's sea cow—should make us painfully sensitive to the plight of the manatees and dugongs. Unless protective measures are initiated quickly, they warn, "many of us could live to witness the extinction of an entire order of mammals—not just any old order, but one that is unique evolutionarily and ecologically."

THE SEA OTTER

The length of the full-grown animal may average five feet, including the tail, which is about ten inches. The head resembles that of the Fur Seal. The eyes of the Sea Otter are full, black, and piercing, and exhibit much intelligence. The color of the female, when "in season," is quite black; other periods, it is a dark brown. The males are usually of the same shade although, in some instances, they are of a jet, shining black, like their mate. The fur is of a much lighter shade inside than upon the surface, and, extending over all, are scattering, long, glistening hairs, which add much to the richness and beauty of the pelage. Some individuals, about the nose and eyes, are of a light brown, or dingy white. The ears are less than an inch in length, quite pointed, standing nearly erect, and are covered with short hair. Occasionally, the young are of a deep brown, with the ends of the longest hairs tipped with white, and, about the nose and eyes, of a cream color.

—Charles Melville Scammon, *The Marine Mammals of the Northwestern Coast of North America,* 1874

Even before Vitus Bering and his crew were shipwrecked, they were perilously short of food, and many of them were severely debilitated by scurvy. The first order of business, therefore, after digging shelters in the sand and shoring them up with ship's timbers and driftwood, was to find something

SEA OTTER
(Enhydra lutris)

to eat. Georg Wilhelm Steller, with two other crew members healthy enough to walk, went down to the beach and clubbed four otters they found sleeping on the rocks. "From the liver, kidneys, heart, and the meat of these animals," wrote Steller, "we made several palatable dishes and ate them gratefully." Steller tried to feed Bering, but the commander lay in the hut, covered with blankets, unable to eat, and died on December 8, a month after the wreck of the *St. Peter*. For the next seven months, the survivors subsisted on the meat of otters, ptarmigans, an occasional seal, and sea cows that they killed and dragged ashore, as well as the meat and blubber of a whale that they found dead on the beach. Between November 1741 and August 1742, Bering's men killed an estimated seven hundred sea otters. Sven Waxell, an officer on the ship (and a survivor), wrote in his journal, "Even if you can perhaps endure the smell of sea-otter meat, it is extremely hard and as tough as sole-leather and full of sinews, so that however much you chew at it, you have to swallow it in large lumps." The men recognized the value of the otter skins, but, wrote Steller, "the precious skins of the sea otters we regarded already as a burden which had lost its value to us, and, as we had no leisure to dry and prepare them, they were thrown about from one day to another, until finally they spoiled, together with many others, and were chewed to pieces by the foxes."

Of the *St. Peter's* original seventy-seven-man crew, thirty-one died before they managed to build a boat from the salvaged wreckage of their ship and sail it back to the Kamchatka Peninsula. During the thirteen-day, sixty-mile voyage, they had to bail almost continuously, and to keep themselves afloat they jettisoned everything they could, including the cannons and grapeshot. In *Where the Sea Breaks Its Back,* a popular account of Bering's voyage, Corey Ford reported that the crewmen brought bales of sea otter skins with them, and even when ordered by Waxell to throw them overboard, Fleet Master Khitrov "had secreted a stack of prime pelts under his bunk . . . and smuggled the skins ashore, to be sold at a fabulous price to the Chinese, and babbled to everyone of the great number of sea otters to be found on Bering Island and the Aleutians." Neither Khitrov's secret stack nor his babbling to the Chinese can be found in Waxell's account or in any available version of Steller's journal, so it is likely that Ford—like others—improvised the specific inspiration for the Russian sealers to return to Bering Island. Whatever the incentive, however, the *promyshlenniki* (fur-hunters) had come to Bering and Copper Islands by the spring of 1743 and begun the wholesale slaughter. They soon expanded the hunt eastward across the Aleutian chain, eventually fetching up on the Alaskan mainland.

This marked the beginning—and almost the end—of the sea otter's unpropitious relationship with human beings. (Sea otters used to breed in Japan, and although the Japanese probably hunted them for fur, they do not seem to have established what would later be called a fishery.) The fur was so fabulously valuable that Russian fur traders almost immediately began hunting otters so that they could sell the pelts to the Chinese, who esteemed them beyond all other furs. Its warmth and luminous beauty made sea otter the imperial fur of China, extraordinarily prized by the royal family, mandarins, and the wealthy classes. Aristocratic ladies wore otter capes, and some made belts or sashes of the fur over which they arranged strings of pearls. The heavy fur was sometimes used to weigh down and border rich silk gowns, and the tails were made into caps, mittens, and small trimmings. For a century, the sea otter trade dominated the commerce of the North Pacific. By 1790, a single skin was bringing the equivalent of $80 to $120 in the Chinese market. Ford claimed that the sea otter "was so highly prized by the early Chinese mandarins that at one time a single skin would bring as high as five thousand dollars." And in his book about the sea otter trade, James Gibson (1992) noted that in 1829 "it took more than ten beaver pelts, the pillar of the continental fur trade of North America, to equal the value of a single sea otter skin."

In Walter Miller's 1899 translation of Steller's "De Bestis Marinis" (Beasts of the Sea), after the description of how tasty the flesh of baby sea otters is, we read Steller's description of the preparation of the skin:

(1) After the skin has been taken from the animal shreds of muscle are cut from it with a knife. . . . (2) Then the skin is stretched to its utmost; for besides the fact that the price increases with the size, the skins thus prepared become lighter, although the fur does become less beautiful. . . . (3) They straighten out the hairs with the bones from the wings of gulls, and sleep upon them naked, for several weeks to make them glossier, nicer, and more beautiful. . . . (4) While the Cossacks are getting the skins from the natives they frequently beat the skins upon the snow with sticks, and if the fur is gray or any other color than black, they color them with alum and epetrum berries cooked to the proper consistency with fish oil. This makes them glossy black.

Steller described the Chinese use of the furs, with a surprising derivation for the name of one of our more common outer garments:

These skins, moreover, being rather heavy, are for that reason dearer to the Chinese than the skins of sables and foxes, and they are better suited to increase the weight of the too light silk gowns. In addition to their beauty they make the silk fit more closely to the body and resist the wind better; and for those reasons the Chinese make of this fur borders of a hand's breadth and put them around their robes on every side; and this has become the fashion also with both sexes, not among the tribes of Kalmuc and Siberia only, but also in Russia. In the land of Kamchatka, nothing is considered a finer ornament than a dress sewed up like a sack (a "*Parka*" they call it), made out of the white skins of reindeer fawns (called "*Püschiki*") and having a border of sea otter fur.

The Aleuts had perfected the art of hunting sea otters, which they called *kalan,* from their baidarkas—narrow, graceful one- or two-man canoes made of marine mammal skin stretched over strips of light wood or whalebone and fastened together with sea lion sinews. The preferred skin was the thick, tough hide of Steller's sea lion, but other pinniped skins were also used. The seams were tightly sewn, and the skin surface was smeared with oil to make it water-proof. Baidarkas were similar in construction to Eskimos' kayaks, and both were equipped with a drip-skirt that fitted over the paddler and the hatch, making the little craft watertight even if it was completely overturned. Where Eskimo kayaks had a simple pointed prow, that of the baidarka was often split into the characteristic bifurcated elements. From their baidarkas (a Russian term, not a native one) the Aleuts hunted sea otters with spears, and they also used the fur to decorate their clothing. The Russian invaders took the Aleuts' elegant hunting techniques and distorted them into a massacre.

A year after the survivors of Bering's expedition returned to the mainland, with their stories of a vast treasure of furs on the bleak islands to the east, a frenzy began that has been compared to the California gold rush. Untrained and underequipped, with only a minimal knowledge of boats or sailing—or of sea otters, for that matter—greedy Cossacks and soldiers headed for Bering Island in anything that could float. Their boats, wrote William Coxe in 1780, were "called in Russian *Shitiki,* or sewed vessels because the planks are sewed together with thongs of leather . . . in general so badly constructed that it is wonderful how they can weather so stormy a sea." The first recorded voyage was made in 1743 by Yemelyan Bassov, a sergeant in the Lower Kamchatka detachment who took a few men to Bering Island and brought back a rich harvest of furs. Two years later, funded by a merchant named Serebrenikov, Bassov again sailed to Bering Island, this time in a barely seaworthy boat named *Kapitan,* and came back with 1,600 sea otter skins, 2,000 fur seal skins, and 2,000 blue fox skins. His triumphant return fanned the flames of avarice even higher, and more and more little boats were hastily assembled for the *promyshlenniki* invasion of the Aleutians.

Island-hopping eastward along the Aleutians, the Russians killed off the sea otters, the fur seals, and the foxes, occasionally meeting some modest resistance from native islanders. Spears and arrows were no match for Russian muskets, however, and the Aleuts were either killed or put to work for the *promyshlenniki.* One tactic was to send the native hunters out to hunt the sea otters for them and then, when they were gone, move into their village, capturing and raping the women who had been left behind. In 1762, the Aleuts of Unimak Island seized and burned three Russian ships and slaughtered the crews, but horrible retribution was visited upon them by one Ivan Solovyev, who destroyed entire settlements by driving the Aleuts into their dugout huts and blowing them up. Solovyev, whom the Aleuts called "the Destroyer," also demolished their baidarkas, hunting equipment, and war weapons. One story told (probably apocryphal) is that he amused himself by packing a dozen Aleuts together and seeing how many could be killed with a single musket ball. (Nine, with the ball stopping at the tenth man.) The Russians found and emptied island after island of much of its sea otter population and, sometimes, its human one, being stopped briefly in 1763 at Kodiak Island, where the more warlike Koniagas put up a valiant fight until a temporary cease-fire was negotiated.

With the ascent to the throne of Catherine the Great in 1762, the Russian government renewed its interest in establishing dominance in the new lands to the east. In 1783, Gregorii Shelikov equipped three vessels and sailed to

America with more than furs on his mind; he intended to create an empire that would stretch from Bering Strait to Prince William Sound, based primarily on the fur trade but also with permanent settlements that would grow their own food, make their own ships, and dominate Russian America. In 1799, Tsar Paul I (who just happened to be a stockholder) granted the company a charter that gave it a complete monopoly over all Russian enterprises in North America. Aleksandr Baranov (1746–1819) was chosen by Shelikov as manager of his interests in Alaska, and he soon became the single most influential Russian in the complex and contentious history of Russian America. Shelikov himself died in 1795, but his intentions were carried out and even expanded by Baranov, who brutally conquered native settlements, consolidated fur-trading operations, and put together the organization that would become the Russian-American Company.

In his initial attempt to get from Kamchatka to Alaska, Baranov was shipwrecked with his fifty-two men on Unalaska Island and spent the winter of 1790–1791 in dugouts roofed with driftwood. In the spring, they set sail in open boats for Kodiak Island, 800 miles away, and on their arrival, Baranov assumed command of Shelikov's "empire" in Alaska. He consolidated the Aleuts' hunting parties, which essentially meant using them as slave labor to hunt sea otters, fur seals, foxes, beavers, minks, wolves, wolverines, and even walruses, the latter for their tusks. After 1799, with the Aleutian and Pribilof Islands under Russian jurisdiction, Aleksandr Baranov was, for all intents and purposes, the governor of Russian America. The Russian settlement at Novoarkhangel'sk (New Archangel, later to be named Sitka) became the de facto capital of the region. In mid-June 1802, however, while Baranov was at Three Saints Bay on Kodiak Island, the native Tlingits, led by a chief named Katlean, rose up against the Russians in New Archangel. Nearly a thousand men overran the stockade, slaughtered almost everyone in it, and burned the fort to the ground.

Baranov struck a deal with the American captain Joseph O'Cain whereby the Russians would supply men and baidarkas if O'Cain would help him retake New Archangel. In the fall of 1804, with four new ships of his own, O'Cain (whose ship was also called *O'Cain*), 800 Aleuts in baidarkas, and the considerable assistance of Captain Yuri Lisianski in the heavily armed brig *Neva*, Baranov led his *promyshlenniki* to avenge the embarrassing loss and reclaim the fort at Sitka. Baranov was wounded in the battle, but the firepower of the Russians and the cannonades of the *Neva* drove the Tlingits off, and the fort was rebuilt. The following year, perhaps in response to their defeat at New Archangel, the Tlingits destroyed the Russian outpost at

Yakutat (on the mainland, north of Sitka), but it would be the last time Russian rule was challenged. By this time, the Russians had killed off the northern populations of sea otters by the tens of thousands, and when they learned of untouched populations far to the south in the coastal waters of Alta and Baja California, they went after them as well. The California otters were smaller, and because they lived in warmer climes their fur was less dense, but their fur was extraordinarily valuable nonetheless.

In 1811, Baranov sent Ivan Kuskov, his chief assistant and a company employee of long standing, on a voyage to locate a site in California for a Russian settlement. After arriving at Bodega Bay in early 1812 aboard the *Chirikov,* Kuskov decided that the most suitable location for the colony was the site of a Kashaya Indian village called Meteni, seventy-five miles north of San Francisco. According to one account, the entire area was acquired from the natives for "three blankets, three pairs of breeches, two axes, three hoes, and some beads." The land offered a harbor of sorts, plentiful water, good forage, and a nearby supply of wood for the necessary construction. It was also relatively distant from the Spanish, who were to be unwilling neighbors for the next twenty-nine years. The fort—named Fort Ross, from *Rossiya,* the name for Russia in tsarist days—was completed in a few weeks and formally dedicated on August 13, 1812. Baranov brought in Aleut hunters with their baidarkas aboard Russian ships to hunt sea otters along the California coast. These otters, however, never as numerous as those in Alaska, were rapidly depleted. By the time of the Monroe Doctrine of 1823, which declared that American lands were no longer open to colonization by Europeans, only four yearlings could be found. In 1841, the settlement at Fort Ross was sold to John Sutter, whose mill near Sacramento was the scene of the first California gold rush.

Farther to the south, California was explored in 1542 by the Spanish navigator Juan Rodríguez Cabrillo and later by the merchant Sebastían Vizcaíno, who named San Diego, Santa Barbara, and Monterey Bay in 1602. There was little European interest in this dry coast, but offshore, floating on their backs, were the little animals that had the finest fur in the world. By the eighteenth century, Spanish traders, anxious to sell the sea otter skins to the Chinese, were vying with the Russians who brought Aleuts and their baidarkas from Alaska. The Americans also joined the fray, and in 1801 fifteen American ships were working the kelp beds from southeastern Alaska to southern California, engaged solely in the hunting of sea otters, often under the noses of the Spaniards. The skins were packed up and carried to Hawaii, where they would be shipped to China. When Mexico became independent in 1821, Alta and Baja California came with it, but only until 1846, when the United States proclaimed victory in the Mexican-American War, stretching its borders from ocean to ocean and putting the sea otters of California in American waters for the first time. Although the Russians had initiated the Aleut-assisted slaughter of the sea otters and the Americans had enthusiastically followed suit, the valuable pelts attracted adventurers from other nations as well.

When Captain James Cook sailed the ships *Resolution* and *Discovery* into Nootka Sound on Vancouver Island in March 1778, his men bought sea otter skins and clothing from the natives and brought the items back to England, where they were sold for an enormous profit. (Cook was killed in Hawaii in January 1779, but Captain James King brought the expedition home.) Of the aboriginal inhabitants of the inlet he named for himself, Cook wrote, "I will be bold to say that the Russians have never been among them; for if that had been the case, we should hardly have found them clothed in such valuable skins as the sea otter." The British East India Company almost immediately dispatched two ships from Canton with trade items for the northwestern coast and returned with 250 sea otter skins, which were sold for a 400 percent profit. Then Captain James Hanna in the brig *Harmon* (renamed *Sea Otter*) set sail for Nootka Sound and procured 560 skins, which fetched $24,000 in Canton. The British trade in sea otter furs lasted only until the end of the eighteenth century, however, when the traders quit Nootka Sound because they were unable to compete with the more aggressive Americans.

After collecting the skins along the northwestern coast, the American vessels—primarily from Boston and Salem, Massachusetts—headed across the Pacific, usually stopping at Hawaii before making for Canton, the gateway to the China trade. "Fuel was scarce and costly in China," Gibson notes, "and in North China winters were long and cold. Even at Canton, all the Chinese [who could] afford it wore woolens or fur-lined camlets during the cool season of March–April, when frost could occur at night." Evidently, the Chinese saved their fuel for cooking, so they piled on the warmest clothing they could afford—and the warmest, densest fur of all was sea otter. In exchange for furs, the traders brought back tea, silks, and Oriental porcelain, the latter popularly known as *chinaware* and, eventually, just *china*.

Of course, any animal that becomes an integral component of commerce will pay the price, and the numbers of otters taken by the Americans continued to fall. Gibson cites the figures from "an unknown and profitable peak in 1795 or 1796, to 18,000 in 1800, 15,000 in 1802, to annual averages of 14,837 in

1804–07 (17,445 in 1805), 9,592 in 1808–12, and 3,100 in 1813–14 to 4,300 in 1815, 3,650 in 1816, 4,177 in 1817, 4,500 to 4,800 in 1818, 3,000 to 3,500 in 1820 and 1821, 2,500 in 1822, 1,100 in 1826, 700 in 1827, and fewer than 500 in 1828." Sea otter specialist James Bodkin (2000) reports that "an estimated 500,000 to 900,000 otters were killed between 1742, when the commercial harvest began, and 1910, when the unsuccessful final hunt was held."

The object of this slaughter was *Enhydra lutris,* the smallest of all marine mammals, not exceeding five feet in length (including tail) and weighing no more than seventy-five pounds. They are almost totally aquatic: they feed, mate, and sleep in the water but may give birth in or out of the water. Males are larger than females and have a more massive head, neck, and shoulders, which become whiter with age. Sea otters have no blubber layer; instead, they are insulated by tiny bubbles of air trapped in a two-layer fur coat. The pelage consists of guard hairs about an inch and a half long and dense underfur that is about a quarter of an inch shorter. Each guard hair is surrounded by approximately seventy underfur hairs, and this makes the pelage of the otter about twice as dense as that of the fur seal. Whereas the average person has about 600,000 hairs on his head, the sea otter has 300,000 hairs *per square inch.* An adult sea otter may have a billion fur fibers.

Sea otters spend a great deal of time floating on their backs, feeding and grooming themselves. They prefer to rest in kelp beds and often wrap themselves in kelp fronds to remain stationary. They usually dive for their food in water less than twenty fathoms deep, but they can dive to fifty-five fathoms (a fathom equals six feet) to forage for invertebrates such as sea urchins, abalone, clams, snails, and crabs. An average dive lasts about ninety seconds, but dives of more than four minutes have been recorded. Otters are also among the few mammals that use tools, breaking open shellfish on their chests with rocks that they hold in their front paws. Their forefeet consist of manipulative "hands" with retractile claws, and their webbed hind feet have the longest toes on the outside, a unique arrangement in mammals.

By 1874, when Charles Melville Scammon published his discussion of the marine mammals of North America, the northern sea otter population had been decimated:

> The hunting of them on the coast of California is no longer profitable
> for more than two or three hunters, and we believe of late some seasons
> have passed without any one legitimately engaging in the enterprise;
> notwithstanding, off Point Grenville, which is an old hunting-ground,
> sixty Otters were taken by only three hunters during the summer of
> 1868—a great annual increase over many past years. It is said the

Russian-American Company restricted the number taken yearly by the Aleutian Islanders, from whom the chief supply was obtained, in order to perpetuate the stock. Furthermore, may it not be that these sagacious animals have fled from those places on the coasts of the Californias where they were so constantly pursued, to some more isolated haunt, and now remain unmolested?

Alas, "these sagacious animals" could not betake themselves to some more isolated haunt, for wherever they went, they were hunted mercilessly. Because they spend much of their time at the surface, for the most part floating on their backs, they were as easy to spear or shoot as ... well, sea otters in a barrel. Shortly after the Pribilof Islands were discovered, in 1786, the resident population of sea otters was exterminated, and their numbers were brought to precariously low levels throughout their range. In his 1875 report to the United States Congress, Henry W. Elliott detailed the methods used in hunting them:

Shooting them in the surf at long range with a rifle, and waiting till they drift ashore if the surf is too rough to permit the launching of a boat; surrounding an otter by a party of spearers in their boats and waiting its return to the surface after it becomes exhausted in several dives; clubbing them in winter when they may at times be stealthily approached among rocks and kelp; and using nets 16 to 18 feet long and 6 to 10 feet wide, of coarse meshes, spread out on the kelp beds. Frequently several at a time are thus taken, for when enmeshed they seem to make little or no attempt to get free.

By 1910, *E. lutris* was in serious trouble, and even though it was protected by the U.S. government, there was not much hope for its survival. From then until about 1930, there was little news of sea otters except for a few scattered sightings in the outlying islands of the Aleutian chain and along the Alaska Peninsula, where the few survivors had taken refuge far from the spears, guns, and nets. However, when Corey Ford, who had been stationed on Amchitka Island during the Battle of the Aleutians in World War II, returned to the island some years after the war, he was surprised to learn that American soldiers stationed there were familiar with sea otters and had even made pets of a couple: "In every sheltered bay and inlet, as I explored the island, otters were feeding or sleeping, or sporting in the breakers, as playful as children. . . . The rate of increase in the two decades after the war has been prodigious." At the time of his book's publication (1966), Ford estimated that on just one island, Amchitka, the otter population had reached 5,000, with the total state population estimated by the Alaska Department of Fish and Game at approximately 30,000. In the 1970s, 1,000 otters were photographed in a single group in the Bering Sea north of the Alaska Peninsula.

The return of the otters wasn't viewed as a good thing by everyone. Commercial abalone divers resented the competition, and the fishery for sea urchins in the absence of their sea otter predators had grown from a total of 200 pounds in 1971 to 3 million pounds in 1974. In a 1974 article, biologist Joel Hedgepeth commented: "The sea otter is a hungry animal. It not only eats sea urchins, abalone, and mussels; it eats almost everything, including limpets and barnacles. There may be lots of things in the sea, but sea otters are so voracious that more than twenty of them per square mile is too many for the carrying capacity of the nearshore." Although most people—and presumably the otters themselves—were happy with their renewed population growth, others worried that they would wreak ecological havoc on the California coastal community. As it turned out, they didn't proliferate all that successfully in the years that followed, and despite the efforts of groups such as Friends of the Sea Otter, they are still threatened in some areas.

A single sea otter was spotted off the western (Pacific) coast of Baja California in 1994 (Rodriguez-Jamarillo and Gendron 1996), at the southern limit of the species' previous range. Attempts to restore the sea otter to parts of its former range that entailed transporting the animals from Alaska's shores to Vancouver Island, and to Washington and Oregon, have been moderately successful, but sometimes the otters were placed in regions where they (and the biologists who moved them) were surprised by shark attacks. Four-foot-long mammals that spend most of their time floating on their backs offer little resistance to great white sharks. In 1980, two researchers (Ames and Morejohn) documented these attacks in the waters of northern California, noting that the sea otters were killed by the sharks but not eaten.

For sea otters, there is no safety in numbers, especially from oil spills. With no blubber layer, they depend almost exclusively on their dense fur for insulation, and matting of the fur by oil makes them dangerously vulnerable. If the coat becomes dirty through contact with oil or other polluting substances, its protection may be lost, and the animal will become chilled in icy waters. Sea otters groom themselves extensively and are thus at risk from swallowing toxins. When, just after midnight on March 24, 1989, the 987-foot-long supertanker *Exxon Valdez* ran aground, dumping 11 million gallons of crude oil into Alaska's Prince William Sound, the event spelled disaster for the local sea otter population, as it did for many other animals in the region. Winds and shifting tides spread the oil over 10,000 square miles along the

Alaska Peninsula, qualifying this ecological disaster as one of the worst in history. The oil moved for 1,500 miles along the coastline of Alaska, contaminating portions of the Kenai Peninsula, lower Cook Inlet, and the Kodiak Island. High winds blew the oil slick onto the shore, creating havoc with living creatures. The actual total will never be known, but it has been estimated that at least 100,000 seabirds died, along with 150 bald eagles and hundreds of seals, sea lions, whales, dolphins, and porpoises and countless fishes. In her 1997 book about oil spills, Joanna Burger described the effects of the *Exxon Valdez* oil on sea otters:

> Since they spend most of their time at the surface of the water, they were
> unable to avoid the oil. When the oil began to penetrate their fur,
> destroying its insulation ability, they may have groomed obsessively,
> increasing their ingestion of oil. Almost a thousand sea otter carcasses
> were picked up in the weeks following the spill, but the number that died
> may have been three or four times as high. . . . Although many otters
> were found dead, others were taken to rehabilitation facilities. Of the 357
> captured alive, 123 died during treatment. Some of their stomachs had
> lesions, many were hemorrhaging badly, and their livers and kidneys
> were damaged. Before the spill, biologists who studied sea otters
> reported that most carcasses they found were either from very young
> otters, or very old ones. In the two years after the spill, many of the dead
> animals were in their prime, between the ages of two and eight. This is
> disturbing, because it indicates that the breeding population may be
> dying from exposure to the oil.

For two more years following the spill, higher than expected numbers of prime-age adult sea otters were found dead in western Prince William Sound. There was also evidence of higher mortality among juveniles in the oiled areas. Although some have been saved, the overall lack of recovery may reflect the extended time required for population growth in a long-lived mammal with a low reproductive rate, but it also may reflect the effects of continuing exposure to hydrocarbons and ingestion of oil-contaminated food, or a combination of both factors. Joanna Burger again:

> In the months following the spill there was a 35 percent decline in the
> number of sea otters in Prince William Sound. In succeeding years there
> appeared to be no recovery, largely because they continued to be
> exposed to the oil. Unweathered oil still remains under and within
> mussel beds, one of their staple food items. Unlike some other animals,
> which change their eating habits when faced with contamination, the

sea otters have not. They continue to eat the contaminated foods in the same contaminated places.

Although more than 2,000 sea otters now live in California waters, they are still listed as threatened under the Endangered Species Act. In 1986, after twenty years of controversy and debate, the Marine Mammal Commission suggested a zonal management system that designated sea otter protection zones and otter-free shellfishing areas. The legislation was intended both to foster California sea otter recovery and to protect valuable southern California shellfish resources from otter predation. In March 1998, a colony of about 150 otters emigrated into the "no-otter" zone south of Point Conception in southern California and swiftly decimated shellfish resources in Little Cojo Bay, a productive area that has sustained shellfisheries for many decades, according to the Sea Urchin Harvesters Association of California. Then, in March 1999, fishermen reported seeing as many as 200 sea otters in the no-otter zone. On moving into new areas, otters quickly reduce exposed populations of their preferred prey (sea urchins, abalone, crabs, and clams), leaving the shells as evidence of their activity. Because they lack blubber for insulation, sea otters must consume 25 percent or more of their body weight in shellfish meat daily. Scientists in California and Alaska have documented a drastic decline of harvestable shellfish in areas that sea otters have recolonized, observing individual otters eating as many as twelve crabs and eighty clams in one day. The battle continues between the people who fish for shellfish and the thick-furred mammals who do the same.

Humans do not have to coat sea otters with oil to affect them. Killer whales feed on a wide range of prey animals, including squid, fish, seals, sea lions, dolphins, and even great whales, but there hadn't been a verified attack on a sea otter until 1991. Then carcasses began appearing regularly, and the number of sea otter sightings dropped alarmingly. The decline was noticed in the Aleutian islands of Adak, Kiska, Amchitka, and Kagalaska, and with the reduction in sea otters, the sea urchin population exploded and promptly grazed the kelp forests into "urchin barrens." "After nearly a century of recovery from overhunting," wrote James Estes and his colleagues in 1998, "sea otter populations are in abrupt decline over large areas of western Alaska." Why did the killer whales suddenly decide to add sea otters to their menu? Estes believes that the decline in their normal prey items—whales and pinnipeds—may have forced them to "fish down the food chain," shifting to smaller and smaller prey animals as the larger ones were removed. Steller's sea lions are in a precipitous decline, and the absence of their usual prey items may have caused the killer whales to behave like the oceans' other top predator, *Homo piscivorus*.

It has recently been learned that California sea otters are succumbing to brain infections caused by the protozoan parasite *Toxoplasma gondii*. In a report published in the *International Journal for Parasitology* in July 2002, veterinarian Melissa Miller and her colleagues noted that 42 percent of the live otters they tested for the parasite and 62 percent of the dead ones were infected. *Toxoplasma gondii* can infect almost any mammal and has been found in virtually every country of the world. The intestinal phase of the parasite's cycle occurs in wild and domesticated cats and produces the parasites' egg cases, which are passed when the cat defecates. How could sea otters be exposed to cat feces? From surface runoff. In some California communities, contaminated water is conducted to coastal streams or directly into the sea from lawns, streets, and open land via storm drains, ditches, and culverts, with virtually no pretreatment. As Josie Glausiusz summarized it in a 2002 article in *Discover* magazine, "curb your cat, save a sea otter."

THE NORTHERN FUR SEAL

Northern fur seals have been known—and thus probably killed for their meat, oil, and skin—for at least 4,000 years. The Aleuts are believed to have colonized the islands at the end of the Alaska Peninsula as early as 2000 B.C., and archaeological evidence indicates that they probably hunted seals there, as well as whales, sea otters, and sea lions. In 1715, Ryoan Terajima published a description and drawing of what Charles Greer and Victor Scheffer (1971) called "the first unambiguous description of a fur seal," but the description contains enough ambiguities, such as "no external ears, only small holes; a forked tail like a goldfish; no forelegs," to open the identification to question. (A fur seal has small but visible external ears, and its foreflippers are plainly visible.) Since aboriginal people are never given credit for "discovering" a species, Georg Wilhelm Steller, the zoologist on Vitus Bering's 1741 voyage, was the one acknowledged as discoverer of the northern fur seal, just as with the jay, sea lion, sea eagle, extinct cormorant, and extinct sea cow that now carry his name.

If one were to place a big male northern fur seal next to its southern counterpart, the difference would be obvious: whereas the southern *Arctocephalus* species all have long, collie-like muzzles, the northern fur seal (*Callorhinus*) has a short pug nose, which, in combination with the seal's powerful neck and shoulders, gives it a characteristic bullnecked, pinheaded appearance. Furthermore, the hairline line ends abruptly at the wrist of *Callorhinus* but extends all the way to the metacarpals in *Arctocephalus*. The

NORTHERN FUR SEAL
(Callorhinus ursinus)

only place the northern and southern species might meet (though without interbreeding) is off the coast of California—for example, at San Miguel, one of the Channel Islands, just off Los Angeles, where a herd of perhaps a hundred northern fur seals has established a beachhead.

Although the northern and southern fur seals are quite different animals in appearance and habit, they share one characteristic: they have a fur coat so luxurious and desirable that it was responsible for their nearly complete elimination. Beneath its grizzled outer coat, *Callorhinus ursinus* has underfur so thick (200,000 hairs per square inch) that water cannot get through to the skin, even when the seal rubs or scratches itself in the water. Of all furbearing animals, only the sea otter has as dense a coat.

The dark-colored, small-headed fur seals with the long, drooping whiskers had fought and bred on their rocky beaches, virtually unmolested by terrestrial predators, for millions of years. No more than a year, however, after the survivors of Bering's expedition returned with reports of hordes of fur seals, sea otters, and foxes just waiting to be harvested, the Russian fur-hunters (*promyshlenniki*) invaded the islands in a slaughtering frenzy; and in the process, as we have seen, they eliminated the sea cow altogether. In the summer of 1786, Russian fur merchant Gerassim Gavrilovich Pribilof came upon an isolated group of fog-shrouded islands in the Bering Sea and saw that they were full of seals—as many as 3 million of them. Pribilof claimed the islands, which consist of St. Paul and St. George, forty miles apart, and almost immediately the *promyshlenniki* began a hunt that netted them 40,000 fur seals and 2,000 sea otters in just the first two years, along with 6,000 blue fox skins and more than 125 tons of walrus ivory.

Shortly after the discovery of the potential riches of the Pribilofs, numerous trading companies began to vie for the lucrative fur trade. The competition was destroying the resource so fast that in 1799, the Russians established the Russian-American Company to bring order to what had become a fur free-for-all. (The company consisted only of Russians, and it was given exclusive rights by the imperial government to trade along the shores of northwestern America.) The slaughter continued more or less unchecked, however, until 1834, when the Russian government prohibited the killing of females. All told, the Russians killed an estimated 2.4 million seals between 1787 and 1867 (Gentry 1980). In 1867, as part of the purchase of Alaska, the United States acquired the Pribilofs, and it handed over the sealing operation to two commercial companies, which escalated the rate of carnage. But they added a new wrinkle: they killed the seals at sea, where it was impossible to differentiate males from females, a particularly wasteful method. Between 1889 and 1909 alone, the heyday of pelagic sealing, more than 600,000 fur seals were collected, the majority of them females, and probably an equal number were wounded, possibly fatally. Under this kind of pressure, northern fur seal populations, which once numbered in the millions, declined dramatically, and by 1911 only an estimated 300,000 were left in the Pribilofs.

Henry W. Elliott surveyed the fur seals in the Pribilof Islands in 1873 and calculated, using an arcane formula he devised, that the islands had 3,200,000 breeding seals and their young and another 1,500,000 nonbreeding seals, making the "grand sum total of the fur-seal life on the Pribilof Islands, over 4,700,000." He reckoned that a million pups were born every year and concluded that "100,000 male seals under the age of five years and over one may be safely taken every year." Unfortunately, his computations, based on his idea that every seal occupied a space two feet square, were much too high. When he returned to the islands in 1890, he found that the fur seal population was only about 20 percent of what he had estimated seventeen years earlier, and he immediately accused the sealers and the government of destroying the herd—which, of course, was exactly what they had done, but largely on the basis of his overestimates.

Even after two hundred years of mass murder on the hauling-out grounds (as distinguished from the rookeries, where the seals mate and give birth), the bulls continued to return, year after year, to the same beaches. Even though, as pinniped expert Roger Gentry (1980) says, "they are highly intelligent, and can learn as quickly as cats or chimpanzees," the bulls learned nothing from the previous experience of their species. Perhaps they were unable to understand that the men with clubs were a threat, but it is more likely that the animals that recognized the approaching danger were killed and were therefore unable to communicate anything at all. Nevertheless, the inability to communicate danger was interpreted as a sign of the seals' "low intelligence" by David Starr Jordan (1898), president of Stanford University and commissioner in charge of the fur seal investigations of 1896–1897:

> The life processes of the fur seal are as perfect as clockwork, but its grade
> of intelligence is low. Its range of choice in action is very slight. . . . A fur
> seal will do what its ancestors have had to do to perfection. If he is forced
> to do anything else he is dazed and stupid. . . . The habits of the fur seal
> are fixed and immutable. No better illustration of this can be cited than
> the fact that having been driven from their hauling ground, culled over,
> and subjected to the excitement of the killing grounds, bachelors* have
> been known to return quietly and take up their positions as if nothing
> had happened. And this thing goes on throughout the season and has
> been going on for half a century.

In the early days of the seal hunt, the skins were used primarily as decorative wall insulation in the homes of the Russian nobility. It was not until the end of the eighteenth century that Catherine the Great, tsarina of Russia from

---

*If northern fur seals were, as Jordan said, fixed and immutable in their behavior, humans could be anything but consistent in their seal designations. In a 1912 report on the northern fur seals, Jordan and George Archibald Clark commented thus on "the eccentricities of the nomenclature of the fur seals": "It is . . . incongruous that a 'cow' should occupy a place in a 'harem' on a 'rookery' and bear a 'pup,' which, if a male, should be known for the first four years of its life as a 'bachelor,' and afterwards a 'bull.' Moreover, it is absurd that this animal, which is in reality more like a bear, should be called a 'seal,' thus confounding it with a distinctly different animal. But these names are all so closely identified with the animal and their history that it is useless to attempt to change them, and so we may expect the 'sea-bears' of the North Pacific to continue to produce 'seal skins,' which although originally and properly taken on land, will remain the product of a 'fishery.'"

1762 to 1796, used them as robes and other outer garments (Murray 1988). Elliott commented as follows in his 1881 study of the fur seal fishery:

> The common or popular notion in regard to seal-skins is that they are worn by those animals, just as they appear when offered for sale; that the fur-seal swims about, exposing the same soft coat with which our ladies of fashion so delight to cover their tender forms during inclement weather. This is a very great mistake; few skins are less attractive than the seal-skin when it is taken from the creature. The fur is not visible; it is concealed entirely by a coat of stiff overhair, dull, gray-brown, and grizzled.

"Prior to 1815, about the only market for the sale of the skins was China, where they were exchanged for tea and other commodities," wrote A. Howard Clark (1887b). "They were mostly dressed in the same manner as hair seal, for the hide. The fur was cut off clean and thrown away as useless, and the hides were used for the manufacture of trunks, valises, &c." An economical way to remove the guard hairs and expose the undercoat seems not to have existed much before 1780, when the Chinese discovered that the underside of the skins could be shaved to loosen the roots of the guard hairs so they could be removed without damaging the dense underfur.

The thick, dark pelts of fur seals (and sea otters) were not for everyday wear; rather, they were luxury items, to be worn conspicuously. The most important nobles wore full fur capes, and lesser lights wore fur belts, sashes, and mittens. If the skin was badly preserved—if it was merely sun-dried rather than salted—the fur was likely to come off eventually. The loose fur, however, could be compressed into felt, a nonwoven fabric made by applying heat, moisture, and pressure to the hairs, causing them to interlock and mat together. The resulting material, though not so soft as that made from the fur of sea otters, was more durable and could be shaped, molded, or cut into different patterns to make clothing, hats, and slippers. It was probably the Americans and British who made the market for sealskins in China, since their desire for tea encouraged the slaughter of the furbearing mammals of northwestern America. Between just 1793 and 1797, 3.5 million sealskins were sent to Canton. Of course, as the furs became scarcer, they became more valuable, and prices soared. The Russians dominated the Chinese market until "Russian America" (Alaska) was sold to the United States in 1867.

The northern fur seal is found as far north of the equator as some of its southern counterparts are found south of it. (In fact, the Pribilof Islands, at latitude 58° N, are farther north than South Georgia, at 54° S, is south.) In early August, after the breeding season ends, the bulls leave their territories and go to sea. Adult females and juveniles follow a few months later, beginning their feeding migration in October. The seals fan out over the North Pacific, some of them getting as far south as Mexico in the eastern Pacific and Tokyo in the west. After spending months at sea, sleeping on the surface by day and feeding on every kind of fish they can catch, including pollock, hake, herring, lanternfish, rockfish, salmon, and cod—as well as squid and even seabirds such as loons and petrels—they begin their return journey. While at sea, northern fur seals are seen either alone or in pairs, rarely in groups of three or four. The great majority return to the rookery of their birth, completing a seven-month migration in which many of them will have traveled more than 7,000 miles. Eighty percent of the 1.2 million living fur seals breed on the Pribilof Islands; the rest breed on Russian-owned islands in the northwestern Pacific, including the Commanders, where some 265,000 breed; the Kuriles (33,000); and tiny Robben Island, twelve miles off Sakhalin in the Sea of Okhotsk, where some 150,000 fur seals come ashore to breed.

The common term for the collective scientific information about a particular animal is *the literature,* as in "the information available in the literature on the breeding habits of the northern fur seal is voluminous." *Callorhinus* also makes several appearances in *real* literature, including Jack London's *Sea Wolf,* in which fur seals are the object of the hunt, and Victor Scheffer's *Year of the Seal,* in which we read about the adventures of the golden seal ("her jacket shines with a yellowish hue, a color variation seen in one of a thousand individuals"). Scheffer, a biologist, studied sealing and seal behavior on Robben Island in 1960 with his interpreter and was the first American to land on the island since Leonhard Stejneger had in 1896. Here is a description from Scheffer's book:

> Robben Island is a low, grassy rock, one-third of a mile long, the summer home of 150,000 seals. The buildings that house the workmen huddle at the base of a plateau covered with nesting murres. . . . At the place where the bachelor seals can be rounded up during the sealing season, the beach is narrow. The workmen cannot easily surround the animals to cut them off from the sea, so they crawl on their hands and knees on the floor of a long sandy tunnel underneath the seals and pop up through a trap door on the water's edge.

Robben Island figures in Jack London's work as well. In 1893, seventeen-year-old London signed aboard the *Sophia Sutherland* out of San Francisco, bound for the seal-rich island of Robben. He worked for twelve weeks as a deckhand and boat-puller, and after the "hunters" had killed the seals, London and the others would peel the skins from the carcasses and salt them away. On his return to California, London won $25 in a writing contest for his description of riding out a typhoon aboard the *Sophia Sutherland,* and his career as a writer was launched (Murray 1988). In 1902, he published *The Sea Wolf,* in which the *Sophia Sutherland* is the *Ghost* and the otherwise anonymous captain is the cruel nihilist Wolf Larsen. The interactions between London's protagonist, Humphrey Van Weyden, and Captain Larsen are obviously fictional; it has been suggested that London saw himself more as Larsen than as the citified Van Weyden. The description of sealers and sealing is probably more accurate for the time, like Herman Melville's account of whaling in *Moby-Dick,* because both of these authors had actually participated— albeit briefly—in the activities they described. Sealing and whaling were bloody and dangerous professions, for the most part discontinued today, but we are fortunate that writers of experience and distinction described the activities that otherwise would have been recorded firsthand only by sea captains or deckhands—if at all. London evidently did not go ashore with the sealing gangs, but he watched as they processed the seals on deck. In his book, Van Weyden, who describes himself as "a scholar and a dilettante" pressed into service aboard the *Ghost,* describes the scene from aboard the sealer:

> It was wanton slaughter, and all for woman's sake. No man ate of the seal meat or the oil. After a good day's killing I have seen our decks covered with hides and bodies, slippery with fat and blood, the scuppers running red; masts, ropes, and rails spattered with the sanguinary color; and the men, like butchers plying their trade, naked and red of arm and hand, hard at work with ripping and flensing-knives, removing the skins from the pretty sea-creatures they had killed.

To the canon of fur seal literature we must add Rudyard Kipling's "The White Seal," included in *The Jungle Book* in 1894. Kipling tells of Kotick, a white seal who travels from his birthplace in the Bering Sea to the Aleutians, where he encounters the seal-hunters. In his search for a safe place unknown to the hunters, the seal goes to the Galápagos Islands ("a horrid place on the Equator"), "the Georgia Islands, the Orkneys, Emerald Island, Little Nightingale Island, Gough's Island, Bouvet's Island, the Crossets, and even to a little speck of an island south of the Cape of Good Hope," only to learn that "seals had come to these islands once upon a time, but men had killed them all off." After completing his world tour, Kotick learns (from the Sea Cows) of a completely protected beach and fights the other males for dominance so he can lead all the seals to "the place where no man comes."

In every one of the *Jungle Book* stories, Kipling appended a poem as an epilogue. To his story of the Aleutian seal rookeries, Kipling added "Lukannon," which he called "a sort of sad seal national anthem":

I met my mates in the morning (and, oh, but I am old!)
Where roaring on the ledges the summer ground-swell rolled.
I heard them lift the chorus that drowned the breakers' song—
The Beaches of Lukannon—two million voices strong.

The song of pleasant stations beside the salt lagoons,
The song of blowing squadrons that shuffled down the dunes,
The song of midnight dances that churned the flame—
The Beaches of Lukannon—before the sealers came!

I met my mates in the morning, (I'll never meet them more!);
They came and went in legions that darkened all the shore,
And through the foam-flecked offing as far as voice could reach
We hailed the landing-parties and we sang them up the beach.

The Beaches of Lukannon—the winter-wheat so tall—
The dripping, crinkled lichens, and the sea-fog drenching all!
The platforms of our playground, all shining smooth and worn!
The Beaches of Lukannon—the home where we were born!

I met my mates in the morning, a broken, scattered band.
Men shoot us in the water and club us on the land;
Men drive us to the Salt House like silly sheep and tame,
And still we sing Lukannon—before the sealers came.

Wheel down, wheel down to southward—O Gooverooska, go!
And tell the Deep Sea Viceroys the story of our woe;
Ere, empty as a shark's egg the tempest flings ashore,
The Beaches of Lukannon shall know their sons no more!

When Kipling wrote "The White Seal," many people believed that the southern and northern fur seals were a single species, and this may be why Kipling assigned it such a wide geographic range. In his 1874 discussion of marine mammals, former whaling captain Charles Melville Scammon wrote that "the Fur Seals have so wide a geographical range—extending nearly to

the highest navigable latitudes in both the southern and northern hemisphere—and are found assembled in such countless numbers at their favorite
resorts that they become at once a source of great commercial wealth; and
among marine mammalia, they are the most interesting we have met with."

By the beginning of the twentieth century, fur seals, wherever they were
taken, were being killed so that people could wear the thick undercoats that
had been the seals' birthright. If eighteenth- and nineteenth-century Chinese
royalty wore fur-trimmed or fur-lined robes, later Americans and Europeans
wanted complete fur coats. In 1893 the Russian fleet visited Toulon, a seaport
in southeastern France, and three years later the tsar himself came to Paris,
setting off a vogue in furs for both men and women. In the past, furs had been
mostly a male prerogative, but now women wanted to wear not only the trimmings but complete fur coats. For those men and women who could afford
them, sealskin coats were the *ne plus ultra*. "In 1900," wrote Busch, "high fashion could demand a full length seal coat, with collar, cuffs, and lapel edging of
sable and ermine lining—adding in the next decade sealskin muffs and hat to
match."

A 1977 report of the National Oceanic and Atmospheric Administration
(NOAA) noted: "From 1889 to 1909, over 600,000 animals were taken—and
at least that many were lost after being wounded and not recovered. The herd
had now been reduced from an estimated two million to probably 300,000."
In 1911, an agreement had been drawn up between Great Britain (which
included Canada at that time), Russia, Japan, and the United States to protect
the seals and prohibit sealing in the North Pacific Ocean except by native
Aleuts. Japan, as a fishing country, regarded the fur seals as competitors for
fish, and thus the agreement never sat well with them. In 1941, they found a
reason (World War II) to abrogate the treaty, and for the next sixteen years
they continued the slaughter. But in 1957, the four nations signed the Interim
Convention on Conservation of North Pacific Fur Seals, which not only outlawed pelagic sealing but also established the International North Pacific Fur
Seal Commission, composed of scientists who would set limits on the number of nonbreeding males that could be taken on the breeding grounds. In
1977, the Fur Seal Commission gave the Soviet Union (now Russia) jurisdiction over the herds of the Commander Islands, Robben Island, and the Kurile
Islands. The United States manages the Pribilof and San Miguel herds, and
Canada and Japan receive a percentage of skins from the other two countries.

Under the treaty, the northern fur seal population slowly climbed from a
low of 200,000 to about 2 million. Then, for reasons not clearly understood,
the population began to drop and then plummeted to approximately 1 million

by 1957, about 870,000 of which lived in the Pribilofs. In its wisdom, the Fur Seal Commission decided that the population was too high and began removing prescribed numbers of breeding females from the Pribilof herd. The 1977 NOAA report explained it thus:

> A reduction of herd size to reach the level of maximum sustainable productivity is based on the premise that if a population is allowed to expand to its natural peak, there is an accompanying increase in the death rate attributable to such factors as insufficient food, disease, and injuries associated with overcrowding.

In other words, they had to kill the seals to save them. This ill-conceived plan was dropped, and the herd once again began to grow.

Nowadays, there is limited subsistence harvesting on the Pribilof Islands, under the jurisdiction of the Marine Mammal Protection Act of 1972. Some 1,400 seals were harvested in the Pribilofs in 1997 and about the same number in 1998, most of them on St. Paul Island. The current fur seal estimate—which includes the populations of the Pribilofs, the Commander Islands, Robben Island, the Kuriles, and San Miguel—is about 1.2 million (Reeves et al. 2002).

~ 6 ~

SLAUGHTER OF THE
SOUTHERN SEALS

The *Seals* are a sort of Creatures pretty well known, yet it may not be amiss to describe them. They are as big as Calves, the head of them like a Dog, therefore called by the *Dutch* the *Sea-hounds*. . . . Their Hair is of divers colors, as black, grey, dun, spotted, looking very sleek and pleasant when they first come out of the Sea. For those at *John Fernando's* have fine sleek short Furr; the like I have not taken notice of any where but in these Seas. Here are always Thousands, I might say probably Millions of them, either sitting on the Bays or going and coming in the Sea round the Island; which is covered with them (as they lie at the Top of the Water playing and sunning themselves) for a Mile or two from the shore. . . . A blow on the Nose soon kills them. Large Ships might here load themselves with Seals-skins, and Trayne-oyl, for they are extraordinarily fat.

—William Dampier, *A New Voyage Round the World,* 1697

William Dampier's mention of *John Fernando's* refers to the Juan Fernández Islands, some four hundred miles west of Valparaíso, Chile, named for the Spaniard who discovered them in 1563. Dampier sailed past the islands in 1684 on his voyage around the world, and the sleek, colorful "Seals" were *Arctocephalus philippii,* now known as Juan Fernández fur seals, so reduced by hunting in the late eighteenth and nineteenth centuries that until recently they were believed to be extinct.

Seven miles long and four miles wide, the Juan Fernández island of Más Afuera (translating to "farther out") is a speck of land hostile to sailors—the crashing surf makes it almost impossible to land—but it was home to the millions of fur seals that crowded its crags and beaches, and if the sealers had to clamber ashore from an overturned boat, well, that was sealing. (The island has been renamed Isla Alejandro Selkirk, after the sailor marooned in 1704 whom Daniel Defoe used as a model for *Robinson Crusoe*.) In 1792, the crew of the sealer *Eliza* killed 38,000 seals on Más Afuera, and in the next six years an extraordinary 3 million skins were taken from there and transported to China. In 1798, Captain Edmund Fanning of the Stonington (Connecticut) sealer *Betsey* took another 100,000 skins and estimated that there were 500,000 to 700,000 seals left on the island. In 1801, a single ship carried a cargo of half a million skins to the London market, but only six years later the islands did not hold enough fur seals to make a visit there profitable. The Spanish authorities then closed the islands to American sealers, a classic case of locking the barn after the horse has been stolen. Sealing ended in the Juan Fernández Islands in the early decades of the nineteenth century, and in modern times the seal population has slowly begun to make a comeback. In 1966, about 200 were seen on Alejandro Selkirk, and now there are believed to be 6,000 seals on the two main islands, the second of which used to be known as Más a Tierra but is now officially Isla Robinson Crusoe.

Like the northern fur seals, whose discovery by Europeans predated theirs, the southern fur seals were slaughtered by the millions for their coats. But unlike *Callorhinus*, which was restricted to the Pribilof and Aleutian Islands, where native hunters had known of them for centuries, southern fur seals of the genus *Arctocephalus* (which means "bear-headed") represented a serendipitous bounty of look-alike species and subspecies. They were "harvested" until they were so close to extinction that the sealers had to scour the Southern Ocean for additional isolated islands with undiscovered fur seal populations. Wherever the early sealers encountered large colonies of *Arctocephalus* fur seals, almost all of which are found in the Southern Hemisphere, they killed them. Mammalogist Joel Asaph Allen summarized the situation in 1898:

> Seal hunting for commercial purposes began here during the closing decades of the last century, and as early as the beginning of the present century the industry had assumed gigantic proportions. The skins at this time and for many years after were taken to the Canton market and exchanged for teas, silks, and other well-known products of the Chinese Empire. . . . The sealing business proved immensely profitable, and led to an indiscriminate and exterminating slaughter. One after another of the populous seal rookeries was visited and reduced to the verge of extermination, followed by new voyages of discovery in search of new sealing grounds, which in turn were quickly despoiled. Every seal that could be obtained was killed, regardless of age or sex.

SUBANTARCTIC FUR SEAL
(Arctocephalus tropicalis)

In the early years of the nineteenth century, as sea otters and northern fur seals were becoming scarcer and scarcer, British and American sealers were discovering the plentiful and equally thick-furred southern versions of the fur seal and heading for the Antipodes. The southern fur seals are all similar in size and shape and differentiated mostly by geography, although some species are larger, some are smaller, and some have longer noses. Charles Repenning, Richard Peterson, and Carl Hubbs (1971) sorted out the various *Arctocephalus* species and subspecies, and their histories turned out to be remarkably—and depressingly—repetitious. The sealers found them, killed a number of them, and then returned home with tales of hordes of seals crowding the beaches, setting off a sealing frenzy that almost always resulted in mass destruction of the resident fur seal population. (Actually, it was in the sealer's interest to keep his discoveries secret and preserve the seals for himself, but word of a crowded beach almost always leaked out.)

The first cargo of fur seal skins obtained south of the equator came from the Falkland Islands in 1784, when Captain Benjamin Hussey of the American ship *United States* returned to Nantucket with 13,000 skins and 300 tons of elephant seal oil. The skins were sold in New York for 50 cents apiece and brought to Canton aboard Captain Simon Metcalfe's brig *Eleanora* in 1787.

There, they were sold for $65,000 ($5 apiece), marking the beginning of the incredibly lucrative fur seal trade with China. (On his return journey, Metcalfe stopped at Nootka Sound and became the first American to trade with the Indians for sea otter skins, amassing 500 skins worth some $20,000.) These seals were *Arctocephalus australis*, known to the sealers as "sea-bears" and to later naturalists as South American fur seals.

A. australis (*australis* means "southern"), known as *lobo de dos pelos* in Spanish, breeds on both coasts of southern South America, from southern Brazil on the Atlantic around Cape Horn and as far north as Peru on the Pacific side. Much of its breeding range overlaps that of the southern sea lion (*Otaria flavescens*), but the fur seals are smaller and have the characteristic pointed muzzle of their kind, whereas the hefty sea lions, especially the bulls, have a thick mane and a short, upturned muzzle. Sea lion skins do not have the dense underfur that inspired the relentless pursuit of the fur seal, but the sealers killed whatever was available, and the two species are completely integrated in catch statistics. Both kinds of eared (otariid) seal were hunted by the indigenous inhabitants of Tierra del Fuego and the southern Chilean fjords. In his 1898 discussion of the southern fur seals, Allen wrote of a Captain Buddington who took 5,000 skins in Tierra del Fuego in 1879–1880 and then only 900 in 1891–1892. When he went back again later, he found that the seals were "practically extinct." From 1876 to 1892, the total "Cape Horn catch," which included all the fur seals taken off the coasts of South America and the various outlying islands and archipelagoes, totaled 113,000 skins.

The British and the Americans were not the only avid sealers in the Southern Ocean. When Spaniard Juan Díaz de Solís explored the coast of Uruguay in 1515, he collected some pelts and brought them back to Spain, which of course encouraged Spanish traders to sail in search of more. The industry has been running since the seventeenth century, and on Uruguay's Lobos Islands it continues today, making it the longest-sustained operation of its kind in the world.

In 1764, when French navigator Louis-Antoine de Bougainville happened upon the Falkland Islands, which lie about 300 miles northeast of Tierra del Fuego, he built a settlement that he called Port Louis. The settlers not only introduced livestock onto the island and cultivated the land but also probably killed the fur seals for their meat, fur, and oil. The following year, Captain John Byron, in HMS *Dolphin*, sailed into a bay that he named Port Egmont, claiming the islands for King George III. In the years of coexistence that followed the initial French and English settlement, visiting sealers clobbered and skinned whatever came ashore, including South American fur seals

(*Arctocephalus australis*) and southern sea lions (*Otaria flavescens*). Adult males (called "wigs" or "bulls") were left alive the longest because their presence ensured that the cows ("clapmatches") would remain on the beach. Young animals were preferred because their skin was softer and unscarred. After the skins were scraped and dried, they were tied into bundles, or "books," and packed in salt in the ship's hold or in barrels. Elephant seals (*Mirounga leonina*) were also killed here, but their skins were not furred. Their insulation against the cold was their blubber, which was boiled down for the oil, similar in quality to whale oil and quite valuable. It was made into odorless lamp fuel and candles and used for waterproofing and dressing leather. The hides, which were thick and strong, were tanned and used to make harnesses, belts, and luggage covers.

Most species of southern fur seal live on subantarctic islands, but one lives on the equator. The Galápagos Islands, off the coast of Ecuador (which of course means "equator" in Spanish), are home to a small population of fur seals of the species *Arctocephalus galapagoensis*. The smallest of all the eared seals, adult females average about four feet in length and weigh no more than 60 pounds; the males (always larger in otariids) are about six feet long and weigh in at about 140 pounds. Hunting in the nineteenth century brought the population to an all-time low, but the seals—like all Galápagos wildlife—are now fully protected as part of an Ecuadorean national park. A 1994 estimate (Bonner 1994) put their number at some 30,000, although they were heavily affected by the El Niño events of recent years. (El Niños, complex meteorologic phenomena that somehow cause the temperature in the tropical Pacific Ocean to rise, which often kills off the small fishes on which fur seals feed; thus, many seals starve.)

The Guadalupe fur seal, *Arctocephalus townsendi,* is the only species of southern fur seal that lives *north* of the equator. It is found only on the remote island of Guadalupe, off the coast of northern Baja California. In the early nineteenth century, hunters killed every one of the fur seals they found there. Either they missed a couple or the survivors were at sea during the holocaust, but somehow this species survived, as did the Juan Fernández fur seal. Guadalupe fur seals were twice thought to have become extinct: no seals were sighted from 1895 until 1926, when sixty were seen, and then again from 1928 until 1949, when a lone male was sighted. Believed to have numbered more than 200,000 before the sealers found it, the Guadalupe fur seal, now fully protected, today numbers only around 2,500 (Riedman 1990).

But these oxymoronic "northern" southern fur seals are an anomaly. The vast majority of this vast multitude lived far below the equator in the

Southern Hemisphere, on such islands as South Georgia. Probably sighted by French explorer Antoine de la Roché in 1675, South Georgia was named after George III by Captain James Cook, the first European to set foot on it a hundred years later. Cook returned to England with tales of abundant elephant and fur seals, and sealers soon turned their attention to the island. Robert Headland wrote this in his 1984 history of the island:

> There were several reasons for the movement of the sealers southwards including: an increasing demand for oil for lighting, textile and leather preparation and other uses prior to the widespread availability of mineral oils; and a demand for fur skins, for fur, felt, and leather preparation. A more unfortunate reason for their spread was that these early sealing operations were of a basically self-limiting nature as virtually no attempt was made at conservation of the stocks by sealers or governments.

Like Bouvet, the Crozets, Kerguelen, Heard, Macquarie, and the South Sandwiches—islands discussed on subsequent pages as we tour the Southern Ocean in search of fur sealing history—South Georgia is considered a subantarctic island, meaning that it is north of the Antarctic continent. Eight hundred miles east of the Falklands and 900 miles from the tip of the Antarctic Peninsula, South Georgia is about 100 miles long and 18 wide. The first sealers arrived there in 1786, led by Thomas Delano of London, captain of the *Lord Hawkesbury.* The next year, the *Lucas,* also out of London, made a similar voyage, and the Yankees soon followed. By 1790, two Connecticut vessels, the *Polly* and the *Nancy,* were sending men ashore with clubs. In 1801, Captain Edmund Fanning's *Aspasia* arrived and then left with 57,000 fur seal skins, the largest number ever taken from South Georgia by one ship (Headland 1984). From November 1800 to February 1801, "sixteen American and British vessels took 112,000 fur-seal skins from this place" (Clark 1887a). Soon thereafter, South Georgia's fur seal stocks had become so depleted that it seemed uneconomical to make voyages there, and the sealers searched elsewhere for something to kill. The respite for the seals was short-lived, though. Soon after the Napoleonic Wars and the War of 1812, as stocks increased again, sealing returned to South Georgia. By 1819, the Russians, led by the intrepid Thaddeus von Bellingshausen, were cruising Antarctic waters in the *Mirnyi* and the *Vostok.* (Bellingshausen, for whom an Antarctic sea is named, was probably the first to sight the Antarctic continent in 1820, even though Americans like to claim it was Nathaniel Palmer, a Connecticut sealer aboard the sloop *Hero.*) In 1825, Captain James Weddell—for whom both a sea and a seal would be named—noted that the take of seals had been so great that "the number of skins brought off from Georgia cannot be estimated at fewer than 1,200,000."

As the South Georgia fur seal populations were again brought low, the South Shetland Islands, just north of the Antarctic Peninsula, were discovered, providing a virgin stock of seals for plundering. The South Shetlands were discovered accidentally in 1819 by Captain William Smith, who was attempting to avoid a gale while rounding Cape Horn in the brig *Williams.* The following year, Captain Christopher Burdick of the Nantucket schooner *Huntress* began killing seals there.* In December 1820 (the Antarctic summer), Burdick and Captain Johnson of New York between them took more than 2,000 seals (Stackpole 1953), and by 1821 no fewer than thirty sealing vessels were anchored off the South Shetlands, sending gangs ashore to kill the fur seals by the hundreds of thousands. Of this fishery, Weddell wrote:

> The quantity of seals taken off these islands by vessels from different parts during the years 1820 and 1821 may be computed at 320,000, and the quantity of sea-elephant oil at 940 tons. . . . The system of extermination was practiced at the South Shetlands; for whenever a seal reached the beach, of whatever denomination, he was immediately killed and his skin taken, and by this means, at the end of the second year, the seals became nearly extinct. The young, having lost their mothers when only three or four days old, of course died, which at the lowest calculation exceeded 100,000.

The subantarctic fur seal (*A. tropicalis*) also breeds on the Tristan da Cunha Islands (pronounced "da *coon*-ya"), a lonely island group in the South Atlantic Ocean roughly halfway between Capetown and Buenos Aires. Its isolation made it no safe haven for fur seals; in 1791 the sealer *Industry* out of Philadelphia took 5,600 skins there, and in 1811 three sealers set up a colony to process sealskins for sale to passing vessels. Edgar Allan Poe mentions these men in his 1838 *Narrative of Arthur Gordon Pym of Nantucket,* a gory horror novel with lengthy digressions on geography, natural history, and history: "In 1811, a Captain Haywood, in the *Nereus,* visited Tristan. He found there three

---

*The South Shetlands, some 560 miles off Tierra del Fuego, consist of two large islands (King George and Livingston) and many smaller ones, including Nelson, Robert, Greenwich, Snow, Smith, Low, Clarence, Gibbs, and Deception, a horseshoe-shaped volcanic caldera that is still active and erupted most recently in 1970. Elephant Island, from which Sir Ernest Shackleton and five men sailed 800 miles to South Georgia in 1914, is one of the South Shetlands.

Americans, who were residing upon the island to prepare sealskins and oil. One of these men was named Jonathan Lambert, and he called himself the sovereign of the country."

Two hundred fifty miles south-southeast of the Tristan da Cunhas, and therefore even more remote, is tiny Gough Island, discovered in 1506 by the Portuguese navigator who also discovered the larger islands, Tristão da Cunha (in Portuguese, *Tristão* is pronounced "tris-*tahng*"). Gough, eight miles long and four miles wide, rises from the South Atlantic as part of the Mid-Atlantic Ridge. Captain Patten of the American schooner *Industry* was the first to visit this island for seals in 1790, collecting 5,500 skins. Its shores are rocky and full of caves, so the sealers hunted by candlelight, locating the seals by the light reflected in their eyes and then clubbing them to death. Few remained by 1820, and from then on, only those sealers who happened to be passing by—perhaps on their way to South Georgia—would anchor off Gough. The same is true of the subantarctic Crozets, the Prince Edward Islands, and St. Paul and Amsterdam Islands: after the initial killing frenzy, too few seals remained to make a stop worthwhile. In 1832, sealing captain Benjamin Morrell observed, "This island used to abound with fur seal and sea elephants, but they were so much annoyed by their relentless persecutors that they have sought more safe and distant retreats, perhaps some lonely isles in the southern ocean as yet unknown to that fell destroyer, man."

Now that the sealing has ended on these tiny outposts, the populations are recovering. Randall Reeves and his colleagues Brent Stewart and Stephen Leatherwood (1992) wrote of modern seals in the region:

> Births increased on St. Paul and Amsterdam islands at annual rates of 16 to 17 percent between 1971 and 1985. Approximately 11,000 pups were born at Amsterdam in 1982. . . . The colony at Gough has increased by 13 percent annually since 1955; nearly 59,000 pups were born there in 1978. . . . The world population was estimated at 270,000 in 1983.

Kerguelen Island, in the southern Indian Ocean, was referred to by sealers as Desolation Island because of its inhospitable remoteness. In Poe's *Narrative of Arthur Gordon Pym,* the eponymous writer, a participant in a mutiny, a shipwreck, and cannibalism, is rescued by the sealer *Jane Guy* and briefly visits Kerguelen and the surrounding islands. "We saw a great many fur seal," says Pym, "but they were exceedingly shy, and with the greatest exertions, we could only procure three hundred and fifty skins in all. Sea-elephants were abundant, especially on the western coast of the mainland [of Kerguelen], but of these we killed only twenty, and this with great difficulty.

On the smaller islands we discovered a good many of the hair seal, but did not molest them." (Because it was Kerguelen, the animals seen by Poe's characters were probably Antarctic fur seals, *Arctocephalus gazella*.) Of the writers who used sealing as a basis for their novels, only Jack London—like Herman Melville before him—actually participated in the "fishery" he chose as the setting for his novel. Like Poe, James Fenimore Cooper never went sealing, but he wrote *The Sea Lions* in 1849, based on the journals of Benjamin Morrell and Edmund Fanning and his early acquaintance with the Connecticut sealers.

Joseph Fuller (1839–1920) was captain of the schooner *Pilot's Bride,* which was wrecked in 1880 on Desolation (Kerguelen) Island. Fuller spent almost a year there before he and his crew were rescued, and in his book (first published in Briton Busch's 1980 *Master of Desolation*) he records the method of killing elephant seals:

> It takes four men to kill a good sized bull. First of all you have to get
> them out of the water holes. This is accomplished by driving them out
> with a stick. You then commence to slaughter bulls first. The reason for
> doing this is because the cows will remain on the beach to protect their
> young, but the bulls will make straight way for the water, and nothing
> but a bullet in the brain or a well-delivered stab will stop them. Some-
> times it takes as high as ten bullets to stop them and then a good
> spearing to kill them. As the elephants do not go over two or three
> hundred feet from the water's edge, they have not far to travel to get
> back. After all of the bulls have been slaughtered, the cows are killed and
> also the young. Those that are small are let go free. Now comes the
> skinning. It takes four men to skin a bull.

The animals were skinned where they lay, and the blubber, with the skin attached, was washed, cut into small pieces, and put into try-pots to be boiled down. These islands are treeless, so what did they use to fuel the fires? Scraps of oil-filled sealskin burned nicely, and so did penguin carcasses. The oil was then casked, and the casks were floated to the ship when it returned, to be stored in the hold and brought home. In the same way New Bedford and Nantucket dominated Yankee sperm whaling, the Connecticut towns of Stonington, New London, and Mystic sent most of the sealers—elephant and fur—to the south.

Fur sealing was not confined to the islands around southern South America. There were seal islands and rookeries throughout the high southern latitudes from New Zealand and Australia to southern Africa. The Cape fur seal or South African fur seal, *Arctocephalus pusillus,* is the largest of the southern fur seals. (*Pusillus* actually means "small," but the name was used because the first specimen was a juvenile.) To differentiate it from the Australian fur seal, *Arctocephalus pusillus doriferus,* which it closely resembles, it has been assigned the subspecific status of *Arctocephalus pusillus pusillus.* The largest bulls can measure almost eight feet from nose to tail and weigh more than 700 pounds; they are dark brownish gray, whereas the females are smaller in size and lighter and softer in color. *A. p. pusillus* breeds along the coast of southern Africa from Namibia to the Cape Peninsula and as far east as Algoa Bay. They are plentiful all along the coast, and twenty-three separate colonies exist on the mainland and offshore rocks and islands. The seals are probably responsible for the numbers of great white sharks in these waters, where entrepreneurs take adventurous divers down in cages for a view of the "man-eater," *Carcharodon carcharias.* In an article about diving with the white sharks off Seal Island, *Jaws* author Peter Benchley observed that "some 84,000 fur seals make their home here, and they covered every inch of the barren rock, barking, lounging, squabbling, and sliding clumsily into the water, where they metamorphosed into creatures of sleek and sinuous beauty."

As with all fur seals, the South African was hunted as soon as it was discovered. In 1488, upon rounding the Cape of Good Hope, Bartolomeu Dias anchored in Table Bay, and João del Infante, in command of Dias' second ship, sailed across the bay to Robben Island and began immediately to slaughter the penguins and seals. The Southern Hemisphere's Robben Island, notorious as a South African political prison (Nelson Mandela spent nearly nineteen years in a tiny cell there), was first named for the seals—*Robben Eiland* in Dutch—as was the Robben Island off Sakhalin. The penguins and seals of Robben Island served as an almost unlimited food supply for the sailors, and by 1503 a massive slaughter of these animals was in progress. For the next two centuries, Robben Island was used as a pantry to feed the sailors on passing ships, as a postbox for their letters, and occasionally as a prison for miscreant sailors. Dutch settlers took 45,000 seals from the islands of the Cape of Good Hope in 1610, and by the eighteenth century the seal population had plummeted. The government took control in 1946, and seals subsequently have recovered such that southern Africa is now the only area where fur seals are still commercially hunted.

More than 2 million Cape fur seals have been killed since 1900, mostly next door to South Africa in what is now Namibia, where an annual commercial hunt of the seals takes place between August and November. Fur seals in South Africa have been protected since 1973 by the Sea Birds and Seal

Protection Act, which affords the seals general protection but allows the government to grant permits to kill them at specific colonies. The average annual pup kill for 1970–1979 was 73,400 (Cressie and Shaughnessy 1987). Between 1973 and 1982, an average of 18,750 pups and 530 adult males were killed each year, and from 1983 until the official suspension of sealing in South Africa in 1990, the annual average was 3,500 pups and 4,300 adult males, although these figures were highly variable between years. In addition, the Food and Agriculture Organization of the United Nations estimates that some 4,000 Cape fur seals are killed every year in pelagic purse seine fisheries for anchovy and pilchard.

In 1994, an estimated 200,000 seals died unexpectedly on the Namibian coast, almost certainly from malnutrition and starvation caused by a fish scarcity brought about by environmental conditions. The Namibian quota for the 2000 season was set at 60,000 pups and 7,000 adult males, almost double the 1999 quota. The Namibian government has claimed that the increased hunt is needed to protect fisheries, a claim countered by environmental groups, which point out that no scientific evidence indicates that an increased seal hunt would actually benefit Namibian fisheries. The pups are clubbed to death and the adult males are shot. The fur seal population that remains after hunting is exploited as a major tourist attraction.

Thousands of miles away, the Cape fur seal's cousin, the Australian fur seal (*A. p. doriferus*), is found off Tasmania and New South Wales and along the coast of Victoria. The females of this species are silvery gray with yellowish underparts, the males are larger and darker, and the pups are black at birth. In 1798, when British surgeon and navigator George Bass (for whom the Bass Strait, between Tasmania and mainland Australia, is named) explored the coast of Victoria, he reported large colonies of fur seals, and it was only a short time before the *Nautilus* left Sydney on Australia's first sealing voyage. The crew brought back 9,000 Australian fur seal skins, marking the beginning of the sealing industry (King 1983). In less than two decades the Australian seal populations were decimated, but it was not until 1891, after most of them were gone, that any official protection was granted to the beleaguered species. The Australian fur seal is not to be confused with the Australian sea lion, *Neophoca cinerea,* a completely different animal that is sometimes known locally as the "hair seal," is more heavily built, and has a chunky muzzle. Although the fact is not visually apparent, *Neophoca*—like all sea lions—does not have the dense underfur of the fur seals. But like the fur seals, *Neophoca* was nearly exterminated by commercial sealers before the end of the nineteenth century (Walker and Ling 1981a).

Macquarie Island is an undulating plateau 21 miles long but only 2 miles wide that lies 600 miles south of New Zealand in the Southern Ocean. No trees or shrubs grow there; the vegetation is primarily tussock grass. Early in the nineteenth century, seal-hunters began coming to Macquarie from all over the world. When Richard Siddons landed on the island in 1812, he found the Russian explorer Thaddeus von Bellingshausen already there. Bellingshausen's journal (1825, translated by Frank Debenham) reads:

> Having killed the sleeping animals the men cut off the blubber with a knife, and put it in a boiler placed on stones with room for a fire beneath it, which they kindle with lumps of the same fat. . . . We then went along the sandy beach so as to observe the sea elephants, which lie dormant for two or three months without moving from their place. One of the sealers accompanied us. He had with him an implement which consisted of a club 4½ feet long and two inches thick. The end was bell-shaped, 4 or 5 inches in diameter, and bound with iron studded with sharp nails. When we approached a sleeping sea elephant the trader hit him . . . over the bridge of the nose; the sea elephant opened its mouth and gave a loud and pitiful roar. It had already lost all power of motion. Then the man took out his knife . . . and stuck it into its thick neck four times.

By 1820, the fur seals of Australia's Macquarie Island had been slaughtered with such ruthless efficiency that scientists today cannot identify the species that lived there. Sealing continued sporadically on the islands in the decades after 1916, when Sir Douglas Mawson, Australia's foremost Antarctic explorer, lobbied successfully for revocation of all sealing licenses. The island was designated a wildlife sanctuary in 1933, and in recent times, the Antarctic fur seal (*A. gazella*) and New Zealand fur seal (*A. forsteri*) have been identified on the island. Penguins and elephant seals have come back, and about 1,000 fur seals land on the island each summer.

Even though the earth's circumference at latitude 50° S is considerably smaller than it is at the equator, there is a lot of open water there, broken only by the southern tip of South America and a few scattered islands. (There is no land at all at 40° S; there, the wind can blow around the world uninterrupted.) It is more than a little difficult to imagine sailing ships, largely at the mercy of the winds, finding all those lonely, isolated islands in the vastness of the Southern Ocean. But find them they did, and they often found them alive with fur seals. Within a couple of years, for example, after the seals of the South Shetlands were discovered by William Smith in the *Williams* in 1819, 940 tons of oil and 32,000 skins were loaded for shipment (Busch 1985). Neither the South Orkney Islands, discovered in 1821 by Captain George Powell in the *Dove,* nor the South Sandwich Islands, discovered by Captain James Cook, had significant seal populations. But Heard Island did. This island in the South Indian Ocean was not found until 1833, when Captain James Heard, in the Boston sealer *Oriental,* accidentally came upon it. But Heard Island is a barren, ice-fortressed rock with raging surf, treacherous rocks, and no safe anchorage, so sealers from Kerguelen Island, 260 miles to the northwest, would be dropped off on the rainy, windswept island and stay for three months or more, killing fur and elephant seals, living in rock-and-canvas huts, and subsisting on a diet of seal flippers, salt beef, and penguin eggs.

After an Australian National Antarctic Research Expeditions station was established on Heard Island in 1947, not a single fur seal birth was recorded until 1963, but there has subsequently been some recovery. In the summer of 1986–1987, there were 172 pups born, and in the next summer, 248. The population seems to be increasing an exponential rate, which may be partly attributable to migrants from South Georgia—more than 4,000 miles away —seeking less crowded conditions (Shaughnessy and Goldsworthy 1990). In any case, by 1993 the number of Antarctic fur seals on Heard Island had grown to an estimated 21,280, according to researchers Peter Shaughnessy, Erwin Erb, and Ken Green (1998).

New Zealand is a thousand miles from Port Jackson (later renamed Sydney) across the Tasman Sea, and whalers and sealers visiting the new colony probably heard about the large islands to the southeast. In 1792, the British sealer *Britannia* under Captain Raven arrived at Dusky Sound, a fjord on the southwestern coast of South Island, and left a gang of a dozen men, who killed 45,000 seals in a ten-month period. Their hut was the first European dwelling in New Zealand (Busch 1985). American and Australian sealers typically would leave a gang ashore at a promising spot, and the men would kill seals, prepare the skins, and store them until the ships returned to pick them up. After 1810, their success at killing was so great that they had to range farther afield to find fur seal colonies, and they sailed to Campbell Island, Macquarie Island, the Antipodes, and the Auckland Islands to the south. But by 1829 they had eradicated those seals too, and Captain Benjamin Morrell of the schooner *Wasp* wrote, "Although the Auckland Isles once abounded with numerous herds of fur and hair seal, the American and

English seamen engaged in this business have made such clean work of it as scarcely to leave a breed; at all events there was not one fur-seal to be found on the 4th of January, 1830" (McNab 1913).

The New Zealand fur seal, *Arctocephalus forsteri,* naturally enough, is found in New Zealand waters, but in another attempt to confuse taxonomists, it also occurs around the South Neptune Islands and Kangaroo Island in South Australia, and, in Western Australia, off the Archipelago of the Recherche. (White sharks, which pay little attention to taxonomic niceties, probably feed on New Zealand fur seals even when they are in South Australian waters.) In New Zealand, these seals are found off the coasts of North Island and South Island and also on nearby island groups. George Forster, the botanist on Captain James Cook's second voyage, sketched a "sea-bear" in 1773 and had his name attached to *Arctocephalus* by French zoologist Rene Lesson in 1828. After Captain Frederick Hasselburg found Macquarie Island and Campbell Island in 1810 and collected 15,000 skins on his first visit, the population was so reduced that sealers bypassed the islands because it was no longer profitable to look for fur seals there (Bailey and Sorensen 1962). Campbell Island was named after the wife of Lachlan Macquarie, governor of New South Wales, as was sealer Richard Siddons's vessel the *Campbell Macquarie* (Rose 1984). The pinnipeds have now recolonized the island, and many rare birds breed there, including the yellow-eyed penguin and the royal albatross. Except for occasional visits by meteorologic station workers, the island is uninhabited.

According to a recent guide to New Zealand, the Chatham Islands are "flung in icy seas east of New Zealand in the Southern Ocean on the way to Antarctica . . . [they are] lonely, windswept places where whalers have been wrecked, where sea mammals and sub-Antarctic bird life have dominion, and where few mainland New Zealanders have ever ventured" (McLauchlan 1985). The islands, 500 miles east of Christchurch (South Island), are the easternmost outpost of New Zealand, first settled around A.D. 1200 by Polynesian mariners known as the Moriori, who became stranded there and developed their own culture. In 1791, Captain William Broughton in the *Chatham,* having become separated from George Vancouver's *Discovery* en route to Tahiti from Dusky Bay, on New Zealand's eastern coast, became the first European to discover the Chatham Islands. Upon landing on the main island (now known as Chatham Island), his crew was greeted by "some 2,000 unarmed natives, most of whom were covered with mattes or sealskins" (Richards 1982). In November 1807, Captain Mayhew Folger of the Nantucket sealer *Topaz* (who three months later would find the last of the *Bounty* mutineers on Pitcairn

Island) landed at Chatham and killed 600 fur seals. When the first sealers arrived there in 1815, they saw that the Moriori were killing the abundant fur seals in small numbers, so they joined in on the carnage and what would eventually be the destruction of the Chatham Island fur seal population.

New Zealand historian Rhys Richards scoured the literature for information about Chatham Island sealing and, in 1982, published *Whaling and Sealing at the Chatham Islands,* surely one of the most meticulous chronicles of any of the Southern Ocean seal fisheries. Of the early period (1807–1830), he wrote:

> As elsewhere, the slaughter would have been total and thoughtlessly without regard for the future. Given that seals, especially females, are migratory rather than pelagic, returning seasonally to the place of their birth in preference to all else, the foreign sealers apparently fulfilled the Morioris' prediction that the rookeries on the main island would be exterminated, and the timid remnants driven off by continuous harassment to insignificant outliers where breeding facilities would not provide for recreation in their former numbers. Certainly Chatham Island appears to have more sites suitable for rookeries than are occupied today, and even on the outliers the replenishment of stocks still seems to have stayed at a level far, far below that which sustained the sealing industry through its initial bonanza and well into the early half of last century.

The Antipodes were named because they are at latitude 50° S, approximately the same latitude south that Greenwich, England, is north. (*Antipodes,* "opposite-footed," as people dwelling on the opposite side of the globe were once believed to be, refers to diametrically opposite parts of the earth.) This barren, uninhabited group of islands about 450 miles southeast of New Zealand was once—and still is—home to a breeding population of New Zealand fur seals. The islands were first sighted by Captain Waterhouse in HMS *Reliance* in 1800, but the first sealing gang did not land there until 1804, when Captain Pendleton of the *Union* put twelve men ashore. In 1806, some 60,000 skins were collected from the Antipodes by the American sealer *Favorite,* at the same time several other vessels were collecting in these islands. Richards (1994) reported that the sealer *Pegasus* collected more than 100,000 skins in the Antipodes (or Penantipodes, as the islands were sometimes called), but they were imperfectly cured and had to be dug out of the hold and sold as manure. It is estimated that, all told, a quarter of a million fur seals were killed and skinned in the Antipodes from 1804 to 1809; this figure, based on skins shipped or sold, does not include the actual number of seals killed (Richards 1982). When the Boston sealer *Topaz* visited the Antipodes in 1807, her gangs found only 3,000 fur seals to kill.

The mass slaughter of southern fur seals—especially the 3.5 million that had been harvested on Más Afuera—caused the Chinese market for sealskins to collapse in 1807, and many of the Sydney merchants who had subsidized the sealers went bankrupt. (For some, the downfall was so rapid that they were unable or unwilling to relieve sealing crews left on the various islands; Richards noted in 1994 that "in several cases it was some years before these abandoned gangs were uplifted. Presumably some never were.") For all intents and purposes, sealing had ended in the Antipodes by 1810: once again, there were not enough seals left to make a visit worthwhile.

Fur seals everywhere in the Southern and Northern Hemispheres are almost entirely predictable with regard to the beaches where they come ashore; they return year after year to the same breeding ground, usually the one where they were born. Once these beaches were discovered, the sealers themselves could return there and continue to massacre the seals until they were either gone altogether or too scarce to bother with. Their methods were brutally simple. They sailed in small ships, rarely more than 300 tons, equipped with a cutter that enabled them to work in shallow water. The crew might number as many as twenty men, who came ashore and clubbed and stabbed the seals, which made no effort to escape. A bull might make a rush at the men, but he was easily dispatched, and the doe-eyed cows lay there and watched until it was their turn to be clubbed, stabbed, and flayed. The bloody skins were pegged out and salted (or left to dry in the sun, if there was any) and carried back to the ship, where they were packed for transport. If the sealing was successful, every available space might be packed with tiers of dry skins, and the little ship would head across the Pacific for Canton, where the prices were much higher than in London.

Because the Chinese had perfected methods of curing them, air-dried skins fetched the highest prices in the Canton markets. An agreement between a Canton merchant and Captain John Ebbets of the *Enterprise* showed that the merchant was willing to purchased Ebbets' cargo, which consisted of sea otter furs, beaver skins, and sealskins, at the price of one dollar for every undressed skin and two dollars for every dressed one. Chinese furriers used the skin, with the thick underfur attached, to make garments for the wealthy; the guard hairs, once removed, were used to make felt clothing for the less privileged classes. At first, the guard hairs were cut off or picked out by hand—labor was cheap in China. But after Thomas Chapman of

London spilled beer on a trunk lined with fur seal skin and the guard hairs came away as he tried to clean up the damage, he developed a chemical process for removing the hairs: the skins were repeatedly soaked in a mixture of soap and pearl ash (potassium carbonate) until the guard hairs were loosened and could be scraped off. Not only did Chapman's process enable the traders to sell the thick underfur to the Chinese, but the loosened guard hairs were used to make felt hats, and these "beaver" hats could be manufactured more cheaply for British and American markets.

The total number of fur seals killed in the Southern Hemisphere will never be known, but in *The War against the Seals: A History of the North American Seal Fishery* (1985), to date the most comprehensive study of this sanguinary chapter in world history, sealing historian Briton Busch attempted a recapitulation:

Más Afuera	3,000,000
Galápagos, Guadalupe, and Baja California	150,000
Farallon Islands	150,000
South Shetlands	250,000
South Georgia	1,200,000
Macquarie and other New Zealand islands	150,000
Bass Strait (Australia)	150,000
Tristan, Bouvet, and other Indian Ocean islands	150,000

Busch's study covers mostly the North American sealers, and the total for the fisheries listed here is 5.2 million. If we add the fur seals killed in South Africa by South Africans, in South America by South Americans, and in Australia and New Zealand by locals, we can probably come close to the total by doubling that figure. The "fatal impact," as writer-historian Alan Moorehead (1966) called it, of the arrival of humans was the near elimination of the fur seals. Moorehead wrote:

No one will ever know how many whales and seals were killed in the southern ocean. . . . Was it ten million or fifty million? Figures become meaningless; the killing went on and on until there was virtually nothing left to kill, nothing at any rate that could be easily and profitably killed. . . . In the South Shetlands a single ship would expect to take as many as 9,000 seals in three weeks, and there is a record of two ships and sixty men demolishing 45,000 in one season. And since every pelt was worth a guinea—in some markets like Canton in China very much more—there was every inducement for the slaughter to go on to the bitter end. An end, however, there had to be; and by the eighteen-thirties fur seals in the southern ocean were virtually extinct, and sea lions and sea-elephants were dying out as well.

Connecticut sealers continued in the Antarctic well into the twentieth century, but there were fewer and fewer seals, and eventually the enterprise was abandoned. (In 1904, when the first Norwegian whalers came to a sealing station in Prince Edward Cove on South Georgia Island, they found the rusting cauldrons the sealers had used to boil down the elephant seals, so they named the place *Grytviken,* or Cauldron Bay. Grytviken eventually became the most important whaling station on South Georgia and did not close until 1964.)

Despite what looked like a concerted effort to eliminate them, no *Arctocephalus* species was finally exterminated, although *A. philippi* and *A. townsendi* came close. Left to their own devices, fur seals are incredibly prolific, and once the killing had ceased, they began to recover. On South Georgia, the population of *A. gazella,* which had been reduced to perhaps 100 animals, has bounced back with such vigor that there are now a million fur seals there, and smaller, thriving colonies breed on the South Shetlands and the South Orkneys as well.

If people had continued to favor the thick, dark fur of fur seals—or if synthetic insulation had not been invented—the fur seals probably would have been eliminated from the face of the earth. Their survival, more a function of changing clothing styles than a manifestation of any sort of conservation imperative, is one of the few bright spots in the shifting conditions pertaining to the welfare of marine mammals.

~ 7 ~

LIONS AND ELEPHANTS

The dense undercoat of the fur seals—northern and southern—made them the targets of a fishery so concentrated that they were hunted to the very ends of the earth, with many species pushed close to annihilation. Fur seals are distinguished from sea lions in that the former have abundant underfur and the latter do not. Like the fur seals, sea lions are otariids—pinnipeds with exterior ear flaps, as opposed to phocids, which have only ear holes—and they were also hunted by the roving sealers. Although their pelts were not nearly as valuable as those of their relatives, they were slaughtered in numbers great enough to endanger the survival of the species. The pelts of elephant seals were worthless, but for the layer of blubber that lay beneath the skin, they too were slaughtered by the tens of thousands.

HOOKER'S SEA LION

The New Zealand, or Hooker's, sea lion (*Phocarctos hookeri*), once found on the beaches of North Island and South Island, is now seen during breeding season only on the scattered and isolated islands south of the two main islands. Most are found on the Auckland Islands, some 290 miles southwest of South Island. The Aucklands, discovered by British whaling captain Abraham Bristow in 1806, consist of six rocky crags: Auckland (the largest), Enderby, Dundas, Adams, and the two Figure-of-Eight Islands. (The entire group was named, as was the capital, for George Eden, earl of Auckland and viceroy of India.) The islands were also home to the New Zealand fur seal, *Arctocephalus forsteri;* with its more valuable fur, it was the pinniped of choice for sealers in the Aucklands. But the massive bulls and svelte cows of *Phocarctos hookeri* were too tempting to ignore. Even if their coats were not so fine, they were just sitting there on the beach, ripe for harvesting. Two decades of concentrated slaughter almost wiped them out, but when Thomas Musgrave of the *Grafton* was shipwrecked on the Aucklands in 1864, there

HOOKER'S SEA LION
(Phocarctos hookeri)

were still enough sea lions for him and his men to subsist on—in fact, his journal was written in sea lion blood (King 1983).

Hooker's sea lion (named for Sir Joseph Hooker, the botanist with the British Antarctic expedition of 1839–1843) is a typical sea lion in that the bulls are considerably larger and darker than the females. The black, 900-pound bull has a mane of longer hair that covers his massive head, neck, and shoulders; the silvery gray female is much more delicate and has large, liquid eyes. When the bulls haul out in early December (the Antipodean summer), they establish and defend a territory against all interlopers, each assembling a harem of ten to twelve cows. About a week after the pups are born, the male mates with the females, and by the end of February they have all moved off the beaches and headed out to sea, where they will feed for the next eight months.

Somewhere around 1870, French settlers introduced rabbits onto one of the Aucklands, Enderby Island, and there are now some 4,000 there, digging deep burrows just above the rookeries. Hooker's pups, naturally curious, as are all little sea lions, wriggle into the burrows, become trapped, and suffocate. It is estimated that 10 percent of the pups die in these burrows every year (Bruemmer 1983). With a total population of approximately 7,000 animals, a loss of 700 per year is significant.

AUSTRALIAN SEA LION

The Australian sea lion, *Neophoca cinerea,* is found along the beaches of southern Australia, from the island known as Houtman Abrolhos on the western coast north of Perth all along the Great Australian Bight to Kangaroo Island and Adelaide in South Australia. The greatest concentration—some 4,000 animals—is around Spencer Gulf and Dangerous Reef. This concentration of sea lions has not gone unnoticed by the great white shark, which also concentrates here, particularly to feed on the sea lions but also because large numbers of sport divers come to this area to submerge themselves in cages and come face to face with the man-eater. In the process, they fill the shark's domain (and belly) with all sorts of tender victuals, such as tasty chunks of tuna and horsemeat, which the shark doesn't have to bother chasing.*

The species was heavily hunted for its hide and oil in the eighteenth and nineteenth centuries, before which time its range extended as far as the islands of the Bass Strait. The Australian sea lion is now listed as rare under South Australian legislation, which has afforded it full legal protection since 1964, and it has Special Protected Species status in Western Australia, where it has been legally protected since 1892. The sea lion has also been protected under Australian national legislation since 1975 and is listed as Rare in the *IUCN Red List of Threatened Species.* Some small colonies in South Australia are protected within the Great Australian Bight Marine Park, which was created in 1996 by the South Australian government and expanded in 1998 by the national government.

Evidence is mounting that the size of the Australian sea lion population has leveled off and may now be declining. Recent research has shown unexplained dramatic fluctuations in pup mortality rates, which may be endangering the species. The pup mortality rate during the 1999 breeding season at the Dangerous Reef colony in South Australia, for example, was 41 percent, a record high for the colony. It is thought that the likely main causes of the high mortality were infanticide by aggressive adult sea lions and entanglement in

---

*There have even been instances of human beings—inadvertently, to be sure—putting themselves on the white shark's menu. In the early 1960s, the Australian spearfishing championships were held off Aldinga Beach, just south of Adelaide, and three consecutive years saw casualties among participants: in 1961, Brian Rodger was attacked; in 1962, Geoff Corner was killed; and in 1963, Rodney Fox was attacked and nearly killed, requiring 462 stitches. Abalone divers are also at risk when diving in these waters; in 1974, Terry Manuel was killed. In March 1985 at Peake Bay, South Australia, Shirley Ann Durdin was bitten in half while snorkeling (Ellis and McCosker 1991).

fishing nets and crayfish pots, with other factors such as food shortages a possibility. Some shooting also occurs, but the extent of this is unknown.

CALIFORNIA SEA LION

Everybody knows the California sea lion, star performer at zoos, oceanaria, and circuses as it toots a horn, claps its flippers, and barks sonorously on command. These "trained seals" are, of course, sea lions, as evidenced by their visible ear flaps and hind flippers that they can rotate forward so as to move quadrupedally on land. (They can also rotate their whiskers, or vibrissae, forward—the ball seen balancing on the animal's "nose" is actually being cradled in a basket of whiskers.) *Zalophus californianus* males are much less amenable to training, so the performers are likely to be either females or males not old enough to have become ornery.

In the wild, California sea lions are found breeding on islands all along the coast. San Miguel hosts the largest breeding colony, but there are others on San Nicolas Island, Santa Barbara Island, the Anacapa Islands, Catalina Island, South Farallon Island, and Año Nuevo Island. (Those pictures of sea

CALIFORNIA SEA LION
(Zalophus californianus)

lions peeking from second-story windows of abandoned buildings were taken on Año Nuevo.) Although noisy sea lions begging for food seem to be permanent residents of some places, such as Santa Cruz, these sea lions do migrate like others of their species, fanning out far offshore for feeding before returning to their breeding grounds.

In 1970, an epidemic of leptospirosis broke out among the sea lions of the California coast, perhaps somehow transmitted by goats, which are known carriers of the bacterium. Symptoms include high fever, loss of appetite, and listlessness. This often fatal disease is spread via urine, allowing rapid transmission among animals in the same region (Steller's sea lions in the same waters were not affected, however).

There is a subspecies of *Zalophus* in the Galápagos Islands that probably numbers around 40,000 animals, and another in Japanese waters that numbers zero. During the early twentieth century, *Zalophus* sea lions evidently were common off the Pacific coasts of the Japanese islands and also in the Seto Inland Sea, off Kyushu, in the Sea of Japan, and even off Korea. By the 1950s, however, the numbers seemed to be plummeting, and they were reported only from Takeshima Island, an isolated speck of rock in the southern Sea of Japan. According to marine mammalogist Dale Rice (1998), *Zalophus japonicus* is "probably EXTINCT; last credible report was 50 to 60 individuals on Takeshima in 1951." The Japanese sea lion and the Caribbean monk seal seem to have become extinct at approximately the same time—the mid-1950s—and they represent the most recent documented extinctions of marine mammals.

SOUTH AMERICAN (SOUTHERN) SEA LION

The South American sea lion, *Otaria flavescens,* has given its scientific name to all the eared seals, now known as otariids. (And with good reason: *otarion* means "little ear" in Greek and refers to the external ear flaps.) The South American sea lion—*lobo marino* to the locals—is found all along the Atlantic and Pacific coasts of South America, from northern Peru around Cape Horn and as far north as Uruguay. The largest concentrations are on the Isla de Lobos and associated Uruguayan islands, Península Valdés in Patagonia, and the Falklands. Unlike most otariids, the *lobos* do not migrate but remain on the same beaches year-round, segregating into bull-dominated harems during the breeding season. Both sexes are golden brown, and the bulls have a thick mane. The adult bull's head and neck look too big and heavy for his body, and his pug-nosed, upturned snout is characteristic. The pups are born

SOUTH AMERICAN SEA LION
(Otaria flavescens)

in December and January, and in some areas—particularly Punta Norte on Península Valdés—they are preyed upon by killer whales that come right out of the water and onto the beach to take them, as shown in those spectacular nature documentaries.

Not nearly as photogenic as the black-and-white orcas, *Otaria*'s other predators have been far more successful in reducing the population. The sea lions around Tierra del Fuego were hunted by prehistoric peoples, who utilized them for food and skins. Sealers have hunted along the coasts of Chile and Argentina since the sixteenth century, killing the sea lions for meat, skins, and oil. The government of Uruguay has been in the sealing business since the early nineteenth century, harvesting *lobos* for skins used to make leather goods. British and American sealers worked the coast of Chile in the early decades of the nineteenth century; between 1821 and 1822, more than 52,000 pelts were collected from the area between Mocha Island and Santa María Island. By the 1860s, Chilean nationals were insisting on their right to kill their own sea lions, and they did so until 1907, when the government closed down the fishery. They reopened it in 1976; today, under a quota system, the hunt concentrates on the pups, which are known as "poppies."

In Argentina, more than a quarter of a million *lobos* were killed between 1917 and 1953, and it has been estimated that sealers killed more than 80 percent of the sea lion population in the northern part of the country. Between

1928 and 1939, the Falkland Island Dependencies Sealing Company killed 40,000 South American sea lions, and the Falklands sea lion population, which ran as high as 300,000 in the 1930s, is now around 30,000. In 1990, the total population of *O. flavescens* was believed to be 275,000 and declining (Riedman 1990, citing Vaz-Ferreira 1981).

When cetologists Giorgio Pilleri and Margarete Gihr visited Uruguay's Isla Verde and Isla Coronilla in 1977, they wanted to observe the behavior of *Otaria flavescens,* but instead they observed the behavior of *Homo sapiens.* The local fishermen believed that the *lobos* were destroying their nets and taking the fish that were their rightful property, so they were systematically killing the adult seals of Isla Verde. From a 1953 population of some 2,400, Pilleri and Gihr discovered, the total population on the two islands had plummeted to 28 animals in just twenty-five years. They issued an urgent plea for conservation measures.

Throughout its range, the population of *Otaria flavescens* is dwindling, probably because of drowning deaths in nets of the increased commercial fisheries for squid and fish. By and large, however, the reduction in hunting has left the species relatively safe for the moment. The latest estimates suggest that there are about 100,000 *lobos marinos* along the coast of Chile; about 20,000 of these are in Peru, 50,000 in Argentina, and 30,000 in Uruguay (Reeves et al. 2002).

STELLER'S SEA LION

The largest of all the eared seals, Steller's sea lion (*Eumetopias jubatus*) is another species first described by Vitus Bering's intrepid naturalist. Also known as the northern sea lion, Steller's is the largest of all sea lions. Bulls can grow to ten feet long and weigh well more than a ton; the dainty females reach a mere seven feet in length and tip the scales at a modest 600 pounds. The bulls are tan or cork-colored, noticeably darker on the head and neck; the females are lighter; and the newborn calves are black. They breed all around the perimeter of the North Pacific Ocean, in a wide arc that runs from the Channel Islands in southern California north past Oregon, Washington, and southeastern Alaska and through the Aleutian Islands, where the largest colonies are found. The arc then sweeps westward to incorporate the Commander Islands, the Kamchatka Peninsula, and the Sea of Okhotsk, including Sakhalin Island. *Eumetopias jubatus* also establishes breeding colonies on the Kurile Islands and the northern Japanese island of Hokkaido.

It is hard to imagine such abundant, massive animals as being "incidental,"

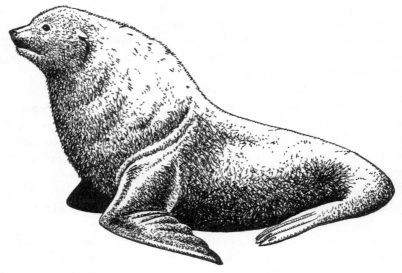

STELLER'S SEA LION
(Eumetopius jubatus)

but because their range overlaps that of the northern fur seal and the northern elephant seal in so many areas, sealers would often kill Steller's sea lions during their sealing and "elephanting" harvests. Compared with that of the fur seal, the pelt of Steller's sea lion is almost of a noncommercial quality, but the sealers killed the sea lions anyway. For the Aleutian natives, however, the sea lion was necessary to their way of life, as Henry W. Elliott (1887b) described:

> Although the sea-lion has little or no commercial value for us, yet to the service of the natives themselves . . . it is invaluable; they set great store by it. It supplies them with its hide, mustaches, flesh, fat, sinews, and intestines, which they make up into as many necessary garments, dishes, &c. They have abundant reason to treasure its skin highly, for it is covering to their neat "bidarkies" and "bidarrahs," the former being the small "kyak" of Bering Sea, while the latter is a boat of all work, exploration, and transportation. These skins are unhaired by sweating in a pile; then they are deftly sewed and carefully stretched over a light keel and frame of wood, making a perfectly water-tight boat that will stand, uninjured, the softening influence of water for a day or two at a time, if properly air-dried and oiled.

In California in the early 1900s, northern sea lions were killed because fishermen complained that they were eating the fish that belonged to the fishermen, and later, in the Aleutians, pups were killed for their skins to make clothing. Most pinnipeds have a baculum, or penis bone, and it is not surprising that these bones were ground up and the powder sold as an aphrodisiac in some Asian countries. In *The War against the Seals,* an aptly named study of North American sealing, Briton Busch discusses "trimmings," which were composed of the bull seals' genitals, gallbladder, and whiskers. The penis and testicles were powdered and believed to impart virility to humans; the gallbladder was used as medicine, and the whiskers made toothpicks or opium-pipe cleaners. The whole "set"—genitals, gallbladder, and whiskers—brought $2 to $5 in San Francisco. Because the pelts were not particularly useful, the animals were often killed just for the "trimmings" and the carcasses left on the beach to rot. Charles Melville Scammon, who was a sealer before he turned to whaling, wrote about a herd of northern sea lions killed on Santa Barbara Island in 1852:

> The herd at this time numbered seventy-five, which were soon dispatched, by shooting the largest ones, and clubbing and lancing the others, save one Sea Lion, which was spared to ascertain whether it would make any resistance by being driven over the hills beyond. The poor creature only moved along through the prickly pears that covered the ground, when compelled by his cruel pursuers; and at last, with an imploring look and writhing in pain, it held out its fin-like arms, which were pierced with thorns, in such a manner as to touch the sympathy of the barbarous sealers, who instantly put the sufferer out of his misery by the stroke of a heavy club. As soon as the animal is killed, the longest spires of its whiskers are pulled out, then it is skinned, and its coating of fat cut in sections from the body and transported to the vessel, where, after being "minced," the oil is extracted by boiling. The testes are taken out, and, with the selected spires of the whiskers, find a market in China—the former being used medicinally, and the latter for personal ornaments.

In recent years, the Bering Sea and Gulf of Alaska populations of Steller's sea lion have taken a nosedive, and no one is quite sure why. In the 1960s, the total population was estimated to be some 192,000 animals, but by 1994, it had dropped to an estimated 52,000, a reduction of about 75 percent in a twenty-year period. Under the Endangered Species Act of 1973, the species was listed as threatened in the eastern portion of its range and endangered in the western. As of 1999, the population had fallen to around 20,000 animals, and the dreaded word *extinction* had begun to appear in discussions. Suggested causes for this decline include "redistribution, disease, environmental perturbations (which may influence the quality and quantity of prey), and the synergistic effects of fisheries" (Loughlin, Perlov, and Vladimirov 1992), the latter of which seems the most likely. The "synergistic effects of fisheries" is just a fancy reference to the fact that if you remove the food supply of an animal, it is likely to starve.

Like northern fur seals, Pacific harbor seals, spotted and ringed seals, and some of the world's largest breeding colonies of kittiwakes, murres, and puffins, Steller's sea lions rely on walleye pollock (*Theragra chalcogramma*) for their diet. The giant Alaska pollock trawl fisheries are hauling in the fish, however, on an unprecedented scale. The annual pollock catch in the Bering Sea rose from about 220,000 tons in the late 1970s to 880,000 tons in 1995. It has been estimated that nearly 90 billion pounds of pollock have been mined from the eastern Bering Sea since 1964. Unregulated pollock fishing in critical sea lion foraging habitat soared to record levels in the mid-1990s, with much of the winter catch concentrated in pollock spawning grounds near the sea lion population center. A recent study (Thomas and Thorne 2001) revealed a heretofore unreported aspect of the sea lions' feeding habits: they were observed to feed at night on Pacific herring, not pollock, at least in Prince William Sound, Alaska. This revelation, however, does not explain the fall in sea lion numbers: even though the herring are not being overfished, the sea lion population continues to dwindle.

As sea lion stocks continued to fall, the pollock fishery grew exponentially, increasing by 45 percent from 1990 to 2001. The Alaskan pollock fishery accounts for about 40 percent of all commercially harvested seafood in the United States and represents the country's largest fishery as well as the world's largest single-species commercial fish harvest. Pollock appears in stores as frozen whitefish, fish sticks, the patties used in fast-food fish sandwiches, and "imitation crab meat." In the spring of 1998, Greenpeace, the American Oceans Campaign, and Sierra Club Alaska joined forces to sue the National Marine Fisheries Service (NMFS) under the Endangered Species Act of 1973 for failing to protect the critical foraging habitat of Steller's sea lion. Since lack of food is the problem, they argued, it makes no sense to allow major fisheries to target pollock within the sea lions' critical habitat. The Endangered Species Act requires that "reasonable and prudent alternative (RPA) measures" be taken to avoid inflicting any "adverse modification" on the critical habitat of a species. In December 1998, the NMFS sent shock waves through the fishing industry by agreeing with the plaintiffs representing sea lions that fishery operations did create a situation of "food web competition." In July 1998, Judge Thomas Zilly of the United States District Court for the Western District of Washington upheld this finding and ordered the NMFS to revise its "reasonable and prudent alternative" in order to reduce the pollock catch. Pollock fishing in critical sea lion areas has been curtailed as a result, but it is not clear whether the reduction will allow the severely depleted Steller's sea lion populations to recover.

ELEPHANT SEALS

Unlike the thick, luxurious pelt of the fur seal, the skin of an adult elephant seal is sparsely covered with stiff hairs. It was the elephant seal's blubber—which was boiled down into oil—that the eighteenth- and nineteenth-century sealers wanted, and they slaughtered these gigantic seals by the tens of thousands to get it. Then—as now, but with significant interruptions—more than 50 percent of the world's southern elephant seals lived on South Georgia Island and another 30 percent lived on Kerguelen and Heard Islands. The only mainland population of southern elephant seals is found on the Península Valdés of Patagonia; all other rookeries are located on islands in the South Atlantic Ocean: the Falklands, South Georgia, the Crozets, the South Shetlands, Heard, Macquarie, and Kerguelen. There was once a colony on King Island in the Bass Strait (between mainland Australia and Tasmania), but it was completely eradicated in the nineteenth century. The breeding grounds of the northern elephant seal are located about 5,000 miles from those of the southern variant, primarily along the coast of California from the Farallon Islands, near San Francisco, to Guadalupe Island, off Baja California.

The southern elephant seal (*Mirounga leonina*) is a different species from its northern relative and somewhat larger in size, making it the largest of all the pinnipeds—and, in fact, the largest carnivorous *land* mammal in the world. (Sperm whales and killer whales are considerably larger.) The bull of the southern species may reach a length of twenty feet, three or four feet longer than the average northern male, and weigh as much as four tons. The females of both species are about half the length of the males and typically weigh about 1,300 pounds—larger than the bulls of all other pinnipeds except the walrus and Steller's sea lion. (The disparity in size between adult males and females—sexual dimorphism—is greater in elephant seals than in any other mammal.) Differences between the northern and the southern species include variations in the configuration of the skull, in the flexibility of the back (the southern species can bend itself backward into a V shape, whereas the northern variety seems able only to raise itself straight up), and in the

NORTHERN ELEPHANT SEAL
(*Mirounga angustirostris*)

trunk-like proboscis from which the animals get their name, which is longer in the northern species.

The dominance of the alpha males is almost absolute. Males rarely hold positions of power for more than one season, but during that time they might inseminate as many as 100 females. The protests of the females also serve a strategic function. If a female is being mounted by a subordinate male, she barks and squeals, attracting the attention of the alpha male, who then charges over and chases off the intruder. Intruders, usually operating around the fringes of the harem, rarely complete copulation. On tiny Año Nuevo Island, just off the California mainland north of Santa Cruz, there have been situations in which a single male has sired all the pups in a given harem, and most of the other bulls, unable to consummate a single mating, died without ever having bred. This situation is compounded by the fact that most males die before they reach the breeding age of eight. (Even though they look as if they have lived for centuries, elephant seals rarely survive beyond thirteen or fourteen years of age.)

After a gestation period of about eleven months, eighty-five-pound pups are born about a week after the cows arrive on the beaches. Virtually every female bears a single, curly-coated black pup, which she nurses for about four weeks. During this period, pup mortality is extremely high: in some cases, as many as 50 percent of the newborn pups die before they are a month old. They are either abandoned by their mothers or, more frequently, crushed by rampaging bulls. This might seem to contradict the principle of maximizing reproductive potential—what kind of father crushes his own offspring? However, since aggressive breeding behavior is necessary for multiple inseminations, the frequency of copulation offsets the occasional death of a pup. Therefore, aggressive mating—which may result in the death of one of the bull's own offspring—is more important to the breeding males in the long run than protecting individual pups.

The pups have developed a strategy for maximizing their potential for survival. Ordinarily, the arrangement is one baby to a mother. Some of those already weaned, however, become "milk stealers," finding another lactating female—usually one that has lost her pup, but sometimes one that is still nursing—and suckling from this foster mother as well as from their own. The milk stealers, always males, put on twice as much weight as the other pups, giving them a pronounced head start in life.

If the pup survives the first four weeks of life, it is abandoned by its mother when she returns to the sea. The weaners remain on the beach for another two months on their own, living off their accumulated fat and learning to swim and dive in the shallow tide pools. At this time, they also shed their black coats for a silvery, shorter-haired style in the first of what will be an annual molt.

Until recently, the destinations of elephant seals leaving the breeding beaches were completely unknown, but by attaching radio transmitters to individuals, researchers have been able to track their migrations. Even though their wanderings were surprising—they appear to spend most of their time at sea, which explains why they are not found at hauling-out sites other than breeding beaches—their feeding dives astonished everyone. Brent Stewart and Robert DeLong affixed time-depth recorders to six adult male elephant seals off San Miguel Island, California, in February 1991 and recorded dives that lasted as long as seventy-seven minutes, with a maximum recorded depth of 5,105 feet, "the deepest yet measured for air-breathing vertebrates." The greatest documented depth for a southern elephant seal, as recorded by Mark Hindell, David Slip, and Harry Burton in 1991, was 3,936 feet. Sperm whales and northern bottlenose whales (*Hyperoodon ampullatus*) are believed to dive as deep or even deeper, but so far the deepest dive recorded for a bottlenose whale is 4,765 feet.

Marine mammals that dive to great depths to feed usually do so in pursuit of prey. Because sperm and bottlenose whales have long been the objects of directed fisheries, their stomach contents have been closely examined, and it is known that squid make up a large proportion of their diet: by a process known as stomach lavage, in which the stomach contents are pumped out without the animal being killed, it was learned that northern elephant seals feed primarily on squid but also take octopuses, starfishes, crabs, and assorted fishes (Antonelis et al. 1987).

Northern elephant seals are big and yield abundant oil, and lots of them come ashore in one place. Despite their size and ferocious demeanor, even the bulls are relatively placid, so they have been particularly easy to kill. Humans have probably been doing that for 10,000 years, but they really didn't get warmed up until sealers and whalers from various countries began slaughtering them in earnest for their oil, killing most of them on California's Año Nuevo Island, Farallon Islands, and Channel Islands, and the Mexican islands as well. In 1872, Scammon wrote: "We have reliable accounts . . . of the Sea Elephant being taken for its oil as early as the beginning of the present century. At those islands, or upon the coast of the main, where vessels could find shelter from all winds, the animals have long since been virtually annihilated." Captain Scammon (1874), our authority on the methodology of killing, told of his experiences with the sea elephant in 1852:

> The sailors get between the herd and the water; then, raising all possible noise by shouting, and at the same time flourishing clubs, guns, and lances, the party advance slowly toward the rookery, when the animals will retreat, appearing in a state of great alarm. Occasionally an overgrown male will give battle, or attempt to escape; but a musket-ball through the brain dispatches it; or some one checks its progress by thrusting a lance into the roof of its mouth, which causes it to settle on its haunches, when two men with heavy oaken clubs give the creature repeated blows about the head, until it is stunned or killed. After securing those that are disposed to show resistance, the party rush on the main body. The onslaught creates such a panic among these peculiar creatures, that, losing all control of their actions, they climb, roll, and tumble over each other, when prevented from farther retreat by the projecting cliffs. We recollect in one instance, where sixty-five were captured, that several were found showing no signs of having been either clubbed or lanced, but were smothered by numbers of their kind heaped upon them. The whole flock, when attacked, manifested alarm by their peculiar roar, the sound of which, among the largest males, is nearly as loud as the lowing of an ox, but more prolonged in one strain, accompanied by a rattling noise in the throat.

In 1880, Joel Allen wrote, "The [northern] Sea Elephant seems to have been formerly very abundant on the coast of California and Western Mexico, whence it became long since nearly extirpated." Annihilated, extirpated, eliminated . . . whatever the term, the elephant seals were slaughtered for the high-grade oil that was obtained from their blubber, as much as 200 gallons from a large bull. By 1884, no northern elephant seals were seen anywhere. In 1892, an expedition led by Charles H. Townsend of the Smithsonian Institution visited Guadalupe Island specifically to locate elephant seals—if any were to be found. They located eight animals and killed seven, even though Townsend (1912) realized that these animals represented "the last of an exceedingly rare species." There were now study specimens in the collection of the U.S. National Museum, but there was no longer a viable population left in the wild. In a 1977 article, Burney LeBoeuf coined the term *extation* in reference to the northern elephant seal "to describe the status of a species whose population has been reduced to such a low level that it can no longer function as a significant part of its own ecosystem . . . or to the point where there is considerable doubt as to whether the species remains extant."

Subsequent researchers, recognizing that a single animal would have been unlikely to preserve an entire species, have suggested that twenty to fifty elephant seals may have been alive at that time, probably swimming offshore or hauled out on islets that the researchers didn't find. We can safely assume, however, that all the northern elephant seals alive today are descendants of this remnant group on Guadalupe. In 1911, the Mexican government officially protected *el elefante marino,* and twenty years later, the U.S. government did the same for this species in its waters. Since then, the comeback of the northern elephant seal has been nothing short of astonishing. In 1922, the total population was estimated to be about 250 animals. In 1957, there were about 13,000, and by 1977, approximately 30,000. In 1990, Marianne Riedman estimated the number of Northern Hemisphere elephant seals at 120,000 and growing, and in 2002, Randall Reeves and colleagues wrote, "By 2000, the population may have numbered more than 150,000." The expanding population is establishing new beachheads and recolonizing old ones. The Farallon Islands were recolonized in 1972, and in 1975, a pregnant female came ashore at Año Nuevo Point and gave birth to what was possibly the first elephant seal born on the North American mainland. The population has now established such a firm foothold on the mainland that bull elephant seals occasionally appear on the fairways, the greens, and, especially, the sand traps of the famous Pebble Beach golf course, which conveniently overlooks the Pacific Ocean on the Monterey Peninsula.

Although this would seem to be an unqualified success story, problems still give biologists cause for concern. If the current population of northern elephant seals is descended from a single male, or even a few, the species doesn't have the genetic diversity that might help protect it from disease and changes in the environment. Even a relatively slight variation in environmental conditions—a change in climate, a problem with the food supply— normally dealt with by the adaptation of one genetic variation or another within the population, might endanger the entire species.

At the beginning of the eighteenth century, sealers plied the Southern Ocean in search of new places to kill seals. Indeed, many of the more remote islands were discovered during this search for new sealing grounds. South Georgia was discovered in 1775 by Captain James Cook (who was not searching for sea mammals to kill), and his reports of plentiful whales and seals brought the hunters there shortly thereafter. When Captain Edmund Fanning arrived on South Georgia in the *Aspasia* in 1801, he collected 57,000 fur seal skins and learned that a British "elephanter" had already left with a cargo of oil. (Fur sealers and so-called elephanters were often the same people; they filled their open holds with fur seal pelts and their casks with elephant seal oil.) In 1904, when Captain Carl Anton Larsen established Grytviken, the first whaling station at King Edward Cove on South Georgia Island, he was after the great blue and fin whales that came to the south to feed on krill, but on his next voyage he took eighty elephant seals. Subsequent Norwegian voyagers harvested elephant seals, but they also killed fur seals for their skins. When Robert Cushman Murphy visited South Georgia in 1912–1913 aboard the whaling brig *Daisy,* he reported not only on the whaling (in his 1947 *Logbook for Grace*) but also on the transgressions of the captain, Benjamin Cleveland, who had elephant seals killed indiscriminately, with little or no regard for the restrictions in place. In his summary of the "second sealing epoch (1909–64)," Robert Headland (1984) wrote that "approximately 260,000 seals were taken which yielded 84,000 tons of oil." Commercial sealing continued at South Georgia until 1964, when shore-based whaling closed down, forcing the sealing industry also to close because of its inability to sustain itself economically (Reeves et al. 2002).

Even though they were slaughtered by the hundreds of thousands during the sealing frenzies, the southern elephant seals survived. In a few places, such as Heard Island, most of them were killed, but the world population of *Mirounga leonina* was too remote, too large, and too scattered to have been threatened like that of its northern cousin, *M. angustirostris.* After centuries of killing, southern elephant seal populations are rebounding. According to Reeves and colleagues (2002), "the species may now number around 750,000, with the highest number of seals centered at South Georgia."

～ 8 ～

SEALS

Of the several kinds of seals frequenting the northwestern approaches when the European invasion began, four were pre-eminent: hood, harp, harbour, and horsehead by name. Although hoods and harps were the most numerous, they were of small importance to the human newcomers, being present only during the winter and early spring and even then mostly staying so far offshore as to be seldom seen. Horsehead and harbour seals, on the other hand, lived year round in astonishing profusion almost everywhere along the northeastern coasts of the continent.

—Farley Mowat, *Sea of Slaughter,* 1984

Because they are quadrupedal and move with all four flippers, the fur seals and sea lions were sometimes able to escape the sealers' clubs by waddling into the water. Unfortunately, this mobility didn't save many of them because they obviously didn't understand the extent of the danger, often waiting placidly on the beach as their neighbors were clubbed to death. Of course, when the sealers were armed with rifles, no amount of high-speed waddling could save the fur seals. The true seals—those that move only by pulling themselves forward with their foreflippers—were hunted differently, first by the Inuit people and then by the sealers. Taking their cue from polar bears, the Inuit would wait motionless by the seals' breathing holes in the ice, but whereas the bear would swipe the seal out of the water with its powerful clawed forefoot, the Inuit would harpoon it and then drag it onto the ice. The Inuit hunted bearded seals, harp seals, hooded seals, ribbon seals, and ringed seals for meat, oil, sinews, and fur, and they used virtually every part of the seal.

The early Arctic voyagers originally killed seals out of need, but soon a vast industry developed for the sole purpose of hunting seals. The massive seal slaughter was conducted purely for monetary gain. Like an invading army, the sealers descended on the hordes of seals, clubbing, shooting, and

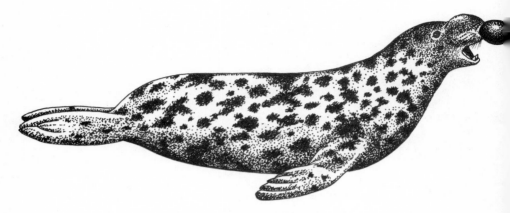

HOODED SEAL
(*Cystophora cristata*)

skinning them in an orgy of killing. Not that it would have made any difference, given the size of the invading forces, but the seals that became the primary objects of the sealers' killing frenzies could barely get away from their
attackers, and unless a breathing hole was nearby, they bayed pitifully at their
attackers before they were clubbed senseless on the ice.

HARPS AND HOODS

Harp seals are phocids. They have no visible ear flaps, and they cannot rotate
their hind flippers forward, so they move on land or ice by pulling themselves
ahead with their sharp-clawed foreflippers. Adult harp seals are blimp-like,
with fat bodies and small heads, but in the water they are surprisingly lithe
and graceful. A well-fed adult will weigh 300 pounds. The hooded seal
(*Cystophora cristata*), named for the inflatable sac on the male's nose, occupies much of the same North Atlantic territory as the harp seal, but it is not
nearly as numerous. Baby hooded seals (known as "bluebacks") do not have
the fluffy white coats of harp seal pups, but their shorthaired coat is also
highly valued. Alongside the harp seals, they are slaughtered by Canadian,
Russian, and Norwegian sealers.

   At birth, the harp seal is yellowish from being covered in amniotic fluid,
but in three days its coat turns the fluffy white that gives it the name "whitecoat." In three or four weeks, the white coat is shed in patches—at this time
the sealers call them "ragged-jackets"—revealing a shorthaired coat of gray
with darker spots. Once the white fur has completely molted, the seal is

known as a "beater," and juveniles marked with large spots are called "bed-lamers" (from *bête de la mer*). By the age of four, the young seal has developed the characteristic harp pattern, consisting of a horseshoe-shaped band running from the flanks up and across the back of the silvery gray coat. It is not so distinct in adult females, and in some it may be broken up into spots or even nonexistent. The head is dark in both sexes, black in the males and lighter in the females.

The harp seal's scientific name, *Pagophilus groenlandicus,* means "ice-lover from Greenland" and accurately describes its lifestyle. Those portions of the harp seals' existence not spent swimming are spent on large chunks of frozen water; "dry land" plays no part in their lives. During storms, they dive through holes in the ice they've made with their claws. Occasionally, these holes are closed by the shifting ice, and the seals, unable to surface, are drowned. The females give birth on the ice, and the newborns' thick, fluffy coats insulate them from the cold. (Adults lie on the ice for hours, protected by a two-inch layer of blubber and a circulatory system that keeps their internal temperature at a steady 92.2°F while their skin is only slightly above freezing.) Immediately after giving birth, the female nuzzles her newborn pup, and the memory of the scent—or perhaps recognition of its pitiful bleating—enables her to recognize her pup when she returns from feeding. Mothers nurse only their own pups; if the mother is lost at sea, the pup will starve. Feeding regularly on the mother's rich, thick milk, the pup can triple its twenty-pound birth weight in three weeks. Once it has packed on enough insulation and lost its buoyant white coat, the pup enters the sea to supplement its diet with small crustaceans such as euphausiids, mysids, and amphipods.

In the North Atlantic and Arctic Oceans, harp seals form three separate herds: the Newfoundland herd, by far the largest; the White Sea herd, also known as the East Ice herd; and the Jan Mayen (West Ice) herd. In September, as the ice begins to form in the north, the entire Newfoundland herd begins its southward migration and splits in two. The Newfoundland seals that breed on the ice in the Gulf of St. Lawrence, usually in the vicinity of the Magdalen Islands, is known as the Gulf herd; those that breed on the drifting pack ice between Labrador and Newfoundland are known as the Front herd. By December, the pregnant females of each herd are ready to deliver their twenty-pound pups. For two centuries, the sealers have arranged to meet them on the ice.

"The commercial hunt for harp seals was probably the most highly publicized form of marine mammal exploitation, with the possible exception of commercial whaling," wrote Randall Reeves, Brent Stewart, and Stephen Leatherwood in 1992. The image of heartless sealers bashing fuzzy white baby seals on the head is an accurate one; in the earlier days of this two-centuries-old fishery, sealers killed pups and adults indiscriminately and in awesome numbers. Large-scale harp sealing began around 1800 and reached an early peak in 1831, when the sealing ships brought in 680,000 pelts. During the nineteenth century, the yearly average was 350,000; in the twentieth, it was around 200,000. In his 1977 *Life of the Harp Seal*, writer-photographer Fred Bruemmer observed:

> Two centuries ago when the females hauled out to give birth to their pups, hundreds of square miles of ice were dotted with their dark shapes. And the hunt of the harp seals has no equal. It has now lasted two hundred years, and about fifty or sixty million seals have been killed of the Front and Gulf herds alone. If one adds to this the killed harp seals of the two other herds—the one east of Greenland, the other in Russia's White Sea—the total rises to about 70 million, the greatest, most protracted mass slaughter ever inflicted on any wild mammal species.

When the Basques crossed the Atlantic Ocean in the sixteenth century to search for codfish and whales, they found harp seals along the coasts of Canada, and they decided to catch them too. Early settlers in Labrador trapped seals in nets, but when they realized it was more practicable to go to the seals instead of waiting for the seals to come to them, they headed for the ice with their rifles loaded. Shooting seals on the ice, however, usually meant several lost for every one recovered. Later, Arctic whalers searching Spits-

HARP SEAL
(Pagophilus groenlandicus)

bergen waters for the "polar whale" or "Mysticetus" (now known as the bow-head whale) found the Jan Mayen herd of harp seals and collected them for their skins and oil. By the mid-nineteenth century, the enterprising Norwegians had come to dominate the Arctic sealing industry, and it was sealers—such as Carl Anton Larsen and Svend Foyn—who developed the techniques of mechanized whaling. In 1863 alone, Norwegian sealing vessels working the ice at Jan Mayen took 120,000 harp seals. When these catches fell off, the fleet headed east to the White Sea grounds. Although they needed heavier ships to penetrate the thicker ice, the hunters were able to kill harp seals by the tens of thousands.

During the eighteenth century, the British in Newfoundland killed an average of 80,000 seals every year, the catches fluctuating with the vicissitudes of weather, conflicts with the French, and other factors. But by the beginning of the nineteenth century, the Newfoundlanders had honed their new industry to a remarkable and deadly efficiency. Small schooners took men to the ice to hunt seals on the whelping patches in winter and early spring, providing supplementary employment and income for the men who fished for cod in the summer and fall. By 1816, the average annual catch of Newfoundland seals was 117,000, and it would continue to grow. In *Harps and Hoods,* their study of the ice-breeding seals of the northwestern Atlantic, David Lavigne and Kit Kovacs commented, "For all intents and purposes, 1818 marks the beginning of the Golden Age of Sealing in the northwest Atlantic." In that year, 200,000 seals were landed, a record that would be broken repeatedly during the next forty years.

The scale of the industry in its heyday was enormous. W. Nigel Bonner (1928–1994), a lifelong student of pinnipeds and the author of numerous papers and books—including *Seals and Man*—reported in 1982 that "catches of 680,000, 740,00, and 686,000 seals were reported in 1831, 1832, and 1844 respectively." In 1857, 400 vessels with a total of 13,000 men went to the hunt. They killed nearly half a million seals that year, worth more than $1.2 million (Bruemmer 1977). The number of seals "landed," however, was often significantly lower than the number killed. Lavigne and Kovacs wrote:

> During the entire period of 1818–1862, more than 18.3 million seals were landed by the Newfoundland sealers. This works out to an average of 400,000 per year over the entire period. Unbelievable as these figures may seem, they actually represent a minimum estimate of the number of seals that actually died at the hands of the sealers. . . . In those days, the sealers routinely collected the seal pelts in a central location on the ice rather than loading them directly onto the ships. Because of

inclement weather or drifting ice, many of the pelts, in some years numbering in the tens of thousands, were never recovered and therefore were not reported in the landed catches.

Around 1863, the "wooden walls" were introduced to Newfoundland. These wooden-hulled, ship-rigged vessels with small auxiliary steam engines proved more efficient than the newfangled steel-hulled vessels, which cracked under pressure. The wooden walls concentrated the sealing industry in St. John's, the capital of Newfoundland (then a British colony and not part of Canada), and carried more men to the ice than ever before.* Crews of as many as three hundred would work a patch, and it was said that such a crew could kill 20,000 seals in a single day. But by this time, the seal populations were so decimated that even this greater efficiency could not produce numbers like those of the "Golden Age." Catches dropped to around 300,000 per year and continued to fall. In the 1860s, the fleet, which at its height had numbered more than 370 ships, was halved, and by 1884, only 50 vessels were engaged in harp sealing. The heavier Dundee and Peterhead whaling ships were pressed into action, and they penetrated the ice until the more efficient steel-hulled vessels with icebreaker bows were introduced, around the turn of the century.

Even though they wore thick-furred, waterproof coats, harp seals were not killed for their pelts. (Fur seals and sea otters, of course, were killed *only* for their coats.) Newfoundlanders did not walk around in fashionable seal-skin coats, and neither did the swells of New York and Boston. In the harp seal fishery, what really mattered was the oil. Boiled out of the skins, seal oil, like whale oil, was used to fuel lamps, for lubrication, for cooking, in the tanning of leather, in rope making, and in the manufacture of soap. Petroleum, which would eventually supplant whale and seal oil as a lubricant and fuel, was not discovered until 1859, when Colonel Edwin Drake of Titusville, Pennsylvania, drilled the first producing oil well.

Sealing was dangerous work, and the men were consistently underpaid and underfed; they were cold, wet, and uncomfortable most of the time. The

---

*The 700-ton, wooden-walled *Terra Nova* had participated in nineteen consecutive sealing seasons when she was selected by Robert Falcon Scott to serve as a relief ship for his 1901–1903 expedition to the Antarctic. She returned to Newfoundland to participate in the seasons of 1906–1909, but in 1910 Scott again chose the *Terra Nova* to take his team south, this time for his attempt on the South Pole. Scott and his four companions perished, after learning that Roald Amundsen had reached the Pole a month before they did. The *Terra Nova* returned to her original mission and continued sealing until 1941.

ice was always a threat, capable at any time of destroying ships and men. Approximately four hundred vessels and a thousand men were lost between 1800 and 1865. On the ice, some of the Newfoundland "swilers" carried rifles, but every one of them was armed with a gaff, a six- to eight-foot stick with a hook at one end. The Norwegians in their diesel-powered ships, who would eventually displace the Newfoundland "landsmen," preferred to carry a pickax-like instrument called a *hakapik*. It was used as a boat hook, or to pull a man from the icy water if he slipped in, or even to assist the men in jumping from floe to floe, but its most important function was seal-killing. Sometimes the whitecoats were bashed on the head; sometimes they were gaffed through the brain, and sometimes they were swatted as if with a baseball bat. It was in the swilers' interest to work as quickly as possible, so they didn't always wait until the seal was dead before skinning it. The skins, known as "sculps," were tied together and dragged back to the waiting vessel, where the fat was removed for oil and the skins prepared for processing. The oil was the primary product, but the skins, even those from the whitecoats, were tanned and turned into fine-grain leather, used for gloves, pocketbooks, wallets, and belts (Busch 1985).

The harp seal hunt continued through World War I, but many of the steel steamers were transferred to war work, so the old wooden walls were bought back into service. In 1915, the total catch was a relatively modest 47,000 seals, but because petroleum was needed for the war effort, seal oil was again at a premium, and sealing remained a profitable business. By 1920, the catch had dropped to 34,000, the lowest since the beginning of the nineteenth century. Around 1937, having depleted the harp seals of the Jan Mayen population, the Norwegians came to Newfoundland and began killing seals there. Even the German occupation of Norway in 1941 did not stop them; instead of returning to Norway with their catch, they simply sold the skins in Newfoundland. After the war, the Norwegians prosecuted the Newfoundland seal hunt with Viking zeal, and even after 1949, when Newfoundland joined the Dominion of Canada, the hunt still belonged to the Norwegians. In 1951, the twentieth-century high of 430,000 was achieved, and during the remainder of the 1950s, catches averaged around 300,000 per annum. Sealers from the USSR joined the Newfoundland harp seal hunt in 1960, but they stayed only one season before returning to their traditional hunting grounds on the White Sea. In a 1976 article, seal researcher David Lavigne estimated that during the 1950s, the western Atlantic harp seal population was more than halved, from an estimated 3.3 million to 1.25 million seals.

Despite massive efforts on the part of various conservation groups to shut it down, the Newfoundland harp seal hunt continues even today. That tens of thousands of harp seals were being killed was bad enough, but the method of killing the cuddly whitecoats—clubbing them and perhaps even skinning them alive—brought out conservationists' heavy artillery. Among the early leaders of the battle to save the seals was Paul Watson, founder of the Sea Shepherd Society and a one-man wrecking crew dedicated to putting commercial whalers and sealers out of business. On the ice in Labrador, Watson tried to spray-paint the whitecoats green so their coats would be useless for commerce, but the sealers nearly killed him, and the Canadian government arrested him. He was later expelled from Greenpeace for "being too much of an activist."*

In response to a film showing baby harp seals being skinned alive in 1966, Dr. Bernhard Grzimek, director of the Frankfurt Zoo and an ardent conservationist, initiated a worldwide protest society that he called Campaign Against the Apathy of the Canadian Government. The film, made by a small Montreal-based company called Artek, was intended to show the eternal struggle between man and nature, but instead, as Farley Mowat wrote, "not only did it show the stark vista of crimson slush on white ice, which is the hallmark of the seal hunt, it captured harrowing scenes of sealers with steel-hooked staves gaffing what may well be the most appealing young creature in the animal kingdom, together with stunning close-ups of one of these attractive little animals—being skinned alive." The embarrassed Canadian government made some efforts to curb the hunt—or at least conceal it from newsmen and filmmakers—but the sealers would have none of it and continued to kill the whitecoats. Although the 1967 quotas were set at 50,000 for the Gulf of St. Lawrence, the actual number of harp and hood seals slaughtered that year was 232,000, the largest since World War II.

In 1968, after falling in love with the harp seal pups on the ice at the Gulf of St. Lawrence, Brian Davies founded the International Fund for Animal Welfare (IFAW), now based in Yarmouth, Massachusetts. In 1978, Davies pub-

---

*There are those who defend the whitecoat clubbing as being no worse than the killing of cattle in a slaughterhouse; and besides, they argue, the embattled Newfoundland sealers have to earn a living somehow, don't they? William McCloskey, a journalist and commercial fisherman, shipped out twice on Newfoundland sealing vessels and concluded that there was nothing particularly reprehensible about the practice. In 1983, he wrote, "It's easy for city people to 'save a baby seal' with a ten dollar tax-deductible contribution, and afterwards, feeling all warm inside, they can reward themselves with a hamburger." In 1985, Janice Henke published an entire book (*Seal Wars!*) about what she saw as self-serving millionaire conservationists pitted against the poor but noble Newfoundlanders, who were only doing what came naturally.

lished *Seal Song*, with an introduction by Roger Caras, a preface by Ray Bradbury, and photographs by Eliot Porter. In this book, Davies commented:

> Unthinkingly, we exploit animals in many ways—in the name of science, food, companionship, and whatever else we feel is necessary to our own survival or comfort. We do awful things to animals, but the worst that we do, it seems to me, is to kill them for the sake of luxury or novelty. This is why I believe that the seal hunt is a tragedy that should fill us all with shame.

In January 1972, Jack Davis, Canada's minister of the environment, announced that the government would impose a partial ban on seal hunting in the Gulf of St. Lawrence the following spring. Brian Davies submitted a petition with a million and a half signatures, claiming that the ban was "a victory for the little people all over the world," but Davis replied that his action was based not on popular opinion but on conservation principles. Besides, said Davis, the ban would apply only in 1972. Then French actress Brigitte Bardot joined the mêlée. She auctioned off her jewelry and other items to raise the 3 million francs required by the French government to start a foundation; then she donated her house to the Brigitte Bardot Foundation. She protested the "barbarian" slaughter of all animals, but she devoted her greatest efforts to the Canadian seal hunt. In 1977, the star of *And God Created Woman* was in Newfoundland, and Greenpeace activists took her by helicopter to the ice where the seals were being killed. The campaign to save the seals saw the union of Greenpeace, IFAW, and La Bardot, all trying to protect the cuddly whitecoats from the heartless sealers. It helped the campaign to have such an adorable symbol, but the activists' hope—that no more baby harp seals would be killed—never became a reality.

In the United States, the Marine Mammal Protection Act of 1972 was passed primarily to control the number of dolphins being killed in tuna purse seines, but also out of revulsion over the clubbing of seal pups. In 1983, the battle heated up to the point that Greenpeace and IFAW engineered a boycott of Canadian fisheries products, forcing Canada's minister of fisheries and oceans to ask the sealers to stop killing baby seals. The sealers did not: 5,609 whitecoats were clubbed and skinned that year. (The ban didn't apply to adult seals, and the Canadian government set a quota for 1983 of 186,000 animals.) Brian Davies spearheaded a campaign to convince the countries of the European Community to ban importation of the white pelts so the sealers would have no market for the skins, and on March 11, 1982, the EEC parliament voted 160 to 10 in favor of such a resolution.

Paul Watson returned to the Gulf of St. Lawrence in the *Sea Shepherd* in March 1983 with his siren blaring, threatening to plow through the ice and disrupt the seal hunt taking place. In defense of the seal hunt, the Canadian Coast Guard icebreaker *John A. Macdonald* trapped the *Sea Shepherd,* and she was rammed by another icebreaker. Mounties arrested Watson and his crew, who were charged with violating seal protection regulations, fined, and sentenced to jail time. The threat of a U.S. boycott of Canadian fish nevertheless forced the sealers to declare a moratorium on whitecoat hunting in 1984, and the hunting of whitecoats for commercial purposes was banned in Canada in 1987, yet juveniles and adults are still being killed in prodigious numbers.

In addition to the numerous reported harp seal kills, there are many unreported kills representing those seals not included in official reports of the number of "landed" seals. This category includes seals that are "struck and lost," which means that for some reason—usually because they are wounded and enter the water—the carcass is not collected; those taken by hunters north of Newfoundland; and those caught in fishing nets. Seals are also taken as a result of high-grading, wherein the animals are killed by sealers for certain products (e.g., the penises, which are ground up and used in powder form in traditional Chinese medicine) and their remains discarded. David Lavigne (1999) found that in some fisheries, as in Greenland, the loss rate approached 50 percent, which means that for every seal reported, one was lost. In the net fishery for lumpfish (*Cyclopterus lumpus,* from which we get lumpfish caviar), 25,000 to 30,000 seals are killed each year. Incorporating all age categories of seals (except whitecoat babies, which are no longer officially hunted), Lavigne concluded that whereas the 1994 catch for Canada and Greenland was officially reported at 292,888 to 310,148 harp seals, the total kill was 376,220 to 478,177. In 1997, the figures were as follows: reported, 332,696 to 349,956; total kill, 417,170 to 533,491. The Canadians killed 10,048 hooded seals in 1998, and the quotas for 1999 and 2000 were set at 10,000 per annum.

An IFAW publication dated March 21, 2000, suggests that whitecoats may still be illegally killed in Canada. In addition, the Norwegians and Russians still take a sizable number of whitecoats from the East and West Ice herds, respectively. Bardot's foundation (on the Internet at http://www. fondationbrigittebardot.fr) is still actively campaigning against the seal kill and the wearing of furs. In 1998, when the Canadian government announced that it was authorizing a quota of 275,000 seals, Bardot announced that she was going to join the protest in Ottawa. A delayed Air France flight caused her to miss the rally, but in a press release she stated: "The massacre of the seals has started again in Canada. Twenty-one years after my first protests, the Canadians have begun to slaughter these peaceful animals again. . . . Listen to their cries! They are massacred with picks and skinned alive!" At the rally, which was organized by IFAW, some 2,500 people protested, but the government ignored them.

The harp seal hunt takes place wherever these animals make the mistake of coming out of the water. Greenland's waters harbor some 5.5 million harp seals, and a story in the *New York Times* dated October 17, 2000, was titled "As Greenland's Seal Population Surges, Its Fishermen Look to Revive the Hunt." Like many fishermen, the Greenlanders believe that the seals are eating their fish, and so the way to protect their fishing industry is to eliminate the competition. (Some fishermen even blame seals for the collapse of the Grand Banks cod fishery.)

The newest threat to harp seals seems to be rising temperatures associated with global warming. If there is no ice, the seals will have no place to breed. In the winter of 2000, unusually warm conditions melted most of the ice in the Gulf of St. Lawrence, leaving the remaining ice bunched against the shore. The whitecoats were huddled on small floes, and according to IFAW reports, few mothers were to be seen. All over the world, rising temperatures are causing a reduction in ice. For example, the North Pole, usually under some ten feet of ice in summer, was under open water in August 2000. As James McCarthy and Malcolm McKenna wrote that year in their discussion of this surprising condition, "Loss of ice at the North Pole is symbolic—like the loss of a signature species in a particular region—of a profound change in the order of nature."

Harp seals have been killed by sealers by the millions, drowned in fishing nets, shot by fishermen, and killed by polar bears and killer whales. But incredibly, despite two hundred years of concentrated slaughter, *Pagophilus groenlandicus* is not officially endangered. Nigel Bonner believed that it is possible for harp seals and men to coexist. In 1994, he wrote:

> Harp seals represented a depleted but not in any way endangered species and quota controls could have maintained the population in a steady state. Conservation interests would have better looked at the general exploitation of the North Atlantic rather than the seal hunt. But there is inevitably less concern for fish than for cuddly seal pups. For most people nowadays, there is a deep feeling that it is wrong to bash the heads of baby seals.

It is almost as difficult to estimate the population as to monitor the illegal traffic in whitecoat pelts. Harp seals live in some of the most inhospitable (to humans) regions on the earth, with shifting ice, subzero temperatures, and no place of refuge save for the icy water. We certainly did everything we could to drive the harp seals into extinction, but we failed. Their fecundity and our difficulties in reaching their remote habitat probably saved them. Recent estimates of the number of harp seals alive today range from 5 million to 8 million, and as far as we can tell, that number is holding steady. But should the ice on which they breed disappear, as much harm will befall the harp seals as was done by the centuries of hunting.

THE GREY SEAL

For the most part, seal-hunters have had to range far and wide, often to remote, ice-choked lands. One seal species, however, is threatened because it lives too close to human habitation and industry. The common name for *Halichoerus grypus* is most often spelled in the British fashion because the seal is found throughout the British Isles, but the grey seal is "gray seal" in eastern Canadian and New England waters. Its scientific name comes from *halios,* which is Greek for "sea," *khorios,* for "pig," and *grypus,* which means "hook-nosed." Thus, the grey (or gray) seal is the hook-nosed sea pig. The large nose and distinctive profile are also responsible for its common Canadian name, "horsehead."

The grey seal is a large, irregularly spotted phocid that occurs in many variations of the color gray, ranging from very light (almost white) through olive, silver, brown, and even black. Males are usually darker and considerably larger than females and can weigh upward of 700 pounds. At birth, babies are a creamy yellowish white, a color that lasts until the first molt, when the animal is two to four weeks old. There are three populations in the North Atlantic Ocean: in Canada's Maritime Provinces, including the Gulf of St.

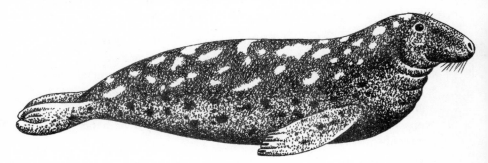

GREY SEAL
(*Halichoerus grypus*)

Lawrence, Nova Scotia, Newfoundland, and Labrador; in New England, from Maine to Cape Cod; and in northwestern Europe, from Iceland to Norway, Sweden, and Finland and throughout the Faroe Islands and the British Isles. The largest of the British rookeries are on the Inner and Outer Hebrides and the Orkney, Shetland, and Farne Islands, but there are smaller colonies along the southwestern coasts of England, Wales, and Ireland.

When the first settlers arrived in North America, one of the welcoming committees consisted of seals. As Farley Mowat wrote in 1984, "gregarious and polygamous, horseheads used to gather in January and February in enormous numbers on myriad islands and even mainland beaches from Labrador to Cape Hatteras, there to whelp and breed." At first they were killed, like the whales, for their oil, with the center of the industry at lonely Sable Island, a swath of sand and rock 100 miles east of Halifax, Nova Scotia. Canadian and New England sealers vied for the privilege of extirpating the horseheads from Sable and the Magdalen Islands, and they surely would have succeeded had they not been distracted by the harp seals that became the object of the fishery in the 1860s.

Gavin Maxwell, an English writer who operated a basking shark fishery in the Hebrides and kept otters that he described in *Ring of Bright Water,* also wrote a book about the seals of the world (1967). "The grey seal," he wrote, "is the largest surviving carnivore in Britain. It is also the most controversial—the centre, from time to time, of passionate arguments. On the one hand it is damned as a criminal creature, the slayer of salmon, and the ruination of the fisherman's livelihood. On the other hand, it is defended with a degree of emotion peculiar to the British people—especially since the Government has permitted the selective killing (culling) of the species."

The grey seal is a fish-eater, and therein lies its problem because it feeds in waters that fishermen believe belong to them. And no fish is more precious to fishermen than the Atlantic salmon. When it was seen that the seals were gobbling up the salmon in prodigious quantities, the Canadian government offered a $5 bounty for each seal killed, and the fishermen, who didn't know the difference between harbor seals and grey seals, killed everything that came into their sights. Grey seals were believed to be extinct in Canada until 1949, when a couple were spotted sunning themselves on a sandbank in New Brunswick's Miramichi River. The Canadian population of grey seals is now estimated at about 30,000.

The northern Baltic Sea (Gulf of Bothnia) is the home of another population of grey seals, which has been hunted by Swedish and Finnish hunters for thousands of years. The Scandinavians were subsistence hunters and never took enough seals to threaten the Baltic population. Most of the grey seals of Britain are found in the far north, in the Hebrides, the Shetlands, and the Orkneys, but there is a population of about 8,500 on the Farne Islands, offshore just south of Berwick-upon-Tweed. West of the Orkneys is the tiny island of Sule Skerry, where the grey seals breed, and where the folk song was born about the man who shoots a seal (known there as a *selchie*), only to learn that it is his son:

> I am a man upon the land,
> I am a selchie in the sea,
> An' when I'm far from every strand,
> My dwellin' is in Sule Skerrie.

The grey seal is the definitive host (the host on which a parasite reaches sexual maturity) for the codworm, *Phocanema decipiens,* the larvae of which infest food fishes, especially cod. Where there are dense seal concentrations, the cod show a high incidence of worms, and although they are not harmful to humans, they are unsightly and have to be removed laboriously by hand. The seals also steal fish from nets and lines and damage the nets, so they are considered especially harmful to fisheries. In 1962, in an attempt to protect fish and fishermen, the British government initiated a system of culling—a term that Mowat (1984) called "one of the most abhorrent of the newspeak phrases devised by 'wildlife resource managers' in order to conceal the true intentions of the political and commercial masters"—but public outrage at the murder of mothers and pups caused the program to be suspended in 1979. Culling to protect the salmon began in Canada in 1967 and continued until 1983. There are now some 200,000 grey seals, half of which breed in Great Britain and the others in Canada and the Baltic.

CARIBBEAN MONK SEAL

Altogether, there are some thirty-three species of pinniped, ranging in size from the ponderous elephant seal, as heavy as its terrestrial namesake, to the little ringed seal of the Arctic, which can weigh just more than 200 pounds. Of all the pinnipeds, only a few species were heavily hunted, and one—the Caribbean monk seal—was completely eradicated.

When Christopher Columbus arrived at the island of Alta Vela, south of Haiti, on his second voyage in 1494, he saw a group of eight "sea wolves" on the beach. A shore party killed them all, and, as Peter Knudtson wrote in 1977, "thus ended, in a prophetically bloody manner, the first recorded encounter between Europeans and the sea mammal now known as the Caribbean monk seal, *Monachus tropicalis*." The seals' placid and unaggressive nature made them easy to kill, and there was already a fishery for these animals in 1675 when William Dampier (1699) visited the Bay of Campeche on the western Yucatán Peninsula:

> ... there being such plenty of Fowls and Seals (especially of the latter) that the Spaniards do often come hither to make Oyl of their fat; upon which account it has been visited by Englishmen of *Jamaica,* particularly by Capt. *Long;* who, having command of a small Bark, came hither purposely to make Seal-Oyl, and anchored on the North side of one of the sandy Islands, the most convenient Place for his design.

Monk seals are the only seals that live in warm waters year-round; this fondness for tropical waters meant that they were likely to inhabit the very locations where human beings from colder climates wanted to spend their vacations. (Earlier, these fat little seals were killed for their oil, as were so many pinniped species.) In the latter years of their existence, Caribbean monk seals found themselves on beaches that developers wanted for hotels and condominiums, and these shy and inoffensive creatures proved no match for the land sharks.

In addition to the Caribbean species, there are monk seals in Hawaiian waters and also in the Mediterranean Sea. All three species look very much alike; if one were to somehow transplant a Hawaiian monk seal to, say, the eastern Mediterranean, nobody would be able to tell the difference. So it is only the caption that identifies the forlorn-looking Caribbean monk seal in a

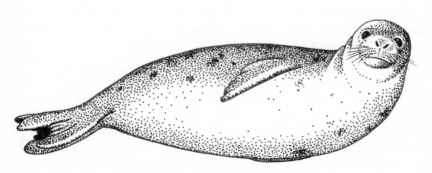

CARIBBEAN MONK SEAL
(Monachus tropicalis)

photograph in the New York Aquarium's 1937 guidebook as a "West Indian Seal." This lonely creature, described by the aquarium's director, Charles H. Townsend, as "now approaching extinction," was probably one of the last of its kind. In his 1942 study of extinct and vanishing mammals of the Western Hemisphere, Glover Allen penned a plaintive cry for the waning members of this species:

> It would appear to be a simple matter for the British Government to pass protective regulations for the preservation of any that might still exist in the Bahamas and for the Mexican Government to prohibit their killing on the islands of the Yucatan so that they might breed up to numbers placing them less close to the danger line.

No such luck. In 1973, under the auspices of the U.S. Fish and Wildlife Service, biologist Karl Kenyon (1977) carried out a 4,000-mile aerial survey of the Caribbean basin in search of monk seals. He visited almost every island where they had been seen in the past and interviewed fishermen, sailors, and anyone else who might provide information on the missing monk seal. Concluding that they were gone, he wrote wistfully, "Man has now dominated the environment." The final sighting of a wild Caribbean monk seal occurred in 1952, Kenyon tells us, off the Serranilla Bank, 250 miles southwest of Jamaica.

The fur seals and harp seals were killed for their coats, the elephant seals for their oil, and some sea lions for their whiskers and testicles. Along with harbor seals, which have the widest distribution of any pinniped and, at an estimated Northern Hemisphere population of 500,000 (Reeves et al. 2002), are not considered endangered, grey seals were killed because they were a nuisance to fishermen. Some species had the misfortune to wear thick fur coats that humans coveted, and others had a blubber layer that humans needed for industry. The walrus of the Arctic, neither seal nor sea lion (it has no ear flaps but moves with all four flippers), was sought for its giant tusks, which are used, like elephant ivory, to make decorative carvings. A number of other Arctic seals have been spared the predations of *Homo industrialis*. The ringed, ribbon, and bearded seals are hunted by polar bears and Inuit people, but they have nothing that Europeans crave, and although some are killed for their meat and hides, for the most part they continue to live out their lives on the Arctic ice, untroubled by guns and harpoons.

The phocids of the Antarctic have been protected by the remoteness and inaccessibility of their habitat. Sealers could not get at the seals that lived on the ice because conditions around the Antarctic continent make ship travel difficult and more than a little hazardous. The fat Weddell seals would have provided a tidy harvest for sealers, but with a couple of exceptions, such as the Norwegian sealing expedition of 1893–1894, few serious attempts were made to hunt them in the vastness of their icy habitat. Crabeater seals, whose population estimates range from 10 million to 70 million animals, are usually considered the most numerous large mammals in the world—except for us, of course. If anyone could have figured out how to hunt crabeaters economically they surely would have done so, but so far the crabeaters have been protected by their frigid fortresses. Ross seals are another Antarctic species; they are essentially solitary in nature and so little known that Randall Reeves, Brent Stewart, and Stephen Leatherwood (1992) could write: "Guesses at the total number of Ross seals in the Antarctic have ranged from a few tens of thousands to several hundreds of thousands. However, the truth is that no satisfactory census has been made."

Whether they moved on all fours or dragged themselves forward with their clawed foreflippers, seals and sea lions in fur coats have been the objects of concentrated hunts—curiously called fisheries—for centuries. So far, the Caribbean monk seal is the only pinniped species that we have successfully extirpated, but our "failures" with fur and elephant seals were not for want of trying. The northern elephant seal, hunted, like its southern counterpart, for its oil, was once reduced in number to single digits, and the Juan Fernández fur seals were so reduced by hunting in the late eighteenth and nineteenth centuries that they were considered extinct. If Brummer's estimate of 70 million harp seals killed is correct, the total number of pinnipeds killed in the last two centuries probably exceeds 120 million. Of all the earth's sea mammals, only whales and dolphins have been killed in comparable numbers.

~ 9 ~

LITTLE CETACEANS IN PERIL

Through the windows of history, literature, and cinema, we have become familiar with images of intrepid whalemen lowering boats in pursuit of the mighty sperm whale, harpooning it, and then being towed in the famous "Nantucket sleighride" until the great beast tired and could be killed and towed back to the ship, where it would be rendered into oil and its teeth pulled for scrimshaw. Later whalers modernized the process, using diesel-powered catcher boats to chase the whales and harpoon cannons to shoot them; the carcass would be towed back to a factory ship, dragged aboard, and processed at sea. For a thousand years, men have been killing whales for meat, oil, and baleen plates, which were made into skirt hoops and corset stays. The heroic tale of the all-conquering whaleman is known to everyone, yet few people know that some small cetaceans (whales and dolphins) have also been hunted for centuries. Unlike their larger cousins, however, they are on the very brink of extinction.

On February 18, 1914, Charles M. Hoy, the son of an American missionary in Hunan Province, China, was duck hunting in Tung Ting Lake. When a school of dolphins passed within range, Hoy shot one in the back. When he neared the wounded animal, it "gave out a subdued bellow somewhat after the nature of a noise made by a buffalo calf." He described the animal as weighing 297 pounds, with jaws that showed a distinct upward curve. He said the creature was pale blue gray in color, but from a distance it looked white. (In Chinese, this animal is known as the *baiji*, from *bai*, "white," and *ji*, "dolphin.") From its stomach he removed "about two quarts of a single species of eellike catfish that inhabits the mud at the bottom of the lake." Hoy retained the skull and the cervical vertebrae, which he delivered to the U.S. National Museum (Smithsonian Institution) on his return to America. The material was examined and described by G. S. Miller, who realized that it represented a new species of dolphin and named it *Lipotes vexillifer* (from the Greek *lipos*, "fat," and Latin *vexillifer*, "flag bearer"). The cervical vertebrae that Hoy had saved were unfused, one of the diagnostic characteristics of this family. It also had a long snout, broad flippers, and tiny eyes that were practically useless. Other than its basic physical appearance and restricted habitat, however, hardly anything was known about it. In their 1938 book *Giant Fishes, Whales, and Dolphins,* John R. Norman and Francis C. Fraser noted that "the Chinese River Dolphin is never seen except in Tung Ting Lake and around its mouth"; they then quoted at some length from Miller's 1918 paper on the species. In Remington Kellogg's 1940 *National Geographic* article on whales and dolphins, we read that "the Chinese White Flag Dolphin today is restricted to the fresh-water Tung Ting Lake in Hunan Province, China, some 600 miles up the Yangtze River." Fishermen were reluctant to capture this dolphin, Kellogg commented, because they believed it to be descended from a princess who flung herself into the lake. In subsequent mentions of *Lipotes vexillifer,* the story of the princess was usually repeated and its restricted habitat was always included. In the popular literature, some elaboration on its habits even began to appear, presumably the result of an author's having to describe an animal about which hardly anything was known. For example, in Ivan Sanderson's 1958 *Living Mammals of the World,* the following description appears: "Although the lake is connected to the main river, the animals never go downstream; on the other hand, at certain seasons they leave the lake and go up small tributary streams and even into ditches, so that it is hard to see how they ever turn round and get back again."

When China was opened to westerners in the mid-1970s, Giorgio Pilleri, a brain anatomist and authority on the freshwater dolphins known as platanistids, was able to participate in two *Lipotes* expeditions with Chinese scientists. During these expeditions, the scientists saw fewer than thirty animals, usually in groups of ten or fewer individuals, but they made a number of observations. *Lipotes* tended to remain in deeper waters but occasionally traveled into river branches in search of food, and the dolphins could become

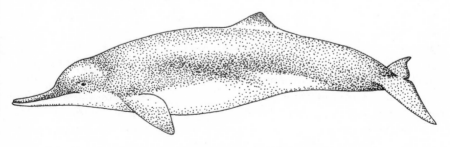

CHINESE RIVER DOLPHIN
(Lipotes vexillifer)

stranded there. At the surface, the baiji is particularly difficult to see because it raises only its melon (the "forehead"), its blowhole, and part of its back out of the water when it breathes. The beak and tail are rarely seen, but infrequently an animal will lift the front half of its body out of the water so that the snout and flippers are clearly visible. The Chinese river dolphin is often seen in mixed schools with the finless porpoise, but the behavior of the two animals is totally different. The finless porpoise is much more abundant in the river and considerably less shy; it even approaches boats occasionally. *Lipotes* is shy, avoiding boats and people; whenever a ship comes near, it dives, splitting into small groups, only to re-form as a larger group after the ship has passed (Zhou, Pilleri, and Yuemin 1979). Fishermen often find specimens that have been killed or badly wounded by boat propellers. One Chinese scientist reported that "the greatest threat . . . is the hook fishery which is the most common practice in the river. We have investigated the causes of the death of nearly one hundred individuals between 1950 and 1980, and found that nearly 50 percent were killed by the hooks. It seems very likely that *Lipotes* was caught while ingesting fish that had already been hooked up." (Yangtze fishermen employ "rolling hooks," which consist of finely pointed hooks attached to a long, slack bottom setline. The hooks snag fish on the bottom, and the baiji, attracted by the struggling fish, become entangled and drown.)

The Chinese river dolphin has small but functional eyes located higher up on the head than those of any other freshwater dolphin. Its eyes are also oriented forward, which enables it to see better when swimming closer to the surface of the river. Like all platanistids, *Lipotes* has a well-developed capability for echolocation. According to Shochi Yeh and Giorgio Pilleri (1980), because of the increasing turbidity of the baiji's habitat, a result of deforestation and erosion, this species has had to rely increasingly on its sonar to navigate.

Edward Mitchell, in his 1975 "Review of Biology and Fisheries for Smaller Cetaceans," wrote that "the status of the [Chinese river dolphin] population is unknown." It now appears that the Chinese have long been aware of the declining population of their only endemic freshwater dolphin—the finless porpoise is also found in Indian waters and in the Inland Sea of Japan—and have assigned it first-grade protection, the same granted the giant panda. Pilleri (1979), discussing the possibility of saving this species, commented that "the Chinese have enormous experience in breeding both land and water animals, having developed skills which are seldom to be found in other countries. If they succeed in saving *Lipotes vexillifer* in this way, it will certainly be a splendidly original achievement." They didn't, and it wasn't.

In a 1999 study of cetaceans in danger, zoologist William F. Perrin commented: "What is most remarkable about the baiji is that it exists at all. It is a river dolphin that shares the Yangtze River drainage with approximately 10% of the world's human population and suffers from all the attendant river traffic, overexploitation of fish and water resources, and pollution." Although efforts are being made to protect this animal, its fatal propensity for becoming entangled in fishermen's gear has greatly reduced its numbers, and it is now among the most endangered of all cetaceans. Researchers in 1998 counted only 30 baiji on a 310-mile stretch of the river. Adding in likely numbers from other stretches of this river, which bisects China from Tibet to the East China Sea, they estimated the species total to be 150. Pollution and shipping accidents are killing off this rare dolphin at an alarming rate; there are now half as many as there were in 1990. Concluding his 1999 discussion, Perrin stated, "The results to date of the concerted rescue effort for this species have not been good, and there is little reason for optimism." In a letter to me in 2000, Perrin wrote, "There may be less than 100 baiji left now."

Like the Chinese river dolphin, the vaquita (*Phocoena sinus*) was not known to western science until the twentieth century. In 1950, a skull was found on a lonely beach in the Gulf of California, the body of water that separates the Baja California peninsula from mainland Mexico. In a paper published in 1958, Ken Norris and W. N. McFarland noted that the vaquita "could not be referred to as *P. phocoena* [the harbor porpoise] because of numerous osteological differences," and they therefore reported it as a new species. The cranial distinctions between this species and the harbor porpoise are indeed consistent and significant enough to separate the two species. The specific name *sinus* is Latin for "bay" or "gulf" and refers to the body of water in which the animal is found. The vaquita (Spanish for "little cow") is somewhat

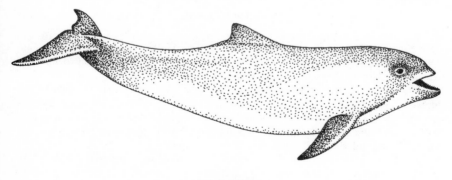

VAQUITA
(*Phocoena sinus*)

smaller than the harbor porpoise, which makes it one of the smallest of all cetaceans. Mature individuals have been measured at 4.9 feet, and it is thought that they do not get much larger. Whereas the harbor porpoise is lead black or gray, however, the vaquita is brownish, with dark markings around the eyes and lips. Vaquitas travel in small groups, sometimes only in pairs, and feed on grunts, croakers, and squid. When surfacing to breathe, they exhale with a loud puff that is characteristic of the genus.

The primary threat to the vaquita's existence are the Mexican fishermen, particularly those who fish for the large sea bass known as the totoaba.* Because this chubby little porpoise is limited to the northern region of the Gulf of California and has the most limited range of any marine mammal, even a small number killed annually may have a detrimental effect on the total population. Along with the baiji, the vaquita is listed as Critically Endangered in the 1996 *IUCN Red List of Threatened Species.* Since researchers Jay Barlow, Tim Gerrodette, and Greg Silber (1997) began counting the

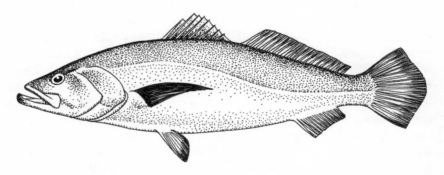

TOTOABA
(Cynoscion macdonaldi)

---

*The totoaba (*Cynoscion macdonaldi*) lives only in the Gulf of California, between Baja California and mainland Mexico. This fish, a member of the drum family (Sciaenidae), reaches a maximum length of six feet and weight of 225 pounds, which means it may actually grow larger than the little porpoise that shares its habitat. Earlier in the century, the totoaba (also spelled *totuava*) was caught for its large air bladder, which was used in the preparation of soups in Asian countries, but more recently it was simply considered a popular food fish. Before the construction of dams on the Colorado River, fresh, muddy water flowed regularly into the gulf, providing the necessary spawning conditions for the totoaba, but now this inflow is greatly reduced. In addition, commercial fishing—first with hook and line, then with dynamite, and finally with gill nets—has reduced its numbers to a dangerously low level, and the totoaba is now believed to be one of the few marine fish actually on the brink of extinction.

vaquita population in 1986, it has been plummeting. From 1986 to 1988, they counted a total of 503 animals, but by 1993, they were able to find only 224.

Rivers seem to be unpropitious places for dolphins to earn a living. River dolphins are usually close to people, and too much familiarity usually does not end well for the dolphins. Before people recognized the intelligence of dolphins and enjoyed their antics in captivity, the little cetaceans were regarded as just another item to be hauled out of the water—if they could be caught. There were net fisheries for bottlenose dolphins (Flipper was a bottlenose) off Cape Hatteras and off Cape May, New Jersey, in the 1880s; at the same time, large schools of pilot whales—which are actually large dolphins— were driven into shallow water to be killed for the oil in their heads. Of the five recognized species of freshwater dolphin, four are in trouble. Only the bouto, or Amazon River dolphin (*Inia geoffrensis*), is prospering. Found close to shore in the coastal waters of Uruguay, Argentina, and Brazil, the Franciscana, also known as the La Plata River dolphin (*Pontoporia blainvillei*), is so often trapped in gill nets that it is now considered endangered.

The baiji has suffered because of its unfortunate proximity to Chinese fishermen, and in the rivers of the Indian subcontinent there are two species of blind freshwater dolphin that are in almost as much trouble. The Ganges River dolphin, or susu (*Platanista gangetica*), and its close relative the Indus River dolphin (*Platanista minor*), sometimes considered subspecies, live only in the rivers for which they are named, separated by hundreds of miles of land in northern India. The Ganges dolphin lives mostly in eastern India and Bangladesh, whereas the Indus dolphin lives in western India and Pakistan. Seven or eight feet long as adults and weighing about 185 pounds, both species are gray and have broad, fan-like flippers, a low, triangular dorsal fin, and a long, tooth-studded beak. The eyes are mere pinholes; because vision would be useless in the turbid waters they inhabit, these dolphins use a highly sophisticated acoustic system to locate the fish they eat.

It was *Platanista gangetica* that piqued Giorgio Pilleri's interest in freshwater dolphins, and in 1969 he organized an expedition to the Indus and Brahmaputra Rivers to collect living specimens for the Institute of Brain Anatomy in Berne, Switzerland. On the basis of his extensive studies of these animals, Pilleri began publishing a journal called *Investigations on Cetacea*, which became a virtual textbook on the biology, habits, taxonomy, and history of this heretofore little-studied group of dolphins. In the wild as well as in captivity, these dolphins tend to swim on their sides with one fin touching the bottom, an adaptation that seems to facilitate swimming in very shallow water: if a river dolphin were to swim upright, its tail would come out of the water on the upstroke and hit the bottom on the downstroke (Herald et al. 1969).

Both species are endangered. They live in some of the most heavily polluted waters in the world, and even though dolphins breathe air and are not directly affected by tainted water, their prey is. The dolphin populations have been fragmented by irrigation dams on the rivers; subpopulations trapped upriver of the dams cannot escape and are hunted for food. Dolphin oil is valued as an aphrodisiac, is used as a liniment for livestock ailments, and is mixed with minced dolphin meat to attract a highly esteemed species of catfish. Like the baiji, India's river dolphins occasionally become trapped in fishing gear, especially gill nets (Reeves 2002b). Although the counts are imprecise, it is believed that there are about 1,000 Indus dolphins and perhaps twice that number of Ganges dolphins.

It is not surprising that the dolphins are losing the battle with the human occupants of the riverbanks. People build dams, pollute rivers, fish out the prey species, and both accidentally and intentionally kill the dolphins. One might assume, therefore, that pelagic dolphins, living their entire lives thousands of miles from land, ought to be well out of range of man the despoiler. For the inhabitants of the eastern tropical Pacific, that assumption would be tragically wrong.

~ 10 ~

THE TUNA-PORPOISE "PROBLEM"

When the Sea Life Park oceanarium opened in Hawaii in 1963, four spinner dolphins were exhibited that had been caught offshore nearby. Since they were so rare, they quickly became the focus of intensive studies, and cetologists from all over the world came to look at the world's first captive spinners. The animals were small, slender dolphins with long, narrow snouts and perky dorsal fins. They were *Stenella longirostris*. (*Stenella* is from the Greek *stenos,* meaning "narrow," and *longirostris* means "long beak.") The maximum length for this species is about seven feet, and adults weigh 120 to 135 pounds. The general coloration of Hawaiian spinners consists of a dark dorsal field or "cape," a lighter band below, and lighter underparts (which accounts for the name "white-belly spinners"); an eye-to-flipper stripe; and, usually, darker coloration on the upper part of the beak than on the lower. In the eastern Pacific Ocean, the color scheme is more muted, described in 1972 by William F. Perrin as "predominantly dark gray." These timid, gentle animals are renowned for their spinning leaps into the air, and when it was discovered that they would perform their unique aerial maneuvers in captivity, they quickly became the stars of the show.

While those spinners were entertaining the visitors at Sea Life Park, others, far from Hawaii, were tragically drowning in tuna nets and being unceremoniously chucked overboard. Tuna fishermen were "setting on porpoise," using the highly visible schools of dolphins—mostly spinners and spotters, or spotted dolphins (*Stenella attenuata*)—to indicate the presence of yellowfin tuna (*Thunnus albacares*) and skipjack (*Katsuwonus pelamis*). The association between dolphins and tuna is still poorly understood, but in the late 1950s, when it was discovered that the presence of dolphins signaled the presence of tuna, the tuna fishermen changed their tactics from a hook-and-line to a purse seine operation. As the nets were drawn around the tuna, the dolphins became entangled in the mesh and drowned or were hauled aboard the boats

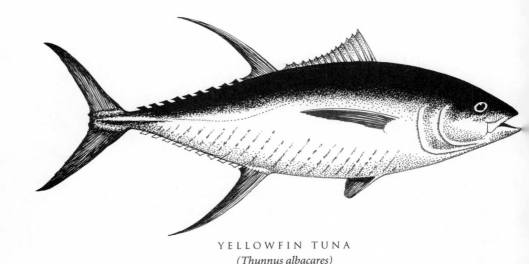

YELLOWFIN TUNA
(Thunnus albacares)

alive and then thrown overboard, often being fatally injured in the process. The purse seines were not so selective as to catch only full-sized tuna and dolphins, however. Other animals caught and discarded in the bycatch included small or undersized tuna of various species, billfishes, mahi-mahis, wahoo, rainbow runners, yellowtails, snappers, jacks, triggerfishes, and various sharks, rays, and sea turtles (Garcia and Hall 1996).

Throughout the tropical oceans of the world can be found a group of slender, spotted dolphins that have been a source of confusion to cetologists for centuries. Because they are creatures of the open ocean—and also because they are found far from the normal shipping lanes as well as far from land—they are not often seen. Early studies of small cetaceans gave these animals short shrift. Examining only skeletal material and other scientists' descriptions, Frederick True (1889) combined the three known species into one, *Prodelphinus attenuatus.* In 1938, British dolphin expert Francis C. Fraser was still referring to the species as *Prodelphinus,* and aside from identifying the characteristic that separates this genus from the otherwise similar *Delphinus*—the palate of the common dolphin is deeply grooved, whereas that of *Prodelphinus* (*Stenella*) shows no such grooving—he supplied very little information. Of the six species Fraser named, none was identified as occurring in the Pacific Ocean, an indication of a lack of observers, not a lack of dolphins. (They all turned out to be variations of the species now known as the pantropical spotted dolphin, *Stenella attenuata.*) In 1940, Remington

Kellogg wrote that "great schools . . . are frequently seen in the Pacific Ocean in coastal waters northward at least to Acapulco, Guerrero, Mexico, and southward to Gorgona Island off Colombia." In a 1966 discussion of the genus *Stenella*, Fraser wrote that cetologists needed more than the "sporadic trickle" of specimens available to them over the past two hundred years. Unbeknownst to Fraser, at the very time his remarks were published, the tuna fishermen of the eastern tropical Pacific were killing hundreds of thousands of the spotters, just as they had every year since 1959.

The fishermen initially look for a commotion on the horizon that might indicate the presence of feeding seabirds, leaping dolphins, or both, which in turn might indicate the presence of tuna. Schools of tuna congregate beneath the dolphins, which sometimes number in the thousands and, because of their characteristic leaping and splashing, are not particularly difficult to see. When the tuna boat is within range, crew members lower pongas—small boats with high-powered outboard motors—into the water and use them to corral the dolphins into a tightly milling herd. When the dolphins have been compactly herded, the seiner lowers its net and surrounds the herd to trap the tuna, and in the process captures the dolphins still congregating above them.*

At first, the mile-long purse seine remains open, making a "wall" around the dolphins and tuna that is open at the bottom, but for some reason—perhaps having to do with the much colder water at the 200-yard depth at the bottom of the net—the animals being herded rarely escape beneath it. During this circling operation, the pongas continue to roar around the perimeter of the school, creating an additional barrier with their noise and wake. When the tuna, and the dolphins, are completely encircled by the net, it is "pursed": the fishermen close it at the bottom by means of a cable that passes through a series of rings, and everything inside is trapped. The net is then drawn in through a power block, one of the inventions that made this sort of operation possible, and section by section is stacked methodically on deck as the enclosure gets smaller. In the early history of this fishery,

---

*Not only is the association of dolphins and tuna poorly understood, but the association of dolphins and dolphins is equally enigmatic. In a 1998 study of the aggregations of pelagic dolphins and tuna in the eastern Pacific, Michael Scott and Karen Cattanach of the Inter-American Tropical Tuna Commission commented, "The questions of whether the tuna seek the dolphins or the other way around, and what advantages are gained by each species, remain to be answered." The timid spinners may also associate with the more powerful and aggressive spotters as a means of protection from predators. "And yet," wrote the authors, "groups may contain hundreds or even thousands of individuals, larger than one might expect would be necessary for protection."

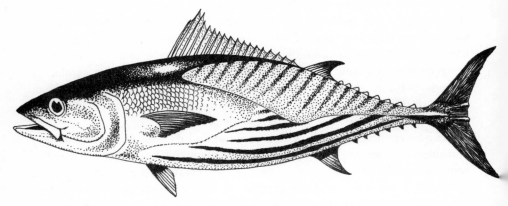

SKIPJACK TUNA
(Katsuwonus pelamis)

everything in the net was hauled aboard; the valuable tuna were kept and the dolphins and "trash fish" were dumped overboard.

In the mid-1960s, William F. Perrin, then a young graduate student in zoology at the University of California, Los Angeles, working on his Ph.D. dissertation on *Stenella,* heard that the species was somehow involved in the tuna fishery. In the past, fishermen had caught tuna by chumming them with bait until the fish were feeding in such a frenzy that they would bite anything, even unbaited hooks; then they were hauled out of the water as fast as the men on the rods could yank them up. By about 1960, setting on porpoise had largely replaced hook-and-line techniques, and by 1966—the same year Fraser's plaint was published—62 percent of the tuna caught in the Pacific were caught in association with dolphins, spinners and spotters mostly. Fraser's "sporadic trickle" of specimens had become a roaring waterfall.

Although the tuna fishermen didn't want to publicize the massive slaughter of dolphins, the information began to leak out, and it soon became apparent that the dolphins were dying in numbers almost impossible to imagine. Extrapolating from the early—and irregular—data accumulated by the fishermen, scientists have postulated that as many as 100,000 dolphins were killed in 1959, even before the entire U.S. fleet had converted to purse seining (Smith 1979). The following year, when more boats had been converted, an estimated half million dolphins died in the nets. No records were kept of the different species at this time. Later studies revealed that the commonest species used for setting on porpoise was the spotter, followed by the spinner, the common dolphin, and some other species in much lesser numbers. Eventually, the U.S. government—under tremendous pressure from various humane and conservation groups—began to monitor the tuna fishery. In a report published in 1979 by the National Marine Fisheries Service's Southwest Fisheries Science Center at La Jolla, California, the total number of dolphins killed between 1959 and 1972 was estimated at 3.8 million. Even this astonishing figure is considered low because it included only dead animals, not the injured ones thrown back into the water.

In a careful examination of the specimens collected in the tuna fishery and elsewhere, Perrin, Sloan, and Henderson (1979) identified two races of spotted dolphin from the eastern tropical Pacific, one from Hawaii, and a fourth from south of the Galápagos Islands. However many varieties there are—and whatever their names—all the spotted dolphins share certain characteristics. They are slender animals, reaching a maximum length of about eight feet and a weight of 250 pounds. The spotting pattern varies from population to population, but it generally consists of a lightly spotted dark dorsal area and a lighter ventral area covered with dark spots. Mature animals have a "cape" and an eye stripe, as well as variations in coloration of the beak. One identifying characteristic of the species (singular or plural) is the white-tipped beak of adults. (This appears in adolescent animals about the age of four but does not seem quite as prevalent in the eastern Pacific races.) After a gestation period of about eleven and a half months, a calf is born that is a dark or purplish gray in color, with a white ventral surface and no spots. As the animals mature, they pass through various stages, including a "two-tone" phase, and as they approach sexual maturity, more and more spots appear. Fully mature individuals are often seen in what has been called a "fused stage," in which the spots have converged and overlapped to such an extent that the animal appears almost solid gray (Perrin 1969b).

The eastern spotted dolphin is an offshore species that has been observed from strandings and sightings in the South Atlantic Ocean; at the Cape of Good Hope and Cape Horn (Hershkovitz 1966); at Durban, South Africa (Best 1969); and around the Solomon Islands (Dawbin 1966). It has also been reported from the Seychelles and Sri Lanka in the Indian Ocean. Masaharu Nishiwaki (1966) discussed two groups of dolphins that he identified as *Stenella attenuata,* which had been driven ashore in Japan by the *oikomi,* or drive, method. (In the drive method, dolphins are herded toward shore into water shallow enough that they cannot dive to escape men with spears, axes, and knives.) He asserted that this species was "very rare; this report is the first one from Japanese waters." But in 1974, Nobuyuki Miyazaki, Toshio Kasuya,

SPOTTED DOLPHIN
(Stenella attenuata)

and Nishiwaki stated that spotted dolphins were "fairly common, and [along with *Stenella coeruleoalba,* had] been the object of commercial hunting at several places on the Pacific coast of Japan." For their detailed study reported in "Growth and Reproduction of *Stenella attenuata* in the Pacific coast of Japan" (1974), Kasuya, Miyazaki, and William Dawbin examined 750 specimens from a total of 2,239 that were "caught by the driving method at Kawana or Futo on the east coast of Izu Peninsula, or at Taiji on the coast of Kii Peninsula." In Japan in the 1970s, each year approximately 17,000 dolphins of various species—mostly spotters and striped dolphins—were killed for human consumption.

Although spotters have been identified in the southwestern Pacific between Japan and New Guinea, the greatest concentration of these animals so far reported has been in the eastern tropical Pacific, where millions have been caught in the tuna nets since 1959. Most of this activity has taken place in the region west of Mexico and Central America, from Cabo San Lucas (the southern tip of Baja California) south to Lima, Peru, and as far offshore as the Revillagigedo Islands and Clipperton Island. This area encompasses millions of square miles of open ocean, and it appears to be the primary habitat of the pantropical spotted dolphin. Clearly, it is impossible to count dolphins in an area of this size, but various attempts have been made to estimate the total population, primarily to determine the number that could be removed by the tuna fishermen. (Prior to the interest shown by conservationists in preserving the dolphins, population estimates were, at best, academic exercises.) The most recent estimates of pantropical Pacific spotters range from 2.5 million to 3 million.

A drive fishery for spotters also existed in the Solomon Islands, but there the animals were destroyed for their teeth. As recently as 1966, when William Dawbin studied this phenomenon, porpoise teeth were a valid currency; approximately 1,000 teeth were required to make a necklace worth $50 in Australian currency. Each spotter has about 150 usable teeth, so six or seven animals had to be killed to make one necklace. Those collecting the dolphins would drive them into shallow water by striking stones together. Dolphins communicate by generating underwater sounds; Dawbin wrote that "noise is intensely disturbing to most of the local species of porpoise . . . some schools will not cross between two noise-making canoes spaced a half mile apart." He further described the scene: as the noise intensifies and the canoes close in, the dolphins "mill about frantically until some of those in the shallows of three or four feet of water suddenly plunge vertically and bury part of their heads in the softish sandy mud bottom. Here they remain with tails oscillating above the surface" until the people in the canoes and those on the beach rush in and drag them ashore. The heads are cut off and cooked to loosen the teeth, and some of the meat is eaten, "but there is far more meat than can be used and the wastage is great."

From its inception, the killing of various small cetaceans in tuna nets was known as the "tuna-porpoise problem," though it is now sometimes referred to as the tuna-dolphin problem.* How large a problem was it? In 1972, the first year an attempt was made to gather information about the number of porpoises killed, the total was well more than 300,000. Between 1959—about the time the tuna fishery converted from pole-and-line fishing to setting on porpoise—and 1972, the number of porpoises killed was an estimated 5 million, an average of 347,082 per year (Wade 1995). By far the most common

---

*The change in nomenclature points out the difficulties inherent in giving common names to various animals. Even though Ken Norris, perhaps America's foremost cetologist—and one of the first scientists to identify the problem—insisted on calling all small cetaceans porpoises, only a few scientists agreed with him. Cetaceans of the family Phocoenidae are indeed commonly called porpoises. They are small, beakless animals with spade- or chisel-shaped teeth. A different and much larger family, the Delphinidae, includes most of the better-known dolphins, including the bottlenose, the common dolphin, and the spinners and spotters involved with the tuna fishery. All members of this family have conical teeth, shaped like the canine teeth of a dog. To add to the confusion, also classified as dolphins are various so-called whales, such as the killer whale, the pilot whale, the false killer whale, and the like. These animals are beakless, as is Risso's dolphin (*Grampus griseus*), the Irrawaddy River dolphin (*Orcaella brevirostris*), and the various small dolphins of the genus *Cephalorhynchus*. Throughout this discussion, I have retained whichever term—*dolphin* or *porpoise*—the user employed.

species caught in the nets was the Pacific spotter, with the spinner a distant second. Also involved, but to a lesser degree, were common dolphins, bottlenose dolphins, and the very rare Fraser's dolphin. It was not only U.S. fishing boats that ensnared and killed the dolphins but also the fleets of Canada, the Congo, Costa Rica, Ecuador, South Korea, Mexico, the Netherlands Antilles, New Zealand, Nicaragua, Panama, Senegal, Spain, and Venezuela (Allen and Goldsmith 1980).

The American public and its congressional representatives were becoming aware of this egregious slaughter of the dolphins, and, under great pressure, the United States Congress passed the Marine Mammal Protection Act of 1972 (MMPA). With passage of the MMPA, it became illegal in the United States to harm cetaceans or other marine mammals. Initially, the tuna fishermen were exempted from the provisions of the act and were required only to abide by quotas to be set in 1974. In the two years granted the fishermen to research and resolve their problem and reduce their porpoise kills to a "near-zero level," they did absolutely nothing but fish in the same manner, although the totals fluctuated because of environmental conditions and the vicissitudes of fishing. The number of spotters and spinners killed in 1972 was estimated at 334,800, and in 1973 the number was 175,300, though this did not take into consideration animals that were irreparably harmed but released (Perrin, Smith, and Sakagawa 1975). After the two-year grace period had expired, conservation groups brought suit against the National Marine Fisheries Service for allowing fishermen to operate in direct contravention of the MMPA. After a nineteen-month court battle during which the fishing went on as usual, Judge Charles Richey of the United States District Court for the District of Columbia handed down a decision in favor of the porpoises in *Committee for Humane Legislation, Inc. v Richardson*, C.A. No. 74-1465 (D.D.C. May 11, 1976). Part of that decision reads as follows:

> The court realizes that the per-ton cost of catching tuna in some ocean areas may rise if purse-seiners are prevented from fishing "on porpoise" until the requirements of the MMPA are satisfied. But steps which ensure the protection and conservation of our natural environment must, almost inevitably, impose temporary hardships on those commercial interests which have long benefited by exploiting that environment. The people of this country, speaking through their Congress, declared that porpoise and other marine mammals must be protected from the harmful and possible irreversible effects of man's activities.

An appeal by the tuna fishermen allowed them to continue unrestricted fishing until the end of 1975, by which time another 100,000 dolphins had been killed. By then, however, the fishermen knew how to release dolphins from their nets: they would throw the engines into reverse when approximately half the net had been hauled in, a process known as "backing down." This sinks the corkline at the far end of the net, allowing the dolphins to escape over the line, which is now below the surface. (The tuna remain lower in the nets and do not swim out over the top.) Addition of the "Medina panel" and the "super apron," both of which are fine-meshed net sections that prevent dolphins from becoming entangled, also helped to lower the dolphin kill figures. These techniques were developed not to protect the dolphins but to reduce the labor required to get the dead dolphins out of the nets and, probably even more important, to preserve at least some dolphins for the future of the tuna fishery. After all, if there were no more dolphins to set on, crews would have to revert to the old hook-and-line style of fishing, and these multimillion-dollar purse seiners, now capable of bringing in a million dollars' worth of tuna on a single voyage, were not going to have a horde of fishermen hanging over the rails with bamboo poles in their hands. The backdown technique was mentioned by Perrin as early as 1969, but in that year a total of 518,407 porpoises of all species were killed, and in 1970 the number was 502,815 (Smith 1979). Obviously, some captains were less interested in getting the porpoises out of their nets than in keeping the tuna in (sometimes the tuna escaped during backdown), and with half a million porpoises dying annually, it would be difficult to say that the system to protect them was working very well.

The U.S. government did not know how many porpoises there were and therefore could not predict whether these huge kills would endanger the species. The fishermen were trying to lower the porpoise mortality rate without sacrificing their all-important profits. The scientists were attempting to discover the answers to all sorts of critical questions: What kinds of porpoises are these? How many are there? What do they eat? Why do the porpoises and the tuna stay together? How do we get the porpoises out of the nets—or, better, how do we keep them from coming into the nets in the first place? As the behaviorists and zoologists wrestled with these and other problems, the fishermen continued setting on porpoise. Although the government had now assigned maximum kill figures to the fishermen, the compromise was satisfactory neither to the fishermen nor to those who would protect the porpoises. For 1977, the limit was 62,429; for 1978, it was 51,945; for 1979, it was 41,610; and for 1980, it was 31,150. (Although these figures may seem high for "incidental" kills, it is important to remember that the number of porpoises killed in 1972 was more than ten times the quota for 1980.)

Backdown procedures, Medina panels, and super aprons contributed to the reduction in kills, but the most important factor was pressure—congressional, judicial, and public—on the fishermen. From 1972 onward, the American public was becoming more and more sensitive to the plight of cetaceans, and it was painfully apparent that the United States, a leader in whale conservation, was paradoxically responsible for more cetacean deaths than any other nation, even the modern pelagic whalers. With the dramatic reduction in kills, it seemed that the problem was being solved, even though there were those who believed that any porpoise deaths were too many. As of October 1980, an annual quota of 20,500 porpoises (of all species) was set by the U.S. government, and since the previous years' kills did not even reach the permitted quota, it appeared that the problem had subsided.

One by-product of the tuna-porpoise controversy was development of the Dedicated Vessel Program, wherein a tuna boat would perform its regular functions with a team of biologists aboard, not only to monitor porpoise kills but also to study the behavior and biology of the porpoises in the nets. Researchers aboard the *Elizabeth C.J.* in 1977, for example, observed porpoise behavior from a helicopter, from the ship, and even underwater in the nets themselves (Norris, Stuntz, and Rogers 1978). Another team of researchers went aboard the *Queen Mary*, a tuna seiner out of San Diego, in 1978 and observed the social behavior and school structure in pelagic spotters and spinners (Pryor and Kang 1980). These studies and others contributed substantially to the information about these heretofore little-known animals and

SPINNER DOLPHIN
(Stenella longirostris)

enabled us to see the dolphins as something more than simply creatures that seemed to share the same habitat as the yellowfin and skipjack tuna.

From the air, for example, it was seen that the "undisturbed" dolphins—those not being herded or chased—swam slowly and spread out, with twenty to thirty body lengths separating the individuals. When chased by speed-boats, however, they crowded together, with only two to three lengths between them. In this "running mode," they also began moving much more rapidly—as might be expected—making long, low leaps out of the water. In a study published in 1980, Whitlow Au and Daniel Weihs demonstrated mathematically that these long leaps are the fastest and most efficient mode of swimming. Even though more energy is required for jumping, the time spent out of the water, and therefore with no water resistance, compensates for the additional expenditure of energy.

Once the dolphins are surrounded by nets, their behavior changes radically. Ken Norris, W. E. Stuntz, and W. Rogers (1978) described a variety of behaviors, including "milling," wherein "a large percentage of the school remains essentially in one area while swimming and diving." They also saw some leaping activity, but this appeared to take place early in the set and soon subsided. In the nets, they saw dolphins at the surface with their heads out of the water (they called this "head-up" behavior) and also with their tails out of the water ("tail up"). In the nets, the animals also aligned themselves into discrete horizontal "layers," and after coming to the surface to breathe, they would return to their original positions: "The exception to a horizontal orientation were rafting individuals which tended more toward a vertical orientation relative to the surface. As many as four individual layers, at depths estimated to be 5 m, 9 m, 12 m, and 15 m, could be detected at any one time in a set" (Norris, Stuntz, and Rogers 1978). In most cases, spinners and spotters remained segregated from each other, forming small groups of four or five animals, but the behavior of the two species was similar in many respects. The "passive behavior" of both spinners and spotters in the nets, with the dolphins sinking slowly to the bottom of the net, the observers suggested, was probably a reaction to a situation of great stress induced by the boats, nets, noise, wake, and the like, and may be comparable to the behavior of spotters in the Solomon Islands, where the animals buried their heads in the sand to escape the loud noises made by the rock-striking hunters. The investigators were in the water with the dolphins and carefully recorded their observations, often writing underwater on specially prepared slates. Since most previous descriptions of the behavior of small cetaceans have been the result of observations of captive animals or of animals viewed from a distance,* this exercise represented a new and unique opportunity in cetology.

Special care was taken on these dedicated vessel cruises, and very few dolphins died. Ken Norris (1977) reported that during twenty sets made when he was aboard the *Elizabeth C.J.*, eleven porpoises were killed. In the seventeen sets of the *Queen Mary*, Pryor and Kang recorded the deaths of three animals. Many of the dolphins observed during the *Queen Mary*'s fishing seemed to know when they were going to end up in the net, and they stopped swimming. They also appeared to know how to escape over the corkline during the backdown maneuver, which indicated that at least some of the animals had been entrapped before and did not panic when they were in the nets.

At a workshop on porpoise stocks held in La Jolla, California, in August 1979, some of the earlier data were analyzed, and some disturbing results emerged. A more careful analysis of the population data indicated that the earlier estimates—on which the quotas were based—were seriously flawed, and the actual number of spotters in the eastern tropical Pacific was much lower than previously assumed. The figures and formulas are (as usual) particularly convoluted, but as an example, the 1979 report stated that the offshore population of spotted dolphins was at 34 to 55 percent of its 1959 level, below the optimal sustainable population (OSP)† range, whereas the same population analyzed in 1973 (for the 1976 report) was at "92 to 95 percent of the 1959 level, which would imply that it is in the OSP range" (Smith 1979). In real terms, the number of spotters in the eastern tropical Pacific was not 4

---

*Würsig and Würsig (1977, 1979) reported on bottlenose dolphins observed from the cliffs of Golfo Nuevo, Argentina; Saayman and Tayler (1973) did the same in South Africa; Norris and Dohl (1980) watched Hawaiian spinners at Kealakekua Bay; and Randy Wells (1991) has been observing the bottlenose dolphins of Sarasota Bay since 1970, but for the most part, these observations were restricted to behavior that could be seen from the surface. Karen Pryor and Ingrid Kang (1980) were in the water with temporarily captive wild dolphins. More recently, Rachel Smolker (2001) observed the behavior of bottlenose dolphins both inshore and offshore at Monkey Mia, Western Australia. Inshore, the wild dolphins came close to people, who fed and even petted them; offshore, the biologists observed the complex interactions of a resident group of bottlenose dolphins over a fifteen-year period.

†This is the definition of OSP in the "Report of the Status of Porpoise Stocks Workshop" (Smith 1979): "Optimum sustainable population is a population size which falls within a range from the population level of a given species or stock which is the largest supportable within the ecosystem to the population level that results in maximum net productivity. Maximum net productivity is the greatest net annual increment in population numbers of biomass resulting from additions to the population due to reproduction and/or growth less losses due to natural mortality."

million, as estimated in 1959, but a figure probably closer to 3 million. This sounds like a lot of dolphins until it is placed alongside the number believed to have been killed throughout the fishery: from 1959 to 1978, a total of 4,180,613 spotted dolphins were killed. The "recruitment rate," or reproductive ability, of the dolphins makes up for the apparent discrepancy, but if more than 4 million spotters were killed in twenty years, it can be seen that the actual numbers—and the OSP—are critical.

There is also a directed fishery for spotted dolphins for human consumption in Japan. In 1982 and 1983, respectively, 3,799 and 2,945 animals were taken. In 1992, 1993, and 1994, the takes were 637, 565, and 449 animals (International Whaling Commission 1996). A large number of spotted dolphins have been killed as incidental catch in the eastern tropical Pacific tuna fisheries. The following numbers, from the National Research Council (1992), include the take of American as well as foreign fleets (in the period 1959–1972, an estimated 350,000–653,751 dolphins of all species were killed per year):

1979	21,426
1980	31,970
1981	35,089
1982	29,104
1983	13,493
1984	40,172
1985	58,847
1986	133,174
1987	99,187
1988	78,927
1989	96,979
1990	52,531

Note that these figures are total dolphin mortalities in the tuna fisheries. They include incidental catches of pantropical spotted dolphins, spinner dolphins, and common dolphins; the spotted dolphins are killed most often in these fisheries. Average yearly mortalities for 1986–1990 were 33,900 spotted dolphins, 12,400 spinner dolphins, and 4,900 common dolphins.

Although the 1986 dolphin kill by American tuna fishermen was 21,000, foreign fishermen killed another 110,000. The reduction in quotas meant a reduction in the size of the U.S. tuna fleet, and other countries, with no restrictions on the number of dolphins that could be killed, took up the slack. As the fleets of Mexico, Venezuela, Ecuador, and other Latin American countries increased, so did the number of dolphins killed. Congress responded by tightening the MMPA and imposing additional requirements on U.S. fishers and importers. By 1986, activists were concluding that the American people were becoming complacent about the dolphin kill; 133,000 dolphins died in the nets that year.

In October 1987, to demonstrate that illegal killing of dolphins was still going on, biologist and activist Sam LaBudde, working undercover for the Earth Island Institute, signed aboard the tuna boat *Maria Luisa,* registered in Panama. With a camcorder, which he explained was a toy given to him by his father, he filmed dolphins struggling in the nets and being cruelly gaffed and kicked overboard. In one shot, the nets surround a school of spinners and kill more than a hundred dolphins; it is then revealed that there are only twelve tuna in the net. LaBudde's gruesome film was shown on national television; it created such an uproar that a massive tuna boycott was initiated, attracting assorted celebrities and executives in the film industry. More significantly, LaBudde sent a copy of the film to Theresa Heinz, chair and chief executive officer of the Heinz Family Foundation, whose family company owned StarKist, the largest tuna cannery in the country, and Heinz convinced StarKist to sell only "dolphin-free" tuna. Kenneth Brower wrote a cover story about LaBudde and the tuna fishermen, which was published in the *Atlantic Monthly* in July 1989.With the story brought to a wider audience, it seemed as if the dolphin-killers were about to be restrained.

In 1990, with the total foreign and American kill at 52,000, Congress enacted the Dolphin Protection Consumer Information Act, which established procedures for labeling tuna as "dolphin safe," meaning that the tuna had to be caught, even by foreign fleets, in accordance with U.S. regulations that prohibit setting on dolphins. By law, "dolphin-safe tuna" had to be identified on the can. The International Whaling Commission (1996) reported incidental catches of pantropical spotted dolphins for 1992 as 6,531–6,790, for 1993 as 1,896, and for 1994 as 2,160. By 1993, the U.S. fleet had reduced its dolphin kill to 115 animals.

In 1998, tuna-fishing countries in the eastern tropical Pacific reached an agreement to provide further protection for dolphins during encirclement fishing. Releasing dolphins that were caught in fishing nets (using the backdown method and the Medina panel) before they were brought on board was part of the improved protection plan. The signatory nations agreed that if the United States amended previous import restrictions, the countries would enter into a binding agreement to continue dolphin protection. The International Dolphin Conservation Program Act, which included a requirement that the U.S. government come up with a "dolphin-safe" label, was passed on March 3, 1999.

About a hundred purse seiners now work the eastern Pacific; they are floating factories that can stay at sea as long as three months and load as much as 2,000 tons of tuna in their freezers. Forty-five of these are from Mexico, and the rest are from Panama, Venezuela, Colombia, and Vanuatu. From a 1976 high of 106 American tuna boats working the eastern tropical Pacific, there are now only 4. Under the terms of the 1993 North American Free Trade Agreement (NAFTA), open trade with Mexico was given the highest priority, which meant a complete relaxation of the restrictions on encircling tuna in the eastern tropical Pacific for Mexican boats. In August 1999, environmental activists filed suit in federal court to stop what one critic called the "animal genocide" that could result from weakened U.S. standards for dolphin-safe tuna. The suit, brought by a coalition of ten groups, sought to block labeling changes that would allow tuna caught by a previously banned method of encirclement to be sold in the United States under the dolphin-safe label. Environmentalists said that the changes, approved by Secretary of Commerce William Daley on April 29, 1999, would give the green light to Mexican and Latin American tuna boats that chase, harass, net, and kill dolphins using purse seines, a practice they alleged had killed an estimated 7 million dolphins over the previous forty years.

In January 2000, backed by the administration of President Bill Clinton and a handful of conservationists, the United States issued an interim final rule for a set of standards for dolphin-safe tuna that allows the encirclement method of fishing in the eastern tropical Pacific. As long as no dolphins are killed or injured by the encirclement method, the tuna can be labeled dolphin safe. In addition to allowing U.S. vessels to set their purse seine nets on dolphins in the eastern tropical Pacific, the interim final rule also changes the standard for the use of dolphin-safe labels on tuna products and establishes a tuna-tracking program to ensure adequate tracking and verification of tuna harvested there. Encirclement fishing has been banned in the United States since 1994, but the practice was continued by foreign fisheries, including those of Mexico and Venezuela. Incidental catch is still limited by U.S. law to 20,500 per year, but it is usually lower than that because of declining tuna seining efforts and the recent adoption of a porpoise mortality reduction program. This international agreement by all major tuna seining countries has a goal of reducing the total incidental catch to fewer than 5,000 dolphins per year by 2000. As of late 2002, the goal had not been reached.

In a recent study conducted by U.S. government biologists, Frederick Archer and colleagues (2001) reported an insidious side effect of the tuna fishery in which thousands of dolphin deaths went unreported. They wrote, "Although the reported dolphin bycatch has drastically decreased, the populations are not recovering at expected rates." One factor might be the stress of the high-speed chase and encirclement, during which calves would be unable to keep up with their mothers. If the mothers were caught in the nets, the calves, having fallen behind, would have escaped, only to starve because their mothers were gone. Thus, the counts, showing only the adults caught in the nets, did not account for the mortality of thousands of calves, now calculated to represent the loss of 10–15 percent more spotted dolphins and 6–10 percent more spinners than originally estimated.

According to an August 2002 report of the Southwest Fisheries Science Center of the National Marine Fisheries Service, "northeastern offshore spotted dolphins are at 20% and eastern spinner dolphins are at 35% of their pre-fishery levels; and neither population is recovering at a rate consistent with these levels of depletion and the reported kills." The death of uncounted baby dolphins in the nets has contributed substantially to this decline, but the stress induced by the netting process has also resulted in drowning, decreased births, and impaired health. Tuna fishing in the eastern tropical Pacific is now being conducted mostly by boats out of Mexico, Colombia, Ecuador, Venezuela, and Peru, countries not required by law to avoid causing stress to dolphins. The Southwest Fisheries Science Center report, released by the Earth Island Institute in December 2002 (available on the Internet at http://www.earthisland.org/immp/secret_report.pdf), cites figures showing that tuna fishers set on dolphins about 5,000 times per year, which means that some 6.8 million dolphins are pursued each year and 2 million are netted. Further broken down, these figures indicate that each offshore spotter is chased 10.6 times per year and captured in a net 3.2 times. Each eastern spinner is chased 5.6 times per year and captured 0.7 times. For the surviving dolphins, this is probably the functional definition of *stress*.

So with all this information in hand—some of it generated by the National Marine Fisheries Service—what did the U.S. government do? It concluded that encircling dolphins in nets was harmless, and it threw open the door to allow Mexican fishermen to sell tuna in the United States under a dolphin-safe label. A report issued on January 6, 2003, by the Environment News Service, an Internet watchdog of ecological issues, read: "On December 31, the National Marine Fisheries Service announced that after new research, it had concluded that the tuna purse seine industry of encircling dolphins to catch tuna has 'no significant adverse impact on dolphin populations in the Eastern Tropical Pacific Ocean'" (Lazaroff 2003). Outraged environmentalists planned to contest the new ruling in court. David Phillips of the Earth Island Institute said, "The Bush administration's claim that chasing and netting of dolphins is 'safe' for dolphins is fraudulent and must be overturned."

In the tuna fishery, another reason for killing cetaceans was invented. The fishermen didn't even want the dolphins; they were "incidental" consequences of fishing for skipjack and yellowfin tuna. Millions of spotters and spinners died because of their unpropitious inclination to associate with tuna. If this many dolphins could be killed unintentionally, imagine what men could do if they actually *intended* to kill cetaceans.

~ 11 ~

THE HUNTING
OF WHALES

In many recent cases in which animals have become extinct, people have been responsible, whether by eliminating the last individuals inadvertently (e.g., Steller's sea cow, passenger pigeon), by reducing the population below the level at which it is able to overcome the effects of ordinary attrition, or by so reducing the animals' available habitat that the remainder of the population does not have enough space and sustenance to live. Although Tasmanian sheepherders probably didn't think they could kill all the Tasmanian wolves, they succeeded in doing just that.

It would be poor business practice indeed to kill off the source of one's revenue, but that nearly describes what was surely the most infamous direct attack on a particular group of animals, the merciless human predation on whales. In some cases, such as early-twentieth-century whaling in the Antarctic, it appeared as if it were the determined goal of the industrial whalers to eliminate the blue, fin, sei, right, and humpback whales from the face of the earth. That they did not succeed can be attributed only to their inefficiency, not to any concern for conserving the whales. Only the California gray whale, also hunted to near extinction, has rebounded to numbers approximating its preexploitation levels. The blue, fin, right, and humpback whales are now reduced to relict populations, and some may never recover. What we do or don't do, now and in the future, may determine the fate of these and many other species. As evolutionary theorist David Archibald (1996) wrote, "the process of extinction . . . was occurring well before the emergence of *Homo sapiens,* although we certainly have accelerated it to breakneck rates."

The Egyptians used olive oil for lighting and lubrication, and candles made of other oils such as tallow and beeswax have been in use for thousands of years. Primitive lamps consisted of a vessel that held oil of some sort and a wick that allowed for controlled burning. Certain seeds, such as castor bean, sesame, cottonseed, linseed, and rapeseed, yield so-called vegetable oils when pressed, and when geographic expansion led to discovery of the coconut palm, its oil was used alongside the others for lubrication and the manufacture of foodstuffs, soaps, varnishes, and various other products. Fats and oils are indispensable to domestic life, and the discovery that there was a source of these unguents that did not have to be cultivated, only harvested, had a salutary effect on the development of European civilization, and a correspondingly devastating effect on the whales.

Instead of teeth, baleen whales have long strips of fibrous material hanging from their upper jaw that enable them to filter small organisms from the seawater. With the exception of the sperm whale, which has teeth only in its lower jaw, all the other "great" whales—the blue, fin, sei, Bryde's, minke, humpback, gray, right, and bowhead—are classified as baleen whales. (Another term for them is *mysticetes,* which means "mustache whales," a direct reference to the fringed baleen plates.) The oil of the baleen whale is of a type commonly found in a variety of plants and animals, and in fact it is identical in composition to human fat. Whale oil is a true fatty acid, consisting almost entirely of triglycerides, one molecule of glycerol in combination with three of fatty acids. The fatty acids can be combined with an alkali to produce soap, and the glycerol (also known as glycerine) can be used in the manufacture of emollients and explosives. It is also edible, but it was not utilized extensively until the beginning of the twentieth century, when the process known as hydrogenation was developed. When two hydrogen atoms were added to the oleic acid, the commonest fatty acid in whale oil, the oil was changed into a solid fat. Hydrogenated whale oil can be used in the manufacture of margarine, the discovery of which fact had a devastating effect on the world's baleen whale populations in the 1930s.

The "oil" of the toothed whales—particularly that found in the heads of the sperm whale and various species of dolphin—is not technically an oil at all but a wax, a condensation product (ester) of monoalcohols and fatty acids, that yields the finest candles ever made. Ever innovative, humankind quickly developed more and better uses for sperm whale oil, incorporating it into steelmaking (for the process known as quenching), leather dressing, textile sizing, and, again, soapmaking. When treated with sulfur, sperm whale oil becomes one of the best lubricants known, and it was regularly used as a component in automatic transmission fluids. In a 1977 article about cetacean oils, biochemist Ron Scogin wrote, "This oil has been regarded as so crucial to our national defense that a large stockpile is probably still being maintained for national emergencies."

As soon as he could (women do not figure in the history of whaling until well into the sixteenth century, when they began demanding that their husbands bring home whalebone for corsets), man took to the sea to begin a thousand-year war against the whales. The first skirmishes occurred in the relatively secluded Bay of Biscay at least a thousand years ago, but when the Basques recognized that the killing of whales was good business and that they were fishing out their native waters (realizations that would govern whalers for the rest of their variegated careers), they expanded their killing to another front. They headed across the Atlantic Ocean to Newfoundland, where they found more of the "right" whales to kill, and while they were at it, they discovered the bountiful cod-fishing grounds of Newfoundland. On the lookout for oil and the stuff they called whalebone—in reality the baleen—whalers from Britain and Holland headed north, originally with Basque harpooners aboard, and threw themselves enthusiastically (albeit coldly) into the business of killing all the Greenland whales they could.

It was the nature of some of these whales—called by the whalers the "right" whales because they had thick blubber, didn't swim too fast for their little boats, and floated when they were killed—to come close to certain shores to breed. (Science now knows the right whale as *Eubalaena glacialis*, from the Greek *eu*, meaning "true" or "original," and *balaena*, "whale." *Glacialis* is self-explanatory.) They preferred bays and inlets that were protected from the open sea, a preference they shared with the settlers who would establish a beachhead for "civilization" in these same protected bays and inlets. Unlike the aborigines whom these settlers sometimes encountered, the whales never disputed ownership of the land; they innocently required only breeding and calving grounds away from the rough seas and the possible predations of sharks and killer whales.

The settlers looked at the broad backs of the right whales and saw not their grace and beauty but floating oil factories—more enticingly, floating oil factories they didn't have to maintain. All they had to do was harvest the limitless bounty, usually for the price of a boat. The right whales died in Siberian waters as soon as these areas were discovered by Russian explorers; in Massachusetts at the hands of the first American settlers; in Table Bay and False Bay in South Africa when the Huguenots arrived there; in Tasmania and Botany Bay when the British transported their first shiploads of convicts; and in the Pacific Northwest when Alaska and Vancouver were settled. At least the right whale females with calves were spared by the early Japanese whalers, who exhibited an ecological sensitivity their descendants do not seem to share. Only off the barren coast of southern Argentina were the right whales untroubled; here, nobody was interested in settling the land. (Even today,

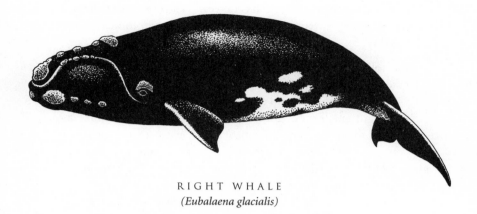

RIGHT WHALE
(Eubalaena glacialis)

there are but a few sheep ranches along the remote South Atlantic coasts of Patagonia, and the sole undisturbed population of right whales in the world still comes to breed in the bays of Golfo San José and Golfo Nuevo.)

In a 1986 publication devoted exclusively to the status of right whales, the International Whaling Commission (IWC) published, among other data, the number of right whales killed since the inception of whaling by various whalers in the North Atlantic Ocean:

The Basque fishery, 1059–1720	Fewer than 100 per year
Newfoundland and Labrador, 1530–1610	25,000–40,000
Davis Strait, 1719–1748 (mostly by French whalers)	623
Long Island, 1656–1733	3,423
The Massachusetts coast, 1820–1929	450

Although the North Atlantic right whale has been protected worldwide since 1935, in recent years it has shown a precipitous decline in numbers, unexplainable except in terms of its imminent extinction. In a report of their 1999 study, Hal Caswell, Masami Fujiwara, and Solange Brault warned:

> The North Atlantic northern right whale (*Eubalaena glacialis*) is considered the most endangered large whale species. Its population has recovered only slowly since the cessation of commercial whaling and numbers about 300 individuals. . . . Population growth rate declined from about 1.053 in 1980 to about 0.976 in 1994. Under current conditions the population is doomed to extinction; an upper bound on

the expected time to extinction is 191 years. The most effective way to improve the prospects of the population is to reduce [human-caused] mortality.

Researchers have recorded sightings annually since 1980 in calving areas off Florida and in waters off New England and into the Bay of Fundy in Nova Scotia. Until the 1999 study, no one suspected that the survival probability for northern right whales was diminishing or that the population was actually declining. As the report notes, the most effective way to improve the prospects for population persistence is to reduce mortality; among human causes, the right whale seems particularly at risk from entanglement in fishing gear, from collisions with ships, and from pollution.

In 1997, the National Oceanic and Atmospheric Administration (NOAA) introduced a 500-yard protection zone to reduce the chances of human activity disturbing or altering the behavior of northern right whales. Since July 1995, at least fourteen right whales have died, nine of which are known to have died or sustained serious injury from entanglements in fishing gear, ship strikes (a euphemism used to denote a ship running into a whale and often killing it), or other human-induced activities. This rate is about five times greater than in previous years, when one or two right whales died annually as a result of human interaction.

Two years later, at the National Marine Fisheries Service's Northeast Fisheries Science Center at Woods Hole, Massachusetts, the IWC convened a workshop to discuss the "status and trends of western North Atlantic right whales." Participants observed that although some other whale populations (Southern Hemisphere right whales and humpbacks, California gray whales) had recovered from very low observed abundance, the North Atlantic right whales had not—possibly a result of the Allee effect, in which the population growth rate declines *because* of low numbers (Courchamp, Clutton-Brock, and Grenfell 1999). A total of 263 right whales were counted in this intensively searched area stretching roughly from the Bay of Fundy to northeastern Florida. "The population," the researchers concluded, "appears to be decreasing at present as a result of (i) a decreased rate of survival in the 1990s versus the 1980s; (ii) an increase in effective calving interval in the 1990s, and (iii) known direct anthropogenic removals (ship strikes and entanglements in fishing gear) that have been increasing in recent years."

Right whales seem to be particularly susceptible to ship strikes. Since 1976, there have been ten recorded fatal strikes of right whales in the northwestern Atlantic from Maine to Florida; seven of these whales were juveniles.

In their 2001 discussion of ship collisions with whales, David Laist and colleagues noted that "young animals may be more vulnerable to being hit by ships. This could be caused by the relatively large amount of time that calves and juveniles spend at the surface . . . it may also indicate that whales learn to avoid vessels as they mature." A team from the Woods Hole Oceanographic Institution attached noninvasive recording devices to North Atlantic right whales in order to analyze their swimming, diving, and acoustic behavior. Right whales were found to be positively buoyant (they float) near the surface, whereas other marine mammal species are negatively buoyant (they sink). Although right whales glide during the ascent portion of their dives, they maintain a similar or greater ascent rate than other species, which they could achieve only with the assistance of some buoyant force. These results provide insight into how the natural behavior of this whale species may increase its risk of being hit by ships. Even if a right whale correctly perceives a ship as a threat, its ability to maneuver may be compromised by its buoyancy, leaving it vulnerable to ship strikes. It is the whales' misfortune that the waters of their traditional breeding and feeding grounds are filled with tankers, freighters, cruise ships, and pleasure boats of all descriptions. The region inhabited by these whales includes such major ports as Boston, New York, and Miami and is one of the busiest in the world. Just as when the technology was designed to kill them, in ships versus whales, the whales come out the losers.

Humpbacks were far from being the "right" whales to kill; they were comparatively skinny, had negligible baleen, and sank when they were killed. Nevertheless, the whalers picked them off whenever and wherever they found them. It was not until 1970—when most of the world's humpbacks had been annihilated—that we learned humpback whales were unique in that they sang complex, mysterious songs, but we had virtually eliminated the whales before we could learn what, if anything, the songs meant. After whalers had reduced the inshore populations of right whales and humpbacks, they discovered that some whales in the far north were even *more* right: they had all the attributes of their smaller relatives, but they were bigger and therefore had more fat that could be boiled into oil, as well as longer baleen plates to satisfy the bottomless maw of Dame Fashion. These whales, known variously as Greenland whales, polar whales, and bowheads, are found only in the circumpolar Arctic, and from the sixteenth century to late in the nineteenth, they were killed with such celerity and determination that there are hardly any left. In some areas, there may be none. In a paper published in 2001, Robert Allen and Ian Keay argued that by 1828, the stock of resident bowhead whales off the eastern coast of Greenland had been hunted to the brink of extinction. Today, there are no bowhead whales there.

The story of commercial whaling is a story of unrelieved greed and insensitivity. In no other activity has our species practiced such a relentless pursuit of wild animals, and if no species has become extinct at the hands of the whalers, it has not been for want of trying. *Homo sapiens* came close with the right whales and the humpbacks; we killed off the bowheads until it was uneconomical to look for any more; we followed the gray whales into their breeding areas in Korea, China, Japan, and California and killed so many that by 1930 the species was thought to be gone from the face of the earth. The proud Yankee whalers in their square-rigged ships scoured the seven seas so that they could decimate the world's sperm whale populations.

The early whalers achieved these dubious victories with primitive weapons; imagine what they might have done given the ordnance to wage war properly on the whales. For 850 years of this thousand-year war, the whalers depended on hand-thrown harpoons. Progress for the early-nineteenth-century whaler meant a new toggle design for the harpoon head or a previously undiscovered stock of whales to throw it at. Of the ten species of great whale, five—the gray, humpback, right, bowhead, and sperm—were slaughtered to the brink of extinction in those first eight and a half centuries. The other five—the blue, fin, sei, Bryde's, and minke—were designed differently, and although the whalers sighted them with disconcerting regularity, they swam tantalizingly outside the harpooners' range and competence. These species belong to a group known collectively as rorquals (from the Norwegian for "grooved whale"), and they are characterized by a series of longitudinal pleats along the throat and belly that enable them to expand their throats as they engulf huge quantities of seawater containing small sea creatures. All these whales are slim and graceful—although one species can weigh as much as 150 tons—and they are capable of speeds that made them completely inaccessible to men in rowboats.

The rorquals are largely missing from the early history of whaling because the whalers could not catch them, and even if they had succeeded, they had no way of handling an animal that weighed 300,000 pounds. To make matters worse for the whalers—but better for the whales—these animals inconveniently sank if and when they were killed, and the only thing harder than trying to handle a 300,000-pound animal at sea is trying to handle a 300,000-pound animal that has sunk. Whaling historians were almost ready to write *finis* to their subject when the populations of right, bowhead, humpback, gray, and sperm whales seemed to be so low that there was no point in chasing them any more. Besides, petroleum had been discovered in Pennsylvania in 1859, and it appeared that the need to risk life and limb in chases of dangerous whales was passing. It was almost as if the rorquals had received a pardon.

But of course they hadn't; they had received instead a judgment so merciless that it amounted to a generic death sentence. Instead of ignoring the rorquals, the whalers developed a way of chasing and killing them that would bring them to even lower levels than their predecessors in whaling history: the Norwegian Svend Foyn invented the exploding grenade harpoon. From 1868 to the present day, virtually every whale killed by the hand of man has been killed by Foyn's invention. (The exceptions are the occasional whales killed by aborigines, who can't afford the heavy artillery.) With the grenade harpoon and the bow-mounted cannon with which to fire it from a steam-powered catcher boat, the heretofore inaccessible rorquals were brought within range.

Now, armed with 200-pound iron shafts that spread foot-long toggles into the body of the whale, and equipped with tubes through which compressed air could be pumped into the body of the dead whale to keep it afloat, powerful catcher-killer boats roamed the oceans in search of the great blue and fin whales, the smaller sei and Bryde's whales, and the relatively small minke whales. (In fact, the animals are small only by cetacean standards; a full-grown minke can be thirty-three feet long and weigh ten tons.) As technology provided them with more ways to kill and process the rorquals, whalers added to their arsenal. Once they had found a way to kill the giants, they began to process them in a more modern fashion. The Dutch and British whalers of the seventeenth century had peeled the carcasses at sea, minced the blubber, and stuffed it through the bungholes of wooden barrels. Then the Nantucket sperm whalers "tried out" the whales in iron cauldrons on the decks of their sailing ships, even feeding the fires with the whales' own kindling by using unburned scraps of skin to feed the try-pot fires. Various other whalers did their dirty work on the shore, dragging the bloody carcasses up ramps to be reduced to their components in the heat of the Australian or New Zealand sun.

When progress came to whale processing, it came in a swift and deadly form: invention of the stern slipway. This gaping chute in the rear of a factory ship meant that 100-foot whales could be hauled up on deck and flensed at sea; the whalemen were no longer tied to land stations. Ten-ton pressure cookers received the chopped-up bone and meat and reduced it to meal for use as fertilizer. The oil was stored in steel tanks and transported across the world to be turned into margarine, soap, and pharmaceuticals. For World

War I, whale oil was reduced to its glyceride components, which in turn were used in the manufacture of nitroglycerine. The second time the industrial nations of the world trained their guns on one another, they concurrently killed whales for oil, meat, and margarine.

In war or in peace, whalers always managed to find a way to justify the slaughter. The discovery of petroleum, instead of sparing the whales, provided fuel for the steamers and diesel-powered catcher boats to get to the far reaches of the globe where the whales could be found. We needed oil for candles or for lighting or for soap and margarine; corsets and skirts had to be braced with whalebone strips; hungry people wanted the meat; the livers provided vitamins; men needed work; national pride would be affected if another country caught more whales. And throughout the history of whaling, as the catch began to decline, the whalers simply escalated their hunting efforts. It appeared that everyone knew the whales were being hunted out of existence, but nobody wanted to acknowledge it. Besides, it was clear that if one nation stopped whaling or even reduced its effort, the others would move in.

From the day in 1868 when Svend Foyn of Vestfold, Norway, first trained his primitive harpoon cannon on the blue whale, the numbers of *Balaenoptera musculus* began to decline. Not until it was far too late did anyone recognize that whalers were methodically eliminating the grandest animals that ever lived. They killed them in the North Atlantic and the North Pacific, in the South Atlantic and the Indian Ocean. But the greatest concentration of these magnificent creatures was in the high latitudes of the Antarctic, and when the whalers found their way there after the turn of the twentieth century, they commenced to murder these gentle giants. Because the whalers' ingenious scheme concentrated all their efforts on the blue whales, they ignored the other species until the blues became too scarce. Then they turned on the next smallest species, and the next and the next.

Throughout this millennial war on whales, various nations have risen to an uncertain ascendancy. Circumstances allowed the Dutch, the British, the Yankees, the Norwegians, or the Japanese to take the lead in the race to eliminate the whales, but other factors usually knocked them from their precarious domination and allowed another nation to pass them in the statistical sweepstakes. (Aboriginal whaling was primitive; these whalers couldn't have affected whale populations even if they wanted to.) When the specter of commercial greed appeared, however, the stakes were raised. What had been a subsistence activity became a business, and the whales suffered in direct proportion to the prosperity of the whaling communities—the more successful the whaling was, the more whales died. It has been said that a rational management scheme, instead of uncontrolled hunting, which allowed the whalers to decide what was best for business, could have provided an almost endless supply of whale meat and oil to the world. Instead, the whaling nations fought among themselves for the right to eliminate whale species. Although their economies suffered—often as a function of bad management—the consequences were nothing compared with the suffering of the whales. If the whaleman was lonely, uncomfortable, cold, or hungry, or even if his life was threatened, those were minor inconveniences in contrast to the massive agony visited upon the whales. Trusting creatures whose size probably precluded a knowledge of fear, the whales were chased until they were exhausted and then stabbed and blown up; their babies were slaughtered; their numbers were halved and halved again. And still the whalers persisted, convincing themselves that the killing was being done in the name of progress, commerce, gross national product, gross national pride, or whatever gods technological man invokes to justify his atrocities against nature.

Are there now, or were there ever, reasons for this senseless slaughter? Some men died in pursuit of the whale, but a vastly disproportionate number of whales died in this cetacean world war, a war in which one side was heavily armed and the other almost defenseless and unaware a war was going on. Volumes have been written about the courage of the "warriors" who risked their lives so that the whales might die for technology and fashion. At one time, whale oil was used to light the lamps of Europe and America, but even if we allow for the expediency of whale-killing to avoid darkness, we must still search for a rationale for the prodigious slaughter that followed the discovery and development of petroleum. Whales were killed by the hundreds of thousands in perhaps the most callous demonstration history offers of humankind's self-appointed dominion over animals. One searches almost in vain for an expression of sympathy, compassion, understanding, or rationality. In their place were only insensitivity and avarice.

In their voluminous logbooks and journals, the whalers documented the slaughter of the innocents in the name of progress. Was there ever another course? Could the whales have been saved? Yes. It is only when the signals are clear and unequivocal and still we do not act that we can be held fully accountable. The whaling nations might be excused for not focusing on the whaling problem in 1937; there were other cases before the world court. But when World War II was over and the whalers came to Washington to hammer out an agreement to control the whaling industry, they ended up producing a document that virtually guaranteed the elimination of the whales—and the industry, as it turned out. It was one of the most shortsighted exercises in the history of international negotiations. With a thousand years of history to guide them, the whalers condemned themselves to repeat all the mistakes made before. By 1946, the framers of the International Convention for the Regulation of Whaling knew all about the destruction of the right whales and the disappearance of the Arctic bowheads. They had before them the bitter documentation of the decline of the Pacific gray whale. And yet they persisted: they designed a system to oversee the destruction of the world's remaining whales.

The history of whaling is marked by some significant dates, only a few of which we can pinpoint. The first day a human being encountered a beached whale carcass is lost, and the moment the Basque lookouts spotted their first right whale will never be known. But we can identify 1596 as the year that Dutch explorer Willem Barents discovered Spitsbergen. Dutchmen and Englishmen in high-pooped sailing vessels braved Arctic cold and ship-crushing ice to hunt the bowhead for its baleen "finnes," used in the manufacture of corset stays and busks for ladies of fashion. In the seventeenth century, halfway around the world, an enterprising Japanese fisherman named Kakuemon Taiji threw a wisteria-vine net over a whale and launched his countrymen on a course of cetacean destruction that would continue uninterrupted for four hundred years. When the *Mayflower* arrived at Cape Cod on November 21, 1620, the Pilgrims found themselves in the company of black right whales and decided to stay rather than continue on to Virginia, their original destination. In 1712, Captain Christopher Hussey may have been blown off the Nantucket shore in a storm and may have killed the first sperm whale in New England waters. Even if the story is apocryphal, there is no doubt that shortly thereafter the Nantucketers began to roam the world in search of the mighty, square-headed cachalots, in the process developing an industry that would change the way the Western world was lit and lubricated. When the British shipped their first load of convicts to Botany Bay in 1788, they could not have known that the captains would find the waters of Australasia thick with whales. Quick to capitalize, whalers rounded Cape Horn in 1789 and discovered the rich whaling grounds of the eastern Pacific. The Nantucket whaler *Maro* encountered more than the riches of Cipango in 1820 when concentrations of sperm whales were found on Japan's whaling grounds. Captain Thomas Welcome Roys, who blew off his own hand testing a rocket harpoon, sailed through the Bering Strait in 1848 and found these heretofore unexplored waters filled with fat bowheads. In 1855, Charles Melville Scammon, another whaling captain, sailed over the barrier bar at an isolated lagoon on the lonely peninsula that is Baja California, and another whale species was marked for slaughter. Four years later, just when it seemed the world's whales were destined to provide their fat to lubricate the industrial revolution, Colonel Edwin Drake drilled the Western world's first oil well at Titusville, Pennsylvania.

The discovery of petroleum did not save the whales, of course; instead, it provided the impetus for the whalers to mechanize and modernize their industry. Armed with exploding grenade harpoons, they took out after the whales with a vengeance fueled by equal portions of greed, bloodlust, and technology. The great rorquals, long considered too fast and too powerful for the whalers in their open rowing boats, were now within firing range. They were harpooned, shot, blown up, poisoned, and electrocuted in numbers that defy the imagination. Millions of tons of whales were reduced to their components for the lights, machines, wars, fashions, and tables of the world. Deep in the bone-chilling cold of the Antarctic, the great whales had remained unmolested since the morning of the world, but in fifty years' time, the rapacious whalers slaughtered them to near extinction. They shot them under the lowering skies of the Ross Sea, and they hauled them aboard factory ships with gaping maws that swallowed these 100-ton creatures and reduced them to oil and fertilizer in an hour.

When it appeared the whalers would run out of whales if they kept up the carnage, they convened to figure out a way to preserve their industry. On May 30, 1949, representatives of fifteen nations met in London, and the International Whaling Commission was born. For the next forty years, the commissioners, who were supposed to preserve whales for the industry, sat and watched as the whales vanished and the industry deteriorated before their uncomprehending eyes. Compared with the millennium it took the whalers to reduce the whale stocks to vestigial, scattered populations, the end came remarkably quickly. One by one, the whaling nations quit their deadly, costly, anachronistic business. In 1972, the United Nations unanimously passed a resolution calling for a complete cessation of worldwide whaling. The United States passed its own legislation, the Marine Mammal Protection Act of 1972, which protected all whales, dolphins, and seals in American waters and closed down the last of the American whaling stations. South Africa shut down Durban's whaling station in 1975, and the Australians conducted an inquiry in 1978 that resulted in the elimination of Australian whaling. In 1982, only the Soviets and the Japanese were killing whales on the high seas.

From the inception of the IWC in 1949 until around 1970, member nations awarded themselves quotas of various whales to kill. (Before that, there were no controls whatsoever; whaling was conducted by any country,

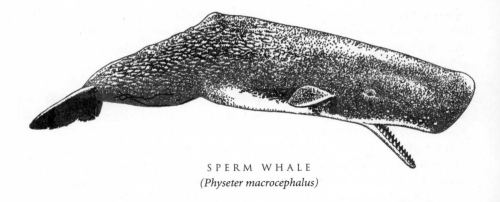

SPERM WHALE
(Physeter macrocephalus)

with any equipment, and on any species of whale the hunters were inclined or able to kill.) Blue whales, already in a steep decline, were not officially "protected" by the IWC until 1966. The whalers then turned their harpoons on the remaining baleen whales in the Antarctic in descending order of size: fin whales, sei whales, and then the lowly minke, all the time reenergizing the sperm whale hunt.

All during the nineteenth century, square-rigged whaling ships from New England plied the seas in search of the sperm whale, but in the great scheme of things, they actually didn't kill all that many, largely because chasing down a single whale from a rowboat and then throwing a spear at it may be picturesque and dangerous (and the stuff of great literature), but it is hardly an efficient way of reducing whale populations. In a 1935 study, Charles H. Townsend, whom we have met before (in the discussions of the Patagonian toothfish and the disastrous—and almost final—hunt of elephant seals on Guadalupe Island), analyzed the logbooks of 744 American vessels that carried out 1,665 whaling voyages from 1792 to 1913, and he accounted for the deaths of 36,908 whales, an average of 305 whales per year. His time frame included the start of the sperm whale fishery, when few ships were engaged in it, and the end of the fishery, when mechanized whalers had forsaken sperm whales for the blue and fin whales of the Antarctic, but even at the height of the fishery, in the mid-nineteenth century, there was never a year in which 10,000 sperm whales were killed. (Other nations were engaged in sperm whaling, of course, but none approached the number of whales killed by the doughty Yankees.)

Were sperm whale populations decimated by nineteenth-century longboat whaling? Not nearly as much as they were during the 1960s, when fleets of Soviet and Japanese catcher boats worked the North Pacific south of the

Aleutians, hunting sperm whales with techniques and in numbers that would have astonished Captain Ahab. Cannons mounted on the catcher boats shot eight-foot-long exploding grenade harpoons into the whales. Then the whalers towed the dead whales to the 500-foot-long factory ship, where they were winched aboard through the stern slipway and processed on deck. Although the Yankee fishery could account for 36,000 whales in a 121-year period, the Soviet and Japanese whalers killed almost that many in the North Pacific in 1968 and 1969 alone.* Under pressure from anti-whaling governments and conservation organizations, the IWC continued to reduce sperm whale quotas for Japan and the USSR until 1980, when the number fell to zero. It was probably the first time in two centuries that commercial whalers were not killing sperm whales. Despite 200 years of slaughter, the sperm whale was not considered endangered then, but is considered endangered now.

Despite decades of optimistic estimates, the global sperm whale population suffered heavy losses from mechanized whaling. Estimates of the total sperm whale population during the onslaughts of the North Pacific Soviet and Japanese whaling fleets were based on the traditional "catch per unit effort" methods, which only estimated the difficulty in finding and killing whales from one year to the next. "The estimates of 1.5 to 2 million animals," stated Hal Whitehead of Dalhousie University in Nova Scotia, in a paper presented at the 2002 meeting of the International Whaling Commission, "have no valid scientific basis." Before the advent of sperm whaling in the mid-eighteenth century, there were about 1.11 million animals, Whitehead suggests, but on the basis of mark-and-recapture techniques, acoustic censuses, and visual censuses, Whitehead estimates that there are now only some 360,000 sperm whales in the world's oceans. The revised estimate now means—among other things—that twentieth-century whalers, grossly mistaken in their estimates of the numbers of sperm whales, were actually hunting a declining species, and the remaining whalers, such as the Japanese, who continue to argue for a quota of sperm whales, will be targeting a depleted population.

In 1966, Scott McVay wrote an article for *Scientific American* titled "The Last of the Great Whales," which brought the plight of the whales to the attention of the general public for the first time. Two years later, *Natural History* magazine published another of his articles, "Can Leviathan Long Endure So

---

*In a 1980 IWC report, Japanese sperm whale expert Seiji Ohsumi provided the totals for sperm whaling in the North Pacific from 1910 to 1966. The numbers are broken down into the categories of "Japan, coastal" (total for those years was 78,220); "Kuril Islands" (28,399); "Japan, pelagic" (48,232); and "USSR, pelagic" (106,654). The grand total of sperm whales killed in the North Pacific during this sixty-six-year period was 261,505.

Wide a Chase?" (a quote from Herman Melville's *Moby-Dick*). Both articles revealed the extent of the killing being conducted under the aegis of the IWC, and readers were outraged at the revelations. At approximately the same time, acousticians Roger and Katy Payne were recording and analyzing the eerie "songs" of Hawaiian humpbacks; the tuna-porpoise problem was receiving nationwide publicity; and Flipper was appearing in movies and on television. We began to believe that whales and dolphins were something very special, and we weren't going to sit idly by while they were being slaughtered out of existence.

In 1978, succumbing to international pressure from environmentalists, the IWC agreed to admit nongovernmental observers (NGOs) to their proceedings, and a couple of years later the press was admitted for the first time. (The IWC did not conduct its business in secret, but it also did not go out of its way to publicize its activities.) The NGOs and the press let the cat out of the bag, and before long a worldwide anti-whaling movement had arisen. Petitions were circulated and demonstrations were staged in Washington, London, even Tokyo. By this time too, various nations—usually those such as the United States, Britain, Australia, and New Zealand, which had a violent whaling history—emphatically denounced whaling and, with the NGOs, lobbied for a reduction of quotas or the complete elimination of commercial whaling.

On July 23, 1982, perhaps the most important date in the thousand-year history of whaling, the IWC voted for a moratorium on all commercial whaling.* Many of the whaling countries protested, objected, and litigated; they invented myriad subterfuges and excuses to continue their business. Faced with declining profits, declining whales, and a manifold increase in global criticism, however, the Soviets quit in 1987. The Japanese quit officially in 1988, though as of this writing, they are still in the whaling business but on a smaller scale. Since the moratorium took effect, whaling has diminished considerably, but whales are still being killed by Alaskans, Japanese, and Norwegians, and various dolphins, not under the jurisdiction of the IWC, are still dying in tuna nets. A decade after passage of the moratorium, commercial whaling appeared to be over, and the IWC, deprived of its dedicated func-

---

*As a representative of the National Audubon Society, I was a member of the American delegation to the IWC from 1980 to 1990. I was present in Brighton, England, in July 1982 at the meeting in which the moratorium was passed. Several of us reacted noisily to the event, and we were asked to leave the meeting room to celebrate elsewhere. Many of us who had campaigned for the moratorium—and cheered its passage—believed we were witnessing the end of commercial whaling. We were wrong.

tion "to provide for the proper conservation of whale stocks and thus make possible the orderly development of the whaling industry," appeared redundant. It began as an organization that encouraged the slaughter of the whales, passed through a stage in which some of its member nations opposed others on basic whaling issues, and came out of the tunnel into an age of conservation. Those who believed whaling would be replaced by whale-watching did not recognize that the whalers—as grimly determined to hang on as any harpooner on a Nantucket sleighride—were not about to give up their battle for the opportunity to kill more whales.

All the great whales were decimated to the point that they may never recover. Right whales, humpbacks, and bowheads have been reduced to sparse shadow populations throughout the world. We do not know how many sperm whales there are—although there are many fewer than we once thought. Even with worldwide protection, the rorqual species are struggling to survive, and we may witness the death of the last blue whale in our lifetime.

Estimation of whale numbers was not helped by the Soviets' tremendous underreporting of their catches. This admission was made in 1994 by Alexei Yablokov, one of the USSR's foremost cetologists, in the esteemed British journal *Nature*. As Phil Clapham and C. Scott Baker noted in 2002, "former soviet biologists revealed that the USSR had conducted a massive campaign of illegal whaling beginning shortly after World War II. Soviet factory fleets had killed virtually all the whales they encountered, irrespective of size, age, or protected status." In the Southern Hemisphere, while reporting a total catch of 2,710 humpbacks, the Soviets had actually taken more than 48,000.

Whaling, mercifully, has ended for Russia, one of the major players in the latter half of the twentieth century, but the intransigent Japanese and Norwegians have not retired from the field of battle, and in one way or another they are still killing whales. The Norwegians, who never actually quit, are still taking some hundreds of minkes every year off their northern coasts, claiming that their fishermen need the money and need to protect their fish stocks from the hungry whales. In 2001, they took 552 minke whales; Norway's self-assigned quota for 2002 is 671. In June 2002, after a fourteen-year hiatus, Iceland announced the resumption of international trade in whale products, which meant that Norwegian whale meat could be imported into Iceland. Negotiations were also under way to reopen trade in whale meat with Japan, last implemented in 1988.

In 2000, the Japanese awarded themselves a "scientific research permit" for minke whales, Bryde's whales, and sperm whales and then went out and began killing them. It's just a happy coincidence, of course, that the meat ends up in the fish markets, ostensibly to provide money for continued research projects. In early 2002, the Japanese decided to double their self-assigned quota for "research" whaling. In addition to the 440 minkes that Japanese whalers kill every year in the Antarctic, on February 22, 2002, they notified the IWC that they were going to take 50 minkes and 50 sei whales in the North Pacific.

The fifty-fourth annual meeting of the IWC was held in Shimonoseki, Japan, from May 20 to May 23, 2002. Neither the whaling nations nor the anti-whalers gave an inch. At this meeting, Masayuki Komatsu, head of Japan's Fisheries Agency, referred to whales as "cockroaches of the sea," a statement not designed to bring harmony to the meeting. Presumably in retaliation for the defeat of previous Japanese proposals, Japan introduced a resolution that would deny quotas on the bowhead whales hunted by Siberian and Alaskan aborigines, which passed. It was the first time in fifty-six years that there was no authorized aboriginal whale hunt. As usual, the subject of Japanese "research whaling" was hotly contested, and despite observations that this killing—which has resulted in the deaths of more than 5,000 minke, Bryde's, and sperm whales since 1987—is only an excuse to keep Japan's whaling industry afloat, the IWC again failed to take any action. In their 2002 discussion of the future of cetaceans in a changing world, William Burns and Geoffrey Wandesforde-Smith wrote:

> Despite all the threats of recrimination and withdrawal that have swirled around the IWC in recent years, most of the parties, even including Japan in the aftermath of Shimonoseki, still seem to find it far more perilous to set out on their own than to continue to fight over their differences within the framework of the IWC. Thus, the IWC is likely to remain the focal point for the management of commercial whaling in the future.... Whatever compromise is ultimately reached on the resumption of commercial whaling, the IWC's legacy in the twenty-first century will depend primarily on its ability to confront emerging issues, including environmental impacts and the ever growing threats to small cetaceans. Whether the IWC is up to the challenge remains an open question whose ultimate answer will have momentous implications for many of the world's cetacean species.

Five months later, on October 14, a special meeting of the IWC was convened in Cambridge, England, to reconsider the issue of limits for the aboriginal subsistence catch of bowhead whales. In addition, an item was to be included regarding an interim relief allocation for Japanese coastal whaling.

Quotas for Siberian and Alaskan aborigines were accepted by consensus, allowing Alaskan Eskimos and the native people of Chukotka, Russia, to hunt 280 bowhead whales over the next five years, with an annual average of 51 bowheads for the Eskimos and 5 for the Russians. Relief for Japanese coastal whaling villages was defeated.

It didn't take long, however, for the fragile house of cards erected at Shimonoseki to come crashing down. At this special meeting, only five months after the conclusion of the annual meeting, Iceland was readmitted to the IWC despite an earlier denial of its petition and despite its avowed intention to resume commercial whaling. The vote for admittance was nineteen to eighteen, with many supporters of the proposal being nations with no direct interest in whaling (such as Benin, Gabon, Mongolia, and Palau) that had been brought into the IWC by Japan with the promise of economic assistance. (Similar tactics for increasing votes were employed in the 1980s by the anti-whaling nations when they brought in Austria and Switzerland— countries as landlocked as Mongolia.) A three-fourths majority is required to rescind the moratorium, so the anti-whalers still have an edge. However, it has been demonstrated that the balance of power can be shifted, and with Iceland now ready to join Norway in whale-killing, the respite afforded the whales by the moratorium may soon be history.

There must be something in man that, upon his seeing a whale offshore or at sea, unleashes an almost uncontrollable desire to kill it. In his 1966 article, Scott McVay asked questions that the whaling industry—and the world that let them kill its whales—should have asked itself:

> What is it in our nature that propels us to continue a hunt initiated in earlier times? Are we like some lethal mechanical toy that will not wind down until the last bomb explodes in the last whale's side? What is it that makes so small a thing of eliminating in our lifetime the oceanic role of the largest creature that has ever lived on our planet? What is it that kills the goose that lays the golden egg? Is our own obituary scrawled in the fates of the bowhead and the right whale, the blue and the humpback— all species that no longer contribute to the biological systems of which they were a part for millions of years? What is the true use of whales beyond bone, beef and blubber?

Edward O. Wilson of Harvard University is probably the scientist most closely associated in the public mind with the concept of biodiversity, and our most eloquent spokesman for its preservation. In his *Future of Life,* he wrote of the blue whale:

At 100 feet and 150 tons in full maturity, the species is the largest animal that ever lived on the land or sea. It is among the easiest to hunt and kill. Over 300,000 were harvested during the twentieth century, with a peak haul of 29,649 in the 1930–31 season. By the early 1970s the population had plummeted to several hundred individuals. The Japanese were especially eager to continue the hunt even at the risk or total extinction. So [economist Colin] Clark asked, What practice would yield the whalers and humanity the most money: cease hunting and let the blue whales recover in numbers, then harvest them sustainably forever, or kill the rest off as quickly as possible and invest the profits in growth stocks? The disconcerting answer: kill them all and invest the money.

"But," Wilson pointed out, "there are many other values, destined to grow along with our knowledge of living *Balaenoptera musculus* in science, medicine, aesthetics, in dimensions and magnitudes still unforeseen. What was the value of a blue whale in A.D. 1000? Close to zero. What will be its value in A.D. 3000? Essentially limitless, plus the gratitude of the generation then alive to those who in their wisdom saved the whale from extinction."

ECOLOGY IN TROUBLE

～ 12 ～

WHAT IS KILLING
THE CORAL REEFS?

"Coral reefs are the most structurally complex and taxonomically diverse marine ecosystems, providing habitat for tens of thousands of associated fishes and invertebrates," wrote marine ecologist Jeremy Jackson and his colleagues in 2001. They continued: "Recently, coral reefs have experienced dramatic phase shifts in dominant species due to intensified human disturbance beginning centuries ago. The effects are most pronounced in the Caribbean, but are also apparent on the Great Barrier Reef in Australia, despite extensive protection over the past three decades."

Corals, the building blocks of reef formations, are a variety of small, sedentary marine organisms characterized by an external skeleton of a stone-like, horny, or leathery consistency. They are classified as cnidarians, along with the jellyfish, hydroids, sea fans, and sea anemones. There are true or stony corals (scleractinians, order Scleractinia), which are the most familiar forms, occurring in various shapes, as in brain coral, mushroom coral, star coral, staghorn coral, and elkhorn coral; black and thorny corals (antipatharians, order Antipatharia); horny corals, or gorgonians (order Gorgonacea); and blue corals (order Coenothecalia). The body of a coral animal consists of a polyp, a hollow, soft cylinder ending in a mouth surrounded by tentacles; at the opposite end, the polyp is attached to some surface. The tentacles are equipped with stinging cells (nematocysts) that paralyze the coral's prey. At night, the animal withdraws into its external skeleton, a cylindrical container known as a corallite or theca. Corals reproduce either sexually, by releasing eggs and sperm into the water, or asexually by budding, wherein a finger-like extension matures into a new polyp.

Coral reefs are formations composed of the skeletons of dead corals bound together by their own limestone. Over thousands of years, coral growth, death, and cementing build a structure on which the living corals continue to attach themselves, but contributors to the reefs also include

ELKHORN CORAL
(Acropora palmata)

plants such as coralline algae as well as protozoans, mollusks, and tube-building worms. Most reefs occur within a band thirty degrees north or south of the equator. The corals' success as reef builders depends on their association with tiny single-celled plants called zooxanthellae, which live in the polyps' tissues. Because they are plants, the zooxanthellae require sunlight for photosynthesis, the processing of the carbon dioxide produced by the polyp. If the zooxanthellae die, the coral polyps die, and the reef, once a host of living creatures, becomes nothing more than a stony, lifeless structure. There are deepwater corals, however, that lack zooxanthellae—they are known as azooxanthellate corals—and live below the level at which light penetrates the ocean, at depths as low as 5,000 feet. These animals cannot photosynthesize, and they capture their prey with tiny, sticky tentacles.

The living corals form only a thin veneer of the coral reefs, measured in millimeters, but, as Charles Birkeland of the University of Guam wrote in 1997, "this film of living tissue has shaped the face of the Earth by creating limestone structures sometimes over 1,300 m thick, from the surface down to its base on volcanic rock (Enewetak Atoll), or over 2,000 km long (Great Barrier Reef)." Bruce Hatcher (1997) continues: "Everything that is useful about reefs (to humans and the rest of nature) is produced by this organic film, which is approximately equivalent (in terms of biomass and carbon) to a large jar of peanut butter (or Vegemite) spread out over each square meter of reef."

What is killing the world's corals? Anything and everything, but mostly us. "Coral reefs," wrote Callum Roberts and colleagues in 2002,

> fringe one-sixth of the world's coastlines and support hundreds of thousands of animal and plant species. Fifty-eight percent of the world's reefs are reported to be threatened by human activities. Terrestrial agriculture, deforestation, and development are introducing large quantities of sediment, nutrients, and other pollutants into coastal areas, causing widespread eutrophication and degradation of biologically productive habitats. Coral reefs are often fished extensively, and in regions of the Indian and Pacific Oceans, fishing with dynamite and poisons has devastated reef habitats.

Fishing with dynamite has to be one of the most harmful techniques ever devised. Sticks of dynamite, dropped from small boats, detonate underwater in an explosion that ruptures the swim bladder of fishes, kills them, and causes them to float to the surface. They are then scooped up and hauled to shore to be cleaned and sold. If possible, the use of Alfred Nobel's invention to collect seashells is even worse.

Most people don't fully realize that the colorful and decorative shells they collect were once living animals; marine snails do not simply move into the shells, as hermit crabs do; they *manufacture* them. Moreover, most shells for sale in souvenir shops or on the Internet are collected not by beachcombers but by professional collectors. Because some of these snails (technically referred to as gastropods) live deep in rock and coral crevices, it is utterly uneconomical to dive and collect them one by one, so the collectors poison or blow up the reefs and harvest the shells of the dead snails.*

After the ubiquitous *Homo sapiens,* far and away the most dangerous and destructive creature the planet has ever known, the animal most threatening to coral is *Acanthaster planci,* the crown-of-thorns starfish. Taking its name

---

*I began my marine painting career by painting seashells. In 1973, I had a one-man show at a gallery on Sanibel Island, off the coast of Florida, generally considered the shell-collecting capital of the United States. But when I realized that in some small way, my glorification of shells was encouraging collecting—and therefore encouraging the dynamiters—I stopped painting shells. In 1975, *Audubon* magazine published "Why I Became an Ex-Shell Painter," in which I explained the reasons for my decision to quit.

from its long, sharp, toxic spines, the crown-of-thorns is a reddish brown, heavy-spined starfish; its seven to twenty-one arms can reach a length of eighteen inches. Females produce 12 million to 60 million eggs per spawning season. These starfish live on Pacific Ocean coral reefs from Australia to Hawaii and as far east as the Gulf of California. Their primary food item is coral polyps, but they can and will eat almost anything that crawls along the ocean bottom. Beginning about 1950, the *Acanthaster* population increased enormously on reefs off Japan, and in 1963, on Australia's Great Barrier Reef, there was a population explosion attributed to the decimation by shell collectors of the crown-of-thorns' chief predator, a large marine snail known as the Pacific triton (*Charonia tritonis*). (At a length of more than sixteen inches and with an intricate color pattern, the triton—also known as Triton's trumpet—is one of the largest and most prized of all marine snails.) Thereafter, the starfish multiplied throughout the southern Pacific, reaching Hawaii about 1970, seemingly threatening destruction of coral reefs and islands. Major outbreaks have also been recorded in Micronesia, Samoa, Fiji, the Society Islands, Malaysia, Thailand, and the Maldives (Brown 1997b). During invasions, when large numbers of this starfish appear on a coral reef,

CROWN-OF-THORNS STARFISH
(*Acanthaster planci*)

they consume most of the living polyps, leaving behind a severely altered coral community (the plants and animals that live in the reefs). During several months in 1968 and 1969, for example, along the northwestern coast of Guam, the crown-of-thorns consumed 90 percent of the living corals. Although other starfish eat corals, only the crown-of-thorns is able to reduce so dramatically the coral cover of an entire reef. Crown-of-thorns outbreaks have been increasing in recent years, throughout the starfish's range. These outbreaks occur most often near high islands and after exceptionally severe rainstorms, usually associated with tropical cyclones, have introduced large amounts of sediments into the water.

Concern among scientists and environmentalists prompted an attempt to control the crown-of-thorns' proliferation; many were killed by formaldehyde injection, and others were simply removed from the reefs and destroyed. In the late 1970s, however, new research data indicated that similar expansions, or blooms, had occurred previously, followed by periods of decline. Thus, it seemed likely that the sudden growth of the starfish population during the 1960s represented a phase in the organism's natural cycle. After crown-of-thorns outbreaks, their numbers appeared to decline, and only recently was anyone able to identify the possible cause of this decline. In 1999, Morgan Pratchett of James Cook University in Queensland examined a specimen that showed numerous dermal (skin) lesions, collapsed spines, and a completely debilitated water-vascular system. When he put pieces of the infected starfish into separate tanks with six healthy starfish, all of them died in eight to nine days. The pathogen remains unidentified.

The corals the starfish eats are often the dominant competitors for space on the reef; by removing them, the star may help to encourage and maintain coral diversity. Given that most *Acanthaster* outbreaks occur about three years after a period of abnormally high rainfall (as documented by Charles Birkeland in 1982), it can be said that coral reef diversity may be due to heavy rains—as mediated and modified by sea stars. These heavy rains cause significant runoff and nutrient enrichment in coral lagoons, and this in turn causes a plankton bloom, which feeds *Acanthaster* larvae swimming in the lagoons. It generally takes the stars about three years to grow large enough to come out and forage during the day, at which point they are noticed. "There are no early records of *Acanthaster* in undisturbed fossil deposits," wrote Jackson and colleagues (2001), "or in accounts of European explorers or fishers." This lack of evidence of *Acanthaster* outbreaks in the distant past suggests that they are a recent phenomenon, perhaps related to overfishing of prawns that feed on juvenile forms of the crown-of-thorns.

In the South Pacific Ocean and Southeast Asia, fishermen squirt cyanide into reef areas and then rip open the reefs with crowbars to get at the fishes that have taken refuge in the crevices. Because it only stuns the fish, cyanide poisoning was previously used to collect colorful tropical fishes for hobbyists, but the catch has escalated exponentially to meet the demand for live fish in restaurants in mainland China, Hong Kong, Taiwan, and other Asian countries. In researching his brilliant—and profoundly disturbing—*Song for the Blue Ocean* (1997), Carl Safina visited fisheries in Palau and the Philippines and then went to the Hong Kong fish market. He wrote:

> In Hong Kong you can see coral reef fishes—groupers, parrotfishes, surgeon-fishes and many others—in numerous locations throughout the city, looking like aquarium displays. Their proximity to restaurants hints otherwise. Looking at them, you would never guess that getting them here entails ecological disruption and human suffering on faraway reefs, nor would you likely guess the staggering sums of money involved. . . . An expanding fishery that poisons reefs with sodium cyanide is engulfing this richest one-third of the world's coral habitats, across an area spanning a quarter of Earth's circumference. Ironically, cyanide that is being used to stun fish so they can be delivered to markets alive leaves reefs dead in its wake.

Cyanide is one of the most toxic of all poisons, capable of killing coral polyps and their symbiotic algae, the zooxanthellae. In addition to being enormously destructive, cyanide fishing is enormously profitable. Charles Barber and Vaughan Pratt (1998), in an article published in the journal *Environment,* estimated that "the live reef fish trade in Southeast Asia has an estimated retail value of $1.2 billion (US dollars), $1 billion of which consists of exports of food fish (mostly to Hong Kong), and $200 million of which consists of exports of aquarium fish to Europe and North America." The fishing, a large proportion of which is done in the Philippines and Indonesia, is quite simple: Fishermen descend onto coral reefs with squirt bottles loaded with crushed cyanide pellets mixed with seawater. They squirt the solution into crevices in the reef and the fish are stunned by the mixture, at which point they are easily captured in plastic bags. Sometimes the fishermen shatter the coral heads with hammers or crowbars to make the fish easier to retrieve.

For the restaurants and the aquarium trade, the fish have to be alive, but it has been estimated that half of the poisoned fish die on the reef, and 40 percent of the survivors die in transit. The South Pacific harbors some 30 percent of the world's coral reefs, and the cyanide kills organisms that make up the reefs. According to two regional surveys, only 4.3 percent of reefs in the Philippines are unaffected by poison, and only 6.7 percent of Indonesian reefs are unaffected. So far, there have been no studies on the cumulative effects of cyanide on those who eat the fish, but it stands to reason that regular ingestion of the cyanide-laced flesh of fishes would not be beneficial to the diner.

Although the fish in Japanese fish markets are offered dead or fresh-frozen, the tastes of Hong Kong businessmen run toward the flaky flesh of reef fishes, which they must see swimming alive in a tank before they order them for dinner. Because the fisheries are uncontrolled and unregulated, no one knows how many fish are being caught for Asian restaurants. Safina quotes one estimate of 4,600 tons and another of 15,000 tons coming into Hong Kong every year. And that says nothing of the fish caught for restaurants in Singapore, Taiwan, and mainland China—the flesh of some of which is toxic.

The dinoflagellate *Gambierdiscus toxicus* is believed to be the cause of a type of poisoning known as ciguatera, in which not the fish but the eater of the fish is stricken. The dinoflagellate attaches itself to dead or damaged coral, and its toxins are passed up the food chain from coral-grazing to carnivorous fish. When humans eat these top predators—snappers, jacks, groupers, or barracudas—they develop symptoms such as tingling in the lips, nausea, vomiting, diarrhea, weakness, and temporary blindness. The toxin is not diminished by cooking or freezing, and the affected fish, cooked or raw, is not tainted by bacteria in any way. Ciguatera poisonings, which kill some 7 percent of people affected, are connected to the destruction of coral reefs, whether natural or unnatural.

Hurricanes, cyclones, and tsunamis can, of course, inflict major physical damage on shallow-water corals, but these have been part of the natural cycle for eons, and the affected reefs have traditionally rebuilt themselves. Sewage runoff, which contains everything from human waste to phosphates and nitrates, encourages the overgrowth of microalgae, which asphyxiates coral and other marine life. Sediment washed into the sea from rivers clouds the waters and prevents sunlight, necessary for photosynthesis, from reaching the corals; pesticides such as DDT also wash into the sea from shoreside communities, poisoning the coral. Coral mining, once a big business on tropical islands, supplying coral for use in building blocks, runways, and the like, has not helped much either.

In addition to the painfully obvious degradation of shallow-water corals by fishermen who dynamite reefs or poison them with cyanide to collect fish or shellfish, corals around the world are being adversely affected by harmful bacteria and viruses. Some of these coral pathogens have been introduced by humans through sewage runoff, oil spills, and other environmental pollutants, but others appear to have arisen naturally, perhaps in response to weaknesses in the coral imposed by human activities. In an article about the worldwide degradation of coral reefs (but particularly the Great Barrier Reef), Eric Wolanski and his colleagues (2003) pointed out:

> Some human influences are acute—for example, mining reefs for limestone, dumping mine tailings on them, fishing with explosives and cyanide, and land reclamation. Pollutants, including pesticides, heavy metals and hydrocarbons, also degrade coral reefs. They can interfere with the chemically sensitive processes of reproduction and recruitment in corals and other reef organisms, such as synchronization of spawning, egg-sperm interactions, fertilization, embryological development, larval settlement, larval metamorphosis and acquisition of symbiotic zooxanthellae by young corals following recruitment.

In 1999, the Coral Reef Alliance, a California-based nonprofit organization dedicated to the preservation of coral reefs around the world, issued the following statement:

> Coral reefs are home to over 25 percent of all marine life and are among the world's most fragile and endangered ecosystems. In the last few decades, mankind has destroyed over 35 million acres of coral reefs. Reefs off of 93 countries have been damaged by human activity. If the present rate of destruction continues, 70% of the world's coral reefs will be killed within our lifetimes.

In a 2001 article discussing new methods of measuring the extent of coral damage, coastal systems analyst Peter Mumby and his colleagues wrote: "Almost three quarters of the world's coral reefs are thought to be deteriorating as a consequence of environmental stress. . . . It is predicted that coral reefs will suffer mounting stress associated with a global increase in atmospheric carbon dioxide over the coming decades, and from local disturbances such as overfishing and disease."

About 10 percent of the world's coral has already died, according to James Porter, an ocean studies specialist at the University of Georgia, and if present trends and conditions continue, another 20 to 30 percent of the world's coral will be lost by 2005. There has been a 446 percent increase in disease at 160 coral sites being monitored along the Florida coast since 1996 (Porter et al.

2001). Overall, 37 percent of all corals in Florida have died since 1996 (Porter and Porter 2002), but some species, such as the magnificently branched elkhorn coral, have suffered even higher rates of loss. On average, 85 percent of all elkhorn corals in the Florida Keys have died since 1996, and on some reefs off Key West, the mortality is more than 98 percent (Patterson et al. 2002). Elkhorn corals are the giant sequoias of the reef, and their loss would be equivalent to the loss of all the redwood forests in California. In a letter to me on January 8, 2003, Porter wrote, "These loss rates are caused by a new disease which we call white pox. The culprit is a bacterium, *Serratia marcescens*, which is commonly found in human fecal wastes. Evidence is mounting that the origin of this disease is untreated sewage. . . . It is unlikely that we are seeing a natural cycle. It seems more and more likely that we have unleashed these plagues upon the planet ourselves."

The health of the world's shallow-water corals is now in grave danger from an imposing roster of frightening diseases. So far, the coral diseases that have been identified are aspergillosis, black-band disease, dark spots disease, red-band disease, tumors and skeletal anomalies, white-band disease, white plague, white pox, yellow-blotch or yellow-band disease, rapid wasting, and bleaching. Of these, the most common are black-band disease (BBD), white-band disease (WBD), plague, and bleaching.

BBD was first reported in reefs off Belize and Bermuda in the mid-1970s, but it has since been found throughout Caribbean and Indo-Pacific waters. A sulfate-reducing cyanobacterium, *Phormidium corallyticum*, invades the coral tissue and deprives the zooxanthellae of oxygen; the bacteria then nourish themselves on the organic compounds released as the coral cells die. The result, BBD, appears as a thin black band that spreads at a rate of a few millimeters a day, killing the coral and leaving behind bare coral skeletons, which are eventually colonized by filamentous algae (Peters 1997).

In a 1997 study of the corals of St. Ann's Bay, Jamaica, Andrew Bruckner, Robin Bruckner, and Ernest Williams found that BBD had destroyed 5.2 percent of the large reef-building coral in the area and was spreading from infected to uninfected colonies in the direction of prevailing currents, an occurrence not previously documented. In a deadly circularity, as the corals died, algae moved in to colonize the skeletons, and the corals most susceptible to the disease were those overgrown by algae.

It now appears that BBD is caused not by a single organism but by several acting in concert. Examining corals in the laboratory as well as in the wild, Laurie Richardson and her colleagues (1997) concluded that the consortium of black band microbes consists of the aforementioned *P. corallyticum*, the sulfide-oxidating *Beggiatoa,* the bacterium *Desulfovibrio,* and several other microorganisms that together create a toxic, sulfide-rich environment that prevents the zooxanthellae from photosynthesizing. In his investigation of BBD in the reefs of St. Annabaai, Curaçao, Bruce Fouke of the University of Illinois at Urbana-Champaign made the surprising discovery that several of the bacteria types in the consortium were known only from human beings (Harder 2001). How people-infecting bacteria might jump to corals remains a mystery, but it has been suggested that human waste material flushed into the ocean might be the vector.

In the early 1980s, Caribbean elkhorn and staghorn corals (genus *Acropora*), which come in many colors, began to show areas of white, and by 1989, 95 percent of the elkhorn corals on St. Croix had died. These spectacular corals, the predominant corals in much of the Caribbean, are susceptible to WBD throughout their range. William Gladfelter, who described this phenomenon in 1982, wrote: "The overall decrease in live coral tissue during this time [1977–1979] was 16% while the increase in dead standing colony surface was 11%. . . . The impact of such an agent of mortality on this coral community as well as on reef growth is thus potentially catastrophic." Although Gladfelter himself could find no "consistent possible causative organism," he suggested, following Esther Peters, that bacteria could be the culprit. By 1998, the causative pathogen (or suite of pathogens) for WBD had been identified, though writing in the 1997 *Life and Death of Coral Reefs,* Peters acknowledged that "much remains to be learned about the nature of tissue sloughing in corals and how many conditions caused by different pathogens or environmental stresses may actually be represented by the same disease signs."

Another of the coral diseases is known generically as plague. In the 1980s, a "white plague" epizootic hit the corals of the Florida Keys and infected seventeen of the area's forty-three scleractinian coral species (Richardson 1998). The symptoms of this disease resemble those of WBD, but it spreads much faster—as fast as three millimeters per day, in contrast with two millimeters for WBD—and can kill an entire colony in days, whereas WBD usually takes months. A fungus of the genus *Aspergillus* is probably the agent for the epizootics that have killed sea fans (gorgonians) over the past decades. As with many other coral diseases, aspergillosis opportunistically strikes animals that have been weakened by stresses imposed by pollution, other pathogens, or environmental factors such as fluctuating water temperatures, increased salinity, and the like.

In 1998, in a study of Florida corals decimated in 1995 by a new "band" disease, Laurie Richardson and eight colleagues isolated the responsible pathogen and identified it as a potential new species of *Sphingomonas,* a widespread bacterium that can survive and grow at low temperatures, under low nutrient concentrations, and even in toxic chemical environments. *Sphingomonas* species have been recovered from seawater, sea ice, river water, polluted groundwater, mineral water, and even the "sterile" water used in hospitals and as drinking water. In humans, it is associated with infectious septicemia, wound infections, and peritonitis. In the 1995 outbreak, which occurred at the Florida Reef Tract (a coral reef ecosystem extending from Key West to the Dry Tortugas), the disease infected seventeen species of scleractinian corals, in some cases killing as much as 38 percent of the colonies. Its primary victim was the elliptical star coral, *Dichocoenia stokesi*—a species previously unknown to be susceptible to any coral disease. This virulent disease, identified as "plague type II" by Richardson and three colleagues in 1998, began at the base of the coral and moved upward, an unusual pattern of tissue loss. Corals infected with plague type II exhibited a sharp line that marked the boundary between healthy and diseased tissue, and tissue was destroyed much more rapidly than in other line or band diseases. Four months after it was first spotted, the disease had killed corals to the north and south of the initial site, and by 1997 it had spread to most of the reefs in the Florida Reef Tract.

In a 2002 study, researchers identified a pathogen they suggested might be responsible for decimation of the elkhorn coral (*Acropora palmata*) in the Florida Keys. Kathryn Patterson and her colleagues identified a human fecal bacterium, *Serratia marcescens,* as a likely cause of the death of as much as 85 percent of the elkhorn corals of the Florida reefs. White pox, which specifically targets the giant elkhorn coral, is one of the fastest spreading of all coral diseases, capable of devouring ten square centimeters of living coral per day. (It differs from WBD in that it kills the whole coral rather than attacking in bands.) One of the most common bacteria known, *S. marcescens* is found in the gut of humans and other animals as well as in soil and water. It was shown to be present in corals infected with white pox but not in healthy corals, and it is believed to enter the water via sewage runoff. "This is the first time," wrote the authors, "that a bacterial species associated with the human gut has been shown to be a marine invertebrate pathogen."

When patches of dead or dying coral spread at a rate of several inches per day, the corals are said to be victims of rapid wasting disease. It was first identified on Bonaire, an island off the coast of Venezuela, in January 1997, and it has since been spotted in Mexico, Aruba, Curaçao, Trinidad, Tobago, Grenada, and the U.S. Virgin Islands, an area spanning 2,000 miles. James

Porter summed up the issue thus for the *New York Times:* "We're all stunned at the rapidity with which these new diseases are occurring. The problems are occurring at all depths, and the number of species affected is increasing as well as the number of individuals" (Yoon 1997). As with WBD, the pathogen responsible for rapid wasting disease is unknown.

Coral bleaching, another major marine threat to coral, differs from WBD in that no pathogen infects the living coral; instead, stress—induced by high ocean temperatures, low ocean temperatures, elevated ultraviolet light, sedimentation, changes in salinity, or toxic chemicals—causes the zooxanthellae to be expelled from the coral, leaving it a ghostly white as the calcium carbonate skeletons of the coral colony are exposed. Coral bleaching has been known since the mid-1980s. Describing what the reefs of the Virgin Islands were like in 1987, Barbara Brown and John Ogden, director of the Florida Institute of Oceanography, wrote in 1993: "The normally golden-brown, green, pink and gray corals, sea whips and sponges had become pure white. In some cases, entire reefs were so dazzlingly white that they could be seen from a considerable distance." Although most corals survive infrequent bleaching episodes, repeated or sustained events will eventually kill them. Warm water temperatures related to the El Niño of 1983, for example, resulted in widespread bleaching, mortality, and even extinction of corals in the eastern Pacific and bleaching at many sites in the western Atlantic and the Caribbean. The warm waters that spawned or strengthened hurricanes in the western Atlantic that year were associated with this outbreak of coral bleaching. Some reefs in Belize and many neighboring countries in the western Caribbean and the Gulf of Mexico region were mysteriously spared, however.* In 1997–1998, high ocean temperatures around the world initiated another major episode of coral bleaching, and at least in the Mediterranean Sea, researchers have tentatively identified the causative pathogen as *Vibrio shiloi.*

Corals tolerate a narrow temperature range between 25°C and 29°C (77°F to 84.2°F), depending on location. They bleach in response to prolonged temperature change but not in response to rapidly fluctuating temperatures.

---

*In 2001, Andrew Baker of the New York Aquarium's Osborn Laboratories of Marine Sciences published the results of a study in which he found that bleaching may be a "high-risk ecological opportunity strategy for reef corals to rid themselves rapidly of suboptimal algae and to acquire new partners." Deepwater corals transplanted to shallow sites off Panama bleached but survived by recovering new algae. "Bleaching," wrote Baker, "may ultimately help reef corals to survive the recurrent and increasingly severe warming events projected by current climate models of the next half-century. Bleaching is an ecological gamble in that it sacrifices short-term benefits for long-term advantage."

Laboratory experiments show that corals bleach when water reaches a constant 32°C (89.6°F), but the exact mechanism by which they bleach or the trigger that induces bleaching is unknown. Experiments have shown that the zooxanthellae are released into the gut of the polyp and then expelled through the mouth, but this has not been observed in nature. Algae may produce oxide toxicity under stress (e.g., stress caused by pathogens or temperature increases), and these toxins may induce the polyps to expel their symbiotic zooxanthellae (Brown and Ogden 1993). Another hypothesis is that stressed corals give algae fewer nutrients and thus the algae leave the polyp, which results in bleaching.

Ariel Kushmaro and colleagues (1997) conducted experiments with the coral *Oculina patagonica* by introducing the bacterium *Vibrio* AK-1 under controlled conditions to determine whether it could cause bleaching in healthy corals. When they increased the temperature to 25°C, the healthy corals exhibited observable bleaching after twenty days; at 26°C, all the corals showed bleaching after ten days, and colony death was observed shortly after fifty-two days. In 2001, William Wilson and his colleagues isolated a virus from the temperate sea anemone *Anemonia viridis;* the viral infection had been induced by elevated temperature. "We propose," they wrote, "that zooxanthellae harbor a latent viral infection that is induced by exposure to elevated temperatures. If such a mechanism also operates in the zooxanthellae harbored by reef corals, and these viruses kill the symbionts, then this could contribute to temperature-induced bleaching."

In 1997, coral reef expert John Ogden suggested that coral bleaching was afflicting nearly every reef system in the world, along the coasts of more than twenty countries, including Australia, China, Japan, Panama, Thailand, Malaysia, the Philippines, India, Indonesia, Kenya, the Red Sea states, Puerto Rico, Jamaica, and the Bahamas. Corals are inevitably among the first organisms to show the consequences of a sustained increase in sea surface temperature because of the fragile temperature dependence of the tiny zooxanthellae, which live in the coral's cells and without which the coral dies. Global warming raises sea temperatures and, as melting occurs at the poles, raises sea levels as well. "Under scenarios of global warming," James Porter wrote, "the vertical carbonate accretion rates [i.e., vertical growth] of protected coral-reef flats may be insufficient to keep up. These zones will become inundated and subjected to erosion by progressively larger waves. Seagrass and mangrove communities will be eroded and will become less effective as buffers, releasing nutrients, turbidity, and sediments, further slowing coral-reef growth rate."

In October 2000, at a symposium in Bali, the Global Coral Reef Monitoring Network issued a report stating that two years after it announced that 11 percent of the world's coral reefs had been destroyed, a subsequent assessment had raised the estimated total to 27 percent. The network further identified another 14 percent of coral reefs as in danger of being so bleached as to be lost in the next ten years—and another 18 percent not expected to last another thirty years. In addition to the usual suspects—overfishing by explosion and poisoning and polluted runoff—we can now add the *bête noire* (or, in the case of corals, *bête blanche*) of all things environmental: global warming. Greenhouse gases have raised temperatures, particularly in the Indian Ocean, to the point that there has been a 59 percent loss of living shallow-water corals (Pockley 2000). In a discussion of the Bali symposium, Dennis Normile suggested that the corals' sensitivity to rising temperatures makes them the "silent sentinels" of global warming. At Heron Island in the Great Barrier Reef in March 2002, scientists met in an attempt to develop a research strategy to combat coral bleaching. A report in *Nature* (Dennis 2002) indicates that a major occurrence of mass coral bleaching in 1998, attributed to mild increases in ocean temperatures, destroyed one-sixth of the world's coral colonies. The 2002 rise in water temperature and resulting coral death in northeastern Australia is not related to any El Niño event, suggesting that the events are growing in frequency. "If coral adaptation cannot keep pace with increasing sea temperatures," wrote Dennis, "the survival of the world's reefs is in jeopardy."

Corals, some might say, are pretty things for snorkelers to look at when they dive at tropical reefs, and if they are threatened, well, that's too bad for the corals—and maybe even the colorful fishes that live in and around the reefs—but what does coral disease have to do with us? Everything. Whatever affects coral reefs affects the gigantic worldwide diving industry, which depends on clear waters, colorful fish species, and spectacular coral formations to attract enthusiasts. But even without this anthropocentric view, the degradation of coral reefs affects the creatures that live in them, including fishes, cephalopods, gastropods, and myriad others, because without healthy reefs, these animals cannot survive. There are increasing reports of dying coral, diseased shellfish, and waters infected with human viruses as the sea temperature rises and pollution from the land intensifies. Dying coral can even cause islands to sink. "Without coral to keep them afloat," wrote Julia Whitty in a 2001 article in *Harper's*, "atoll islands eventually disappear altogether, a fate dangerously near for the people of the Maldives—an archipelago of 1,200 atolls in the Indian Ocean so badly hit by the 1997–98 coral bleaching that virtually all coral life here has died."

As if coral diseases were not enough, a massive insult was added to the injury when the corals' housecleaners also began to die. Sometime around 1983, a still-unidentified pathogen arrived in the western North Atlantic Ocean and began killing off the superabundant sea urchin known as *Diadema antillarum.* The herbivorous, nocturnal *Diadema,* a black, long-spined urchin, kept the reefs clean of "turf algae" and permitted the corals of the Caribbean, the Gulf of Mexico, the Bahamas, and Bermuda to proliferate. In an area of more than 2 million square miles, more than 93 percent of the urchins died, an event described as "the most extensive and severe mass mortality ever reported for a marine organism" (Knowlton 2001). With the urchins gone, the algae enveloped vast tracts of the underwater landscape, smothering the corals. Parrotfish, triggerfish, and surgeonfish also graze on algae, and these ordinarily would have helped keep the algae population down, but many of them had been overfished, and without *Diadema,* they alone could not compensate for the lack of algae consumption. Bleached coral was prime real estate for the pernicious algae, and without the urchins to perform their scouring functions, more and more of the reefs were swathed in the thick blanket of greenery.

In some places—Barbados, for example—*Diadema* made a comeback (Hunte and Younglao 1988); in others, researchers tried to reintroduce the urchins, but with little success. Then, in Jamaica, Peter Edmunds and Robert Carpenter (2001) noticed that *Diadema* was experiencing a revival, unassisted by humans. At Discovery Bay, on the northern shore of the island, arguably the most extensively studied reef in the Caribbean region, microalgae had blanketed the reef, leaving less than 5 percent of the coral exposed. By the 1990s, after the disappearance of *Diadema* and two major hurricanes, the corals of Discovery Bay were believed to be hopelessly lost. In 1992, however, small colonies of *Diadema* began to appear, and by 1995–1996, the urchins had become locally abundant in shallow water. By January 2000, wrote Edmunds and Carpenter, "the expansion and coalescence of microalgae-free areas formed contiguous zones hundreds of meters in length, suggestive of a reversal in community structure."

With coral reefs in decline all over the world, even a small reversal is cause for celebration. In her 2001 article about the Edmunds and Carpenter study, coral reef specialist Nancy Knowlton wrote, "The report . . . is the best news to emerge from the Caribbean in decades, and any good news is welcome indeed." As far as we can tell, the disappearance of *Diadema* from Caribbean and western Atlantic reefs was not initiated by humans, and there was nothing anyone could do to reverse it. Because there is no evidence that the unidentified pathogen responsible for the death of millions of black urchins was introduced by people, the lesson we might learn from the recovery of *Diadema* is that nature can (sometimes) repair "natural" disasters, perhaps because they do not involve the introduction of alien or toxic organisms. Where the cause is human intrusion, however, repair or recovery is often difficult or even impossible.

As the oceans get warmer, they also get murkier, and that's bad for coral reefs. Sunlight is essential for the growth of coral: the zooxanthellae must be able to photosynthesize in order to produce the carbohydrates the corals use to build calcium carbonate. If the sunlight is blocked, the entire process is affected. Researchers led by Charles Yentsch of the Bigelow Laboratory for Ocean Sciences in Maine have found that some reefs in the Florida Keys are getting barely enough sunlight to sustain themselves, to say nothing of further growth. Diminished sunlight, however, is not the only cause of coral depletion. "Competing hypotheses for the cause of coral loss include removal of grazers, nutrient enrichment, disease, coral bleaching, increase in temperature, and excess light/ultraviolet exposure," noted Yentsch and colleagues in their 2002 study.

And now comes the news that human waste, flushed into waterways, is having a worse effect on corals than anyone imagined. In a 2002 article in *Marine Pollution Bulletin,* Erin Lipp and her colleagues at the University of South Florida found that corals off Florida's coast are being tainted with human feces containing bacteria and viruses, as well as prescription drugs, that can wreak havoc with the coral ecosystem. They wrote: "Corals and reef environments are under increased stress from anthropogenic activities, particularly those in the vicinity of heavily populated areas such as the Florida Keys. The potential adverse impacts of wastewater can affect both the environment and human health." In a *New Scientist* article, Mark Schrope (2001) pointed out, "Over 24,000 septic tanks and 10,000 illegal cesspools drain into the Florida Keys alone." The accompanying bacteria and chemicals are killing not only the corals but also the zooplankton that forms the base of the marine food chain.

In her 1997 discussion of the role of coral reefs in the earth's history—and the savage destruction of them that is occurring today—Pamela Hallock, a marine scientist at the University of South Florida, wrote:

> It can be argued that humans are simply part of nature; that exploding human populations are naturally generating another episode of mass extinction from which the Earth will recover in 20 or 30 million years. But from a human perspective there is a difference between a mass

extinction event caused by meteor impact and the ongoing one caused by human activities. Human intelligence has reduced biological limitations on both the growth rate of human populations and the environmental damage that any individual human can cause. Is it too much to hope that human intelligence can be utilized to bring an end to the current human-generated mass extinction event before the most specialized communities, like reefs and rain forests, are lost to future human generations? After all, many so-called "primitive" human cultures, including Micronesian and Polynesian inhabitants of atolls and coral pinnacles, thrived in resource-limited habitats. Can "modern" humans develop a sustainable global society based on recognition of globally limited resources? Or do humans represent the latest in the series of "disaster" species that proliferate globally at mass extinction events?

When Joan Kleypas and her colleagues (1999) analyzed the effects of increased atmospheric carbon dioxide on coral reefs, they wrote that "a coral reef represents the net accumulation of calcium carbonate ($CaCO_3$) produced by coral and other calcifying organisms. If calcification declines, then reef-building also declines." Coral reefs are particularly threatened because reef-building organisms secrete substances that are unstable in the absence of certain conditions, and the effects on other calcifying marine ecosystems may be severe. In 2001, Kleypas, Robert Buddemeier, and Jean-Pierre Gattuso suggested that even if the reefs die off, the coral community could survive, perhaps enduring a sort of "life in exile" until conditions are propitious again for reef building. Corals can survive without reefs; in Hawaii and Florida, for example, corals grow on lava flows or carbonate rock rather than the skeletons of their immediate predecessors. "No matter how hard we try to care for corals, though, our children or our children's children may be the last generation to see the awesome spectacle of flourishing tropical coral reefs," Scott Norris wrote in "Thanks for All the Fish" (2001). "But if the creatures that once inhabited the reefs survive an ecological diaspora to reunite far in the future, the tragedy of the coming century may not matter much 50,000 years hence. In a strange way, that's comforting."

The news of the incipient demise of the world's coral reefs only gets worse. A report published by the National Oceanic and Atmospheric Administration titled *The State of Coral Reef Ecosystems of the United States and Pacific Freely Associated States* (Turgeon et al. 2002) included a breakdown of the problems facing those regions adjacent to the United States as well as reefs surrounding former U.S. territories in Micronesia, the Marshall Islands, and Palau. The report revealed even more damage than was suspected and confirmed many of the biologists' worst fears about the effects of global warming, disease, overfishing, storms, and pollution. Of the report, John Ogden (quoted in Elizabeth Pennisi's 2002 article in *Science*) said, "It is the most sweeping statement of concern by a [U.S.] federal agency about the trajectory of coral reefs to date." In his view, the first order of business has to be preservation of the reefs, even before any more research studies are commissioned.

～ 13 ～

DEEPWATER CORALS

The deep oceans make up the least known—and the largest—habitat on the earth, so it should come as no great surprise that deepwater corals have been poorly studied. Living at depths of more than 1,000 feet off Alaska, the Atlantic coast of Canada, Ireland, Norway, Sweden, Australia, and New Zealand, and even in the Antarctic, these corals of darkness have no symbiotic zooxanthellae because no light is available for photosynthesis at those depths. Their carnivorous polyps take in the "rain" or "snow" of minute marine detritus that is constantly falling through the sea, capturing from it the minute zooplankton they feed on. Whereas the polyps of shallow-water corals emerge at night to feed, the deepwater corals know only darkness and feed both night and day. There are deepwater soft corals (gorgonians), but the predominant types are the hard (scleractinian) corals, with polyps that look like tiny anemones sitting in limestone cups. In the deep Atlantic Ocean, the bottom is (or was) covered in many places with thickets of yellow *Madrepora* and *Lophelia*—what Greenpeace has called the rain forests of the sea. Around the world, these various azooxanthellate corals—those without zooxanthellae—are in danger.

Deepwater corals have actually been known, at least in a fragmentary way, for centuries: in 1755, Bishop Erik Pontoppidan of Norway referred to *Lophelia* collected by fishermen and used for medicinal purposes, and Carolus Linnaeus listed the same species in the tenth edition of his *Systema Naturae* in 1758. Until very recently, deepwater corals were known only from broken bits and pieces dredged up in fishing nets and bottom trawls. Like their shallow-water counterparts, they often form "trees," but fishermen who found these fragments, unaware of what they were, usually regarded them as fossils of some sort and threw them overboard. Indeed, trawler crews regard *Lophelia* as a nuisance because it snags and damages their nets. With the introduction of research submersibles and robotic cameras, however, the world of cold-water corals has been revealed in depth, and it is not a pretty one.

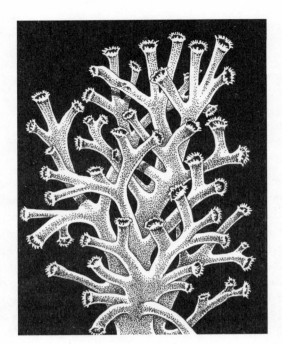

DEEP-SEA CORAL
(*Lophelia pertusa*)

Although most azooxanthellate corals do not build reefs, some of them do. One of these is *Lophelia,* which typically lives at sunless depths of 650 to 6,000 feet, in temperatures that range from about 10°C (50°F) at 2,000 feet to −4°C (25°F) at 4,500 feet. *Lophelia,* which ranges in color from white to orange red, builds a hard, branched skeleton of calcium carbonate with tiny polyps that extend their tentacles into the water to catch microscopic animals. The largest known deepwater coral complex in the world is at latitude 64° N—roughly the latitude of Iceland—in the Norwegian Sea, where one would not ordinarily expect to find a coral reef, given that we usually associate coral reefs with warm, tropical waters. Discovered by Statoil, the Norwegian state oil consortium, the Sula Reef, about 800 feet below the surface, is estimated to be eight miles long, more than 110 feet high, and more than three-quarters of a mile wide. Parts of it may be 8,000 years old.

In a 1995 study of the scleractinian coral *Lophelia pertusa* at latitude 64° N on the Norwegian Shelf, Pal Mortensen and colleagues found that the predominant megafauna around the *Lophelia* constructions were assorted sponges, gorgonians, squat lobsters, redfish, and saithe (*Pollachius virens*). In

1992, the Faroese research vessel *Magnus Heinason* collected twenty-five chunks of *Lophelia* at depths ranging from about 650 to 3,000 feet, which were studied by Andreas Jensen and Rune Frederiksen of the Zoological Museum of the University of Copenhagen. When the chunks of coral were examined, they proved to be home to an incredible variety of animal life. More than 4,000 individual animals were found, representing 256 species of polychaete worms (the major component of the *Lophelia* fauna), sponges, hydroids, gastropods, bivalves, crustaceans, starfish, and even a couple of bony fishes. Thus, operations that would effectively strip-mine *Lophelia* would have a catastrophic effect on the animals that make their home in its nooks and crannies.

During a 1998 survey of some coral reefs along the Norwegian coast, the Norwegian Institute of Marine Research discovered that deep trawling had totally destroyed some deep-sea reefs formed by *Lophelia pertusa*. Fishermen had reported similar damage in other areas along the coast, and the researchers feared widespread destruction of the reefs. As they reported in 2002, Jason Hall-Spencer, Valerie Allain, and Jan Helga Fosse examined the "catch" of deep-sea trawlers off Ireland, Scotland, and Norway and found chunks of broken coral from reefs estimated to be 4,500 years old. Using seabed photographs and acoustic surveys, they identified scars on the seafloor 2.4 miles wide where unregulated trawlers were scouring the ocean bottom.

When oil prospects were being investigated in the northeastern Atlantic in the early 1990s, it was thought that drilling would have a destructive effect on *Lophelia*, but that would have been minimal compared with the effects of trawling.* Raking the sea bottom in pursuit of groundfish such as cod, haddock, pollock, redfish, and grenadier, trawlers have been mowing down the fragile corals like bulldozers. In her 1999 testimony before the United States Congress on the subject of endangered oceans, Sylvia Earle cited the country's "absurdly destructive" methods of fishing, particularly trawling, which sweeps away everything in its path. She likened trawling to dragging nets through marshes to capture ducks and geese, bulldozing forests to take

---

*In one instance, at least, the oil industry proved beneficial to *Lophelia pertusa*. In the summer of 1999, when researchers Niall Bell and Jan Smith examined the decommissioned Brent Spar oil storage facility off the Shetland Islands in the North Sea, they found large quantities of healthy *Lophelia* growing on it. The platform at Brent Spar had been decommissioned in 1991, at which time the Shell Oil Company announced plans to dismantle it and sink it into the sea. However, after three months of mounting protest by Greenpeace, Shell announced it would not sink the Brent Spar as planned but recycle it instead, leaving it for the deepwater coral.

songbirds, or dynamiting trees to catch squirrels. In a letter to the *New York Times* on September 26, 2000, Elliot Norse made clear just how huge was the damaged area: "On an annual basis trawlers scour an area equivalent to twice the size of the lower 48 states. . . . An activity that each year disturbs an area of seabed as large as Brazil, the Congo, and India combined must affect the structure, species composition, and biogeochemistry on both local and global scales."

Off the western coast of Scotland, a formation known as the Darwin Mounds is home to a forty-square-mile colony of *Lophelia* under 3,000 feet of the cold North Atlantic Ocean. The reefs provide a rich habitat for other marine life, such as crabs, sea cucumbers, sponges, and sea spiders. Sonar and video images collected by a British exploratory expedition revealed deep gouges made by trawlers along with fragments of dead *Lophelia* strewn over the damaged landscape.

The Atlantic Frontier, an area of the Atlantic Ocean north and west of the British Isles that includes the Darwin Mounds, contains a great diversity of marine organisms. It is also an important breeding and rearing ground for twenty-two species of migrating whales and dolphins. The nearly 900 species of marine life identified in the area include sponges, corals, bryozoans, barnacles, and xenophyophores (large single-celled protozoans), many of which depend on the habitat provided by the cold-water coral *Lophelia pertusa* for survival. Unfortunately, *Lophelia* is now in retreat in many oceans of the world because of its high vulnerability to pollution and its low growth rate.

In addition to its great ecological importance, the Atlantic Frontier has great economic importance. The region's oil reserves are estimated at 1.2 billion barrels, enough to supply England's factories and vehicles well into the twenty-second century. The Atlantic Frontier was opened for oil and gas licensing in April 1997, and by October 1999, twenty-eight of the sixty-eight available "blocks" (areas on a grid) had been licensed for oil production, which commenced on December 9, 1997, at BP Amoco's Foinaven field with a floating production, storage, and offloading facility. BP Amoco soon followed this with a similar operation at the Schiehallion field, north of Scotland. Greenpeace funded survey work in 1998 that resulted in the discovery that the Darwin Mounds were near blocks licensed to Marathon Oil UK and Conoco. Greenpeace and Alex Rogers of the Southampton Oceanography Centre maintain that, even aside from harm caused by possible oil spills, new drilling operations would pollute the Darwin Mounds with toxic drill cuttings and increase sedimentation, both of which reduce the fecundity and life span of *Lophelia*. Moreover, drilling and exploration in special areas of conservation would cause irreparable damage to coral reefs and damage the breeding and resting grounds of dolphins and whales.

As a result of a lawsuit filed in November 1999 by Greenpeace and the World Wide Fund for Nature, the British government was told by the High Court that it must protect whales, dolphins, and deep-sea corals from the effects of oil exploration in the northeastern Atlantic. The case confirmed that rare species must be protected for 200 miles around the British coastline under European legislation. *Lophelia pertusa* is among the rare species environmentalists hope to protect under the directive.

At the First International Symposium on Deep Sea Corals, held at Dalhousie University in Halifax, Nova Scotia, in August 2000, scientists issued a joint statement proclaiming, "It is essential that existing national laws and international conventions for the protection of biodiversity and the regulation of fisheries be extended to cover these unique and vulnerable deep-water habitats."

We mourn the loss of rain forests and timberlands; we watch helplessly as urban sprawl encroaches on meadows and prairies; we are unable to control chemical emissions that rip the atmosphere's protective ozone layer to tatters; but the rampant destruction of the ocean floor and its endemic fauna is one of the greatest environmental disasters in history, and it is occurring virtually unnoticed. Hidden even from the eyes of those perpetrating the horror, the inhabitants of the ocean floor and the ocean floor itself are being demolished at a rate that defies comprehension. Les Watling and Elliot Norse concluded their 1998 study of the effects of fishing gear on the ocean bottom with these words:

> At present, people trawl anywhere they want, and the sea's equivalents of ancient forests are becoming cattle pastures by default, not by design. Merrett and Haedrich (1997) put it this way: "there still seems to be a frontier mentality that operates in high seas fisheries." Governments generally do not apply the precautionary principle to the sea; individuals and corporations do what they wish unless some governing authority demonstrates conclusively that they should not, decides to prohibit the activity and enforces its prohibition.

When scientists examined the Coral and Tasman Seas bordering New Caledonia and Tasmania, they discovered hundreds of previously unknown species on extinct underwater volcanoes rising from the seafloor. Some are "living fossils" derived from groups believed extinct since the Mesozoic era, the time of the dinosaurs. The unique biological communities on seamounts are dominated by corals adapted to life in the deep sea, as well as sponges, sea fans, and other organisms that filter their prey from the strong currents characteristic of this environment. Based on a sample of fewer than twenty-five seamounts in the Tasman and Coral Sea region, the study uncovered more than 850 species, 42 percent more than previously reported in all studies of seamounts over the previous 125 years. However, "seamounts are increasingly being targeted by international deep-water trawling operations," noted Bertrand Richer de Forges, J. Anthony Koslow, and G. C. B. Poore in 2000. "The spread of trawl fisheries for orange roughy, alfonsino and other deep-water fish threatens seamount communities worldwide," they wrote.

Who will miss the lowly *Lophelia*? The sponges, polychaete worms, crabs, gastropods, and bivalves will—but, more significantly, we will. Every species lost diminishes us, and a massive loss such as this is a major environmental insult. Ninety percent of the world's ocean is more than two miles deep, which means that deep ocean is the predominant habitat on the planet. We know more about the far side of the moon than we do about this ecosystem, but we appear to have dedicated our most sophisticated technology to its destruction. The undeclared war on deepwater corals, combined with the epizootics that threaten the shallow-water varieties, means that corals, previously considered material for jewelry or pretty backdrops for underwater photography, have come to symbolize everything that is injurious and insulting about our approach to the natural world.

~ 14 ~

BIOLOGICAL INVADERS

> Migration, dispersal, and colonization are natural processes that play key
> roles in evolution, but the pace and scale of human-caused "migrations,"
> along with our ability to virtually eliminate geographic barriers, makes
> the current wave of species movements quite unprecedented, and, in
> places, enormously damaging to the species, systems, and natural
> processes we value.
>
> —Yvonne Baskin, *A Plague of Rats and Rubbervines,* 2002

The conodonts, trilobites, ammonites, belemnites, plesiosaurs, ichthyosaurs, mosasaurs, pakicetids, archaeocetes, and desmostylians are long gone from the marine environment, and although we cannot explain their disappearance, we can predict some future marine extinctions with a degree of certainty. We have lost the white abalone and probably the barndoor skate, and the leatherback turtle and northern right whale seem to be on the off-ramp to extinction. In addition to actively—and in some cases intentionally— eliminating species, we have introduced "alien" animals into the environment, which often do the same job. Introduced species (also known as exotic, nonindigenous, or invasive species) are organisms that have moved—or have been moved—beyond their natural geographic range or habitat. Representing all phyla, from microorganisms to terrestrial and aquatic plants and animals, they have displaced, replaced, or even eaten the resident species. An invading species is the functional opposite of a depleted one: instead of leaving a space, it fills one. If no room is available, it shoves something out of the way or eats it up. Whatever their method, bioinvaders are an integral part of the degradation of the world's biological resources.

To underscore the global concern about this problem, the journal *Biological Invasions* was initiated in 1999, with James Carlton as its first editor. In the opening editorial, Carlton (1999a) outlined the origins of the problem:

A rapidly and vastly increasing human population in the 20th century has resulted in the equally increasing need for transglobal movement of huge amounts of commercial goods. Permitting this is the advent of the modern airplane and the modern ship—technological developments that now permit the movement of virtually any commodity anywhere in the world within a matter of hours or days. Accompanying these commodities—or intentionally part of them—are an immense suite of living organisms.

Except in the destruction of entire ecosystems—as with deepwater trawling—there is probably no other area in which human beings have upset nature's balance more than in the introduction of alien species. Left alone over time, a damaged ecosystem might be able to reconstitute its original diversity, but as invaders proliferate, time only exacerbates the problem. Because we are land creatures ourselves and cannot see very well under water, the effects of bioinvasions are most clearly evident on land.

The black rat (*Rattus rattus*) originated in Asia and now lives virtually everywhere humans live, bringing with it massive destruction of food supplies and spreading diseases such as plague, typhus, and rabies. It has correctly been called the most dangerous animal in the world. In cooler regions, it has largely been replaced by the Norway (brown) rat, *R. norvegicus,* which is larger and a better climber and swimmer. (The typical laboratory rat is an albino strain of the brown rat.) Brown rats have spread around the world through their common practice of stowing away on seafaring vessels. They have invaded every continent except Antarctica, and they will eat almost anything that does not bite back. They can be found in sewer systems, at garbage dumps, in barns and houses, and on the plains, in woodlands, and in forests. They are aggressive, intelligent, adaptable, and incredibly fecund. Females can produce as many as eight litters per year, with as many as twelve young per litter. Massive efforts to reduce rat populations have not succeeded, and there are now believed to be approximately as many house rats in the world as people. Where rats have been introduced, they have wreaked havoc on native populations of birds, small mammals, and even some large mammals, such as us. It is a humbling thought that even though we have driven so many species to extinction or close to it, in a few cases in which we have actually *tried* to eliminate a species, as with the rat, we have failed utterly.

Second only to the rat, the paradigmatic bioinvader is the rabbit. That invasion occurred only in Australia, but the bunny's arrival on the island continent permanently altered the ecology of this vast, isolated tract. Domestic rabbits were probably introduced into Australia from England with the first fleet in 1788, but they did not begin to run wild until 1859, when a man named Thomas Austin brought twenty-four wild rabbits from England and released them on his property in southern Victoria so his fellow sporting Englishmen would have something familiar to shoot at. In 1866, more than 14,000 rabbits were shot for sport on Austin's property. This was Australia's first intimation of the amazing reproductive capability of the Old World, or European, rabbit (*Oryctolagus cuniculus*), from which the saying *breeding like rabbits* would work its way into the world's lexicon. By 1869, it was estimated that 2.033 million rabbits had been destroyed on Austin's property, yet they were as thick as ever. They spread from Austin's property and from other release points in both Victoria and South Australia, and from there they moved across the continent in the ensuing fifteen years.

The rabbits' effect on native wildlife was vast, varied, and pernicious. They directly competed for food and habitat with many small to medium-sized marsupials, such as the greater bilby, *Macrotis lagotis* (now an endangered species), and the burrowing bettong, *Bettongia lesueur* (now extinct on the mainland). In their spread across Australia, rabbits took advantage of existing burrows and evicted various burrowing mammals. Moreover, a colony of rabbits will support a high number of predators such as feral cats and foxes, which of course put stress on small populations of native mammals. Other animals, such as rat kangaroos, tiger cats, and magpies, were often killed by poisons and traps set for rabbits (Rolls 1969).

To see just how pervasive bioinvaders can become, let's have a look at one of the worst of the terrestrial cases—the brown tree snake (*Boiga irregularis*), a native of Australia, Papua New Guinea, and the Solomon Islands. It is about fifteen inches long at hatching and may reach a length of eight to ten feet, but most are only three to four feet long. It uses constriction and venom to immobilize its prey, which consists of rodents, frogs, lizards, and birds and their eggs. *Boiga irregularis* is active at night and lives in trees, spending most of its days coiled in a cool, dark place such as a treetop or a rotted log. This snake has become a very serious problem on Guam since its accidental introduction, sometime in the late 1940s, by means of U.S. military cargo planes, probably from the Solomon Islands. *B. irregularis* now numbers as many as 10,000 per square mile in some Guam forests—among the highest densities ever recorded for a species of snake—for a total of 1 million to 3 million snakes on the island. Having virtually wiped out the island's native forest birds, the brown tree snake has turned its focus on Guam's lizards and small mammals.

Hawaii, Saipan, Tinian, Rota, Kwajalein, Diego Garcia, Okinawa, Cocos

Island, and Wake Island have also experienced accidental introduction of the brown tree snake. In August 1997, shortly after a cargo plane landed at Hickam Air Force Base in Honolulu, a young airman reported seeing a brown snake about three feet in length slither from the airport tarmac into a nearby canal. In most parts of the world, such an event would have gone unnoticed, but because Hawaii is serpentless and the transport plane was from *Boiga*-infested Guam, an intensive hunt by state and federal authorities ensued. Experts warn that just one pregnant female brown tree snake hiding in an aircraft cargo hold or wheel well and slipping through import checks could begin a colonization capable of devastating Hawaii's environment and its tourist-dependent economy.

The marine extinctions we know about are largely restricted to vertebrates, but in 1991 the first historical extinction of a marine invertebrate was reported. James Carlton and his colleagues described the demise of the eelgrass limpet (*Lottia alveus*), a half-inch-long single-shelled gastropod once found in brackish inshore waters of the western Atlantic Ocean from Labrador to Long Island Sound. *L. alveus* (once known as *Acmaea alvaeus*) fed only on the epithelial cells of the eelgrass *Zostera marina,* and when the eelgrass itself precipitously disappeared between 1930 and 1933 as a result of a wasting disease (probably caused by a slime mold), the limpet, unable to adapt to the change in conditions, disappeared along with it.

The decline of the eelgrass and the disappearance of *Lottia alveus* do not appear to have been connected with any human activity, unless the slime mold *Labyrinthula zosterae* was somehow introduced into those western Atlantic waters. Although wasting diseases and mold-caused blights had been recorded well back into the nineteenth century, none was as extensive as the blight of 1930. The problem of so-called marine bioinvasions—in which organisms are carried around the world, typically via ships in the medium of ocean-water ballast, and then released in foreign climes—has been going on for centuries. James Carlton (1999) pointed out:

> These introductions have led to a profound alteration of the diversity and structure of many coastal communities, including exposed rocky shores, sublittoral soft bottom habitats, sandy beaches, marshes, and estuaries. More than 1,000 species of nearshore marine plants and animals that are now regarded as naturally cosmopolitan may represent overlooked pre-1800 invasions. . . . In contrast to ancient vessels, modern vessels may be playing an even larger role, carrying between 3,000 and 10,000 species globally in any given 24-hour period in their ballast water.

The giant brown kelp *Macrocystis pyrifera,* for example, was originally found only in the northeastern Pacific along the coasts of California and Mexico. In the eighteenth century, Spanish vessels sailing from North to South America may unwittingly have transported this hardy alga from one hemisphere to another. In any case, *Macrocystis* is now well established in the southern Atlantic and has also been reported in Tasmanian waters.

It may appear that the problems with bioinvaders have to do only with such exotic creatures as mussels or jellyfish, but there are far more insidious threats to humans in the global spread of potentially harmful microorganisms by ships. A recent article in *Nature* (Ruiz et al. 2000) details the dangers posed by invading organisms and potential pathogens in the 79 million tons of water transported annually as ballast in ships. The investigators examined the ballast water of vessels arriving in Chesapeake Bay and found that one prevalent microorganism was *Vibrio cholerae,* the bacterium that causes human epidemic cholera. Is this going to be a problem? The authors conclude, "Given the magnitude of ongoing transfer and its potential consequences for ecological and disease processes, large scale movement of microorganisms by ships merits attention from both invasion biologists and epidemiologists."

Sometime around 1985, a bulk cargo vessel left a Black Sea port for North America, carrying in its ballast water the planktonic larvae of hundreds, even thousands, of alien animals. Among these was the zebra mussel, *Dreissena polymorpha,* a freshwater inhabitant whose proliferation in recent years has caused major problems for ships, power plants, harbor facilities, and water treatment facilities. Since their arrival in 1988, zebra mussels have spread to the St. Lawrence River system and all the Great Lakes, and they are threatening every state east of the Mississippi River as well as the Canadian provinces of Ontario and Quebec. They can be spread by commercial and recreational boats, amphibious airplanes, scuba equipment, and fishing gear. Zebra mussels are D-shaped, striped bivalves about the size of your thumbnail. They cluster in colonies of hundreds of thousands per square yard and can clog the opening of any underwater pipe, eventually closing it off altogether. To combat this alien invasion, everything from chlorination, chemicals, ozone, and heat to ultraviolet radiation, anti-fouling paints, sonic vibrations, electric shock, and parasites has been tried, but nothing works very well, and the mussels keep on spreading.

Mnemiopsis leidyi is a ctenophore, a transparent creature that looks something like a jellyfish but is not in the same phylum. It is a comb jelly, named for its comb plates—rows of fused cilia that beat synchronously and propel

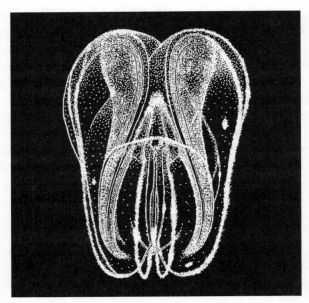

COMB JELLY
(Mnemiopsis leidyi)

the animal through the water. In Chesapeake Bay, the fist-sized *Mnemiopsis* is a voracious planktivore, or plankton-eater—and itself a common summertime constituent of the plankton. As long as they have suitable transportation, bioinvaders can cross any ocean in any direction, and in the mid-1980s, *Mnemiopsis leidyi* was accidentally introduced into the Black Sea from the eastern seaboard of the United States in the ballast water of a cargo ship. The fishery for anchovies, the Black Sea's largest, fell by more than two-thirds as a consequence.

But this wasn't because the ctenophores were eating the anchovies; instead, they were gobbling up the anchovies' food—fish larvae and planktonic animals—at such a prodigious rate that they rapidly became the dominant planktonic organism in the Black Sea. By 1988, they had reached "an estimated biomass of 1.10^9 t [tons] wet weight in the entire Black Sea, *a number ten times larger than the world's annual fish landings.*" (The italics are mine: the comb jellies in the Black Sea weighed ten times more than all the fish caught in the world in a year.) This astonishing estimate comes from a paper by Vladimir Ivanov, several Russian biologists, and others from the United States and Europe (Ivanov et al. 2000) who were discussing the invasion of the *Caspian* Sea by *Mnemiopsis*. Five years earlier, Henri Dumont of

Belgium, one of the contributors to the Ivanov paper, had predicted that it would be only a matter of time before *Mnemiopsis* invaded the Caspian from the Black Sea—and it certainly wasn't much time. When *Mnemiopsis* reached the Caspian Sea, it proliferated even faster than it had in the Black Sea. Ivanov and colleagues' discussion, published in *Biological Invasions,* is a chilling foretaste of what might lie ahead. The Caspian Sea has no access to other seas, but through a narrow strait called the Bosporus, the Black Sea joins the Sea of Marmara, which in turn is connected to the Mediterranean Sea through the Dardanelles.

The voracious comb jelly is characterized as a "superfluous feeder," meaning that it eats far more than it needs and regurgitates the excess. According to Ivanov and his colleagues, *Mnemiopsis* "can consume up to ten times its own weight per day." This unchecked gluttony caused the collapse of the populations of anchovies, horse mackerel, and sprats of the Black Sea, and its effects are being felt in the Caspian. Already heavily overfished, the fish fauna of the Caspian Sea now consists predominantly of various herring species, known collectively as *kilka.* When *Mnemiopsis* eats all their food, the *kilka* will disappear too. Most likely to be noticed as a casualty of the invasion of the comb jellies, however, is the Caspian Sea's top predator, the Caspian seal, *Phoca caspica.* Already threatened by high levels of organochlorines, which may have contributed to their being stricken by canine distemper virus (Kennedy et al. 2000), Caspian seals now face elimination of their primary food source.

In the Black Sea, *Mnemiopsis* has no natural predator, so ecologists are debating the wisdom of introducing *Beroe ovata,* another ctenophore that eats only comb jellies, or the Atlantic butterfish (*Peprilus triacanthus*), a fish with little commercial value but a diet that includes *Mnemiopsis* in the eastern North Atlantic. The intentional introduction of predators to feed on alien species that have run wild brings a whole new set of problems to the table, not the least of which is how to control the predators. Ivanov and his colleagues noted, "One challenge in the case in hand is the immediate threat to the potential survival of many endemic Caspian species versus the possibility that a species introduced for bio-control could directly or indirectly impact those same species."

"During the 1980s and early 1990s," wrote Turkish ecologist Ahmet Kideys in 2002,

> . . . the Black Sea ecosystem was in a catastrophic condition. The deterioration of this ecosystem was the result of two principal factors: eutrophication (that is, nutrient enrichment due to domestic or

agricultural waste), and invasion by the comb jelly *Mnemiopsis*. . . .
Remarkably, since the mid-1990s, the impact of eutrophication and
Mnemiopsis has declined, and virtually all ecosystem indicators now
show signs of recovery, suggesting that the Black Sea has returned to a
healthier state.

The nutrient input from rivers decreased in the mid-1980s because of declining production in factories along the Black Sea, itself a result of the weak
economies of the former Iron Curtain countries that border the Black Sea
and the River Danube—Turkey, Bulgaria, Romania, Moldova, Ukraine,
Russia, and Georgia. Several countries introduced programs to reduce
eutrophication, which led to a decrease in phytoplankton and an increase in
diatoms, "indications of a healthier ecosystem" (Kideys 2002). The predatory
ctenophore *Beroe ovata* appeared in the Black Sea, introduced not to combat
Mnemiopsis but by accident, probably via ballast water, and recent studies
show that both *Mnemiopsis* and *Beroe* are now almost gone from the Black
Sea. The prey was killed off by the predator, and the predator died off because
there was nothing left to eat. Black Sea anchovy landings are on the rise, but
now attention must be directed to the Caspian Sea, which is almost as large as
the Black Sea but has no water exchange with other oceans. (As mentioned
earlier, the Black Sea connects indirectly with the Mediterranean at the
Bosporus.) *Mnemiopsis* has now appeared in the Caspian Sea, with a resulting decline in endemic species such as the white sturgeon and the Caspian
seal, both of which feed on *kilka*.

Usually found in the waters of China, Japan, Thailand, and Myanmar
(Burma), the Asian swamp eel, or *belut* (*Monopterus albus*), is a fish (not a
true eel because it does not migrate to the ocean to spawn) capable of leaving
the water and slithering along the ground, relying on its ability to breathe air
while out of the water. In and out of the water, it is a voracious nocturnal
predator, feeding on worms, insects, shrimp, crayfish, frogs, and other fishes.
The Asian swamp eel, which grows to a length of three feet, is sometimes kept
as an exotic aquarium fish, and scientists now speculate that somebody
released one or more in the vicinity of Tampa Bay, on the Gulf Coast of
Florida. (Another theory is that Asian immigrants who consider the *belut* a
delicacy released one or more so they could have a supply of familiar food.)
Since 1997, *Monopterus albus* has been found in significant numbers in canals,
ditches, streams, and ponds in Florida and Georgia, and ecologists fear the
eels may be on their way to the Everglades (Robichaux 2000). Overland, they
travel in "packs" of fifty or more, and they can literally empty waterways of
small fishes. Even though they are tropical in origin, they can evidently

endure freezing temperatures, and their only natural enemies would appear to be alligators. They seem impervious to traditional fish poisons, since they can simply raise their heads out of the water and breathe air.

On October 5, 2000, while fishing at a residential pond in Tamarac, a city in Broward County, Florida, an angler pulled in what he initially thought was a bowfin, a fish common in stagnant waters from the St. Lawrence River to Florida. But the bowfin is characterized by an orange-rimmed black spot at the base of the tail, and this fish—and others caught nearby—did not have this ocellus. Fisheries biologists identified the fish as a snakehead, *Channa asiatica*, another powerful predator that can reach a length of three feet, and usually found in China, Thailand, Sri Lanka, the Philippines, and India. Snakeheads are so durable that they are kept alive in Philippine fish markets in trays with no water and then clubbed into submission before being sold. Like the swamp eel, the snakehead is imported live into the United States and sold in fish markets as an Asian delicacy or an exotic aquarium fish. Within a year of that first sighting, more than 100 snakeheads were caught in Florida, and in July 2002, newspapers picked up reports of an exotic predatory fish that had somehow been released into a drainage pond in suburban Crofton, Maryland. Identified as a snakehead, it was described as a three-foot-long fish that could survive icy winters and travel overland.

Because the snakehead is an evil-looking fish with an evil-sounding name, its arrival in a Maryland pond became an occasion for overheated tabloid-style prose. Columnist Maureen Dowd of the *New York Times* quoted a fisheries biologist as saying that the "Frankenfish ... has the potential to displace a species and create significant problems in the ecosystem." The front-page headline in the *New York Daily News* for July 13, 2002, screamed "THE FISH FROM HELL," and a wanted poster with a picture of a snakehead was put up around the pond in Crofton, where the first snakehead had been caught. "Have You Seen This Fish?" asked the poster. Beneath a picture of the suspect and a list of its distinguishing features—"long dorsal fin, small head, large mouth, big teeth"—was a warning and a death warrant: "If you come across this fish, PLEASE DO NOT RELEASE. Please KILL this fish by cutting/bleeding as it can survive out of water for several days and REPORT all catches to the Maryland Department of Natural Resources Fisheries Service." In fact, *Channa asiatica* is a freshwater species that might threaten the inhabitants of a given pond or even a pond system, but is unlikely to pose a significant danger to the fishes of North America.

Without question, the most harmful invader is humankind. We are also the world's deadliest predator, and, at 6.25 billion and rising, by far the most numerous large vertebrate. From their humble beginnings, Mr. and Mrs. H. Sapiens have invaded every possible biome on the earth, including every island, whether volcanic, ice-covered, jungle-clad, or coral-based. We have "conquered" both poles, as well as mountaintops 29,000 feet above sea level and underwater canyons 35,000 feet below. We can live where it is hot, cold, wet, dry, high, or low, and we are able to disregard or overcome conditions that make places inhospitable to most other living things. Whereas other species cannot successfully occupy a beachhead if the climate is unsuitable, we just modify the circumstances. If native species get in the way, we shove them aside or eliminate them. We are the most adaptable species on the planet because we have an almost limitless capability to modify the environment to suit our purposes. With our air-conditioning, central heating, fiberglass insulation, aircraft, high-altitude balloons, deep-sea bathyspheres, submarines, all-terrain vehicles, snowmobiles, Gore-Tex, and thermal insulation, we modify the way we occupy otherwise hostile or unwelcoming climates. There is no place on the earth we have not gone, often for no better reason than having developed the technology that enabled us to do so. And if colonizing much of the earth was not enough, we have already landed on the moon and are making noises about landing on Mars.

Indeed, one of humankind's most deleterious contributions to the once respected balance of nature is the introduction of alien species. By competing with native species—and sometimes eliminating them—invasive species not only change the ecological balance in a particular environment but may also alter the evolutionary pathways of competing organisms. (Elimination, of course, permanently alters the evolutionary pathways.) Despite their often placid appearance (Vasco Núñez de Balboa, who named the Pacific, had obviously never seen a storm there), the world's oceans have been under siege, threatened by alien invaders that can infect, poison, and destroy life-forms that have survived for ages.

IS THIS THE END?

Imagine an entire *country* dedicated to the elimination of its marine wildlife. This appears to be the case in Greenland, where, according to John Bonner (2002), "hunting has always been a way of life for the Inuit in one of the world's great wildernesses, but now they have far greater mobility and firepower. . . . Companies set up by the Greenland government will buy the carcasses or valuable parts of any animal that strays within shooting distance of the island's 10,000 registered hunters." In *A Farewell to Greenland's Wildlife*, published in 2002, Danish author and environmentalist Kjeld Hansen documents that country's wanton and irresponsible slaughter of seabirds, marine mammals, fish, and mollusks, a slaughter that spares only those species— large mammals such as caribou and musk ox—that are terrestrial and can be easily counted. Even the Greenland harp seal fishery, so much smaller than its Canadian counterpart, dumps 5,700 tons of skinned carcasses into the sea because no use for the meat has been found.

A little bird known as Brünnich's guillemot used to nest on the rocky cliffsides of Greenland in uncountable numbers, but the population is now reduced to a few thousand, and "sixteen of the forty Brünnich's guillemot colonies in West Greenland are already presumed extinct—destroyed by illegal summer hunting and egg collecting" (Hansen 2002). The common eider, sought by Greenlanders for hundreds of years for its meat, eggs, and down, is now considered endangered. In 1998, hunters in Greenland killed 221,783 Brünnich's guillemots, 72,109 common eiders, 43,713 black-legged kittiwakes, 746 narwhals, 187 minke whales, 198 polar bears, 610 walruses, 82,108 ringed seals, and 82,491 harp seals. These kills and others amount to 17,500 tons of animals and birds killed annually, which works out to 770 pounds of meat for every one of Greenland's 58,000 people. "Meat wastage from Greenland kills is enormous," Hansen observed. "Thousands of tons of meat from killed animals and birds are not used at all. At the same time, the quantity of beef and pork imported from Denmark satisfies three quarters of the population's needs." As for the fish, Hansen wrote:

> Beneath the waves the situation looks no better. All the economically valuable stocks of fish are either overfished or completely destroyed. Halibut stocks had already folded 60–70 years ago, never to recover. In

the mid 1970s cod stocks collapsed and have not recovered. During the 1960s "salmon boom," some Danish, Norwegian, and Faroese fishermen became millionaires, but in just 10 years stocks were exhausted—with the majority of North American salmon rivers laid waste as a result.

Few other nations could be accused of *intentionally* setting out to destroy their own marine resources, but the Greenlanders may serve as an unintentional paradigm for the rest of the world. A history of their depredations gives a sense of the problems that could—indeed, *will*—be writ larger if we do not heed the warnings so clearly placed before us.

Once upon a time, the sea was considered threatening. Its unknown tides, currents, waves, and weather often spelled doom for early seafarers, and until the sixteenth century, few European adventurers were willing to sail out of sight of land. Sailors feared the monsters and serpents that might be lurking in the depths, and even today, many people are afraid to swim in deep water. We still know little about the oceans, and, for the most part, what we do know is restricted to the surface layers. As the oceanographer said to the young student who was marveling at the amount of water he could see from shore, "And that's only the top of it." We are only now beginning to explore the depths.

Of the two-thirds of the planet's surface that is covered by water, two-thirds of *that* is more than two miles deep, so it can be said that the predominant habitat for living things on Planet Earth is deep ocean, and most of it remains unexplored. The immensity of the sea that thwarted so many explorers for so long has also provided a haven for its wildlife. Yes, we have fished some species too heavily—anchovies off Peru, for example, and now codfish in the North Atlantic Ocean—but wasn't the ocean wide and deep and protective of its own? Couldn't the sea's creatures escape the predations of fishermen by roaming farther afield or descending lower into the depths? In a word, no. Our species has never called the sea home, but it has served us in myriad ways and provided us with sustenance for eons. We have expressed our gratitude by emptying and poisoning it.

When the Basques arrived in Newfoundland in the sixteenth century, the codfish were not only more plentiful but also much larger. There are reports of cod "as big as a man," and the record is that 211-pounder, bigger than most men, caught in 1895. After the larger individuals were caught, it was the smaller ones whose genes came to predominate, and the population continued to diminish in average size. By 1923, David Starr Jordan could write: "Many examples weighing 100 to 175 pounds have been recorded [in the past], but cod weighing even 75 pounds are not at all common. The average weight of the large-size cod caught in the shore-waters of New England is about 35 pounds; on Georges Bank, 25 pounds; on the Grand Bank and other eastern grounds, 20 pounds." Because cod are groundfish, they tend to stay within a few feet of the seafloor, feeding on mollusks such as clams, cockles, and mussels as well as crabs, lobsters, shrimp, and even sea stars. But as the cod fishermen knew, they also feed on fishes higher in the water column, so hooks would be baited with pieces of fish, hunks of clam, or simple fishing lures. Codfish eat just about anything they can swallow; there are even reports of large codfish taken with ducks in their stomach (Bigelow and Schroeder 1953).

As we have seen, codfish in the eastern North Atlantic are all but gone. With their removal, species such as skates have expanded rapidly in response to the changing species dynamics, with as yet unknown consequences for the ecosystem. Some have become new targets of commercial fishermen, but others, like the barndoor skate, regarded for so long as a trash fish, have also been wiped out. While local fishermen grumble about boats lying idle along the New England coast, political pressure to loosen regulations is unending and heedless of nature's timetable. "The problem with the people out here on the headlands of North America," commented Mark Kurlansky in *Cod: A Biography of the Fish That Changed the World*, "is that they are at the wrong end of a 1,000-year fishing spree."

If everybody is fishing in unregulated waters, some fishers will harvest more than others because of better technology, bigger nets, or the favorite fickle ally of fishermen everywhere, plain luck. It is almost axiomatic that commercial fishermen have been among the most shortsighted of all consumers of natural resources, taking what they can for short-term profit and then moving on. Until the introduction of the exclusive economic zone (EEZ), which limited fishing in waters that bordered on a particular country, almost anyone could fish almost anywhere. The United Nations Convention on the Law of the Sea was adopted at Montego Bay, Jamaica, on December 10, 1982, to codify international law regarding territorial waters, ocean dumping, fishing and fish stocks, endangered species, sea lanes, and ocean resources. According to the treaty, each nation's territorial waters extend 12 miles beyond its coasts, but foreign commercial vessels are permitted "innocent passage" through the 12-mile zone. In addition, every sovereign nation has exclusive rights to the fish and other marine life in waters extending 200 miles from shore; in those cases where countries are separated by less than 400 miles, a mutual agreement must be negotiated.

Overfishing has become the prime example of what Garrett Hardin identified as "the tragedy of the commons" in a classic paper published in *Science* in 1968. Hardin spoke of pastures, but the ideas are applicable—and on a considerably larger scale—to the oceans. He wrote:

> The tragedy of the commons develops in this way. Picture a pasture open to all. It is to be expected that each herdsman will try to keep as many cattle as possible on the commons. Such an arrangement may work reasonably satisfactorily for centuries because tribal wars, poaching, and disease keep the numbers of both man and beast well below the carrying capacity of the land. Finally, however, comes the day of reckoning, that is, the day when the long-desired goal of social stability becomes a reality. At this point, the inherent logic of the commons remorselessly generates tragedy.
>
> As an economically self-interested rational being, each herdsman seeks to maximize his gain. Explicitly or implicitly, more or less consciously, he asks, "What is the utility to me of adding one more animal to my herd?" This utility has one negative and one positive component.
>
> 1.   The positive component is a function of the increment of one animal. Since the herdsman receives all the proceeds from the sale of the additional animal, the positive utility is nearly +1.
>
> 2.   The negative component is a function of the additional overgrazing created by one more animal. Since, however, the effects of overgrazing are shared by all the herdsmen, the negative utility for any particular decision-making herdsman is only a fraction of –1.
>
> Adding together the component partial utilities, the rational herdsman concludes that the only sensible course for him to pursue is to add another animal to his herd. And another. . . . But this is the conclusion reached by each and every rational herdsman sharing a commons. Therein is the tragedy. Each man is locked into a system that compels him to increase his herd without limit—in a world that is limited. Ruin is the destination toward which all men rush, each pursuing his own best interest in a society that believes in the freedom of the commons. Freedom in a commons brings ruin to all.

With regard to the cod fishery as a commons, Stuart Pimm (2001) noted:

> Nations have long recognized this problem. Its resolution is politically popular and ecologically sensible. Extend the economic exclusion zone as far out to sea as your gunboats can effectively patrol. Take possession

of the commons. . . . Canada declared its 200-mile exclusion zone in 1977, but not all fish live within the protected zones. Cod also live outside the zone, where foreign trawlers fish. Canada's own massive offshore trawlers were simultaneously working the commons within that limit, while the inshore catch declined almost annually. Economic exclusion zones may turn an international commons into a national commons, but it is still a commons.

In 1997, Callum Roberts, a marine conservation biologist at the University of York, made a statement that is as true today as it was then:

> The world's fisheries have been in the headlines again but the news gives little comfort: declining yields, stock collapse, crisis, conflict, and social dislocation. Almost every way you look at fisheries, the trends are in the wrong direction: decreasing catch per unit effort despite improved technology, reduced fish abundance, average size and reproductive output, loss of genetic variation, replacement of high-value species by "trash" fish, increased by-catch mortality, recruitment failures, habitat degradation . . . the litany continues. How can fisheries scientists have gone so badly wrong?

Roberts's article, which appeared in the journal *Trends in Ecology and Evolution* (*TREE*), is titled "Ecological Advice for the Global Fisheries Crisis," and it actually offers a solution, at least to some of the problems. The answer? Marine reserves that incorporate no-take zones, which means no fishing by anybody. Roberts maintains that in effect we had reserves until recently—those areas people could not get to—and these refuges helped to keep populations healthy. One of the more recently established marine reserves that Roberts cites is located near the island of St. Lucia in the eastern Caribbean. He noted that generations of fishermen have fished there using handlines or nets, but by the mid-1990s the reefs had become almost barren. Conservationists cordoned off an eleven-mile stretch of reef and prohibited fishing there, and five years later, the refuge was bursting with fish, which lived longer and grew larger. Moreover, big fish produce more offspring than smaller ones, and the extra fish are transported out of the refuge on ocean currents, making the reserve a nursery for nearby fisheries. The article concludes:

> Despite an impressive theoretical underpinning and a rapidly expanding body of field evidence supporting the benefits of reserves, there is still enormous resistance to their implementation. People almost reflexively oppose restrictions on what they can do on the global commons. Critics

often argue that other alternatives should be exhausted before setting up reserves. But time is running out, conventional management is failing us and the seas are rapidly being stripped of their biological resources. It is time to trust the insights of ecologists for once, press for the establishment of marine reserves and place fisheries management and marine conservation on a sound basis at last.

Even though it is becoming evident that marine reserves would help the fishermen in the long run, there is great resistance to the idea because of its short-term consequences and the economic interests involved. And because there are so many complexities in fisheries control, closing areas to fishing will not always produce the desired results quickly. A 1989 ban on trawler fishing in the Gulf of Castellammare on the northern coast of Sicily was supposed to give depleted fish stocks an opportunity to recover. Thirteen years later, Fabio Badalamenti and his colleagues (2002) found that although there was a decided increase in small species, the larger ones that fed on them—Mediterranean hake (*Merluccius merluccius*) and red mullet (*Mullus barbatus*)—did not increase in number or size. Only the goosefish (*Lophius budegassa*) showed an increase in size. "What this shows us is that the timescale of recovery is going to be a lot longer than people thought," said Nicholas Polunin, one of the authors of the study (Randerson 2002). Protected areas can still be made to work, but they will not solve the larger problems of overfishing.

In their 2001 article about historical overfishing, Jeremy Jackson and colleagues commented:

> Ecological extinction caused by overfishing precedes all other pervasive human disturbance to coastal ecosystems, including pollution, degradation of water quality, and anthropogenic climate change. Historical abundances of large consumer species were fantastically large in comparison with recent observations. Paleoecological, archaeological, and historical data show that time lags of decades to centuries occurred between the onset of overfishing and consequent changes in ecological communities, because unfished species of similar trophic level assumed the ecological roles of overfished species until they too were overfished or died of epidemic diseases related to overcrowding. . . . Whales, manatees, dugongs, sea cows, monk seals, crocodiles, codfish, jewfish, swordfish, sharks, and rays are other large marine vertebrates that are now functionally or entirely extinct in most coastal ecosystems.

For security reasons, all fishing was banned off Cape Canaveral in 1962. Forty years later, sportfishermen are pulling record numbers of record-sized fish from these waters, demonstrating that a no-fishing zone can be an excellent way to protect fish stocks. When Callum Roberts and his colleagues (2001) studied data kept by the International Game Fish Association (IGFA), they found that in the Caribbean waters of St. Lucia, with every passing year, more large, slow-growing fish were being caught after a refuge had been established. It seems obvious, of course, that if fishing is banned, the fish populations will rise (or at least will not fall), but no one ever looked at the effect that a ban on commercial fishing would have on sportfishing. In their report, Roberts and colleagues stated: "Within 5 years of creation, a network of small reserves in St. Lucia increased adjacent catches of artisanal fishers by between 46 and 90%, depending on the type of gear the fishers used. In Florida, reserve zones in the Merritt Island National Wildlife Refuge [off Cape Canaveral] have supplied increasing numbers of world record-sized fish to adjacent recreational fisheries since the 1970s."

Coral reefs are under assault; cod fishing is finished; overfishing has altered the oceans' ecosystem; green turtles are seriously endangered; the shortage of sea otters in the Aleutian Islands has caused a population explosion among the sea urchins, which have eaten all the kelp; oysters in Chesapeake Bay have been replaced by plankton blooms; and on and on. The solution? European editor Robert Kunzig named it in the January 2002 issue of *Discover* magazine: "Overfishing is a catastrophe, but it's a uniquely tractable one. . . . We can stop it, or at least contain it if we really want to." This can be done, he noted, concurring with Roberts and others, "by establishing 'no-take' reserves where no fishing is allowed, period." Even closing a small section of a coral reef leads to a massive increase in the fish count. Kunzig quoted James Bohnsack of the National Marine Fisheries Service's Southeast Fisheries Science Center in Miami (one of the authors of the 2001 report with Callum Roberts): "A reserve is win-win; the evidence is very strong. . . . It's kind of like we've discovered penicillin for the ocean."

But even penicillin won't work if you don't take it. Just when we learned that no-take zones could solve some of the problems of overfishing, it appeared that China hadn't exactly been leveling with the world's fishing community about its catch totals, a fact that has thrown much of the large-scale analysis of the state of the world's fisheries into turmoil. In an article published in *Nature* in November 2001, for example, Reg Watson and Daniel Pauly of the University of British Columbia reported that China had claimed a catch of twice what it actually caught between the 1980s and 1998, thus inflating the numbers of what was believed to be available. Lower-ranking fisheries officials had strong incentives to report that they had met government quotas, so they had simply exaggerated the count to match the goals. Because the Food and Agriculture Organization of the United Nations relies on numbers voluntarily provided by member governments, it had no way of checking the Chinese figures. Whereas the organization believed that the world catch was rising by 330,000 tons per year, it was actually declining by 360,000 tons per year. (The total worldwide fish catch was in the neighborhood of 90 million tons.) Watson and Pauly concluded, "The present trends of overfishing, wide-scale disruption of coastal habitats and the rapid expansion of non-sustainable aquaculture enterprises, however, threaten the world's food security."

In a massive report published in 2001, Villy Christensen and his colleagues at the Fisheries Centre of the University of British Columbia (including, among others, Watson and Pauly) analyzed the abundance of various high-trophic-level fish (those at the top of the food chain) in the North Atlantic Ocean from 1950 to 1999. They concluded that the biomass of high-trophic-level fish declined by two-thirds during that fifty-year period. In the late 1960s, annual catches increased from 2.4 million to 4.7 million tons, but by the 1990s they had dropped below 2 million tons. The fishing intensity for high-trophic-level fishes tripled during the first half of that period and remained high during the last half, but as we have seen, fishing out the highest-level species is a recipe for disaster. They wrote, "Our results raise serious concern for the future of the North Atlantic as a diverse, healthy ecosystem; we may soon be left with only low trophic-level species in the sea."

"We humans, as 'the new predator on the block,' can take virtually what we like from the sea, and whatever we remove is taken away from other predators," observed Pauly and Jay Maclean in their 2003 book, *In a Perfect Ocean*. "Unlike us, though," they continued,

> . . . the other predators in the system are unable to turn to other parts of
> their own food web and certainly cannot turn to rice or potatoes when
> marine prey are all gone. On our part, over the course of several
> centuries we have removed nearly all the large whales (with no rebound
> in most of their North Atlantic populations), and are presently eating
> into the populations of other top predators, the sharks and tunas, and of
> fishes lower down the food web such as cod and other ground fish, all
> much reduced from their initial abundance. . . . In terms of ecosystems,
> this means that different species will thrive, others diminish or perish,

and the relationship among them will all change. It also means that for the top predator—us—there will be less fish of the kind we like to eat.

Harvard Medical School's Center for Health and the Global Environment, the Consortium for Conservation Medicine, the Wildlife Trust, and the Environmental and Energy Study Institute presented a report to the United States Congress in May 2001 in which they identified the decline of coastal habitats. They pointed out that residential, recreational, and commercial development have increased pressures on the marine coastal environment, in addition to leaks, spills, and other accidents associated with oil extraction. The combined panels testified, "We are witnessing the degradation of coastal marine habitat and excessive nutrient, chemical and pathogen loading from farming, coastal development, animal and human waste, and the burning of fossil fuels." They identified sea otters that were dying from runoff of polychlorinated biphenyls (PCBs); marine birds exposed to marine pollution and chemical contaminants; and sea turtles threatened by a variety of environmental problems, including virus-induced fibropapillomas. They identified coral reefs as vulnerable to disease, "including several diseases that can harm humans." Perhaps they believed that identifying a threat to humans would make their report more meaningful to Congress, but it is obvious that no congressional panel by itself can halt the slide of coastal ecosystems into ecological despair.

At a meeting in Brussels in June 2002, European Union (EU) fisheries officials made arrangements that allowed Europeans to take more fish off the coasts of the western African countries of Angola, Mauritania, and Senegal. Financial and environmental disagreements had caused an eighteen-month hiatus in the "European Union/Senegal fisheries protocol," but most of Senegal's demands were accepted, and EU fishing boats were set to haul in even greater tonnage than before. The same was true of Angola and Mauritania. Intensive fishing in African waters will be a disaster, particularly for the Africans. Having learned nothing from their experience in the Grand Banks, the Europeans will almost certainly fish out the African stocks, leaving the remainder to subsistence fishermen, who obviously cannot give up their livelihood. In an article published in *New Scientist* on July 13, 2002, Debora MacKenzie wrote, "The big worry now, is that if the West African fisheries go the way of the Grand Banks, they will never come back."

Not only have certain marine species been unable to escape the predations of fishermen, but humans have also introduced pathogens into the living body of the sea. We poison and infect mammals, birds, reptiles, and fishes with fatal, contagious diseases, but we have also introduced alien species that

displace, replace, and sometimes eat the native species. We discharge our poi-
sonous or radioactive effluents into the water, contaminating everything
from lakes and streams to bodies the size of the Caspian Sea. No longer a
haven for endangered species, the sea has become the next environmental
battleground. When a panel was convened in late 1999 to testify before the
U.S. Congress on the subject of endangered oceans and the corresponding
threats to human health, Dr. Eric Chivian, director of Harvard Medical
School's Center for Health and the Human Environment, said, "Oceans are
endangered as perhaps never before, and there is mounting evidence that
human activity may be the culprit." On the subject of pollution half a century
earlier, a certain possum had come to the same conclusion: "We have met the
enemy," said Pogo, "and he is us."*

In 2001, the American Museum of Natural History published *The Biodiversity Crisis* to accompany the opening of its multimillion-dollar Hall of
Biodiversity. The book's editor, Michael Novacek, commented in the introduction:

> Biodiversity is the spectacular variety of life on Earth and the essential
> interdependence of all living things. First formally used at a 1986 forum
> of researchers sponsored by the National Academy of Sciences in the
> United States, it has become the most commonly used word of scientists,
> conservationists, educators and policy-makers to describe a scientific
> discipline and an approach, as well as a critical—indeed, life-threatening
> —issue. We know that because we are losing biodiversity at an alarming
> rate.

No single region of the world has a corner on biodiversity loss, although the

---

*In 1953, in the introduction to his fourth "Pogo" book, Walt Kelly (1913–1973) wrote:
"There is no need to sally forth, for it remains true that those things which make us
human are, curiously enough, always close at hand. Resolve then, that on this very
ground, with small flags waving and tinny blasts on tiny trumpets, we shall meet the
enemy, and not only may he be ours, he may be us." In a strip he created for Earth Day
(April 22) 1971, he had Pogo saying the words "We have met the enemy and he is us," and
in 1972 he titled a book *Pogo: We Have Met the Enemy and He Is Us,* thus ensuring that
these words will always be associated with the possum. In his introduction to the 1972
book, which is specifically about pollution, Kelly wrote: "The big polluter did not start
out with smokestacks. He didn't start pumping gunk into the waters of our world when
he was six years old. He started small. Throwing papers underfoot in the streets, heaving
old bottles into vacant lots, leaving the remnants of a picnic in the fields and woodlands.
Just like the rest of us. At last the stuff is catching up to us. Man has turned out to be his
own worst enemy."

tropical rain forests are often cited as the paradigm. Immense as the rain forests are, however, they represent only a fraction of terrestrial habitats and an even smaller fraction of the earth's livable space. By a substantial margin, the ocean is the largest biome on this planet.

Something lives in almost every cubic inch of the ocean—and the seas contain about 326 million cubic *miles* of water. That's a lot of biodiversity. Ocean occupants range in size from microscopic diatoms to the great whales, the largest animals ever to have lived on the planet. Most of the creatures that inhabit this gigantic watery realm breathe dissolved oxygen, not the O of H_2O. The exceptions, minuscule in number but not in size, are the chemosynthetic hydrothermal vent animals, which do not rely on oxygen at all, and the cetaceans and sirenians, which rely on the interface of air and water, extracting oxygen from the air just like all other mammals. All other ocean inhabitants—fishes, sharks, squid, octopuses, cuttlefishes, clams, crabs, lobsters, gastropods, oysters, sea cucumbers, starfish, jellyfish, copepods— even corals—depend on dissolved oxygen for life. Everything that lives in the ocean is intimately connected with every other living thing by a complex arrangement of feeding strategies, which can be simply expressed by chang- ing *flea* to *fish* in Jonathan Swift's little ditty, as so:

> So, naturalists observe, a fish,
> Has smaller fish that on him prey;
> And these have smaller still to bite 'em;
> And so proceed ad infinitum.

Fleas or fishes, the point is the same: everything feeds on everything else, and it is not necessarily the bigger ones that eat the smaller. Very few ocean inhab- itants can be classified as pure predators; among them are probably the larger sharks and killer whales, but with those exceptions, virtually every animal that lives in the sea is vulnerable to predation by another animal at some stage in its life. The food chain, often simplified to show the few larger species feed- ing on the plentiful smaller ones, and so on, ad infinitum, is far more com- plex than that.

Consider the life history of the codfish. Each female lays millions of eggs, which float slowly upward, becoming part of the surface plankton. The hatchlings are provided with a pendulous yolk sac that provides nourishment for them—and for any other creature that gobbles up these quarter-inch-long larvae. Even at that length, cod are already predators, though they can prey only on planktonic creatures smaller than they are, such as the larvae of bar- nacles, shrimp, crabs, and little worms. Some inch-long cod take refuge in the tentacles of the stinging jellyfish *Cyanea*, evidently without being stung as they pick tiny parasites from the jellyfish. At about two months of age, the cod fry begin to look like miniature adults, and they head toward the bottom, where they will spend the rest of their lives. En route, they can be picked off by all sorts of midwater predators, such as dogfish sharks and pollock, and even by larger codfish. (So much for the simplicity of the food chain: prey and predator can be the same species if the size differential is sufficient.) If they survive this sequential predation, codfish spend their lives within a fathom of the ocean bottom, feeding primarily on shellfish but more than willing to eat anything that moves—or doesn't. Cod are infamous for gobbling up inanimate and inedible objects such as tin cans, shoes, pieces of wood, rocks, even a set of false teeth. By the age of two, cod can reach a foot in length, and by three, they are almost two feet long. A cod five feet long might be forty years old. But there are no more five-foot-long cod, and probably very few three-footers. They have been mercilessly removed by the superpredator who has bullied his way to the top rung of the food ladder and announced that the devil can take the hindmost.

Our fishing out the cod from the North Atlantic upset the entire ecosystem and fostered imbalance in the trophic relationships that make up the food web. Prey animals ordinarily kept in check by traditional predators proliferate when those predators are removed. Even as the cod's disappearance spelled doom for the fishermen and the cod themselves, it wrought a special ecological havoc on the system of which the cod was an integral component. Thus are all natural systems integrated in ways we are only now beginning to understand. The assault on the fishes of the sea, the slaughter of the sea otters, the displacement and extinction of the sea cows, the extirpation of the seals, the war against the whales, the drowning of the albatrosses, and the destruction of the world's coral reefs are all massive acts of violence against our Mother Ocean, she who gave us life and has sustained us so selflessly. In *Poor Richard's Almanac* for 1758, Ben Franklin wrote:

> And again, he adviseth to Circumspection and Care, even in the smallest Matters, because sometimes a little Neglect may breed great Mischief; adding, For want of a Nail the Shoe was lost; for want of a Shoe the Horse was lost; and for want of a Horse the Rider was lost, being overtaken and slain by the Enemy, all for want of Care about a Horseshoe Nail.

We are guilty of more than "a little Neglect," and unless we begin exercising "Circumspection and Care," we will surely lose the kingdom and all that goes with it. How poor we will be for its loss is beyond calculation. John Donne warned us in 1623:

> Who casts not up his eye to the sun when it rises? But who takes off his eye from a comet when that breaks out? Who bends not his ear to any bell which upon any occasion rings? But who can remove it from that bell which is passing a piece of himself out of this world? No man is an island, entire of itself; every man is a piece of the continent, a part of the main. If a clod be washed away by the sea, Europe is the less, as well as if a promontory were, as well as if a manor of thy friend's or of thine own were: any man's death diminishes me, because I am involved in mankind, and therefore never send to know for whom the bell tolls; it tolls for thee.

BIBLIOGRAPHY

Ackerman, R. A. 1997. The nest environment and the embryonic development of sea turtles. In *The Biology of Sea Turtles,* edited by P. L. Lutz and J. A. Musick, 83–106. CRC Press.

Adler, J. 2002. The great salmon debate. *Newsweek* 140 (18): 54–56.

Aguayo, L. A. 1979. Juan Fernández fur seal. In *Mammals in the Seas II: Pinniped Species Summaries and Report on Sirenians,* 28–30. Food and Agriculture Organization of the United Nations, Rome.

Aguilar, A. 1981. The black right whale, *Eubalaena glacialis,* in the Cantabrian Sea. *Reports of the International Whaling Commission* 31:457–459.

Aguirre, A. A. 1998. Fibropapillomas in marine turtles: A workshop at the Eighteenth Annual Symposium on Biology and Conservation of Sea Turtles. *Marine Turtle Newsletter* 82:10–12.

Allee, W. C. 1931. *Animal Aggregations: A Study in General Sociology.* University of Chicago Press.

Allen, G. M. 1942. *Extinct and Vanishing Mammals of the Western Hemisphere, with the Marine Species of All the Oceans.* American Committee for International Wildlife Protection. Reprint, Cooper Square Publishers, 1972.

Allen, J. A. 1880. *History of North American Pinnipeds: A Monograph of the Walrus, Sea-Lions, Sea-Bears, and Seals of North America.* U.S. Government Printing Office.

———. 1898. Fur seal hunting in the Southern Hemisphere. In *The Fur Seals and the Fur-Seal Islands of the North Pacific Ocean,* edited by D. S. Jordan, vol. 3, 307–319. U.S. Government Printing Office.

Allen, R. C., and I. Keay. 2001. The first great whale extinction: The end of the bowhead whale in the eastern Arctic. *Explorations in Economic History* 38 (4): 448–477.

Allen, R. L. 1975. A life table for harp seals in the northwest Atlantic. *Rapports et Procès-Verbaux des Réunions du Conseil International pour l'Exploration de la Mer* 169:303–312.

Allen, R. L., and M. D. Goldsmith. 1980. Dolphin mortality in the eastern tropical Pacific incidental to purse seining for yellowfin tunas, 1979. SC/32/SM6. *Reports of the International Whaling Commission* 31:539–540.

Ames, J. A., and G. V. Morejohn. 1980. Evidence of white shark, *Carcharodon carcharias,* attacks on sea otters, *Enhydra lutris. California Fish and Game* 66:196–209.

Anathaswamy, A. 2002. Muddy waters: Corals are being robbed of light. *New Scientist* 173 (2331): 14.

Andersen, T. 1987. The Kemp's ridley puzzle. *Oceans* 20 (3): 42–49.

Anderson, P. K. 1995. Competition, predation, and the evolution and extinction of Steller's sea cow, *Hydrodamalis gigas*. *Marine Mammal Science* 11 (3): 391–394.

Anderson, P. K., and D. P. Domning. 2002. Steller's sea cow. In *Encyclopedia of Marine Mammals,* edited by W. F. Perrin, B. Würsig, and J. G. M. Thewissen, 1178–1181. Academic Press.

Andrews, C. L. 1945. *Sitka: The Chief Factory of the Russian American Company.* Caxton.

Antonelis, G. A., M. S. Lowry, D. P. DeMaster, and C. H. Fiscus. 1987. Assessing northern elephant seal feeding habits by stomach lavage. *Marine Mammal Science* 3 (4): 308–332.

Apple, R. W. 2002. How to grow a giant tuna. *New York Times,* April 3, F1–F2.

Archer, F., T. Gerrodette, A. Dizon, K. Abella, and S. Southern. 2001. Unobserved kill of nursing dolphin calves in a tuna purse-seine fishery. *Marine Mammal Science* 17 (3): 540–554.

Archibald, J. D. 1996. *Dinosaur Extinction and the End of an Era.* Columbia University Press.

Arnould, J. P. Y. 2002. Southern fur seals. In *Encyclopedia of Marine Mammals,* edited by W. F. Perrin, B. Würsig, and J. G. M. Thewissen, 1146–1151. Academic Press.

Aronson, R. B., W. F. Precht, I. G. Macintyre, and T. J. T. Murdoch. 2000. Coral bleach-out in Belize. *Nature* 405:36.

Associated Press. 2001. Giant tuna sells for record $173,600. On-line at http://www.flmnh.ufl.edu/fish/InNews/GiantTuna.htm.

Au, W., and D. Weihs. 1980. At high speeds dolphins save energy by leaping. *Nature* 284:548–550.

Audubon, J. J. 1827–1838. *The Birds of America.* Edinburgh.

Austin, O. L. 1949. The status of Steller's albatross. *Pacific Science* 3 (4): 283–295.

Backhouse, K. M. 1969. *Seals.* Arthur Barker.

Badalamenti, F., G. D'Anna, J. K. Pinnegar, and N. V. C. Polunin. 2002. Size-related trophodynamic changes in three target fish species recovering from intensive trawling. *Marine Biology* 141:561–570.

Bailey, A. M., and J. H. Sorensen. 1962. *Subantarctic Campbell Island.* Denver Museum of Natural History.

Baker, A. C. 2001. Reef corals bleach to survive change. *Nature* 411:765–766.

Balazs, G. 1982. Status of sea turtles in the Central Pacific Ocean. In *Biology and Conservation of Sea Turtles: Proceedings of the World Conference on Sea Turtle Conservation, Washington, D.C., 26–30 November 1979,* edited by K. A. Bjorndal. Smithsonian Institution Press and World Wildlife Fund.

————. 1986. Fibropapillomas in Hawaiian green turtles. *Marine Turtle Newsletter* 39:1–3.

Balazs, G. H., and S. G. Pooley, eds. 1991. *Research Plan for Marine Turtle Fibropapilloma.* NOAA Technical Memorandum NMFS-SWFSC-156. U.S. Department of Commerce, Honolulu.

Baldridge, H. D. 1974a. *Shark Attack*. Berkeley Medallion.

————. 1974b. Shark attack: A program of data reduction and analysis. *Contributions from the Mote Marine Laboratory* 1 (2): 1–98.

Barber, C. V., and V. Pratt. 1998. Poison and profit: Cyanide fishing in the Indo-Pacific. *Environment* 40 (8): 5–34.

Bardach, J. 1968. *Harvest of the Sea*. Harper and Row.

Barlow, J., T. Gerrodette, and G. Silber. 1997. First estimates of vaquita abundance. *Marine Mammal Science* 13 (1): 44–58.

Barnes, L. G. 1984. Search for the first whale: Retracing the ancestry of cetaceans. *Oceans* 17 (2): 20–23.

Barnes, L. G., and S. A. MacLeod. 1984. The fossil record and phyletic relationships of gray whales. In *The Gray Whale, Eschrichtius robustus*, edited by M. L. Jones, S. L. Swartz, and S. Leatherwood, 3–32. Academic Press.

Barnett, A. 2001. Safety in numbers. *New Scientist* 169:38–41.

Baskin, Y. 2002. *A Plague of Rats and Rubbervines: The Growing Threat of Species Invasions*. Island Press.

Beaglehole, J. C. 1966. *The Exploration of the Pacific*. Stanford University Press.

Beebe, W. 1906. *The Bird, Its Form and Function*. Holt.

Belden, A. L. 1917. *The Fur Trade in America*. Peltries.

Bell, N., and J. Smith. 1999. Coral growing on North Sea oil rigs. Nature 402:601.

Bellingshausen, T. F. 1825. *Voyage of Captain Bellingshausen to the Antarctic Seas, 1819–1821*. Translated from Russian by Frank Debenham. Hakluyt Society, 1945.

Benchley, P. 1974. *Jaws*. Doubleday.

————. 1998. Swimming with sharks. *Audubon* 100 (3): 52–57.

————. 2000. Great white sharks. *National Geographic* 197 (4): 2–29.

————. 2002. *Shark Trouble*. Random House.

Benham, H. 1979. *The Codbangers*. Essex County Newspapers.

Bergquist, D. C., F. M. Williams, and C. R. Fisher. 2000. Longevity record for deep-sea invertebrate. *Nature* 403:499–500.

Berzin, A. A. 1972. *The Sperm Whale*. Izdatel'stvo "Pischevaya Promyshlennost" Moskva 1971. Israel Program for Scientific Translation, Jerusalem.

Best, P. B. 1969. A dolphin (*Stenella attenuata*) from Durban, South Africa. *Annals of the South African Museum* 52 (5): 121–135.

Beston, H. 1928. *The Outermost House*. Holt, Rinehart and Winston.

Bickham, J. W., T. R. Loughlin, D. G. Calkins, J. K. Wickliffe, and J. C. Patton. 1998. Genetic variability and population decline in Steller sea lions from the Gulf of Alaska. *Journal of Mammalogy* 79 (4): 1390–1395.

Bigelow, H. B., and W. C. Schroeder. 1953. Fishes of the Gulf of Maine. *Fishery Bulletin of the Fish and Wildlife Service* 74:1–577.

Bigg, M. A. 1981. Harbour seal—*Phoca vitulina* Linnaeus, 1758 and *Phoca larga* Pallas, 1811. In *Handbook of Marine Mammals*, edited by S. H. Ridgway and R. J. Harrison. Vol. 2, *Seals*, 1–27. Academic Press.

Birkeland, C. 1982. Terrestrial runoff as a cause of outbreaks of *Acanthaster planci* (Echinodermata: Asteroidea). *Marine Biology* 69:175–185.

———. 1997a. Geographical differences in ecological processes on coral reefs. In *Life and Death of Coral Reefs,* edited by C. Birkeland, 273–287. Chapman and Hall.

———. 1997b. Implications for resource management. In *Life and Death of Coral Reefs,* edited by C. Birkeland, 411–435. Chapman and Hall.

———. 1997c. Introduction. In Life and Death of Coral Reefs, edited by C. Birkeland, 1–10. Chapman and Hall.

———, ed. 1997. *Life and Death of Coral Reefs.* Chapman and Hall.

Bjorndal, K. A. 1997. Foraging ecology and nutrition of sea turtles. In *The Biology of Sea Turtles,* edited by P. L. Lutz and J. A. Musick, 199–231. CRC Press.

———. 1999. Conservation of hawksbill sea turtles: Perceptions and realities. *Chelonian Conservation and Biology* 3 (2): 174–176.

———, ed. 1995. *Biology and Conservation of Sea Turtles.* Smithsonian Institution Press.

Bjorndal, K. A., A. B. Bolten, J. Gordon, and J. A. Camiñas. 1994. *Caretta caretta* (loggerhead) growth and pelagic movement. *Herpetological Review* 25:23–24.

Bjorndal, K. A., A. B. Bolten, and H. R. Martins. 2000. Somatic growth model of juvenile loggerhead sea turtles *Caretta caretta:* Duration of pelagic stage. *Marine Ecology Progress Series* 202:265–272.

Black, L. T. 1988. The story of Russian America. In *Crossroads of Continents,* edited by W. W. Fitzhugh and A. Crowell, 70–82. Smithsonian Institution Press.

———. 1999. Russian America: A place to start. *Alaska Geographic* 26 (4): 4–17.

Black, L. T., and R. G. Liapunova. 1988. Aleut: Islanders of the North Pacific. In *Crossroads of Continents,* edited by W. W. Fitzhugh and A. Crowell, 52–57. Smithsonian Institution Press.

Block, B. A., H. Dewar, S. B. Blackwell, T. D. Williams, E. D. Prince, C. J. Farwell, A. Boustany, S. L. H. Teo, A. Seitz, A. Walli, and D. Fudge. 2001. Migratory movements, depth preferences, and thermal biology of Atlantic bluefin tuna. *Science* 293:1310–1314.

Block, B. A., H. Dewar, C. Farwell, and E. D. Prince. 1998. A new satellite technology for tracking the movements of Atlantic bluefin tuna. *Proceedings of the National Academy of Sciences* 95 (16): 9384–9389.

Bobrick, B. 1992. *East of the Sun: The Epic Conquest and Tragic History of Siberia.* Poseidon.

Bodkin, J. 2000. Sea otters. *Alaska Geographic* 27 (2): 74–92.

Bolten, A. B., and G. H. Balasz. 1995. Biology of the early pelagic stage—the "lost year." In *Biology and Conservation of Sea Turtles,* edited by K. A. Bjorndal, 579–581. Smithsonian Institution Press.

Bolten, A. B., K. A. Bjorndal, H. R. Martins, T. Dellinger, M. J. Biscoitto, S. A. Encalada, and B. W. Bowen. 1998. Transatlantic developmental migrations of loggerhead sea turtles demonstrated by mtDNA sequence analysis. *Ecological Applications* 8 (1): 1–7.

Bolten, A. B., H. R. Martins, K. A. Bjorndal, M. Cocco, and G. Gerosa. 1992. *Caretta caretta* (loggerhead) pelagic movement and growth. *Herpetological Review* 23:116.

Bolten, A. B., H. R. Martins, K. A. Bjorndal, and J. Gordon. 1993. Size distribution of pelagic-stage loggerhead sea turtles (*Caretta caretta*) in the waters around the Azores and Madeira. *Arquipélago* 11A:49–54.

Bonner, J. 2002. Bloody Greenland. *New Scientist* 174 (2338): 49.

Bonner, W. N. 1979a. Antarctic (Kerguelen) fur seal. In *Mammals in the Seas II: Pinniped Species Summaries and Report on Sirenians*, 49–51. Food and Agriculture Organization of the United Nations, Rome.

————. 1979b. Grey seal. In *Mammals in the Seas II: Pinniped Species Summaries and Report on Sirenians*, 90–94. Food and Agriculture Organization of the United Nations, Rome.

————. 1979c. Subantarctic fur seal. In *Mammals in the Seas II: Pinniped Species Summaries and Report on Sirenians*, 52–54. Food and Agriculture Organization of the United Nations, Rome.

————. 1981a. Grey seal—*Halichoerus grypus* (Fabricius, 1791). In *Handbook of Marine Mammals*, edited by S. H. Ridgway and R. J. Harrison. Vol. 2, *Seals*, 111–144. Academic Press.

————. 1981b. Southern fur seals—*Arctocephalus* (Geoffroy Saint-Hilaire and Cuvier, 1826). In *Handbook of Marine Mammals*, edited by S. H. Ridgway and R. J. Harrison. Vol. 1, *The Walrus, Sea Lions, Fur Seals, and Sea Otter*, 161–208. Academic Press.

————. 1982. *Seals and Men: A Study of Interactions*. Washington Sea Grant.

————. 1994. *Seals and Sea Lions of the World*. Blandford.

Boulva, J. 1979. Mediterranean monk seal. In *Mammals in the Seas II: Pinniped Species Summaries and Report on Sirenians*, 95–100. Food and Agriculture Organization of the United Nations, Rome.

Bowen, S. L. 1974. Probable extinction of the Korean stock of gray whales (*Eschrichtius robustus*). *Journal of Mammalogy* 55 (1): 208–209.

Bowen, W. D., and D. B. Siniff. 1999. Distribution, population biology, and feeding ecology of marine mammals. In *Biology of Marine Mammals*, edited by J. E. Reynolds III and S. A. Rommel, 423–484. Smithsonian Institution Press.

Bradford, W. 1856. *History of Plymouth Plantation*. Reprint, Modern Library, 1952.

Brady, S. L., and J. Boreman. 1996. Distribution and fishery bycatch of sea turtles off the northeastern United States coast. In *Fisheries Bycatch: Consequences and Management*, 9–10. Alaska Sea Grant College Program Report No. 97-02. University of Alaska.

Branstetter, S. 1996. Status of research leading to the reduction of unwanted bycatch in the shrimp fishery of the southeastern United States. In *Fisheries Bycatch: Consequences and Management*, 115–118. Alaska Sea Grant College Program Report No. 97-02. University of Alaska.

Bratten, D., and M. Hall. 1996. Working with fishers to reduce bycatch: The tuna-dolphin problem in the eastern Pacific Ocean. In *Fisheries Bycatch:*

Consequences and Management, 97–100. Alaska Sea Grant College Program
Report No. 97-02. University of Alaska.

Brill, R. W., G. H. Balazs, K. N. Holland, R. K. C. Chang, S. Sullivan, and J. C.
George. 1995. Daily movements, habitat use, and submergence intervals of
normal and tumor-bearing juvenile green turtles (*Chelonia mydas* L.) within
a foraging area in the Hawaiian Islands. *Journal of Experimental Marine
Biology and Ecology* 185 (2): 203–218.

Brodeur, R. D., and M. S. Busby. 1998. Occurrence of an Atlantic salmon *Salmo
salar* in the Bering Sea. *Alaska Fishery Research Bulletin* 5 (1): 64–66.

Brody, A. J., K. Ralls, and D. B. Siniff. 1996. Potential impact of oil spills on
California sea otters: Implications of the *Exxon Valdez* spill in Alaska. *Marine
Mammal Science* 12 (1): 38–53.

Brower, K. 1989. The destruction of dolphins. *Atlantic Monthly* 263 (1): 35–58.

Brown, B. E. 1997a. Coral bleaching: Causes and consequences. *Coral Reefs* 16 (5):
S129–S138.

———. 1997b. Disturbances to reefs in recent times. In *Life and Death of Coral
Reefs,* edited by C. Birkeland, 354–389. Chapman and Hall.

Brown, B. E., and J. C. Ogden. 1993. Coral bleaching. *Scientific American* 268 (1):
64–70.

Brown, S. G. 1986. Twentieth-century records of right whales (*Eubalaena glacialis*)
in the northeastern Atlantic Ocean. *Reports of the International Whaling
Commission* (Special Issue) 10:121–127.

Brownell, R. L. 1986. Distribution of the vaquita, *Phocoena sinus,* in Mexican
waters. *Marine Mammal Science* 2 (4): 229–305.

Brownell, R. L., and C. L. Chun. 1977. Probable existence of the Korean stock of
the gray whale (*Eschrichtius robustus*). *Journal of Mammalogy* 58 (2): 237–239.

Brownell, R. L., and A. V. Yablokov. 2002. Illegal and pirate whaling. In
Encyclopedia of Marine Mammals, edited by W. F. Perrin, B. Würsig, and J. G.
M. Thewissen, 608–612. Academic Press.

Bruckner, A. W., R. J. Bruckner, and E. H. Williams. 1997. Spread of a black-band
disease epizootic through the reef system in St. Ann's Bay, Jamaica. *Bulletin of
Marine Science* 61:919–928.

Bruemmer, F. 1972. *Encounters with Arctic Animals.* American Heritage.

———. 1975. A year in the life of a harp seal. *Natural History* 84:42–49.

———. 1977. *The Life of the Harp Seal.* Times Books.

———. 1983. Sea lion shenanigans. *Natural History* 92 (7): 32–40.

———. 1986. *Arctic Animals.* Northword.

———. 1988. A fate unsealed. *Natural History* 97 (11): 59–65.

Bullen, F. 1899. *The Cruise of the "Cachalot": Round the World After Sperm Whales.*
Appleton.

Bundy, A. 2001. Fishing on ecosystems: The interplay of fishing and predation in
Newfoundland-Labrador. *Canadian Journal of Fisheries and Aquatic Sciences*
58 (6): 1153–1167.

Bundy, A., G. R. Lilly, and P. A. Shelton. 2000. A mass balance model of the

Newfoundland-Labrador Shelf. *Canadian Technical Report of Fisheries and Aquatic Sciences* 2301:1–157.

Burger, J. 1997. *Oil Spills.* Rutgers University Press.

Burns, W. C. G., and G. Wandesforde-Smith. 2002. The International Whaling Commission and the future of cetaceans in a changing world. *Review of European Community and International Environmental Law* 11 (2): 199–210.

Burros, M. 2002. Chefs join campaign against altered fish. *New York Times,* September 18, F1, F7.

Busch, B. C. 1980. Elephants and whales: New London and Desolation, 1840–1900. *American Neptune* 40 (2): 117–126.

———. 1985. *The War against the Seals: A History of the North American Seal Fishery.* McGill-Queens University Press.

———, ed. 1980. *Master of Desolation: The Reminiscences of Capt. Joseph J. Fuller.* Mystic Seaport Museum.

Butler, M. J. A. 1982. Plight of the bluefin tuna. *National Geographic* 162 (2): 220–239.

Bychkov, V. A., and S. V. Dorofeev. 1962. Behavior of fur seal bulls during the harem period. *Zoologicheskii Zhurnal* 41 (9): 1433–1435.

Cahn, R. 1980. The porpoises resurface. *Audubon* 82 (1): 5–8.

Calkins, D. G., D. C. McAllister, K. W. Pitcher, and G. W. Pendleton. 1999. Steller sea lion status and trend in Southeast Alaska. *Marine Mammal Science* 15 (2): 462–477.

Cameron, E. 1972. Death on the ice. *Oceans* 5 (2): 64–70.

Camhi, M., S. Fowler, J. Musick, A. Bräutigam, and S. Fordham. 1998. *Sharks and Their Relatives: Ecology and Conservation.* IUCN/SSG Shark Specialist Group. International Union for Conservation of Nature and Natural Resources, Gland, Switzerland.

Carey, F. G. 1973. Fish with warm bodies. *Scientific American* 228 (2): 36–44.

Carlton, J. T. 1993. Neoextinctions of marine invertebrates. *American Zoologist* 33:499–509.

———. 1996. Marine bioinvasions: The alteration of marine ecosystems by nonindigenous species. *Oceanography* 9 (1): 36–43.

———. 1999a. A journal of biological invasions. *Biological Invasions* 1:1.

———. 1999b. The scale and ecological consequences of biological invasions in the world's oceans. In *Invasive Species and Biodiversity Management,* edited by O. T. Sunderland et al., 195–212. Kluwer Academic Publishers.

Carlton, J. T., and J. B. Geller. 1993. Ecological roulette: The global transport of nonindigenous marine organisms. *Science* 261:78–82.

Carlton, J. T., J. B. Geller, M. L. Reaka-Kudla, and E. A. Norse. 1999. Historical extinctions in the sea. *Annual Review of Ecology and Systematics* 30:515–538.

Carlton, J. T., G. J. Vermeij, D. R. Lindberg, D. A. Carlton, and E. C. Dudley. 1991. The first historical extinction of a marine invertebrate in an ocean basin: The demise of the eelgrass limpet *Lottia alveus. Biological Bulletin* 180:72–80.

Carpenter, R. C. 1997. Invertebrate predators and grazers. In *Life and Death of Coral Reefs,* edited by C. Birkeland, 198–248. Chapman and Hall.

Carr, A. 1942. Notes on sea turtles. *Proceedings of the New England Zoological Club* 21:1016.

———. 1965. The navigation of the green turtle. *Scientific American* 212 (5): 79–86.

———. 1967a. *So Excellent a Fishe: A Natural History of Sea Turtles.* American Museum of Natural History.

———. 1967b. *The Windward Road.* Knopf.

———. 1982. Notes on the behavioral ecology of sea turtles. In *Biology and Conservation of Sea Turtles: Proceedings of the World Conference on Sea Turtle Conservation, Washington, D.C., 26–30 November 1979*, edited by K. A. Bjorndal. Smithsonian Institution Press and World Wildlife Fund.

———. 1986. Rips, FADS, and little loggerheads. *BioScience* 36:92–100.

———. 1987. New perspectives on the pelagic stage of sea turtle development. *Conservation Biology* 1:103–121.

Carr, A., and D. K. Caldwell. 1956. The ecology and migration of sea turtles. 1. Results of field work in Florida. *American Museum Novitates* 1793:1–23.

Carr, A., and A. B. Meylan. 1980a. Evidence of passive migration of green turtle hatchlings in sargassum. *Copeia* 1980 (2): 366–368.

———. 1980b. Extinction or rescue for the hawksbill? Oryx 15:449–450.

Carr, A., and L. Ogren. 1960. The ecology and migration of sea turtles. 4. The green turtle in the Caribbean Sea. *Bulletin of the American Museum of Natural History* 121:1–48.

Carr, A., III. 1998. The big green seafood machine. *Wildlife Conservation* 101 (4): 16–23.

Carroll, G. F. 1982. Born again seal. *Natural History* 91 (7): 40–47.

Carroll, R. L. 1988. *Vertebrate Paleontology and Evolution.* Freeman.

Casey, J. M., and R. A. Myers. 1998. Near extinction of a large, widely distributed fish. *Science* 281:690–692.

Castro, J. I. 1983. *The Sharks of North American Waters.* Texas A & M University Press.

Castro, J. I., C. M. Woodley, and R. L. Brudek. 1999. *A Preliminary Evaluation of the Status of Shark Species.* FAO Fisheries Technical Paper No. 380. Food and Agriculture Organization of the United Nations.

Caswell, H., M. Fujiwara, and S. Brault. 1999. Declining survival probability threatens the North Atlantic right whale. *Proceedings of the National Academy of Sciences* 96:3308–3313.

Cederlund, B. A. 1938. A subfossil gray whale discovered in Sweden in 1859. *Zoologiska Bidrag fran Uppsala* 18:269–286.

Chaloner, W. G., and A. Hallam, eds. 1989. *Evolution and Extinction.* Cambridge University Press.

Chaloupka, M. Y., and J. A. Musick. 1997. Age, growth, and population dynamics. In *The Biology of Sea Turtles*, edited by P. L. Lutz and J. A. Musick, 233–276. CRC Press.

Chapin, F. S., E. S. Zavaleta, V. T. Eviner, R. L. Naylor, P. M. Vitousek, H. L.

Reynolds, D. U. Hooper, S. Lavorel, O. E. Sala, S. E. Hobbie, M. C. Mack, and S. Díaz. 2000. Consequences of changing biodiversity. *Nature* 405:234–242.

Charrier, I., N. Mathevon, and P. Jouventin. 2001. Mother's voice recognition by seal pups. *Nature* 412:873.

Chen, P. 1981. *Lipotes* research in the People's Republic of China. *Reports of the International Whaling Commission* 31:475–478.

———. 1989. Baiji—*Lipotes vexillifer* (Miller, 1918). In *Handbook of Marine Mammals*, edited by S. H. Ridgway and R. J. Harrison. Vol. 4, *River Dolphins and the Larger Toothed Whales*, 25–43. Academic Press.

Chesher, R. 1969. Destruction of Pacific corals by the sea star *Acanthaster planci. Science* 165:280–283.

Chivers, C. J. 1998. Empty waves. *Wildlife Conservation* 101 (4): 36–44.

Christensen, V., S. Guénette, J. J. Heymans, C. J. Walters, R. Watson, D. Zeller, and D. Pauly. 2001. Estimating fish abundance of the North Atlantic, 1950 to 1999. In *Fisheries Impacts on North Atlantic Ecosystems: Models and Analyses*, edited by S. Guénette, V. Christensen, and D. Pauly, 1–25. Fisheries Centre Research Reports 9(4). University of British Columbia, Fisheries Centre.

Clapham, P. J., and C. S. Baker. 2002. Whaling, modern. In *Encyclopedia of Marine Mammals*, edited by W. F. Perrin, B. Würsig, and J. G. M. Thewissen, 1328–1332. Academic Press.

Clark, A. H. 1887a. The Antarctic fur-seal and sea-elephant industries. In *The Fisheries and Fishery Industries of the United States*, edited by G. B. Goode. Vol. 2, sec. 5, 400–467. U.S. Government Printing Office.

———. 1887b. The North Atlantic seal fishery. In *The Fisheries and Fishery Industries of the United States*, edited by G. B. Goode. Vol. 2, sec. 5, 474–483. U.S. Government Printing Office.

Clark, T. W. 1979. Galápagos fur seal. In *Mammals in the Seas II: Pinniped Species Summaries and Report on Sirenians*, 31–33. Food and Agriculture Organization of the United Nations, Rome.

Clarke, M. R. 1976. Observation on sperm whale diving. *Journal of the Marine Biological Association of the UK* 56:809–810.

———. 1977. Beaks, nets, and numbers. *Symposia of the Zoological Society of London* 38:89–126.

Clines, F. X. 2002. Battling an alien predator in a suburban pond. *New York Times*, July 13, A7.

Cohen, P. 2002. Transgenic fish: Will one get away? *New Scientist* 175 (2360): 12–13.

Compagno, L. J. V. 1984a. *FAO Species Catalogue*. Vol. 4, *Sharks of the World: An Annotated and Illustrated Catalogue of Shark Species Known to Date*. Part 1, Hexanchiformes to Lamniformes. FAO Fisheries Synopsis 125(4). Food and Agriculture Organization of the United Nations, Rome.

———. 1984b. *FAO Species Catalogue*. Vol. 4, *Sharks of the World: An Annotated and Illustrated Catalogue of Shark Species Known to Date*. Part 2, Carcharhiniformes. FAO Fisheries Synopsis 125(4). Food and Agriculture Organization of the United Nations, Rome.

Courchamp, F., T. Clutton-Brock, and B. Grenfell. 1999. Inverse density dependence and the Allee effect. *Trends in Ecology and Evolution* 14:405–410.

Courchamp, F., B. Grenfell, and T. Clutton-Brock. 1999. Population dynamics of obligate cooperators. *Proceedings of the Royal Society of London* 266:557–563.

———. 2000. Impact of natural enemies on obligately cooperative breeders. *Oikos* 91:311–322.

Cousteau, J.-Y., and F. Dumas. 1953. *The Silent World.* Pocket Books.

Cowen, R. 1996. Locomotion and respiration in aquatic air-breathing vertebrates. In *Evolutionary Paleobiology*, edited by D. Jablonski, D. H. Erwin, and J. H. Lipps, 337–353. University of Chicago Press.

———. 2000. *History of Life.* Blackwell Science.

Coxe, W. 1780. *Account of the Russian Discoveries between Asia and America: To Which Are Added, the Conquest of Siberia, and the History of the Transactions and Commerce between Russian and China.* J. Nichols. Reprint, Readex Microprint, 1966.

Cramer, J. 1996. Effect of regulations limiting landings of swordfish by weight on commercial pelagic longline fishing patterns. In *Fisheries Bycatch: Consequences and Management*, 63–64. Alaska Sea Grant College Program Report No. 97-02. University of Alaska.

Crawley, M. C., and R. Warnecke. 1979. New Zealand fur seal. In *Mammals in the Seas II: Pinniped Species Summaries and Report on Sirenians*, 45–48. Food and Agriculture Organization of the United Nations, Rome.

Cressie, N. A. C., and P. D. Shaughnessy. 1987. Statistical methods for estimating numbers of Cape fur seal pups from aerial surveys. *Marine Mammal Science* 3 (4): 297–307.

Crichton, M. 1990. *Jurassic Park.* Knopf.

Crowley, M. 1978. Bering Sea: Where the ocean coldly breaks its back. *Oceans* 11 (6): 5–11.

Croxall, J. P., P. Rothery, S. P. C. Pickering, and P. A. Prince. 1990. Reproductive performance, recruitment, and survival of wandering albatrosses *Diomedea exulans* at Bird Island, South Georgia. *Journal of Animal Ecology* 59:775–796.

Culliney, J. L. 1976. *The Forests of the Sea: Life and Death on the Continental Shelf.* Sierra Club.

Cushing, D. H. 1988. *The Provident Sea.* Cambridge University Press.

Dale, P. W. 1969. *Seventy North to Fifty South: Captain Cook's Last Voyage.* Prentice Hall.

D'Amato, A. F., and M. Moraes-Neto. 2000. First documentation of fibropapillomas verified by histopathology in *Eretmochelys imbricata. Marine Turtle Newsletter* 89:12–13.

Dampier, W. 1697. *A New Voyage Round the World.* Knapton. Reprint, Argonaut Press, 1927.

Daniel, H., and F. Minot. 1961. *The Inexhaustible Sea.* Collier Books.

Darwin, C. 1845. *Journal of the Researches into the Natural History and Geology of the Countries Visited during the Voyage of H.M.S. 'Beagle.'* London.

Daszak, P., A. A. Cunningham, and A. D. Hyatt. 2000. Emerging infectious diseases of wildlife—threats to biodiversity and human health. *Science* 287:443–449.

Davidson, O. G. 1998. *The Enchanted Braid: Coming to Terms with the Nature of the Coral Reef.* Wiley.

———. 2001. *Fire in the Turtle House: The Green Sea Turtle and the Fate of the Ocean.* Public Affairs.

Davies, B. 1978. *Seal Song.* Viking Press.

Davis, B. S. 1979. Sea otter irony: Overabundant yet endangered. *Oceans* 12 (5): 60–62.

Davis, G. E., P. L. Haaker, and D. V. Richards. 1996. Status and trends of white abalone at the California Channel Islands. *Transactions of the American Fisheries Society* 125:42–48.

Dawbin, W. H. 1966. Porpoises and porpoise hunting in Malaita. *Australian Natural History* 15 (7): 207–211.

Day, D. 1989. *Vanished Species.* Gallery.

Deere-Jones, T. 2001. Pair trawling kills dolphins. *BBC Wildlife* 19 (10): 40.

Del Carmen Rodriguez-Jamarillo, M., and D. Gendron. 1996. Report of a sea otter, *Enhydra lutris,* off the coast of Isla Magdalena, Baja California Sur, Mexico. *Marine Mammal Science* 12 (1): 153–156.

Dellinger, T. 1998. The Atlantic's wandering turtles. *Scientific American* (Special Issue) 9 (3): 88–91.

DeLong, R. L. 1978. Northern elephant seal. In *Marine Mammals of Eastern North Pacific and Arctic Waters,* ed. D. Haley, 206–211. Pacific Search Press.

Dennis, C. 2002. Reef under threat from "bleaching" outbreak. *Nature* 415:947.

DeSalle, R., and D. Lindley. 1997. *The Science of Jurassic Park and The Lost World.* HarperCollins.

De Smet, W. M. A. 1981. Evidence of whaling in the North Sea and English Channel during the Middle Ages. In *Mammals of the Seas.* FAO Fisheries Series No. 5, vol. III, 301–309. Food and Agriculture Organization of the United Nations, Rome.

DeWitt, H. H. 1962. On the probable identity of *Macrias amissus,* a deep-water notothenoid fish from the Chilean coast. *Copeia* 1962 (3): 657–659.

Dickinson, A. 1990. Some aspects of the origin and implementation of the eighteenth-century Falklands Islands sealing industry. *International Journal of Maritime History* 2 (2): 33–68.

Dingus, L., and T. Rowe. 1997. *The Mistaken Extinction: Dinosaur Evolution and the Origin of Birds.* Freeman.

Donnelly, M. 1991. Japan bans import of hawksbill shell effective December 1992. *Marine Turtle Newsletter* 54:1–3.

Donovan, G. P. 2002. International Whaling Commission. In *Encyclopedia of Marine Mammals,* edited by W. F. Perrin, B. Würsig, and J. G. M. Thewissen, 637–641. Academic Press.

Dorofeev, S. V. 1960. Data on population dynamics of fur seals on Tyuleni Island. *Byulletin' MOIP, Odtel Biologii* 65 (1): 29–35.

———. 1961. Soviet investigations of fur seals in the northern part of the Pacific Ocean. *Trudy Soveschanii Ikhtiologicheskoi Komissii Akademii Nauk SSSR*, no. 12. Akademizdat.

Dorofeev, S. V., and V. A. Bychkov. 1964. Biological requisites for regulation of numbers of bulls on Tyuleni Island. *Izvestiya TINRO* 54; *Trudy VNIRO* 51:83–90.

Dowd, M. 2002. Have you seen this fish? *New York Times,* July 7, 4:9.

Dudley, P. 1725. An essay upon the natural history of whales. *Philosophical Transactions of the Royal Society of London* 33:256–269.

Duhamel du Monceau, H. L. 1769. *Traité général des Pesches et Histoire des Poissons.* Saillant et Nyon, Desaint.

Dumont, H. J. 1995. Ecocide in the Caspian. *Nature* 377:673–674.

Duncan, D. D. 1941. Fighting giants of the Humboldt. *National Geographic* 79 (3): 373–400.

Dyson, G. 1986. *Baidarka: The Kayak.* Alaska Northwest Books.

Earle, S. A. 1995. *Sea Change: A Message of the Oceans.* Fawcett Columbine.

———. 2001. *Atlas of the Ocean.* National Geographic Society.

Eckert, A. W. 1963. *The Great Auk.* Signet.

Eckert, K. L. 1995. Anthropogenic threats to sea turtles. In *Biology and Conservation of Sea Turtles,* edited by K. A. Bjorndal, 611–612. Smithsonian Institution Press.

Eckert, S. A., and H. R. Martins. 1989. Transatlantic travel by juvenile loggerhead turtle. *Marine Turtle Newsletter* 45:15.

Eckholm, E. 2001. Study says bad data by China inflated global fishing yields. *New York Times,* November 30, A5.

Edmunds, P. J. 1991. Extent and effect of black band disease on a Caribbean reef. *Coral Reefs* 10:160–165.

———. 2000. Recruitment of scleractinians onto skeletons of corals killed by black band disease. *Coral Reefs* 19 (1): 69–74.

Edmunds, P. J., and R. C. Carpenter. 2001. Recovery of *Diadema antillarum* reduces macroalgal cover and increases abundance of juvenile corals on a Caribbean reef. *Proceedings of the National Academy of Sciences* 98 (9): 5067–5071.

Edwards, R. 2000. Smashing up the seabed. *New Scientist* 167:15.

Elliott, H. W. 1875. The sea otter and its hunting. In *A Report upon the Condition of Affairs in the Territory of Alaska.* 44th Congress, 1st Sess. H. Exec. Doc. 83, 54–62. U.S. Government Printing Office.

———. 1881. *The Seal-Islands of Alaska.* U.S. Government Printing Office.

———. 1887a. The fur-seal industry of the Pribylov Islands, Alaska. In *The Fisheries and Fishery Industries of the United States,* edited by G. B. Goode. Vol. 2, sec. 5, 320–393. U.S. Government Printing Office.

———. 1887b. The sea-lion hunt. In *The Fisheries and Fishery Industries of the United States,* edited by G. B. Goode. Vol. 2, sec. 5, 467–474. U.S. Government Printing Office.

————. 1887c. The sea-otter fishery. In *The Fisheries and Fishery Industries of the United States,* edited by G. B. Goode. Vol. 2, sec. 5, 483–491. U.S. Government Printing Office.

Ellis, R. 1975. Why I became an ex-shell painter. *Audubon* 78 (1): 4–7.

————. 1977. Of men, whales, and Captain Scammon. *National Parks and Conservation* 51 (10): 8–13.

————. 1982. *Dolphins and Porpoises.* Knopf.

————. 1991. *Men and Whales.* Knopf.

————. 2002a. Whaling, early and aboriginal. In *Encyclopedia of Marine Mammals,* edited by W. F. Perrin, B. Würsig, and J. G. M. Thewissen, 1310–1316. Academic Press.

————. 2002b. Whaling, traditional. In *Encyclopedia of Marine Mammals,* edited by W. F. Perrin, B. Würsig, and J. G. M. Thewissen, 1316–1328. Academic Press.

Ellis, R., and J. E. McCosker. 1991. *Great White Shark.* HarperCollins and Stanford University Press.

Erdheim, E. 1979. The immediate goal test of the Marine Mammal Protection Act and the tuna/porpoise controversy. *Environmental Law* 9 (2): 283–309.

Estabrook, B. 2001. Sea turtle secrets. *Wildlife Conservation* 104 (2): 44–49.

Estes, J. A. 1980. *Enhydra lutris.* In *Mammalian Species,* No. 133, 1–8. American Society of Mammalogists.

Estes, J. A., and J. L. Bodkin. 2002. Otters. In *Encyclopedia of Marine Mammals,* edited by W. F. Perrin, B. Würsig, and J. G. M. Thewissen, 843–858. Academic Press.

Estes, J. A., M. T. Tinker, T. M. Williams, and D. F. Doak. 1998. Killer whale predation on sea otters linking oceanic and nearshore ecosystems. *Science* 282:473–476.

Farnsworth, C. H. 1994. Cod are almost gone and a culture could follow. *New York Times,* May 14, 4.

Field, J. G., G. Hempel, and C. P. Summerhayes (eds.). 2002. *Oceans 2020: Science, Trends, and the Challenge of Sustainability.* Island Press.

Fiscus, C. H. 1978. Northern fur seal. In *Marine Mammals of Eastern North Pacific and Arctic Waters,* ed. D. Haley, 152–159. Pacific Search Press.

Fisher, E. M. 1931. Habits of the southern sea otter. *Journal of Mammalogy* 20 (1): 21–36.

Fisher, R. H. 1977. *Bering's Voyages: Whither and Why.* University of Washington Press.

————. 1984. *The Voyage of Semen Dezhnev in 1648: Bering's Precursor.* Hakluyt Society.

Fleischer, L. A. 1978. Guadalupe fur seal. In *Marine Mammals of Eastern North Pacific and Arctic Waters,* ed. D. Haley, 160–165. Pacific Search Press.

Flower, W. H. 1872. On a subfossil whale (*Eschrichtius robustus*) discovered in Cornwall. *Annals and Magazine of Natural History* 4 (9): 440–442.

Ford, C. 1966. *Where the Sea Breaks Its Back.* Little, Brown.

Forsten, A., and P. M. Youngman. 1982. Hydrodamalis gigas. *Mammalian Species* 165:1–3.

Forsyth, J. 1992. *A History of the Peoples of Siberia: Russia's North Asian Colony, 1581–1990.* Cambridge University Press.

Fox, W. W. 1979. Tuna/dolphin program: Five years of progress. *Oceans* 11 (3): 57–59.

Franklin, H. B. 2001. The most important fish in the sea. *Discover* 22 (9): 42–50.

Fraser, F. C. 1970. An early seventeenth century record of the California gray whale in Icelandic waters. *Investigations on Cetacea* 2:13–20.

Frederiksen, R., A. Jensen, and H. Westerberg. 1992. The distribution of the scleractinian coral *Lophelia pertusa* around the Faroe Islands and the relation to internal tidal mixing. *Sarsia* 77:157–171.

Friends of the Earth Scotland. 2001. *The One That Got Away: Marine Salmon Farming in Scotland.* Edinburgh.

Fuller, E. 1999. *The Great Auk.* Errol Fuller.

Garcia, M. A., and M. A. Hall. 1996. Spatial and seasonal distribution of bycatch in the purse seine tuna fishery in the eastern Pacific Ocean. In *Fisheries Bycatch: Consequences and Management,* 39–43. Alaska Sea Grant College Program Report No. 97-02. University of Alaska.

Garrott, R. A., L. L. Eberhart, and D. M. Burn. 1993. Mortality of sea otters following the *Exxon Valdez* spill. *Marine Mammal Science* 9 (4): 343–371.

Geiser, D. M., J. W. Taylor, K. B. Ritchie, and G. W. Smith. 1998. Cause of sea fan death in the West Indies. *Nature* 394:137–138.

Gentry, R. L. 1980. Set in their ways: Survival formula of the northern fur seal. *Oceans* 13 (3): 34–37.

———. 1981. Northern fur seals—*Callorhinus ursinus* (Linnaeus, 1758). In *Handbook of Marine Mammals,* edited by S. H. Ridgway and R. J. Harrison. Vol. 1, *The Walrus, Sea Lions, Fur Seals, and Sea Otter,* 143–160. Academic Press.

———. 1983. Seals and their kin. *National Geographic* 171 (4): 475–501.

———. 2002. Northern fur seal. In *Encyclopedia of Marine Mammals,* edited by W. F. Perrin, B. Würsig, and J. G. M. Thewissen, 813–817. Academic Press.

Gentry, R. L., and D. E. Withrow. 1978. Steller sea lion. In *Marine Mammals of Eastern North Pacific and Arctic Waters,* edited by D. Haley, 166–171. Pacific Search Press.

George, R. H. 1997. Health problems and diseases of sea turtles. In *The Biology of Sea Turtles,* edited by P. L. Lutz and J. A. Musick, 363–385. CRC Press.

Gerrior, P. 1996. Characteristics of the drift gillnet fishery of the United States East Coast, based on 1989–1994 observer data. In *Fisheries Bycatch: Consequences and Management,* 17–20. Alaska Sea Grant College Program Report No. 97-02. University of Alaska.

Gerrodette, T. 2002. Tuna-dolphin issue. In *Encyclopedia of Marine Mammals,* edited by W. F. Perrin, B. Würsig, and J. G. M. Thewissen, 1269–1273. Academic Press.

Gerstein, E. R. 2002. Manatees, bioacoustics, and boats. *American Scientist* 90 (2): 154–163.

Gibbs, W. 2002. Iceland joins whale panel, giving whalers stronger say. *New York Times,* October 21, A2.

Gibson, C. D. 1981. A history of the swordfishery in the northwestern Atlantic. *American Neptune* 41 (1): 36–65.

———. 1998. *The Broadbill Swordfishery in the North Atlantic.* Ensign.

Gibson, J. R. 1969. *Feeding the Russian Fur Trade.* University of Wisconsin Press.

———. 1992. *Otter Skins, Boston Ships, and China Goods.* University of Washington Press and McGill-Queens University Press.

Gilbert, P. W., and C. Gilbert. 1973. Sharks and shark deterrents. *Underwater Journal* 5 (2): 69–79.

Gill, T., and C. H. Townsend. 1901. The largest deep-sea fish. *Science* 14 (363): 937–938.

Gladfelter, W. B. 1982. Whiteband disease in *Acropora palmata:* Implications for the structure and growth of shallow reefs. *Bulletin of Marine Science* 32:639–643.

Glausiusz, J. 2002. Curb your cat, save a sea otter. *Discover* 23 (11): 15.

Glynn, P. W. 1997. Bioerosion and coral reef growth: A dynamic balance. In *Life and Death of Coral Reefs,* edited by C. Birkeland, 68–95. Chapman and Hall.

Golder, F. A. 1914. *Russian Expansion on the Pacific, 1641–1850.* Peter Smith.

———. 1925. *Bering's Voyages: An Account of the Effort of the Russians to Determine the Relation of Asia and America.* American Geographical Society.

Goode, G. B., ed. 1887a. *The Fisheries and Fishing Industry of the United States.* U.S. Government Printing Office.

———. 1887b. The swordfish fishery. In *The Fisheries and Fishing Industry of the United States,* edited by G. B. Goode, 315–326. U.S. Government Printing Office.

Goode, G. B., and A. H. Clark. 1887. The menhaden fishery. In *The Fisheries and Fishing Industry of the United States,* edited by G. B. Goode, 329–415. U.S. Government Printing Office.

Goode, G. B., and J. W. Collins. 1887. The bank hand-line cod fishery. In *The Fisheries and Fishing Industry of the United States,* edited by G. B. Goode, 123–133. U.S. Government Printing Office.

Goodwin, G. G. 1946. The end of the great northern sea cow. *Natural History* 55 (2): 56–61.

Grady, D. 1986. *Sealers and Whalers in New Zealand Waters.* Reed Methuen.

Greenway, J. C. 1958. *Extinct and Vanishing Birds of the World.* American Committee for International Wild Life Protection.

Greer, C., and V. B. Scheffer. 1971. A 1715 picture of a fur seal. *Pacific Northwest Quarterly* 62 (4): 151–153.

Grey, Z. 1927. *Tales of Swordfish and Tuna.* Harper and Brothers.

Grigg, R. W. 1995. Coral reefs in an urban embayment in Hawaii: A complex case history controlled by natural and anthropogenic stress. *Coral Reefs* 14 (4): 253–266.

Groombridge, B., and R. Luxmoore. 1989. *The Green Turtle and Hawksbill (Reptilia: Cheloniidae): World Status, Exploitation, and Trade.* CITES Secretariat, Lausanne, Switzerland.

Gudger, E. W. 1940. The alleged pugnacity of the swordfish and the spearfishes as shown by their attacks on vessels. *Memoirs of the Royal Asiatic Society of Bengal* 12 (2): 215–315.

Guénette, S., V. Christensen, and D. Pauly, eds. 2001. *Fisheries Impacts on North Atlantic Ecosystems: Models and Analyses.* Fisheries Centre Research Reports 9(4). University of British Columbia, Fisheries Centre.

Haley, D. 1978a. Saga of Steller's sea cow. *Natural History* 87 (9): 9–17.

———. 1978b. Steller sea cow. In *Marine Mammals of Eastern North Pacific and Arctic Waters,* ed. D. Haley, 236–241. Pacific Search Press.

———. 1980. The great northern sea cow: Steller's gentle siren. *Oceans* 13 (5): 7–11.

Hall, A. 2002. Gray seal. In *Encyclopedia of Marine Mammals,* edited by W. F. Perrin, B. Würsig, and J. G. M. Thewissen, 522–524. Academic Press.

Hall, M. A. 1996. Dolphins and other bycatch in the eastern tropical Pacific tuna purse seine fishery. In *Fisheries Bycatch: Consequences and Management,* 35–38. Alaska Sea Grant College Program Report No. 97-02. University of Alaska.

Hallerman, E. M., and A. R. Kapuscinski. 1990. Transgenic fish and public policy: II. Regulatory concerns. *Fisheries* 15 (1): 12–20.

———. 1995. Incorporating risk assessment and risk management into public policies of genetically modified finfish and shellfish. *Aquaculture* 137:9–17.

Hallock, P. 1997. Reefs and reef limestones in Earth history. In *Life and Death of Coral Reefs,* edited by C. Birkeland, 13–42. Chapman and Hall.

Hall-Spencer, J., V. Allain, and J. H. Fosse. 2002. Trawling damage to Northeast Atlantic ancient coral reefs. *Proceedings of the Royal Society of London: Biological Sciences* 269 (1490): 507–511.

Hansen, C. A. 1982. Seals and sealing. *Alaska Geographic* 9 (3): 40–73.

Hansen, K. 2002. *A Farewell to Greenland's Wildlife.* Gads Forlag.

Hansen, L. P., M. L. Windsor, and A. F. Youngson. 1997. Interactions between salmon culture and wild stocks of Atlantic salmon: The scientific and management issues. *ICES Journal of Marine Science* 54 (6): 963–964.

Harder, B. 2001. Coral-killing army recruits human bugs. *Science News* 160 (21): 332.

Hardin, G. 1968. The tragedy of the commons. *Science* 162 (3859): 1243–1248.

Harrison, C. 1979. Short-tailed albatross. *Oceans* 12 (5): 24–26.

Hatcher, B. G. 1997. Organic production and decomposition. In *Life and Death of Coral Reefs,* edited by C. Birkeland, 140–174. Chapman and Hall.

Hatfield, B. B., D. Marks, M. T. Tinker, K. Nolan, and J. Pierce. 1998. Attacks on sea otters by killer whales. *Marine Mammal Science* 14 (4): 888–894.

Headland, R. 1984. *The Island of South Georgia.* Cambridge University Press.

Hedgepeth, J. W. 1974. Sea otters: Irresistible ecological bodies. *Oceans* 7 (5): 61.

Hempel, G., and D. Pauly. 2002. Fisheries and fisheries science in their search for sustainability. In *Oceans 2020: Science, Trends, and the Challenge of*

Sustainability, edited by J. G. Field, G. Hempel, and C. P. Summerhayes, 109–135. Island Press.

Henderson, P. A., and R. M. Seaby. 2000. Fishy figures. *New Scientist* 166 (2271): 86.

Hendrickson, J. R. 1979. Totoaba: Sacrifice in the Gulf of California. *Oceans* 12 (5): 14–18.

Heneman, B., and M. Glazer. 1996. More rare than dangerous: A case study of white shark conservation in California. In *Great White Sharks,* edited by A. P. Klimley and D. G. Ainley, 481–491. Academic Press.

Henisch, B. A. 1976. *Fast and Feast: Food in Medieval Society.* Pennsylvania State University Press.

Henke, J. S. 1985. *Seal Wars! An American Viewpoint.* Breakwater.

Herald, E. S. 1961. *Living Fishes of the World.* Doubleday.

Herald, E. S., R. L. Brownell, F. I. Frye, E. J. Morris, W. E. Evans, and A. B. Scott. 1969. Blind river dolphin: First side-swimming cetacean. *Science* 166:1408–1410.

Herbst, L. H. 1994. Fibropapillomatosis of marine turtles. *Annual Review of Fish Diseases* 4:389–425.

———. 2000. Marine turtle fibropapillomatosis: Hope floats in a sea of ignorance. In *Proceedings of the Nineteenth Annual Symposium on Sea Turtle Biology and Conservation,* edited by H. Kalb and T. Wibbels, 39–40. NOAA Technical Memorandum NMFS-SEFSC-443. U.S. Department of Commerce.

Herbst, L. H., R. Chakrabarti, P. A. Klein, and M. Achary. 2001. Differential gene expression associated with tumorigenicity of cultured green turtle fibro papilloma-derived fibroblasts. *Cancer Genetics and Cytogenetics* 129 (1): 35–39.

Herbst, L. H., R. Garber, and P. A. Klein. 1997. Molecular biological evidence for the involvement of a unique herpes virus in the etiology of green turtle fibropapillomatosis. *Proceedings of the Sixteenth Annual Symposium on Sea Turtle Biology and Conservation.* NOAA Technical Memorandum NMFS-SEFSC. U.S. Department of Commerce.

Herbst, L. H., and E. R. Jacobson. 1995. Diseases of marine turtles. In *Biology and Conservation of Sea Turtles,* edited by K. A. Bjorndal, 593–596. Smithsonian Institution Press.

Herbst, L. H., E. R. Jacobson, and P. A. Klein. 1996. Identification and characterization of the green turtle fibropapillomatosis agent. In *Proceedings of the Fifteenth Annual Symposium on Sea Turtle Biology and Conservation,* edited by J. A. Keinath, D. E. Barnard, J. A. Musick, and B. A. Bell, 135. NOAA Technical Memorandum NMFS-SEFSC-387. U.S. Department of Commerce.

Hermannson, H. 1924. Jon Gudmundsson and his natural history of Iceland. *Islandica* 15:I–XXVIII, 1–40.

Hershkovitz, P. 1966. Catalog of living whales. *Bulletin of the U.S. National Museum* 246:1–259.

Hewer, H. R. 1964. The determination of age, sexual maturity, longevity, and a life-table in the grey seal, *Halichoerus grypus. Proceedings of the Zoological Society of London* 142:593–624.

————. 1974. *British Seals.* Taplinger.

Hewer, H. R., and K. M. Backhouse. 1959. Field identification of bulls and cows of the grey seal, *Halichoerus grypus* (Fab.). *Proceedings of the Zoological Society of London* 132 (4): 641–645.

Hibbein, J. 1998. Fish consumption and major depression. *Lancet* 351:1213.

Higginson, F. 1630. *New England's Plantation, Or, A Short and True Description of the Commodities and Discommodities of That Country.* Michael Sparke.

Hindell, M. A. 2002. Elephant seals. In *Encyclopedia of Marine Mammals,* edited by W. F. Perrin, B. Würsig, and J. G. M. Thewissen, 370–373. Academic Press.

Hindell, M. A., and C. R. McMahon. 2000. Long distance movement of a southern elephant seal (*Mirounga leonina*) from Macquarie Island to Peter 1 Øy. *Marine Mammal Science* 16 (2): 504–507.

Hindell, M. A., and D. Pemberton. 1997. Successful use of a translocation program to investigate diving behavior in a male Australian fur seal, *Arctocephalus pusillus doriferus. Marine Mammal Science* 13 (2): 219–228.

Hindell, M. A., D. J. Slip, and H. R. Burton. 1991. The diving behaviour of adult male and female elephant seals, *Mirounga leonina* (Pinnipedia: Phocidae). *Australian Journal of Zoology* 39:595–616.

Hofman, R. J., and W. N. Bonner. 1985. Conservation and protection of marine mammals: Past, present, and future. *Marine Mammal Science* 1 (2): 109–127.

Holloway, M. 2002. Blue revolution. *Discover* 23 (9): 57–63.

Hooker, S. K., and R. W. Baird. 1999. Deep-diving behaviour of the northern bottlenose whale, *Hyperoodon ampullatus* (Cetacea: Ziphiidae). *Proceedings of the Royal Society of London (B)* 266:671–676.

Hoy, C. M. 1923. The "white-flag" dolphin of the Tung Ting Lake. *China Journal of Arts and Science* 1:154–157.

Hubbs, C. L. 1979. Guadalupe fur seal. In *Mammals in the Seas II: Pinniped Species Summaries and Report on Sirenians,* 24–27. Food and Agriculture Organization of the United Nations, Rome.

Hunte, W., and D. Younglao. 1988. Recruitment and population recovery of the black sea urchin *Diadema antillarum* in Barbados. *Marine Ecology Progress Series* 45:109–119.

Hunter, R. 1979. *Warriors of the Rainbow: A Chronicle of the Greenpeace Movement.* Holt, Rinehart and Winston.

Huslin, A. 2002. Maryland fish officials hunt hardy predator. *Washington Post,* June 28, 8.

Hutchings, J. A. 2000. Collapse and recovery of marine fishes. *Nature* 406:882–885.

Hutchinson, G. E. 1961. The paradox of the plankton. *American Naturalist* 95:137–145.

Huxley, T. H. 1883. The Fisheries Exhibition. *Nature* 28:176–177.

Idyll, C. P. 1973. The anchovy crisis. *Scientific American* 228 (6): 22–29.

Innis, H. A. 1940. *The Cod Fisheries: The History of an International Economy.* Yale University Press.

International Whaling Commission. 1996. Report of the sub-committee on small cetaceans. *Reports of the International Whaling Commission* 46:160–179.

———. 2001. Report of the workshop on status and trends of western North Atlantic right whales. *Journal of Cetacean Research and Management* (Special Issue 2), in press.

Ivanov, V. P., A. M. Kamakin, V. B. Ushivtzev, T. Shiganova, O. Zhukova, N. Aladin, S. I. Wilson, G. R. Harbison, and H. J. Dumont. 2000. Invasion of the Caspian Sea by the comb jellyfish *Mnemiopsis leidyi* (Ctenophora). *Biological Invasions* 2 (3): 255–258.

Jackson, J. B. C. 1991. Adaptation and diversity of reef corals. *BioScience* 41 (7): 475–482.

———. 1997. Reefs since Columbus. *Coral Reefs* 16 (5): S23–S32.

Jackson, J. B. C., and K. G. Johnson. 2001. Measuring past biodiversity. *Science* 293:2401–2403.

Jackson, J. B. C., M. X. Kirby, W. H. Berger, K. A. Bjorndal, L. W. Botsford, B. J. Bourque, R. H. Bradbury, R. Cooke, J. Erlandson, J. A. Estes, T. P. Hughes, S. Kidwell, C. B. Lange, H. S. Lenihan, J. M. Pandolfi, C. H. Peterson, R. S. Steneck, M. J. Tegner, and R. R. Warner. 2001. Historical overfishing and the recent collapse of coastal ecosystems. *Science* 293:629–638.

Jacobson, E. R. 1990. An update on green turtle fibropapilloma. *Marine Turtle Newsletter* 49:7–8.

Jacobson, E. R., C. Buergelt, B. Williams, and R. K. Harris. 1991. Herpesvirus in cutaneous fibropapillomas of the green turtle, *Chelonia mydas. Diseases of Aquatic Organisms* 12:1–6.

Jacobson, E. R., S. B. Simpson Jr., and J. P. Sundberg. 1991. Fibropapillomas in green turtles. In *Research Plan for Marine Turtle Fibropapilloma,* edited by G. H. Balazs and S. G. Pooley, 99–100. NOAA Technical Memorandum NMFS-SWFSC-156. U.S. Department of Commerce.

Jamarillo-Legoretta, A. M., L. Rojas-Bracho, and T. Gerodette. 1999. A new abundance estimate for vaquitas: First step for recovery. *Marine Mammal Science* 15 (4): 957–973.

Jameson, R. J. 1983. Evidence of birth of a sea otter on land in central California. *California Fish and Game* 69 (2): 122–123.

Jameson, R. J., and A. M. Johnson. 1993. Reproductive characteristics of female sea otters (*Enhydra lutris*). *Marine Mammal Science* 9 (2): 156–167.

Jensen, A., and R. Frederiksen. 1992. The fauna associated with the bank-forming deepwater coral *Lophelia pertusa* (Scleractinia) on the Faroe Shelf. *Sarsia* 77:53–69.

Jensen, A. C. 1972. *The Cod.* Crowell.

Johnson, A. M. 1972. The status of northern fur seal populations. *Rapports et Procès-Verbaux des Réunions du Conseil International pour l'Exploration de la Mer* 169:455–461.

Jones, M. L., and S. L. Swartz. 2002. Gray whale. In *Encyclopedia of Marine Mammals,* edited by W. F. Perrin, B. Würsig, and J. G. M. Thewissen, 525–536. Academic Press.

Jones, M. L., S. L. Swartz, and S. Leatherwood, eds. 1984. *The Gray Whale, Eschrichtius robustus.* Academic Press.

Jønsson, H. 1982. *Friends in Conflict: The Anglo-Icelandic Cod Wars and the Law of the Sea.* C. Hurst and Archon Books.

Jordan, A. M. 1974. Porpoises and purse seines. *Oceans* 7 (3): 6–7.

Jordan, D. S., ed. 1898. *The Fur Seals and the Fur-Seal Islands of the North Pacific Ocean.* U.S. Government Printing Office.

Jordan, D. S., and G. A. Clark. 1912. *Truth about the Fur Seals on the Pribilof Islands.* Bureau of Fisheries Economic Circular No. 4. U.S. Department of Commerce and Labor.

Jordan, D. S. 1923. *American Food and Game Fishes.* Doubleday, Page and Company.

———. 1926. A review of the giant mackerel-like fishes, tunnies, spearfishes, and swordfishes. *Occasional Papers of the California Academy of Sciences* 12:1–113.

Joseph, J., and J. W. Greenough. 1979. *International Management of Tuna, Porpoise, and Billfish.* University of Washington Press.

Joseph, J., W. Klawe, and P. Murphy. 1988. *Tuna and Billfish: Fish without a Country.* Inter-American Tropical Tuna Commission.

Junge, G. C. A. 1936. Bones of a whale from the Wieringermeer, Zuider Zee. *Nature* 138:78.

Kaiya, Z. 2002. Baiji. In *Encyclopedia of Marine Mammals,* edited by W. F. Perrin, B. Würsig, and J. G. M. Thewissen, 59–61. Academic Press.

Kapuscinski, A. R. 1990. Integration of transgenic fish into aquaculture. *Food Reviews International* 6 (3): 373–388.

Kapuscinski, A. R., and E. M. Hallerman. 1990. Transgenic fish and public policy: I. Anticipating environmental impacts of transgenic fish. *Fisheries* 15 (1): 2–11.

———. 1994. Benefits, risks, and policy implications: Biotechnology in aquaculture. In *Aquaculture: Food and Renewable Resources from U.S. Waters.* Report prepared for U.S. Congress, Office of Technology Assessment.

Kasuya, T. 2002. Japanese whaling. In *Encyclopedia of Marine Mammals,* edited by W. F. Perrin, B. Würsig, and J. G. M. Thewissen, 655–662. Academic Press.

Kasuya, T., N. Miyazaki, and W. H. Dawbin. 1974. Growth and reproduction of *Stenella attenuata* in the Pacific coast of Japan. *Scientific Reports of the Whales Research Institute* 26:157–226.

Kellogg, R. 1940. Whales, giants of the sea. *National Geographic* 77 (1): 35–90.

Kelly, W. 1953. *The Pogo Papers.* Simon and Schuster.

———. 1972. *Pogo: We Have Met the Enemy and He Is Us.* Simon and Schuster.

Kennedy, S., T. Kuiken, P. D. Jepson, R. Deaville, M. Forsyth, T. Barrett, M. W. G. van de Bildt, A. D. M. E. Osterhaus, T. Eybatov, C. Duck, A. Kydyrmanov, I. Mitrofanov, and S. Wilson. 2000. Mass die-off of Caspian seals caused by canine distemper virus. *Emerging Infectious Diseases* 6 (6): 637–639.

Kenyon, K. W. 1969. *The Sea Otter in the Eastern Pacific Ocean.* Bureau of Sport Fisheries and Wildlife. Reprint, Dover Press, 1975.

———. 1977. Caribbean monk seal extinct. *Journal of Mammalogy* 58:979–998.

———. 1978a. Hawaiian monk seal. In *Marine Mammals of Eastern North Pacific and Arctic Waters,* edited by D. Haley, 212–216. Pacific Search Press.

————. 1978b. Sea otter. In *Marine Mammals of Eastern North Pacific and Arctic Waters*, edited by D. Haley, 226–235. Pacific Search Press.

————. 1980. No man is benign: The endangered monk seal. *Oceans* 13 (3): 48–54.

————. 1981a. Monk seals—*Monachus* (Fleming, 1822). In *Handbook of Marine Mammals*, edited by S. H. Ridgway and R. J. Harrison. Vol. 2, *Seals*, 195–220. Academic Press.

————. 1981b. Sea otter—*Enhydra lutris* (Linnaeus, 1758). In *Handbook of Marine Mammals*, edited by S. H. Ridgway and R. J. Harrison. Vol. 1, *The Walrus, Sea Lions, Fur Seals, and Sea Otter*, 209–223. Academic Press.

Kenyon, K. W., and D. W. Rice. 1961. Abundance and distribution of Steller sea lion. *Journal of Mammalogy* 42 (3): 223–234.

Kideys, A. E. 2002. Fall and rise of Black Sea ecosystem. *Science* 297:1482–1483.

King, F. W. 1982. Historical review of the decline of the green turtle and the hawksbill. In *Biology and Conservation of Sea Turtles: Proceedings of the World Conference on Sea Turtle Conservation, Washington, D.C., 26–30 November 1979*, edited by K. A. Bjorndal. Smithsonian Institution Press and World Wildlife Fund.

King, J. E. 1954. The otariid seals of the Pacific coast of America. *Bulletin of the British Museum (Natural History)* 2 (10): 309–337.

————. 1983. *Seals of the World*. Cornell University Press.

King, J. E., and B. J. Marlow. 1979. Australian sea lion. In *Mammals in the Seas II: Pinniped Species Summaries and Report on Sirenians*, 13–15. Food and Agriculture Organization of the United Nations, Rome.

Kleiner, K. 2002. All fished out. *New Scientist* 173 (2331): 11.

Kleypas, J. A., R. W. Buddemeier, D. Archer, J.-P. Gattuso, C. Langdon, and B. N. Opdyke. 1999. Geochemical consequences of increased atmospheric carbon dioxide on coral reefs. *Science* 284:118–120.

Kleypas, J. A., R. W. Buddemeier, and J.-P. Gattuso. 2001. The future of coral reefs in an age of global change. *International Journal of Earth Sciences* 90 (2): 426–437.

Klimley, A. P., and D. G. Ainley, eds. 1996. *Great White Sharks*. Academic Press.

Knight, J. 2000. Frying fish: UV light could be cooking cod larvae to death. *New Scientist* 168 (2269): 21.

Knoll, A. H. 1989. Evolution and extinction in the marine realm: Some constraints imposed by phytoplankton. *Philosophical Transactions of the Royal Society of London (B)* 325:279–290.

Knowlton, N. 2001. Sea urchin recovery from mass mortality: New hope for coral reefs? *Proceedings of the National Academy of Sciences* 98 (9): 4822–4824.

Knudtson, P. M. 1977. The case of the missing monk seal. *Natural History* 86 (8): 78–83.

Kocik, J., and R. Brown. 2001. Atlantic salmon. On-line at http://www.nefsc.nmfs.gov/sos/spsyn/af/salmon/.

Kogai, V. M. 1968. Present condition and dynamics of the fur seal population of Tyuleni (Robben) Island. In *Pinnipeds of the North Pacific*, edited by V. A.

Arsen'ev and K. I. Panin, 39–48. Russian Federal Research Institute of Fishery and Oceanography (VNIRO). Translated from Russian, Israel Program for Scientific Translation, Jerusalem, 1971.

Kovacs, K. 2002. Hooded seal. In *Encyclopedia of Marine Mammals*, edited by W. F. Perrin, B. Würsig, and J. G. M. Thewissen, 612–614. Academic Press.

Kovacs, K. M., C. Lydersen, M. O. Hammill, B. N. White, P. J. Wilson, and S. Malik. 1997. A harp seal x hooded seal hybrid. *Marine Mammal Science* 13 (3): 460–468.

Kring, D. A. 2000. Impact events and their effect on the origin, evolution, and distribution of life. *GSA Today* 10 (8): 1–7.

Kunzig, R. 2002. Year of the ocean. *Discover* 23 (1): 35–38.

Kurlansky, M. 1997. *Cod: A Biography of the Fish That Changed the World*. Walker.

Kushmaro, A., E. Rosenberg, M. Fine, and Y. Loya. 1997. Bleaching of the coral *Oculina patagonica* by *Vibrio* AK-1. *Marine Ecology Progress Series* 147:159–165.

Kuta, K. G., and L. L. Richardson. 1996. Abundance and distribution of black band disease on coral reefs in the northern Florida Keys. *Coral Reefs* 15 (4): 219–223.

Laidre, K. L., R. Jamison, and D. P. DeMaster. 2001. An estimation of carrying capacity for sea otters along the California coast. *Marine Mammal Science* 17 (2): 294–309.

Laist, D. W., A. R. Knowlton, J. G. Mead, A. S. Collett, and M. Podesta. 2001. Collisions between ships and whales. *Marine Mammal Science* 17 (1): 35–75.

Lander, R. H. 1979. Alaskan or northern fur seal. In *Mammals in the Seas II: Pinniped Species Summaries and Report on Sirenians*, 19–23. Food and Agriculture Organization of the United Nations, Rome.

Landsberg, J. 1995. Tropical reef-fish disease outbreaks and mass mortalities in Florida, USA: What is the role of dietary biological toxins? *Diseases of Aquatic Organisms* (June 1995): 83–100.

Landsberg, J. H., G. H. Balazs, K. A. Steidinger, D. G. Baden, T. W. Work, and D. J. Russell. 1999. The potential role of natural tumor promoters in marine turtle fibropapillomatosis. *Journal of Aquatic Animal Health* 11 (3): 199–210.

Lane, I. W., and L. Comac. 1992. *Sharks Don't Get Cancer*. Avery.

Lanza, H. M., and C. R. Griffin. 1996. Seabird entanglement by the commercial fisheries in the northwestern Atlantic. In *Fisheries Bycatch: Consequences and Management*, 11–15. Alaska Sea Grant College Program Report No. 97-02. University of Alaska.

Last, P. R., and J. D. Stevens. 1994. *Sharks and Rays of Australia*. CSIRO Division of Fisheries.

Lauridsen, P. 1889. *Vitus Bering: The Discoverer of Bering Strait*. Griggs. Reprint, Books for Libraries, 1969.

Laver, J. 1986. *Costume and Fashion: A Concise History*. Thames and Hudson.

Lavigne, D. M. 1976. Life or death for the harp seal? *National Geographic* 149 (1): 128–142.

———. 1979. Harp seal. In *Mammals in the Seas II: Pinniped Species Summaries and Report on Sirenians,* 76–80. Food and Agriculture Organization of the United Nations, Rome.

———. 1999. Estimating total kill of northwest Atlantic harp seals, 1994–1998. *Marine Mammal Science* 15 (3): 871–878.

———. 2002. Harp seal. In *Encyclopedia of Marine Mammals,* edited by W. F. Perrin, B. Würsig, and J. G. M. Thewissen, 560–562. Academic Press.

Lavigne, D. M., and K. M. Kovacs. 1988. *Harps and Hoods: Ice-Breeding Seals of the Northwest Atlantic.* University of Waterloo Press.

Laws, D., and R. J. F. Taylor. 1957. A mass dying of crabeater seals, *Lobodon carcinophagus* (Gray). *Proceedings of the Zoological Society of London* 129:315–324.

Laws, R. M. 1979. Southern elephant seal. In *Mammals in the Seas II: Pinniped Species Summaries and Report on Sirenians,* 106–109. Food and Agriculture Organization of the United Nations, Rome.

Laycock, G. 1986. The legacy of Gerassim Pribilof. *Audubon* 88 (1): 94–103.

Lazaroff, C. 2003. U.S. changes meaning of dolphin safe tuna label. Environmental News Service. On-line at http://ens-news.com/ens/jan2003/2003-01-06-06.asp.

LeBoeuf, B. J. 1977. Back from extation? *Pacific Discovery* 30 (5): 1–9.

———. 1979. Northern elephant seal. In *Mammals in the Seas II: Pinniped Species Summaries and Report on Sirenians,* 110–114. Food and Agriculture Organization of the United Nations, Rome.

LeBoeuf, B. J., and S. Kaza, eds. 1981. *The Natural History of Año Nuevo.* Boxwood Press.

LeBoeuf, B. J., K. W. Kenyon, and B. Villa-Ramirez. 1986. The Caribbean monk seal is extinct. *Marine Mammal Science* 2 (1): 70–72.

LeBoeuf, B. J., and K. J. Panken. 1977. Elephant seals breeding on the mainland in California. *Proceedings of the California Academy of Sciences* 61 (9): 267–280.

Lemonick, M. D. 1994. Too few fish in the sea. *Time* 143 (14): 70–71.

Leslie, M. 2001. Tales of the sea. *New Scientist* 169 (2275): 32–35.

Lesser, M. P. 1997. Oxidative stress causes coral bleaching during exposure to elevated temperatures. *Coral Reefs* 16 (3): 187–192.

Lesser, M. P., J. H. Farrell, and C. W. Walker. 2001. Oxidative stress, DNA damage, and p53 expression in the larvae of Atlantic cod (*Gadus morhua*) exposed to ultraviolet (290–400 nm) radiation. *Journal of Experimental Biology* 204 (1): 157–164.

Lessios, H. A. 1988. Mass mortality of *Diadema antillarum* in the Caribbean: What have we learned? *Annual Review of Ecology and Systematics* 19:371–393.

———. 1995. *Diadema antillarum* 10 years after mass mortality: Still rare, despite help from a competitor. *Proceedings of the Royal Society of London* 259:331–337.

Lessios, H. A., D. R. Robertson, and J. D. Cubit. 1984. Spread of *Diadema* mass mortality through the Caribbean. *Science* 226:335–337.

Limbaugh, C. 1961. Observations on the California sea otter. *Journal of Mammalogy* 42 (3): 271–273.

Limpus, C. J. 1995a. Global overview of the status of marine turtles: A 1995 viewpoint. In *Biology and Conservation of Sea Turtles*, edited by K. A. Bjorndal, 605–610. Smithsonian Institution Press.

———. 1995b. The status of Australian sea turtle populations. In *Biology and Conservation of Sea Turtles*, edited by K. A. Bjorndal, 297–304. Smithsonian Institution Press.

Lindquist, O. 2000. The North Atlantic gray whale (*Eschrichtius robustus*): An historical outline based on Icelandic, Danish-Icelandic, English, and Swedish sources dating from ca. 1000 A.D. to 1792. *Occasional Papers, Centre for Environmental History and Policy* 1:1–53.

Linehan, T. 1979. The trouble with dolphins. *National Geographic* 155 (4): 506–541.

Ling, J. K., and M. M. Bryden. 1981. Southern elephant seal—*Mirounga leonina*. In *Handbook of Marine Mammals*, edited by S. H. Ridgway and R. J. Harrison. Vol. 2, *Seals*, 297–327. Academic Press.

Lipp, E. K., J. L. Jarrell, D. W. Griffin, J. Lukasik, J. Jacukiewicz, and J. B. Rose. 2002. Preliminary evidence for human fecal contamination in corals of the Florida Keys, USA. *Marine Pollution Bulletin* 44 (7): 666–670.

Lockley, R. M. 1955. *The Saga of the Grey Seal*. Devin-Adair.

———. 1966a. The distribution of grey and common seals on the coasts of Ireland. *Irish Naturalists' Journal* 15 (5): 136–143.

———. 1966b. *Grey Seal, Common Seal*. Andre Deutsch.

Lohmann, K. J. 1992. How sea turtles navigate. *Scientific American* 266 (1): 100–116.

Lohmann, K. J., S. D. Cain, S. A. Dodge, and C. M. F. Lohmann. 2001. Regional magnetic fields as navigational markers for sea turtles. *Science* 294:365–366.

Lohmann, K. J., and C. M. F. Lohmann. 1993. A light-independent magnetic compass in the leatherback sea turtle. *Biological Bulletin* 185 (1): 149–151.

———. 1994. Acquisition of magnetic directional preference in hatchling loggerhead sea turtles. *Journal of Experimental Biology* 190:1–8.

Lohmann, K. J., B. E. Witherington, C. M. F. Lohmann, and M. Salomon. 1997. Orientation, navigation, and natal beach homing in sea turtles. In *The Biology of Sea Turtles*, edited by P. L. Lutz and J. A. Musick, 107–135. CRC Press.

Loughlin, T. R. 2000a. Northern fur seals. *Alaska Geographic* 27 (2): 46–58.

———. 2000b. Steller sea lions. *Alaska Geographic* 27 (2): 60–73.

———. 2002. Steller's sea lion. In *Encyclopedia of Marine Mammals*, edited by W. F. Perrin, B. Würsig, and J. G. M. Thewissen, 1181–1185. Academic Press.

Loughlin, T. R., A. S. Perlov, and V. A. Vladimirov. 1992. Range-wide survey and estimation of total number of Steller sea lions in 1989. *Marine Mammal Science* 8 (3): 220–239.

Lourie, S. A., A. C. J. Vincent, and H. H. Hall. 1999. *Seahorses: An Identification Guide to the World's Species and Their Conservation*. Project Seahorse.

Lucas, F. A. 1899. The Pribilof fur seal. In *The Fur Seals and Fur-Seal Islands of the North Pacific Ocean*, edited by D. S. Jordan, 1–96. U.S. Government Printing Office.

Luer, C. 1993. "60 Minutes" of shark cartilage: Commercially available product revealed as cancer treatment. *American Elasmobranch Society Newsletter* 1993 (1): 1.

Lutcavage, M. E., and P. L. Lutz. 1997. Diving physiology. In *The Biology of Sea Turtles,* edited by P. L. Lutz and J. A. Musick, 277–296. CRC Press.

Lutcavage, M. E., P. Plotkin, B. Witherington, and P. L. Lutz. 1997. Human impacts on sea turtle survival. In *The Biology of Sea Turtles,* edited by P. L. Lutz and J. A. Musick, 1–28. CRC Press.

Lutz, P. L., and J. A. Musick, eds. 1997. *The Biology of Sea Turtles.* CRC Press.

McCarthy, J. J., and M. C. McKenna. 2000. How Earth's ice is changing. *Environment* 42 (10): 8–18.

McCloskey, W. 1983. Harp seal hunting. *Oceans* 16 (6): 59–63.

———. 1990. *Fishdecks: Seafarers of the North Atlantic.* Paragon House.

McCracken, H. 1942. *The Last of the Sea Otters.* Stokes.

———. 1957. *Hunters of the Stormy Sea.* Oldbourne.

McDowell, N. 2002. Stream of escaped farm fish raises fear for wild salmon. *Nature* 416:571.

McGinnis, S. M., and R. J. Schusterman. 1981. Northern elephant seal—*Mirounga angustirostris.* In *Handbook of Marine Mammals,* edited by S. H. Ridgway and R. J. Harrison. Vol. 2, *Seals,* 329–349. Academic Press.

McGoodwin, J. R. 1990. *Crisis in the World's Fisheries.* Stanford University Press.

McHugh, J. L. 1993. The Magnuson Act and the Middle Atlantic fisheries. *Underwater Naturalist* 22 (1): 3–11.

Mack, D., N. Duplaix, and S. Wells. 1982. Sea turtles, animals of divisible parts: International trade in sea turtle products. In *Biology and Conservation of Sea Turtles: Proceedings of the World Conference on Sea Turtle Conservation, Washington, D.C., 26–30 November 1979,* edited by K. A. Bjorndal. Smithsonian Institution Press and World Wildlife Fund.

Mackal, R. P. 1980. *Searching for Hidden Animals: An Inquiry into Zoological Mysteries.* Doubleday.

MacKenzie, D. 2001a. Cod's last gasp. *New Scientist* 169 (2275): 16–17.

———. 2001b. Will Viagra save the seals? *New Scientist* 170 (2286): 13.

———. 2002. African fisheries on the brink of collapse. *New Scientist* 175 (2351): 5.

McKinnell, S., and A. J. Thomson. 1997. Recent events concerning Atlantic salmon escapees in the Pacific. *ICES Journal of Marine Science* 54 (6): 1221–1225.

McKinnell, S., A. J. Thomson, E. A. Black, B. L. Wing, C. M. Guthrie, J. F. Koerner, and J. H. Helle. 1997. Atlantic salmon in the North Pacific. *Aquaculture Research* 28 (2): 145–157.

McLaren, D. J. 1989. Detection and significance of mass killings. *Historical Biology* 2:5–15.

McLauchlan, G., ed. 1985. *New Zealand.* APA Productions.

McManus, J. W. 1977. Tropical marine fisheries and the future of coral reefs: A brief review with emphasis on Southeast Asia. *Coral Reefs* 16:S121–S127.

McNab, R. 1913. *The Old Whaling Days.* Reprint, Golden Press, 1975.

McNally, R. 1981. *So Remorseless a Havoc: Of Dolphins, Whales, and Men.* Little, Brown.

———. 1984. The short, unhappy saga of Steller's sea cow. *Sea Frontiers* 30 (3): 168–172.

McVay, S. 1966. The last of the great whales. *Scientific American* 215 (2): 13–21.

———. 1971. Can leviathan long endure so wide a chase? *Natural History* 80 (1): 36–40, 68–72.

Maggio, T. 2001. *Mattanza: The Ancient Sicilian Ritual of Bluefin Tuna Fishing.* Penguin.

Magnus, O. 1555. *Historia de gentibus septentrionalibus.* Antwerp.

Magnuson, J. J., C. Safina, and M. P. Sissenwine. 2001. Whose fish are they, anyway? *Science* 293:1267–1268.

Mahadevan, K. 1993. Letter to the editor [about "60 Minutes" of shark cartilage: Commercially available product revealed as cancer treatment]. *American Elasmobranch Society Newsletter* 1993 (1): 1.

Malakoff, D., and R. Stone. 2002. Scientists recommend ban on North Sea cod. *Science* 298:939.

Marcus, G. J. 1981. *The Conquest of the North Atlantic.* Oxford University Press.

Marlow, B. J., and J. E. King. 1979. Hooker's (New Zealand) sea lion. In *Mammals in the Seas II: Pinniped Species Summaries and Report on Sirenians,* 16–18. Food and Agriculture Organization of the United Nations, Rome.

Márquez, M. R. 1990. *FAO Species Catalogue.* Vol. 11, *Sea Turtles of the World.* FAO Fisheries Synopsis 125(11). Food and Agriculture Organization of the United Nations, Rome.

Marsh, H. 2002. Dugong. In *Encyclopedia of Marine Mammals,* edited by W. F. Perrin, B. Würsig, and J. G. M. Thewissen, 344–347. Academic Press.

Marsh, H., H. Penrose, C. Eros, and J. Hugues. 2002. *Dugong: Status Reports and Action Plans for Countries and Territories.* United Nations Environment Programme.

Marshall, P. A., and A. H. Baird. 2000. Bleaching of corals on the Great Barrier Reef: Differential susceptibilities among taxa. *Coral Reefs* 19 (2): 155–163.

Martindale, D. 2000. No mercy. *New Scientist* 168 (2260): 28–32.

Mate, B. 1972. Annual migrations of the sea lions *Eumetopias jubatus* and *Zalophus californianus* along the Oregon coast. *Rapports et Procès-Verbaux des Réunions du Conseil International pour l'Exploration de la Mer* 169:455–461.

———. 1979. California sea lion. In *Mammals in the Seas II: Pinniped Species Summaries and Report on Sirenians,* 5–8. Food and Agriculture Organization of the United Nations, Rome.

Mate, B., and R. L. Gentry. 1979. Northern (Steller) sea lion. In *Mammals in the Seas II: Pinniped Species Summaries and Report on Sirenians,* 1–4. Food and Agriculture Organization of the United Nations, Rome.

Mather, C. O. 1976. *Billfish: Marlin, Broadbill, Sailfish.* Saltaire.

Mathews, J. 1993. Media feeds frenzy over shark cartilage as cancer treatment. *Journal of the National Cancer Institute* 85:1190–1191.

Maxwell, G. 1967. *Seals of the World.* Houghton Mifflin.

Mead, J. G. 1986. Twentieth-century records of right whales (*Eubalaena glacialis*) in the northwestern Atlantic Ocean. *Reports of the International Whaling Commission* (Special Issue) 10:83–105.

Mead, J. G., and E. D. Mitchell. 1984. Atlantic gray whales. In *The Gray Whale, Eschrichtius robustus,* edited by M. L. Jones, S. L. Swartz, and S. Leatherwood, 33–53. Academic Press.

Melvin, E. F., J. K. Parrish, K. S. Dietrich, and O. S. Hamel. 2001. *Solutions to seabird bycatch in Alaska's demersal longline fisheries.* Project A/FP-7. Washington Sea Grant Program.

Merrett, N. R., and R. L. Haedrich. 1997. *Deep-Sea Demersal Fish and Fisheries.* Chapman and Hall.

Merrick, R. L., T. R. Loughlin, and D. C. Calkins. 1987. Decline in abundance of the northern sea lion, *Eumetopias jubatus,* in Alaska, 1956–86. *Fishery Bulletin* 85:351–365.

Meylan, A. 1982a. Behavioral ecology of the West Caribbean sea turtle (*Chelonia mydas*) in the internesting habitat. In *Biology and Conservation of Sea Turtles: Proceedings of the World Conference on Sea Turtle Conservation, Washington, D.C., 26–30 November 1979,* edited by K. A. Bjorndal. Smithsonian Institution Press and World Wildlife Fund.

———. 1982b. Sea turtle migration—evidence from tag returns. In *Biology and Conservation of Sea Turtles: Proceedings of the World Conference on Sea Turtle Conservation, Washington, D.C., 26–30 November 1979,* edited by K. A. Bjorndal. Smithsonian Institution Press and World Wildlife Fund.

———. 1988. Spongivory in hawksbill turtles: A diet of glass. *Science* 239:393–395.

Meylan, A. B., and P. A. Meylan. 1999. Introduction to the evolution, life history, and biology of sea turtles. In *Research and Management Techniques for the Conservation of Sea Turtles,* edited by K. L. Eckert, K. A. Bjorndal, F. A. Abreu-Grobois, and M. Donnelly, 3–5. IUCN/SSC Marine Turtle Specialist Group. International Union for Conservation of Nature and Natural Resources.

Mignucci-Giannoni, A. A., and P. Haddow. 2002. Wandering hooded seals. *Science* 295:627–628.

Milius, S. 1998. Second group of living fossils reported. *Science News* 154 (13): 196.

———. 2000. Pregnant and still macho. *Science News* 157 (11): 168–170.

———. 2001. Streamers could save birds from hooks. *Science News* 160 (8): 117.

Miller, G. S. 1918. A new river dolphin from China. *Smithsonian Miscellaneous Collection* 68:1–12.

Miller, J. D. 1997. Reproduction in sea turtles. In *The Biology of Sea Turtles,* edited by P. L. Lutz and J. A. Musick, 51–82. CRC Press.

Miller, M. A., I. A. Gardner, C. Kreuder, D. M. Paradies, K. R. Worcester, D. A. Jessup, E. Dodd, M. D. Harris, J. A. Ames, A. E. Packham, and P. A. Conrad. 2002. Coastal freshwater runoff is a risk factor for *Toxoplasma gondii* infection of southern sea otters (*Enhydra lutris nereis*). *International Journal for Parasitology* 32 (8): 997–1006.

Miller, M. A., I. A. Gardner, A. Packham, J. K. Mazet, K. D. Hanni, D. Jessup, J. Estes, R. Jamison, E. Dodd, B. C. Barr, L. J. Lowenstine, F. M. Gilland, and P. J. Conrad. 2002. Evaluation of an indirect fluorescent antibody test (IFAT) for demonstration of antibodies to *Toxoplasma gondii* in the sea otter (*Enhydra lutris*). *Journal of Parasitology* 88 (3): 594–599.

Minasian, S. M. 1977. Dolphins and/or tuna. *Oceans* 10 (6): 60–63.

Minasian, S. M., K. C. Balcomb, and L. Foster. 1984. *The World's Whales: The Complete Illustrated Guide*. Smithsonian Books.

Mitchell, E. 1975. *Porpoise, Dolphin, and Small Whale Fisheries of the World*. IUCN Monograph No. 3. International Union for Conservation of Nature and Natural Resources, Morges, Switzerland.

———, ed. 1975. Review of biology and fisheries for smaller cetaceans. *Journal of the Fisheries Research Board of Canada* 32 (7): 875–1240.

Mitchell, E. D., V. M. Kozicki, and R. R. Reeves. 1986. Sightings of right whales, *Eubalena glacialis*, off the Scotia Shelf, 1966–1972. *Reports of the International Whaling Commission* (Special Issue) 10:83–105.

Miyazaki, N., T. Kasuya, and M. Nishiwaki. 1974. Distribution and migration of two species of *Stenella* in the Pacific coast of Japan. *Scientific Reports of the Whales Research Institute* 26:227–243.

Mohanty-Hejmadi, P. 2000. Agonies and ecstasies of 25 years of sea turtle research and conservation in India. In *Proceedings of the Nineteenth Annual Symposium on Sea Turtle Biology and Conservation*, edited by H. Kalb and T. Wibbels, 83–85. NOAA Technical Memorandum NMFS-SEFSC-443. U.S. Department of Commerce.

Momatuk, Y., and J. Eastcott. 1994. Where have all the codfish gone? *Wildlife Conservation* 97 (3): 44–55.

Monson, D. H., and A. R. Degange. 1995. Reproduction, preweaning survival, and survival of adult sea otters at Kodiak Island, Alaska. *Canadian Journal of Zoology* 73 (6): 1161–1169.

Mooney, H. A., and E. E. Cleland. 2001. The evolutionary impact of invasive species. *Proceedings of the National Academy of Sciences* 98 (10): 5446–5451.

Moorehead, A. 1966. *The Fatal Impact: An Account of the Invasion of the South Pacific, 1767–1840*. Hamish Hamilton.

Morgan, R. 1955. *World Sea Fisheries*. Pitman.

Morison, S. E. 1971. *The European Discovery of America: The Northern Voyages, A.D. 500–1600*. Oxford University Press.

Morrell, B. 1832. *A Narrative of Four Voyages to the South Sea etc., from the Year 1822 to 1831*. J. J. Harper. Reprint, Gregg Press, 1970.

Mortensen, P. B., M. Hovland, T. Brattegard, and R. Farestveit. 1995. Deep water bio-herms of the scleractinian coral *Lophelia pertusa* (L.) at 64° N on the Norwegian shelf: Structure and associated megafauna. *Sarsia* 80:145–158.

Mowat, F. 1984. *Sea of Slaughter*. Atlantic Monthly Press.

Muir, W. M., and R. D. Howard. 1999. Possible ecological risks of transgenic organism release when transgenes affect mating success: Sexual selection and the Trojan gene hypothesis. *Proceedings of the National Academy of Sciences* 96:13853–13856.

Muller-Parker, G., and C. F. D'Elia. 1997. Interactions between corals and their symbiotic algae. In *Life and Death of Coral Reefs*, edited by C. Birkeland, 96–113. Chapman and Hall.

Mumby, P. J., J. R. M. Chisholm, C. D. Clark, J. D. Hedley, and J. Jaubert. 2001. A bird's-eye view of the health of coral reefs. *Science* 413:36.

Murphy, R. C. 1947. *Logbook for Grace: Whaling Brig Daisy, 1912–1913*. Macmillan.

Murray, A. G., R. J. Smith, and R. M. Stagg. 2002. Shipping and the spread of infectious salmon anemia in Scottish aquaculture. *Emerging Infectious Diseases* 8 (1): 1–5.

Murray, P. 1988. *The Vagabond Fleet: A Chronicle of the North Pacific Sealing Schooner Trade*. Sono Nis.

Musick, J. A., and C. J. Limpus. 1997. Habitat utilization and migration in juvenile sea turtles. In *The Biology of Sea Turtles*, edited by P. L. Lutz and J. A. Musick, 137–163. CRC Press.

Musick, J. A., and B. McMillan. 2002. *The Shark Chronicles*. Times Books.

Nakamura, I. 1985. *FAO Species Catalogue*. Vol. 5, *Billfishes of the World*. FAO Fisheries Synopsis 125(5). Food and Agriculture Organization of the United Nations, Rome.

National Research Council. 1992. *Dolphins and the Tuna Industry*. National Academy Press.

Naylor, R. L., R. J. Goldburg, H. Mooney, M. Beveridge, J. Clay, C. Folke, N. Kautsky, J. Lubchenco, J. Primavera, and M. Williams. 1998. Nature's subsidies to shrimp and salmon farming. *Science* 282:883–884.

Naylor, R. L., R. J. Goldburg, J. H. Primavera, N. Kautsky, M. C. M. Beveridge, J. Clay, C. Folke, J. Lubchenko, H. Mooney, and M. Troell. 2000. Effect of aquaculture on world fish supplies. *Nature* 405:1017–1024.

Naylor, R. L., S. L. Williams, and D. R. Strong. 2001. Aquaculture—a gateway for exotic species. *Science* 294:1655–1666.

Nerini, M. 1984. A review of gray whale feeding ecology. In *The Gray Whale, Eschrichtius robustus*, edited by M. L. Jones, S. L. Swartz, and S. Leatherwood, 423–450. Academic Press.

Netboy, A. 1974. *The Salmon: Their Fight for Survival*. Houghton Mifflin.

New York Times. 2002. A true fish story. Editorial, October 13, 4:12.

Nicholls, E. L. 1997. Testudines. In *Ancient Marine Reptiles*, edited by J. M. Callaway and E. L. Nicholls, 219–223. Academic Press.

Nikulin, P. G. 1968. Present condition and growth perspectives of the Commander Islands fur seal population. In *Pinnipeds of the North Pacific*, edited by V. A. Arsen'ev and K. I. Panin, 28–38. Russian Federal Research Institute of Fishery and Oceanography (VNIRO). Translated from Russian, Israel Program for Scientific Translation, Jerusalem, 1971.

Nishiwaki, M. 1966. A discussion of rarities among the smaller cetaceans caught in Japanese waters. In *Whales, Dolphins, and Porpoises*, edited by K. S. Norris, 192–204. University of California Press.

NOAA (National Oceanic and Atmospheric Administration). 1977. *The Story of the Pribilof Fur Seals*. U.S. Department of Commerce.

Norman, J. R., and F. C. Fraser. 1938. *Giant Fishes, Whales, and Dolphins.* Norton.

Normile, D. 2000. Warmer waters more deadly to coral reefs than pollution. *Science* 290:682–683.

Norris, K. S. 1977. Tuna sandwiches cost at least 78,000 porpoise lives a year, but there is hope. *Smithsonian* 11:45–53.

Norris, K. S., and T. P. Dohl. 1980. Behavior of the Hawaiian spinner dolphin, *Stenella longirostris. Fishery Bulletin* 77 (4): 821–849.

Norris, K. S., and G. W. Harvey. 1972. A theory for the function of the spermaceti organ in the sperm whale (*Physeter catadon* L.). In *Animal Orientation and Navigation,* edited by S. R. Galler, K. Schmidt-Koenig, G. J. Jacobs, and R. E. Belleville, 397–419. National Aeronautics and Space Administration.

Norris, K. S., and W. N. McFarland. 1958. A new porpoise of the genus *Phocoena* from the Gulf of California. *Journal of Mammalogy* 39:22–39.

Norris, K. S., and B. Møhl. 1983. Can odontocetes debilitate prey with sound? *American Naturalist* 122 (1): 85–104.

Norris, K. S., W. E. Stuntz, and W. Rogers. 1978. *The Behavior of Tuna and Porpoises in the Eastern Tropical Pacific Yellowfin Tuna Fishery: Preliminary Studies.* Final Report for Marine Mammal Commission. Contract No. MM6AC022. Publication No. PB-283-970. National Technical Information Service.

Norris, S. 2001. Thanks for all the fish. *New Scientist* 171 (2310): 36–39.

Northridge, S. 2002. Incidental catches. In *Encyclopedia of Marine Mammals,* edited by W. F. Perrin, B. Würsig, and J. G. M. Thewissen, 612–614. Academic Press.

Novacek, M. J., ed. 2001. *The Biodiversity Crisis: Losing What Counts.* American Museum of Natural History.

Novak, J. A. 1982. Heard Island: Seal's haven, sealer's nightmare. *Sea Frontiers* 28 (4): 194–202.

Ogden, A. 1941. *The California Sea Otter Trade, 1784–1848.* University of California Press.

Ogden, J. C. 1997. Ecosystem interactions in the tropical coastal landscape. In *Life and Death of Coral Reefs,* edited by C. Birkeland, 288–297. Chapman and Hall.

Ohsumi, S. 1980. Catches of sperm whales by modern whaling in the North Pacific. *Reports of the International Whaling Commission* (Special Issue 2) SC/SP1:11–18.

O'Shea, T. J. 1999. Environmental contaminants and marine mammals. In *Biology of Marine Mammals,* edited by J. E. Reynolds III and S. A. Rommel, 485–563. Smithsonian Institution Press.

Ostrander, G. K., K. M. Armstrong, E. T. Knobbe, D. Gerace, and E. P. Scully. 2000. Rapid transition in the structure of a coral reef community: The effects of coral bleaching and physical disturbance. *Proceedings of the National Academy of Sciences* 97 (10): 5297–5302.

Pain, S. 2000. Scary monsters, super creeps. *New Scientist* 166 (2241): 42–45.

Palmer, L. W. 1971. The otter slaughter. *Oceans* 4 (6): 28–33.

Panin, K. I., and G. K. Panina. 1968. Fur seal ecology and migration to the Sea of

Japan during winter and spring. In *Pinnipeds of the North Pacific*, edited by
V. A. Arsen'ev and K. I. Panin, 66–76. Russian Federal Research Institute of
Fishery and Oceanography (VNIRO). Translated from Russian, Israel
Program for Scientific Translation, Jerusalem, 1971.

Parfit, M. 1995. Diminishing returns: Exploiting the ocean's bounty. *National
Geographic* 188 (5): 2–37.

Parry, J. H. 1974. *The Discovery of the Sea*. Dial Press.

Patterson, K. L., J. W. Porter, K. B. Ritchie, S. W. Polson, E. Mueller, E. C. Peters,
D. L. Santavy, and G. W. Smith. 2002. The etiology of white pox, a lethal dis-
ease of the Caribbean elkhorn coral, *Acropora palmata*. *Proceedings of the
National Academy of Sciences* 99 (13): 8725–8730.

Paulay, G. 1997. Diversity and distribution of reef organisms. In *Life and Death of
Coral Reefs*, edited by C. Birkeland, 298–353. Chapman and Hall.

Pauly, D. 1995. Anecdotes and the shifting baseline syndrome of fisheries. *Trends in
Ecology and Evolution* 10 (10): 430.

Pauly, D., V. Christensen, J. Dalsgaard, R. Froese, and F. Torres. 1998. Fishing down
marine food webs. *Science* 279:860–863.

Pauly, D., V. Christensen, R. Froese, and M. L. Palomares. 2000. Fishing down
aquatic food webs. *American Scientist* 88 (1): 46–51.

Pauly, D., and J. Maclean. 2003. *In a Perfect Ocean: The State of Fisheries and
Ecosystems in the North Atlantic Ocean*. Island Press.

Pearce, F. 1999. In hot water. *New Scientist* 164 (2213): 14.

———. 2002. Siren's swan song? *New Scientist* 175:9.

Pennings, S. C. 1997. Indirect actions on coral reefs. In *Life and Death of Coral
Reefs*, edited by C. Birkeland, 249–272. Chapman and Hall.

Pennisi, E. 2002. Diagnosis and R$_x$ for U.S. coral reefs. *Science* 298:39.

Perez, L., and R. Sisk. 2002. Fierce fish dragnet: Chinatown monster loose. *New
York Daily News*, July 13, 2.

Perrin, W. F. 1968. The porpoise and the tuna. *Sea Frontiers* 14 (3): 166–174.

———. 1969a. The problem of porpoise mortality in the U.S. tropical tuna fishery. In *Proceedings of the Sixth Annual Conference on Biological Sonar and
Diving Mammals*, 45–48. Stanford Research Institute.

———. 1969b. Using porpoise to catch tuna. *World Fishing* 18 (6): 42–45.

———. 1972. Color patterns of spinner porpoises (*Stenella* cf. *S. longirostris*) of
the eastern Pacific and Hawaii, with comments on delphinid pigmentation.
Fishery Bulletin 70 (3): 983–1003.

———. 1975a. Distribution and differentiation of populations of dolphins of the
genus *Stenella* in the eastern tropical Pacific. *Journal of the Fisheries Research
Board of Canada* 32 (7): 1059–1067.

———. 1975b. *Variation of Spotted and Spinner Porpoise (Genus Stenella) in the
Eastern Tropical Pacific and Hawaii*. University of California Press.

———. 1999. Selected examples of small cetaceans at risk. In *Conservation and
Management of Marine Mammals*, edited by J. R. Twiss and R. R. Reeves,
296–310. Smithsonian Institution Press.

Perrin, W. F., M. L. L. Dolar, and D. Robineau. 1999. Spinner dolphins (*Stenella longirostris*) of the western Pacific and Southeast Asia: Pelagic and shallow-water forms. *Marine Mammal Science* 15:1029–1053.

Perrin, W. F., and A. A. Hohn. 1994. Pantropical spotted dolphin—*Stenella attenuata*. In *Handbook of Marine Mammals*, edited by S. H. Ridgway and R. J. Harrison. Vol. 5, *The First Book of Dolphins*, 71–98. Academic Press.

Perrin, W. F., and R. Hunter. 1972. Escape behavior of the Hawaiian spinner porpoise (*Stenella* cf. *S. longirostris*). *Fishery Bulletin* 70 (1): 49–60.

Perrin, W. F., E. D. Mitchell, J. G. Mead, D. K. Caldwell, M. C. Caldwell, P. J. H. van Bree, and W. H. Dawbin. 1987. Revision of the spotted dolphins, *Stenella* sp. *Marine Mammal Science* 3 (2): 99–170.

Perrin, W. F., E. D. Mitchell, and P. J. H. van Bree. 1978. Historical zoogeography of tropical pelagic dolphins. Abstract. *Congressus Theriologicus Internationalis*. Brno, Czechoslovakia.

Perrin, W. F., P. A. Sloan, and P. Henderson. 1979. Taxonomic status of the southwestern stocks of spinner dolphin *Stenella longirostris* and spotted dolphin *S. attenuata*. *Reports of the International Whaling Commission* 29:175–184.

Perrin, W. F., T. D. Smith, and G. I. Sakagawa. 1975. Status of populations of spotted dolphin, *Stenella attenuata*, and spinner dolphin, *Stenella longirostris*, in the eastern tropical Pacific. ACMRR/MM/EC/27. Food and Agriculture Organization of the United Nations, Bergen, Norway.

Peters, E. C. 1997. Diseases of coral reef organisms. In *Life and Death of Coral Reefs*, edited by C. Birkeland, 114–139. Chapman and Hall.

Phinney, J. T., F. Muller-Karger, P. Dustan, and J. Sobel. 2001. Using remote sensing to reassess the mass mortality of *Diadema antellarum*, 1983–1984. *Conservation Biology* 15 (4): 885–891.

Pilleri, G. 1970. Observations on the behaviour of *Platanista gangetica* in the Indus and Brahmaputra River. *Investigations on Cetacea* 2:27–60.

———. 1972. Field observations carried out on the Indus dolphin *Platanista indi* in the winter of 1972. *Investigations on Cetacea* 4:23–29.

———. 1979. The Chinese river dolphin (*Lipotes vexillifer*) in poetry, literature, and legend. *Investigations on Cetacea* 10:335–349.

Pilleri, G., and M. Gihr. 1976. The current status of research on the Chinese river dolphin (*Lipotes vexillifer* Miller 1918). *Investigations on Cetacea* 7:149–160.

———. 1977. *Radical Extermination of the South American Sea Lion Otaria byronia (Pinnipedia, Otariidae) from Isla Verde, Uruguay.* Verlag des Hirnanotomischen Institutes, Ostermundigen, Bern.

Pilleri, G., M. Gihr, P. E. Purves, K. Zbinden, and C. Kraus. 1976. On the behaviour, bioacoustics, and functional morphology of the Indus River dolphin (*Platanista indi* Blyth 1859). *Investigations on Cetacea* 6:14–69.

Pimm, S. L. 2001. *The World According to Pimm: A Scientist Audits the Earth.* McGraw-Hill.

Pockley, P. 2000. Global warming identified as main threat to coral reefs. *Nature* 407:932.

Pontoppidan, E. 1755. *The Natural History of Norway.* London.

Popov, L. 1979a. Baikal seal. In *Mammals in the Seas II: Pinniped Species Summaries and Report on Sirenians,* 72–73. Food and Agriculture Organization of the United Nations, Rome.

———. 1979b. Caspian seal. In *Mammals in the Seas II: Pinniped Species Summaries and Report on Sirenians,* 74–75. Food and Agriculture Organization of the United Nations, Rome.

Porter, J. W., P. Dustan, W. C. Jaap, K. L. Patterson, V. Kosmynin, O. W. Meier, M. E. Patterson, and M. Parsons. 2001. Patterns of spread of coral disease in the Florida Keys. *Hydrobiologia* 460 (1–3): 1–24.

Porter, J. W., and K. G. Porter. 2002. *The Everglades, Florida Bay, and Coral Reefs of the Florida Keys.* CRC Press.

Pratchett, M. S. 1999. An infectious disease in crown-of-thorns starfish in the Great Barrier Reef. *Coral Reefs* 18:272.

Pritchard, P. C. H. 1980. The conservation of sea turtles: Practices and problems. *American Zoologist* 20:609–617.

———. 1997. Evolution, phylogeny, and current status. In *The Biology of Sea Turtles,* edited by P. L. Lutz and J. A. Musick, 1–28. CRC Press.

Pritchard, P. C. H., and J. A. Mortimer. 1999. Taxonomy, external morphology, and species identification. In *Research and Management Techniques for the Conservation of Sea Turtles,* edited by K. L. Eckert, K. A. Bjorndal, F. A. Abreu-Grobois, and M. Donnelly, 21–40. IUCN/SSC Marine Turtle Specialist Group. International Union for Conservation of Nature and Natural Resources.

Pryor, K., and I. Kang. 1980. *Social behavior and school structure in pelagic porpoises (Stenella attenuata and S. longirostris) during purse seining for tuna.* Southwest Fisheries Science Center Administrative Report LJ-80-11C. National Oceanic and Atmospheric Administration, National Marine Fisheries Service.

Pryor, K., and K. S. Norris, eds. 1991. *Dolphin Societies: Discoveries and Puzzles.* University of California Press.

Pryor, K., and I. K. Shallenberger. 1991. Social structure in spotted dolphins (*Stenella attenuata*) in the tuna purse seine fishery in the eastern tropical Pacific. In *Dolphin Societies: Discoveries and Puzzles,* edited by K. Pryor and K. S. Norris, 161–196. University of California Press.

Purvis, A., K. E. Jones, and G. M. Mace. 2000. Extinction. *BioEssays* 22:1123–1133.

Pyle, P., D. J. Long, J. Schonewald, R. E. Jones, and J. Roletto. 2001. Historical and recent colonization of the South Farallon Islands, California, by northern fur seals (*Callorhinus ursinus*). *Marine Mammal Science* 17 (2): 397–402.

Quackenbush, S. L., R. N. Casey, R. J. Murcek, T. A. Paul, T. M. Work, C. J. Limpus, A. Chaves, L. duToit, J. V. Perez, A. A. Aguirre, T. R. Spraker, J. A. Horrocks, L. A. Vermeer, G. H. Balazs, and J. W. Casey. 2001. Quantitative analysis of herpesvirus sequences from normal tissue and fibropapillomas of marine turtles with real-time PCR. *Virology* 287 (1): 105–111.

Quackenbush, S. L., T. M. Work, G. H. Balazs, R. N. Casey, J. Rovnak, A. Chaves, L. duToit, J. D. Baines, C. R. Parrish, P. R. Bowser, and J. W. Casey, 1998. Three closely related herpesviruses are associated with fibropapillomatosis in marine turtles. *Virology* 246 (2): 392–399.

Raloff, J. 1998. Biocontrols might not work for jellies. *Science News* 154 (1): 10.

———. 2001. Wanted: Reef cleaners. *Science News* 160 (8): 120–122.

———. 2002. Clipping the fin trade. *Science News* 162 (15): 232–234.

Rand, R. W. 1959. *The Cape Fur Seal (Arctocephalus pusillus): Distribution, Abundance, and Feeding Habits off the South Western Coast of the Cape Province.* Union of South Africa, Department of Commerce and Industries, Division of Fisheries Investigational Report No. 34. Government Printer, Pretoria.

Randerson, J. 2002. Fish in the Med making poor recovery. *New Scientist* 176 (2365): 18.

Ray, C. E., and D. P. Domning. 1986. Manatees and genocide. *Marine Mammal Science* 2 (1): 77–78.

Red Data Book. 1976. *Lipotes vexillifer.* Mammalia 11.92.3.1. International Union for Conservation of Nature and Natural Resources, Gland, Switzerland.

Reeves, R. R. 1984. Modern commercial pelagic whaling for gray whales. In *The Gray Whale, Eschrichtius robustus,* edited by M. L. Jones, S. L. Swartz, and S. Leatherwood, 187–200. Academic Press.

———. 2002a. Hunting of marine mammals. In *Encyclopedia of Marine Mammals,* edited by W. F. Perrin, B. Würsig, and J. G. M. Thewissen, 593–596. Academic Press.

———. 2002b. River dolphins. In *Encyclopedia of Marine Mammals,* edited by W. F. Perrin, B. Würsig, and J. G. M. Thewissen, 1039–1049. Academic Press.

Reeves, R. R., and R. L. Brownell. 1989. Susu—*Platanista gangetica* (Roxburgh, 1801) and *Platanista minor* (Owen, 1853). In *Handbook of Marine Mammals,* edited by S. H. Ridgway and R. J. Harrison. Vol. 4, *River Dolphins and the Larger Toothed Whales,* 69–99. Academic Press.

Reeves, R. R., B. S. Stewart, P. J. Clapham, and J. A. Powell. 2002. *Guide to Marine Mammals of the World.* National Audubon Society and Knopf.

Reeves, R. R., B. S. Stewart, and S. Leatherwood. 1992. *The Sierra Club Handbook of Seals and Sirenians.* Sierra Club Books.

Reid, T. R. 1995. Tsukiji: The great Tokyo fish market. *National Geographic* 188 (5): 38–55.

Reiger, G. 1975. Song of the seal. *Audubon* 77 (5): 6–27.

Repenning, C. A., R. S. Peterson, and C. L. Hubbs. 1971. Contributions to the systematics of the southern fur seals, with particular reference to the Juan Fernández and Guadalupe species. In *Antarctic Pinnipedia,* edited by W. E. Burt, 1–52. American Geophysical Union.

Revkin, A. C. 2001. Virus is killing thousands of salmon. *New York Times,* September 7, A10.

———. 2002. Japan says it will double its annual whale hunt in the Pacific. *New York Times,* February 28, A14.

Reyes, L. M., E. A. Crespo, and V. Szapkievich. 1999. Distribution and population size of the southern sea lion (*Otaria flavescens*) in central and southern Chubut, Patagonia, Argentina. *Marine Mammal Science* 15 (2): 478–493.

Reynolds, J. E., III, D. P. DeMaster, and G. K. Silber. 1998. *Marine Mammals of the World: Systematics and Distribution*. Society for Marine Mammalogy.

———. 2002. Endangered species and populations. In *Encyclopedia of Marine Mammals*, edited by W. F. Perrin, B. Würsig, and J. G. M. Thewissen, 373–382. Academic Press.

Reynolds, J. E., III, and D. K. Odell. 1991. *Manatees and Dugongs*. Facts on File.

Reynolds, J. E., III, and J. A. Powell. 2002. Manatees. In *Encyclopedia of Marine Mammals*, edited by W. F. Perrin, B. Würsig, and J. G. M. Thewissen, 709–720. Academic Press.

Rice, D. W. 1998. *Marine Mammals of the World: Systematics and Distribution*. Special Publication No. 4. Society for Marine Mammalogy.

Ricciuti, E. R. 1973. *Killers of the Seas*. Walker.

Richards, R. 1982. *Whaling and Sealing at the Chatham Islands*. Roebuck.

———. 1991. *Captain Simon Metcalfe: Pioneer Fur Trader in the Pacific Northwest, Hawaii, and China, 1787–1794*. Limestone Press.

———. 1994. "The upland seal" of the Antipodes and Macquarie Islands: A historian's perspective. *Journal of the Royal Society of New Zealand* 24 (3): 289–295.

Richardson, J. 2002. Salmon farming fights for its life. *Portland (Maine) Press Herald*, January 20, 1B.

Richardson, L. L. 1998. Coral diseases: What is really known? *Trends in Ecology and Evolution* 13 (11): 438–443.

Richardson, L. L., W. M. Goldberg, R. G. Carlton, and J. C. Halas. 1998. Coral disease outbreak in the Florida Keys: Plague type II. *Revista de Biología Tropical* 46 (5): 187–198.

Richardson, L. L., W. M. Goldberg, K. G. Kuta, R. B. Aronson, G. W. Smith, K. B. Ritchie, J. C. Halas, J. S. Feingold, and S. L. Miller. 1998. Florida's mystery coral-killer identified. *Nature* 392:557–558.

Richardson, L. L., K. G. Kuta, S. Schnell, and R. G. Carlton. 1997. Ecology of black band disease microbial consortium. *Proceedings of the Eighth International Coral Reef Symposium* 1:579–600.

Richer de Forges, B., J. A. Koslow, and G. C. B. Poore. 2000. Diversity and endemism of the benthic seamount fauna in the southwest Pacific. *Nature* 405:944–947.

Richter, C., M. Wunsch, M. Rasheed, I. Kötter, and M. I. Badran. 2001. Endoscopic exploration of Red Sea coral reefs reveals dense populations of cavity-dwelling sponges. *Nature* 413:726–730.

Riedman, M. 1990. *The Pinnipeds: Seals, Sea Lions, and Walruses*. University of California Press.

Riedman, M. L., J. A. Estes, M. M. Staedler, A. A. Giles, and D. R. Carlson. 1994. Breeding patterns and reproductive success of California sea otters (*Enhydra lutris*). *Journal of Wildlife Management* 58 (3): 391–399.

Risk, M. J., and A. C. Risk. 1997. Reef surveys as an aid in management. *Proceedings of the Eighth International Coral Reef Symposium* 2:1471–1474.

Rivlin, M. 2000. Bad to the bone. *Amicus Journal* 22 (1): 12–18.

Roberts, C. M. 1997. Ecological advice for the global fisheries crisis. *Trends in Ecology and Evolution* 12 (1): 35–38.

Roberts, C. M., J. A. Bohnsack, F. Gell, J. P. Hawkins, and R. Goodridge. 2001. Effects of marine reserves on adjacent fisheries. *Science* 294:1920–1923.

Roberts, C. M., and J. P. Hawkins. 1999. Extinction risk in the sea. *Trends in Ecology and Evolution* 14 (6): 241–246.

Roberts, C. M., C. J. McClean, J. E. N. Veron, J. P. Hawkins, G. R. Allen, D. E. McAllister, C. G. Mittermeier, F. W. Schueler, M. Spalding, F. Wells, C. Vynne, and T. B. Werner. 2002. Marine biodiversity hotspots and conservation priorities for coral reefs. *Science* 295:1280–1284.

Robichaux, M. 2000. A plague of Asian eels highlights the damage from foreign species. *Wall Street Journal*, September 27, A1.

Rojas-Bracho, L., and A. Jamarillo-Legoretta. 2002. Vaquita. In *Encyclopedia of Marine Mammals*, edited by W. F. Perrin, B. Würsig, and J. G. M. Thewissen, 1277–1280. Academic Press.

Rojas-Bracho, L., and B. L. Taylor. 1999. Risk factors affecting the vaquita (*Phocoena sinus*). *Marine Mammal Science* 15 (4): 974–989.

Rolls, E. C. 1969. *They All Ran Wild*. Angus and Robertson.

Ronald, K., and P. J. Healy. 1981. Harp seal—*Phoca groenlandica* (Erxleben, 1777). In *Handbook of Marine Mammals*, edited by S. H. Ridgway and R. J. Harrison. Vol. 2, *Seals*, 329–349. Academic Press.

Rose, L. 1984. *Richard Siddons of Port Jackson*. Roebuck.

Rose, M. R. 1998. *Darwin's Spectre: Evolutionary Biology in the Modern World*. Princeton University Press.

Rousellot, J.-L., W. W. Fitzhugh, and A. Crowell. 1988. Maritime economies of the North Pacific rim. In *Crossroads of Continents*, edited by W. W. Fitzhugh and A. Crowell, 151–172. Smithsonian Institution Press.

Rudloe, A., and J. Rudloe. 1994. Sea turtles: In a race for survival. *National Geographic* 185 (2): 94–121.

Rugh, D. J., M. M. Muto, S. E. Moore, and D. P. McMaster. 1999. *Status Review of the Eastern North Pacific Stock of Gray Whales*. NOAA Technical Memorandum MNFS-AFSC-103. U.S. Department of Commerce.

Ruiz, G. M., T. K. Rawlings, F. C. Dobbs, L. A. Drake, T. Mullady, A. Huq, and R. R. Colwell. 2000. Global spread of microorganisms by ships. *Nature* 408:49–50.

Russell, D. 2001. *Eye of the Whale*. Simon and Schuster.

Saayman, G. S., and C. K. Tayler. 1973. Social organization of inshore dolphins (*Tursiops aduncus* and *Sousa*) in the Indian Ocean. *Journal of Mammalogy* 54 (4): 993–996.

Sægrov, H., K. Hindar, S. Kålås, and H. Lura. 1997. Escaped farmed Atlantic salmon replace the original salmon stock in the River Vosso, western Norway. *ICES Journal of Marine Science* 54 (6): 1166–1172.

Safina, C. 1995. The world's imperiled fish. *Scientific American* 273 (5): 46–53.

————. 1997. *Song for the Blue Ocean.* Henry Holt.

————. 1998a. Scorched-earth fishing. *Issues in Science and Technology* 14 (3): 33–36.

————. 1998b. Song for the swordfish. *Audubon* 100 (3): 58–69.

————. 1998c. The world's imperiled fish. *Scientific American* (Special Issue) 9 (3): 58–63.

————. 2002. *Eye of the Albatross: Visions of Hope and Survival.* Henry Holt.

Sandegren, R. E., E. W. Chu, and J. E. Vandevere. 1973. Maternal behavior in the California sea otter. *Journal of Mammalogy* 54:668–679.

Sanderson, I. T. 1956. *Follow the Whale.* Little, Brown.

————. 1958. *Living Mammals of the World.* Hanover House.

Scammon, C. M. 1874. *The Marine Mammals of the Northwestern Coast of North America; Together with an Account of the American Whale Fishery.* Carmany and G. P. Putnam's.

Scheffer, V. B. 1958. *Seals, Sea Lions, and Walruses.* Stanford University Press.

————. 1970. *The Year of the Seal.* Scribner.

————. 1981. *The Amazing Sea Otter.* Scribner.

Schevill, W. E., W. A. Watkins, and K. E. Moore. 1986. Status of *Eubaleana glacialis* off Cape Cod. *Reports of the International Whaling Commission* (Special Issue) 10:79–82.

Schiermeier, Q. 2002. How many more fish in the sea? *Nature* 419:662–665.

Schrope, M. 2001. Fish out of water: Chinese inflated catches are masking world-wide overfishing. *New Scientist* 172 (2319): 18.

Schusterman, R. J. 1981. Steller sea lion—*Eumetropias jubatus* (Schreber, 1776). In *Handbook of Marine Mammals,* edited by S. H. Ridgway and R. J. Harrison. Vol. 1, *The Walrus, Sea Lions, Fur Seals, and Sea Otter,* 119–141. Academic Press.

Scogin, R. 1977. Sperm whale oil and the jojoba shrub. *Oceans* 10 (4): 65–66.

Scott, M. D., and K. L. Cattanach. 1998. Diel patterns in aggregations of pelagic dolphins and tunas in the eastern Pacific. *Marine Mammal Science* 14 (3): 401–428.

Scott, W. B., and S. N. Tibbo. 1968. Food and feeding habits of the swordfish, *Xiphias gladius,* in the western North Atlantic. *Journal of the Fisheries Research Board of Canada* 25 (5): 903–919.

Seabrook, J. 1994. Death of a giant: Stalking the disappearing bluefin tuna. *Harper's* 288 (1729): 48–56.

Sefton, N. 1974. Now they're farming turtles. *Oceans* 7 (5): 34–35.

Selkirk, P. M., R. D. Seppelt, and D. R. Selkirk. 1990. *Subantarctic Macquarie Island.* Cambridge University Press.

Sergeant, D. E. 1965. Migrations of harp seals *Pagophilus groenlandicus* (Erxleben). *Journal of the Fisheries Research Board of Canada* 22:433–464.

————. 1973. Feeding, growth, and productivity of north-west Atlantic harp seals (*Pagophilus groenlandicus*). *Journal of the Fisheries Research Board of Canada* 30:17–29.

————. 1975. Estimating numbers of harp seals. *Rapports et Procès-Verbaux des Réunions du Conseil International pour l'Exploration de la Mer* 169:274–280.

————. 1976. History and present status of populations of harp and hooded seals. *Biological Conservation* 10:95–118.

Shaughnessy, P. D. 1979. Cape (South African) fur seal. In *Mammals in the Seas II: Pinniped Species Summaries and Report on Sirenians*, 37–40. Food and Agriculture Organization of the United Nations, Rome.

Shaughnessy, P. D., E. Erb, and K. Green. 1998. Continued increase in population of Antarctic fur seals, *Arctocephalus gazella*, at Heard Island, Southern Ocean. *Marine Mammal Science* 14 (2): 384–389.

Shaughnessy, P. D., and S. D. Goldsworthy. 1990. Population size and breeding season of the Antarctic fur seal, *Arctocephalus gazella*, at Heard Island—1987–88. *Marine Mammal Science* 6 (2): 384–389.

Simenstad, C. A., and J. A. Estes. 1980. The historic role of the sea otter in the ecology of the Aleutian Islands. *Alaska Geographic* 7 (3): 56–59.

Simon, N., and P. Géroudet. 1970. *Last Survivors: The Natural History of Animals in Danger of Extinction*. World.

Simpson, S. 2001. Fishy Business. *Scientific American* 285 (1): 82–88.

Siniff, D. B., and K. Ralls. 1991. Reproduction, survival, and tag loss in California sea otters (*Enhydra lutris*). *Marine Mammal Science* 7 (3): 211–229.

Small, M. 2002. The happy fat. *New Scientist* 175 (2357): 34–37.

Smith, C. S. 2002. North Sea cod crisis brings call for nations to act. *New York Times*, November 7, A3.

Smith, E. A. 1966. A review of the world's grey seal population. *Journal of Zoology* 150:463–489.

Smith, G. M., and C. W. Coates. 1938. Fibro-epithelial growths of the skin of large marine turtles *Chelonia mydas* (L.). *Zoologica* 23:93–98.

Smith, J. E., U. Brand, M. J. Risk, and H. P. Schwarcz. 1999. Mid-Atlantic Ridge hydrothermal events recorded by deep-sea corals. *Canadian Journal of Earth Sciences* 36 (4): 511–517.

Smith, J. E., M. J. Risk, H. P. Schwarcz, and T. A. McConnaughey. 1997. Rapid climate change in the North Atlantic during the Younger Dryas recorded by deep-sea corals. *Nature* 386:818–820.

Smith, T., ed. 1979. *Report of the Status of Porpoise Stocks Workshop (August 27–31, 1979, La Jolla, California)*. Southwest Fisheries Science Center Administrative Report LJ-79-41. National Oceanic and Atmospheric Administration, National Marine Fisheries Service.

Smolker, R. 2001. *To Touch a Wild Dolphin*. Doubleday.

Southwest Fisheries Science Center. 2002. *Report of the Scientific Research Program under the International Dolphin Conservation Program Act*. National Oceanic and Atmospheric Administration, National Marine Fisheries Service.

Spotila, J. R., M. P. O'Connor, and F. V. Paladino. 1997. Thermal biology. In *The Biology of Sea Turtles*, edited by P. L. Lutz and J. A. Musick, 297–314. CRC Press.

Spotila, J. R., R. D. Reina, A. C. Steyermark, P. T. Plotkin, and F. V. Paladino. 2000. Pacific leatherback turtles face extinction. *Nature* 405:529–530.

Stackpole, E. 1953. *The Sea Hunters*. Lippincott.

Stejneger, L. 1884. Contributions to the history of the Commander Islands. 2. Investigations relating to the date of the extermination of Steller's sea-cow. *Proceedings of the U.S. National Museum* 8:181–189.

———. 1887. How the great northern sea-cow (*Rytina*) became exterminated. *American Naturalist* 21:1047–1054.

———. 1936. *Georg Wilhelm Steller*. Harvard University Press.

Steller, G. W. 1751. De bestis marinis. *Novi. Comm. Acad. Sci. Petropolitanae* 2:289–398. Reprinted in "Steller's account of the sea otter," in *The Fur Seals and Fur-Seal Islands of the North Pacific Ocean* (1899), edited by D. S. Jordan, 210–218. Translated by W. Miller and J. E. Miller. U.S. Government Printing Office.

———. 1781. *Journal of a Voyage with Bering, 1741–1742*. Translated by O. W. Frost. Reprint, Stanford University Press, 1988.

Steneck, R. S. 1998. Human influences on coastal ecosystems: Does overfishing create trophic cascades? *Trends in Ecology and Evolution* 13 (11): 429–430.

Stewart, B. S., and R. L. DeLong. 1991. Diving patterns of northern elephant seal bulls. *Marine Mammal Science* 7 (4): 369–384.

Stillwell, C. E., and N. E. Kohler. 1985. Food and feeding ecology of the swordfish *Xiphias gladias* in the western North Atlantic ocean with estimates of daily ration. *Marine Ecology Progress Series* 22:239–247.

Stokstad, E. 2002. Engineered fish: Friend or foe of the environment? *Science* 297:1797–1798.

Stone, L. M. 1979. The loggerhead and his friends. *Oceans* 12 (5): 37–41.

Stump, R. 1996. An investigation to describe the population dynamics of *Acanthaster planci* (L.) around Lizard Island, Cairns Section, Great Barrier Reef Marine Park. *CRC Reef Research Centre Technical Report* 10:1–56.

Summers, C. F., W. N. Bonner, and J. L. van Haaften. 1978. Changes in the seal population of the North Sea. *Rapports et Procès-Verbaux des Réunions du Conseil International pour l'Exploration de la Mer* 172:278–285.

Swan, J. G. 1887. The fur-seal industry of Cape Flattery, Washington Territory. In *The Fisheries and Fishery Industries of the United States*, edited by G. B. Goode. Vol. 2, sec. 5, 393–400. U.S. Government Printing Office.

Tendal, O. S. 1992. The North Atlantic distribution of the octocoral *Paragorgia arborea* (L. 1758) (Cnidaria, Anthozoa). *Sarsia* 77:213–217.

Terry, P., P. Lichtenstein, M. Feychting, A. Ahlbom, and A. Wolk. 2001. Fatty fish consumption and risk of prostate cancer. *Lancet* 357:1764–1766.

Thomas, G. L., and R. E. Thorne. 2001. Night-time predation by Steller sea lions. *Nature* 411:1013.

Tibbo, S. N., L. R. Day, and W. F. Doucet. 1961. The swordfish (*Xiphias gladius* L.): Its life history and economic importance in the Northwest Atlantic. *Bulletin of the Fisheries Research Board of Canada* 130:1–47.

Tickell, W. L. N. 1975. Observations on the status of Steller's albatross (*Diomedea albatrus*), 1973. *Bulletin of the International Council for Bird Preservation* 12:125–131.

———. 2000. *Albatrosses.* Yale University Press.

Tickell, W. L. N., and P. Morton. 1975. The albatross of Torishima. *Geographic Magazine* 49:359–363.

Tomich, P. Q. 1969. *Mammals in Hawaii.* Bishop Museum Press.

Townsend, C. H. 1898. Pelagic sealing, with notes on the fur seals of Guadalupe, the Galápagos, and Lobos Islands. In *The Fur Seals and the Fur-Seal Islands of the North Pacific Ocean,* edited by D. S. Jordan, vol. 3, 223–274. U.S. Government Printing Office.

———. 1912. The northern elephant seal. *Zoologica* 1:159–173.

———. 1935. The distribution of certain whales as shown by logbook records of American whaleships. *Zoologica* 29 (1): 1–50.

———. 1936. The largest deep-sea fish: A long-missing photograph of the monster comes to light after nearly half a century. *Bulletin of the New York Zoological Society* 39(1):29–30.

———. 1937. *Guide to the New York Aquarium.* New York Zoological Society.

True, F. W. 1887. The turtle and terrapin fisheries. In *The Fisheries and Fishing Industry of the United States,* edited by G. B. Goode, 493–504. U.S. Government Printing Office.

———. 1889. Contributions to the natural history of the cetaceans: A review of the family Delphinidae. *Bulletin of the U.S. National Museum* 36:1–191.

Tudela, S. 2002a. *Tuna Farming in the Mediterranean: The "Coup de Grâce" to a Dwindling Population?* World Wildlife Fund, Mediterranean Program Office.

———. 2002b. *Grab, Cage, Fatten, Sell.* World Wildlife Fund Program Office.

Turgeon, D. D., R. G. Asch, B. D. Causey, R. E. Dodge, W. Jaap, K. Banks, J. Delaney, B. D. Keller, R. Speiler, C. A. Matos, J. R. Garcia, E. Diaz, D. Catanzaro, C. S. Rogers, Z. Hillis-Starr, R. Nemeth, M. Taylor, G. P. Schmahl, M. W. Miller, D. A. Gulko, J. E. Maragos, A. M. Friedlander, C. L. Hunter, R. S. Brainard, P. Craig, R. H. Richmond, G. Davis, J. Starmer, M. Trianni, P. Houk, C. E. Birkeland, A. Edward, Y. Golbuu, J. Guiterrez, N. Idechong, G. Paulay, A. Tafileichig, and N. Vander Velde. 2002. *The State of Coral Reef Ecosystems of the United States and Pacific Freely Associated States: 2002.* National Oceanic and Atmospheric Administration, National Ocean Service, and National Centers for Coastal Ocean Science.

Tynan, C. T., D. P. DeMaster, and W. T. Peterson. 2001. Endangered right whales on the southeastern Bering Sea shelf. *Science* 294:1894.

Van Deinse, A. B., and G. C. A. Junge. 1937. Recent and older finds of the California gray whale in the Atlantic. *Temminckia* 2:161–188.

VanStone, J. W. 1988. Hunters, herders, trappers, and fishermen. In *Crossroads of Continents,* edited by W. W. Fitzhugh and A. Crowell, 173–181. Smithsonian Institution Press.

Vaughan, T., and B. Holm. 1990. *Soft Gold: The Fur Trade and Cultural Exchange on the Northwest Coast of America.* Oregon Historical Society.

Vaz-Ferreira, R. 1972a. Behaviour of the southern sea lion, *Otaria flavescens* Shaw, in the Uruguayan islands. *Rapports et Procès-Verbaux des Réunions du Conseil International pour l'Exploration de la Mer* 169:219–227.

———. 1972b. Factors affecting numbers of fur seals and sea lions on the Uruguayan islands. *Rapports et Procès-Verbaux des Réunions du Conseil International pour l'Exploration de la Mer* 169:257–262.

———. 1979. South American sea lion. In *Mammals in the Seas II: Pinniped Species Summaries and Report on Sirenians,* 9–12. Food and Agriculture Organization of the United Nations, Rome.

———. 1981. South American sea lion—*Otaria flavescens* (Shaw, 1800). In *Handbook of Marine Mammals,* edited by S. H. Ridgway and R. J. Harrison. Vol. 1, *The Walrus, Sea Lions, Fur Seals, and Sea Otter,* 39–65. Academic Press.

Vidal, O., and J.-P. Gallo-Reynoso. 1996. Die-offs of marine mammals and sea birds in the Gulf of California, México. *Marine Mammal Science* 12 (4): 627–634.

Vincent, A. 1994. The improbable seahorse. *National Geographic* 186 (4): 126–140.

Wacker, R. 1994. Strip mining the seas. *Sea Frontiers* 40 (3): 14–17, 60.

Wade, P. R. 1993a. *Assessment of the northeastern stock of offshore spinner dolphin (Stenella attenuata).* Southwest Fisheries Science Center Administrative Report LJ-93-18. National Oceanic and Atmospheric Administration, National Marine Fisheries Service.

———. 1993b. Estimation of historical population size of the eastern spinner dolphin (*Stenella longirostris orientalis*). *Fishery Bulletin* 91:775–787.

———. 1995. Revised estimates of incidental kill of dolphins (Delphinidae) by the purse-seine fishery in the eastern tropical Pacific, 1959–1972. *Fishery Bulletin* 93:345–354.

Walker, G. M., and J. K. Ling. 1981a. Australian sea lion—*Neophoca cinerea* (Péron, 1816). In *Handbook of Marine Mammals,* edited by S. H. Ridgway and R. J. Harrison. Vol. 1, *The Walrus, Sea Lions, Fur Seals, and Sea Otter,* 99–118. Academic Press.

———. 1981b. New Zealand sea lion—*Phocarctos hookeri* (Gray, 1844). In *Handbook of Marine Mammals,* edited by S. H. Ridgway and R. J. Harrison. Vol. 1, *The Walrus, Sea Lions, Fur Seals, and Sea Otter,* 25–38. Academic Press.

Walker, M. 1999. Waiting to exhale. *New Scientist* 163 (2203): 25.

Wallace, R. K. 1996. Catch and bycatch: Is there really a difference? In *Fisheries Bycatch: Consequences and Management,* 77–80. Alaska Sea Grant College Program Report No. 97-02. University of Alaska.

Ward, F. 1990. The coral reefs of Florida are imperiled. *National Geographic* 178 (1): 114–132.

Warnecke, R. 1979. Australian fur seal. In *Mammals in the Seas II: Pinniped Species Summaries and Report on Sirenians,* 41–44. Food and Agriculture Organization of the United Nations, Rome.

Warner, W. W. 1977. *Distant Water: The Fate of the North Atlantic Fishermen.* Penguin.

Watling, L., and E. A. Norse. 1998a. Disturbance of the seabed by mobile fishing gear: A comparison to forest clearcutting. *Conservation Biology* 12 (6): 1180–1197.

———. 1998b. Effects of mobile fishing gear on marine benthos: Introduction. *Conservation Biology* 12 (6): 1178–1179.

Watson, P. 1982. *Sea Shepherd: My Fight for Whales and Seals.* Norton.

Watson, R., and D. Pauly. 2001. Systematic distortions in world fisheries catch trends. *Nature* 414:534–536.

Waxell, S. 1743. *The American Expedition.* Translated from Danish by M. A. Michael. William Hodge and Company, 1952.

Webb, P. W., and V. de Buffrénil. 1990. Locomotion in the biology of large aquatic vertebrates. *Transactions of the American Fisheries Society* 119:629–641.

Weber, P. 1993. *Abandoned Seas: Reversing the Decline of the Oceans.* Worldwatch.

———. 1994. *Net Loss: Fish, Jobs, and the Environment.* Worldwatch.

Weddell, J. 1827. *A Journey towards the South Pole, 1822–24.* London.

Wells, R. S. 1991. The role of long-term study in understanding the social structure of a bottlenose dolphin community. In *Dolphin Societies: Discoveries and Puzzles,* edited by K. Pryor and K. S. Norris, 199–225. University of California Press.

Wendell, F. E., J. A. Ames, and R. A. Hardy. 1984. Pup dependency period and length of reproductive cycle: Estimates from observations of tagged sea otters, *Enhydra lutris,* in California. *California Fish and Game* 70 (2): 89–100.

Wenk, E. 1969. The physical resources of the ocean. *Scientific American* 221 (3): 166–176.

Went, A. E. J., ed. 1980. Atlantic salmon: Its future. *Proceedings of the Second International Atlantic Salmon Symposium* 1–253.

Werth, A. 2000. A kinematic study of suction feeding and associated behavior in the long-finned pilot whale, *Globicephala melas* (Traill). *Marine Mammal Science* 16 (2): 299–314.

Wesson, R. 1997. *Beyond Natural Selection.* MIT Press.

Whitaker, I. 1984. Whaling in classical Iceland. *Polar Record* 22 (134): 249–261.

———. 1985. The King's Mirror (*Konnungs skuggsjá*) and northern research. *Polar Record* 22 (141): 615–627.

———. 1986. North Atlantic sea creatures in the King's Mirror (*Konnungs skuggsjá*). *Polar Record* 22 (142): 3–13.

White, K. 1996. A tuna spotter's observation of tuna fishing. On-line at http://www.kiwiwhite.com.

Whitehead, H. 2002. Estimates of the current global population size and historical trajectory for sperm whales. *Reports of the International Whaling Commission* SC/54/06:1–18.

Whitmore, F. C., and L. M. Gard. 1977. *Steller's Sea Cow (Hydrodamalis gigas) of late Pleistocene Age from Amchitka, Aleutian Islands, Alaska.* U.S. Geologic Survey Professional Paper 1036. Washington, D.C.

Whitty, J. 2000. Shoals of time. *Harper's* 302 (1808): 55–65.

Whynott, D. 1995. *Giant Bluefin.* North Point Press.

———. 1999. The most expensive fish in the sea. *Discover* 20 (4): 80–85.

Williams, R. J., and N. D. Martinez. 2000. Simple rules yield complex food webs. *Nature* 404:180–183.

Wilson, E. O. 2002. *The Future of Life.* Knopf.

Wilson, W. H., I. Francis, K. Ryan, and S. K. Davy. 2001. Temperature indication of viruses in symbiotic dinoflagellates. *Aquatic Microbial Ecology* 25:99–102.

Winter, A., R. S. Appeldoorn, A. Bruckner, H. E. Williams, and C. Goenaga. 1998. Sea surface temperatures and coral reef bleaching off La Parguera, Puerto Rico (northeastern Caribbean Sea). *Coral Reefs* 17 (4): 377–382.

Witzell, W. N. 1994. The origin, evolution, and demise of the U.S. sea turtle fisheries. *Marine Fisheries Review* 56 (4): 8–23.

Wolanski, E., R. Richmond, L. McCook, and H. Sweatman. 2003. Mud, marine snow, and coral reefs. *American Scientist* 91 (1): 44–51.

Wuethrich, B. C. 1996. Into dangerous waters. *International Wildlife* 26 (2): 44–51.

Würsig, B. 1979. Dolphins. *Scientific American* 240 (3): 136–148.

Würsig, B., and M. Würsig. 1977. The photographic determination of group size, composition, and stability of coastal porpoises (*Tursiops truncatus*). *Science* 198:755–756.

———. 1979. Behavior and ecology of the bottlenose dolphin, *Tursiops truncatus,* in the South Atlantic. *Fishery Bulletin* 77 (2): 399–412.

———. 1980. Behavior and ecology of the dusky dolphin, *Lagenorhynchus obscurus,* in the South Atlantic. *Fishery Bulletin* 77 (4): 871–890.

Wyneken, J. 1997. Sea turtle locomotion: Mechanics, behavior, and energetics. In *The Biology of Sea Turtles,* edited by P. L. Lutz and J. A. Musick, 165–198. CRC Press.

Yablokov, A. V. 1994. Validity of whaling data. *Nature* 367:108.

Yablokov, A. V., and L. S. Bogoslovskaya. 1984. A review of Russian research and commercial whaling of the gray whale. In *The Gray Whale, Eschrichtius robustus,* edited by M. L. Jones, S. L. Swartz, and S. Leatherwood, 465–483. Academic Press.

Yeh, S., and G. Pilleri. 1980. The acoustic properties of the melon of the Chinese river dolphin—biological transmission, aperture, and considerations of the sonar field of *Lipotes vexillifer. Investigations on Cetacea* 11:189–201.

Yentsch, C. S., C. M. Yentsch, J. J. Cullen, B. Lapointe, D. A. Phinney, and S. W. Yentsch. 2002. Sunlight and water transparency: Cornerstones in coral research. *Journal of Experimental Marine Biology and Ecology* 268 (2): 171–183.

Yoon, C. K. 1997. Mysterious new diseases devastate coral reefs. *New York Times,* August 19, C1, C5.

York, A. E. 1994. The population dynamics of northern sea lions, 1975–1985. *Marine Mammal Science* 10 (1): 38–51.

Zemsky, V., Y. Mikhailiev, and A. Berzin. 1996. Supplementary information about

Soviet whaling in the Southern Hemisphere. *Reports of the International Whaling Commission* 46:131–138.

Zhou, K., G. Pilleri, and L. Yuemin. 1979. Observations on the "baiji" (*Lipotes vexillifer*) and the finless porpoise (*Neophocaena asiaeorientalis*) in the Changjaing (Yangtze) River between Nanjing and Taiyandzhou, with remarks on some physiological adaptations of the baiji to its environment. *Investigations on Cetacea* 10:109–120.

Zorpette, G. 1995. More coral trouble. *Scientific American* 273:37–38.

INDEX

International Symposium on, 279; loss of, 279–80; trawling damage to, 277–78, 280; zooxanthellae and, 258

Delano, Thomas, 166

DeLong, Robert, 191

depression, omega-3 fatty acids and, 91n

DeSalle, Rob, 88n

Desulfovibrio, black-band disease of corals and, 266

de Tieve, Diogo, 58

DeWitt, Hugh, 73

Dezhnev, Semyon, 125

Diadema antillarum, sea urchins, coral reefs and, 22

Diamond, Jared, 75

Dias, Bartolomeu, 170

dinosaurs, 88n. *See also* genetic engineering

Dissostichus eleginoides. See Patagonian toothfish

Distant Water (Warner), 67

dodo, 119

Dolphin Protection Consumer Information Act (1990), 232

dolphins: behavioral studies, 228–29; Chinese river, 212–15, *213*; drift nets and, 18–19; drive fishing, 223–25; gill nets and, 99; optimal sustainable populations, 230, 230n; pair trawling and, 20; porpoises *versus,* 225n; purse seines and, 225; river, 217–18; tuna fishing and, 15, 219–20. *See also* spinner dolphins; spotted dolphins; tuna-porpoise (dolphin) problem

Domning, Daryl, 138

Donne, John, 305

Dowd, Maureen, 289

drift nets, 14, 18–19. *See also* nets

drive fishery, for dolphins, 223–24

ducks, pink-headed, 119

Dudley, Paul, 5

Dugong: Status Reports and Action Plans for Countries and Territories (Marsh), 137

dugongs, 136–38, *137;* sea cows *versus,* 133

Dumont, Henri, 285–86

Duncan, David Douglas, 42

Duplaix, Nicole, 111

dusky shark, 49

dynamite fishing, corals and, 259

Earle, Sylvia, 277–78

Earthtrust, on Japanese drift nets of squid fleet, 19

eastern spotted dolphin, 223

Ebbets, John, 176

Eden, George, 179

Edge, Thomas, 5

Edmonds, Peter, 271

eider, common, 293

elasmobranchs, 47, 55–56. *See also* sharks

elephant seals, 165, 169, 179, *190*, 211; breeding, 190–91; habitat, 189–90; hunting, 192; migration, 191; northern, *190;* resurgence of, 193–94

elkhorn corals, 257, *258*, 265, 266, 267

Elliott, Henry W., 153–54, 155, 186

El Niño, coral bleaching and, 267

encirclement fishing, 232–33. *See also* purse seines

Encyclopedia Londonensis, 61

Endangered Species Act (U.S., 1973): hawksbill turtle and, 112; loggerheads and, 116; on reasonable and prudent alternatives, 188–89; Steller's sea lions under, 187–88; white abalone under, 14

English. *See* British

environmental stress: coral bleaching and, 269; coral reefs and, 263–64

Erb, Erwin, 173

Estes, James, 150

European Commission, on swordfishing, 46

European Community, sela skin imports ban, 203

European Union: African fisheries protocols, 301; on cod crisis, 71; on drift netting, 19; western zone tuna fishing, 33

exclusive economic zones (EEZs), 68, 295

extation, 193

"Extinction Risk in the Sea" (Roberts and Hawkins), 14

extinct species, 8

Exxon Valdez, 148–50

Eye of the Albatross (Safina), 17–18

Richard Ellis is the author of 14 books, including *The Book of Whales, Monsters of the Sea, Book of Sharks, Imagining Atlantis, The Search for the Giant Squid,* and, most recently, *Aquagenesis.* A research associate at the American Museum of Natural History in New York and a contributor to many magazines, Mr. Ellis is also a celebrated artist. His paintings and drawings of marine life have been exhibited in museums around the world.

~